Fodor's 21st Edition

Cape Cod

The Guide for All Budgets, Completely Updated, with Many Maps and Travel Tips

THIS BOOK PURCHASED FROM THE

CAROLINE J. TOBEY

MEMORIAL

FOR THE THOMASTON PUBLIC LIBRARY

Fodor's Travel Publications • New York, Toronto, London, Sydney, Auckland
www.fodors.com

Fodor's Cape Cod

EDITORS: Amy Hegarty, Linda Cabasin

Editorial Contributors: Carolyn Heller, Karl Luntta, Laura V. Scheel
Editorial Production: Taryn Luciani
Maps: David Lindroth, *cartographer*; Rebecca Baer and Bob Blake, *map editors*
Design: Fabrizio La Rocca, *creative director*; Guido Caroti, *art director*; Melanie Marin, *photo editor*; Jolie Novak, *senior picture editor*
Cover Design: Pentagram
Production/Manufacturing: Angela L. McLean
Cover Photo: William H. Johnson

Copyright

Twenty-First Edition

ISBN 0–676–90186–7

ISSN 1093–7986

Important Tip

Although all prices, opening times, and other details in this book are based on information supplied to us at press time, changes occur all the time in the travel world, and Fodor's cannot accept responsibility for facts that become outdated or for inadvertent errors or omissions. So **always confirm information when it matters,** especially if you're making a detour to visit a specific place.

Special Sales

Fodor's Travel Publications are available at special discounts for bulk purchases for sales promotions or premiums. Special editions, including personalized covers, excerpts of existing guides, and corporate imprints, can be created in large quantities for special needs. For more information, contact your local bookseller or write to Special Markets, Fodor's Travel Publications, 280 Park Avenue, New York, NY 10017. Inquiries from Canada should be directed to your local Canadian bookseller or sent to Random House of Canada, Ltd., Marketing Department, 2775 Matheson Boulevard East, Mississauga, Ontario L4W 4P7. Inquiries from the United Kingdom should be sent to Fodor's Travel Publications, 20 Vauxhall Bridge Road, London SW1V 2SA, England.

PRINTED IN THE UNITED STATES OF AMERICA

10 9 8 7 6 5 4 3 2 1

CONTENTS

Maps

ON THE ROAD WITH FODOR'S

The more you know before you go, the better your trip will be. Cape Cod's most fascinating small museum (or its most appealing crafts gallery or coziest clam shack) could be just around the corner from your hotel, but if you don't know it's there, it might as well be on the other side of the globe. That's where this book comes in. It's a great step toward making sure your next trip lives up to your expectations. As you plan, check out the Web as well. Guidebooks have been helping smart travelers find the special places for years; the Web is one more tool. Whatever reference you consult, be savvy about what you read, and always consider the source. Images and language can be massaged to make places appear better than they are. And one traveler's quaint is another's grimy. Here at Fodor's, and at our on-line arm, Fodors.com, our focus is on providing you with information that's not only useful but accurate and on target. Every day Fodor's editors put enormous effort into getting things right, beginning with the search for the right contributors—people who have objective judgment, broad travel experience, and the writing ability to put their insights into words. There's no substitute for advice from a like-minded friend who has just come back from where you're going, but our writers, having seen all corners of Cape Cod, are the next best thing. They're the kind of people you'd poll for tips yourself if you knew them.

One of **Carolyn Heller**'s early memories is of digging in the tide pools along Cape Cod Bay, and she's now introducing her own daughters to the Cape's beaches. A travel writer based in Cambridge, Carolyn tracks the area's dining and arts scenes as Boston bureau chief of the online business-travel site *ontheroad.com*. Her writing has appeared in the *Boston Globe,* the *Los Angeles Times,* the *Philadelphia Inquirer,* the *Miami Herald, Family Fun* magazine, and several other Fodor's guidebooks, including *Boston.*

Karl Luntta has lived on Cape Cod for more than 10 years and covered the Cape and islands for such publications as the *Cape Cod Travel Guide, Cape Cod Life,* and the *Cape Cod Times.* Along with having published his own travel guides to Jamaica, St. Lucia, the Virgin Islands, and the Caribbean region, Karl is also a frequent contributor to Fodor's *Caribbean.*

Although **Laura V. Scheel** recently moved to Portland, Maine, much of her heart still remains on Cape Cod. And as her car mileage attests, much of her free time is spent in her former home of eight years. A freelance writer and editor, she has written on travel and the arts for *A-Plus, Cape Cod Life,* the *Cape Cod Travel Guide,* the *Cape Codder,* the *Provincetown Banner,* and *On the Water.*

Don't Forget to Write

Your experiences—positive and negative—matter to us. If we have missed or misstated something, we want to hear about it. We follow up on all suggestions. Contact the Cape Cod editor at editors@fodors.com or c/o Fodor's, 280 Park Avenue, New York, New York 10017. And have a fabulous trip!

Karen Cure

Karen Cure
Editorial Director

Massachusetts

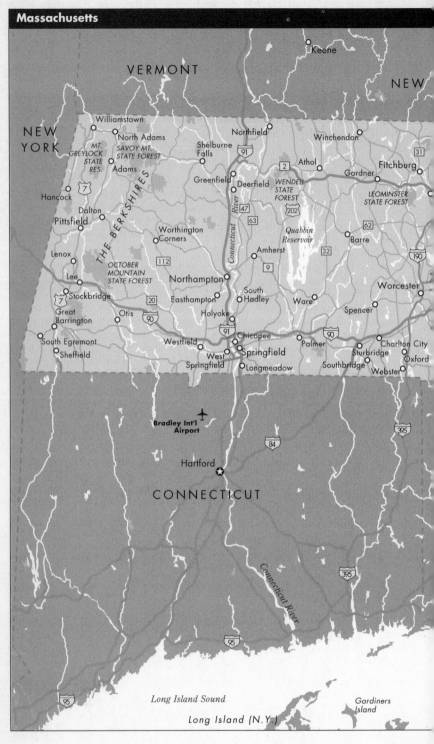

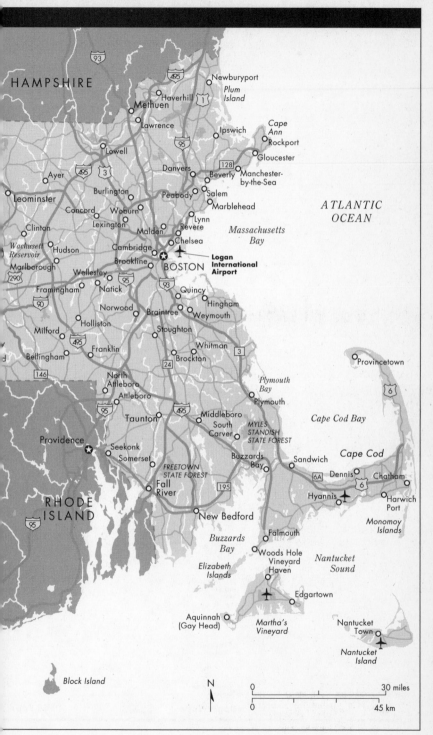

HAMPSHIRE

Newburyport
Plum
Island

Methuen
Haverhill

Lawrence

Ipswich

Cape
Ann
Rockport

Lowell

Gloucester

Ayer

Danvers

Beverly
Manchester-
by-the-Sea

128

Leominster

Burlington

Peabody
Salem

Concord
Woburn

Marblehead

Clinton

Lexington

Malden

Lynn
Revere

ATLANTIC
OCEAN

Wachusett
Reservoir

Hudson

Cambridge

Chelsea

Massachusetts
Bay

Marlborough

Brookline

BOSTON

Logan
International
Airport

290

Wellesley

95

Framingham

Natick

Quincy

90

Hingham

Norwood

Braintree
Weymouth

Milford

Holliston

Stoughton

Bellingham

Franklin

Whitman

3

495

24

Brockton

Provincetown

146

North
Attleboro

Plymouth
Bay

6

Attleboro

Plymouth

Cape Cod Bay

95

Taunton

495

Middleboro
South
Carver

MYLES
STANDISH
STATE FOREST

Providence

Seekonk

Buzzards
Bay

Sandwich

Cape Cod

Somerset

FREETOWN
STATE FOREST

6A
Dennis

Chatham

RHODE
ISLAND

Fall
River

195

6

Hyannis

Harwich
Port

95

New Bedford

Buzzards
Bay

Falmouth

Monomoy
Islands

Woods Hole
Vineyard
Haven

Nantucket
Sound

Elizabeth
Islands

Edgartown

Aquinnah
(Gay Head)

Martha's
Vineyard

Nantucket
Town

Block Island

N

Nantucket
Island

0   30 miles

0   45 km

Cape Cod *(Boxes Refer to Detail Maps)*

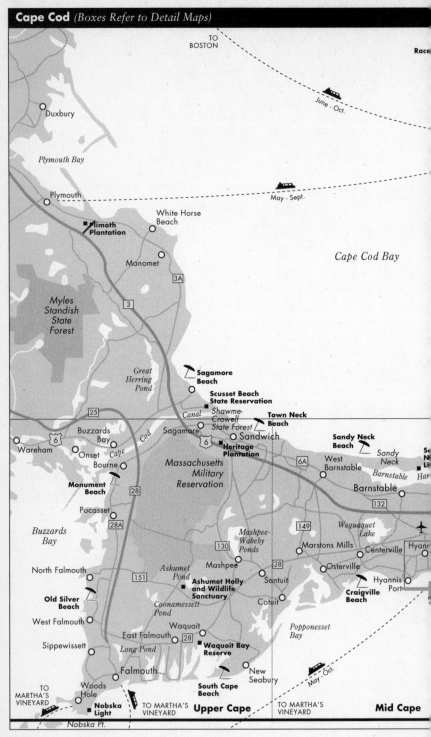

TO
BOSTON

Race

Duxbury

Plymouth Bay

June - Oct.

May - Sept.

Plymouth

Plimoth
Plantation

White Horse
Beach

Manomet

3A

Cape Cod Bay

3

*Myles
Standish
State
Forest*

*Great
Herring
Pond*

Sagamore
Beach

Scusset Beach
State Reservation

25

Canal

*Shawme-
Crowell
State Forest*

Town Neck
Beach

Buzzards
Bay

Cape

Sagamore

Sandwich

Sandy Neck
Beach

*Sandy
Neck*

S
N
Li

Wareham

6

Onset

Cod

6

Heritage
Plantation

West
Barnstable

Barnstable

Har

Bourne

*Massachusetts
Military
Reservation*

6A

Barnstable

Monument
Beach

28

132

Pocasset

28A

*Buzzards
Bay*

149

*Wequaquet
Lake*

Marstons Mills

Centerville

Hyan

North Falmouth

151

*Mashpee-
Wakeby
Ponds*

130

Mashpee

28

Santuit

Osterville

Hyannis

*Ashumet
Pond*

Ashumet Holly
and Wildlife
Sanctuary

Craigville
Beach

Hyannis
Port

Old Silver
Beach

*Coonamessett
Pond*

Cotuit

West Falmouth

Waquoit

*Poppponesset
Bay*

Sippewissett

East Falmouth

28

Long Pond

Waquoit Bay
Reserve

Falmouth

New
Seabury

May - Oct.

TO
MARTHA'S
VINEYARD

Woods
Hole

Nobska
Light

TO MARTHA'S
VINEYARD

South Cape
Beach

Upper Cape

TO MARTHA'S
VINEYARD

Mid Cape

Nobska Pt.

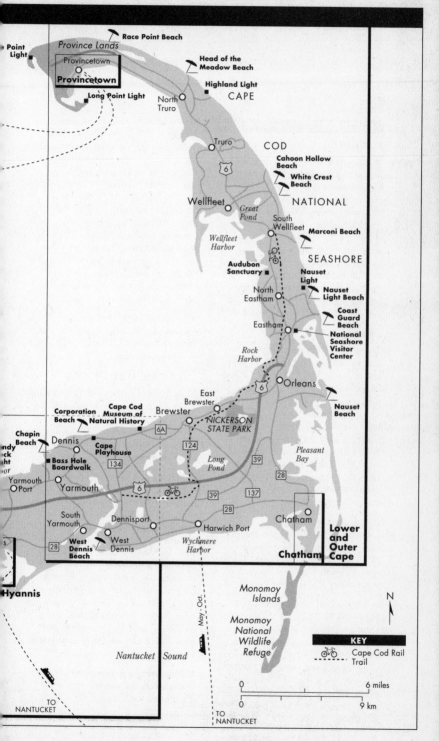

Race Point Beach

Head of the
Meadow Beach

Highland Light

CAPE

Province Lands

Provincetown

Provincetown

Long Point Light

North
Truro

Truro

COD

US 6

Cahoon Hollow
Beach

White Crest
Beach

Wellfleet

*Great
Pond*

NATIONAL

South
Wellfleet

Marconi Beach

*Wellfleet
Harbor*

SEASHORE

Audubon
Sanctuary

Nauset
Light

North
Eastham

Nauset
Light Beach

Coast
Guard
Beach

Eastham

National
Seashore
Visitor
Center

*Rock
Harbor*

Orleans

US 6

Nauset
Beach

East
Brewster

Corporation
Beach

Cape Cod
Museum of
Natural History

Brewster

NICKERSON
STATE PARK

6A

Chapin
Beach

Dennis

Cape
Playhouse

124

*Pleasant
Bay*

Bass Hole
Boardwalk

134

*Long
Pond*

39

Yarmouth
Port

Yarmouth

US 6

28

39

28

137

Chatham

**Lower
and
Outer
Cape**

South
Yarmouth

Dennisport

Harwich Port

28

West
Dennis
Beach

West
Dennis

*Wychmere
Harbor*

Chatham

Hyannis

*Monomoy
Islands*

N

*Monomoy
National
Wildlife
Refuge*

May - Oct.

Nantucket Sound

KEY
Cape Cod Rail Trail

TO
NANTUCKET

TO
NANTUCKET

0   6 miles

0   9 km

ESSENTIAL INFORMATION

AIR TRAVEL

BOOKING

When you book **look for nonstop flights** and **remember that "direct" flights stop at least once.** Try to avoid connecting flights, which require a change of plane. Two airlines may operate a connecting flight jointly, so ask if your airline operates every segment of the trip; you may find that the carrier you prefer flies you only part of the way. For more booking tips and to check prices and make on-line flight reservations, log on to www.fodors.com.

CARRIERS

The major U.S. airlines provide service to Boston, the nearest gateway city to Cape Cod. Providence, Rhode Island—also served by the major carriers—is an easy drive from the Cape. Airline service to Cape Cod itself is extremely unpredictable, however, because of the seasonal nature of travel; carriers come and go, while others juggle their routes. Barnstable Municipal Airport will always know which carriers are currently operating.

For charters, note that Direct Flight is based on Martha's Vineyard and provides charter service off-island. Westchester Air serves Cape Cod (and Martha's Vineyard and Nantucket) from White Plains, New York.

➤ MAJOR AIRLINES: **American** (☎ 800/433–7300, WEB www.aa.com). **Continental** (☎ 800/525–0280, WEB www.continental.com). **Delta** (☎ 800/221–1212, WEB www.delta. com). **Northwest** (☎ 800/225–2525, WEB www.nwa.com). **US Airways** (☎ 800/428–4322, WEB www.usairways. com). **United** (☎ 800/241–6522, WEB www.ual.com).

➤ SMALLER AIRLINES: **Cape Air** (☎ 508/771–6944 or 800/352–0714, WEB www.flycapeair.com) flies between Boston and Hyannis. **Nantucket Airlines** (☎ 508/790–0300 or 800/635–8787, WEB www.nantucketairlines. com), run by Cape Air, has frequent flights between Hyannis and Nantucket. **Island Airlines** (☎ 508/228–7575 or 800/248–7779, WEB www. nantucket.net/trans/islandair) flies between Hyannis and Nantucket. **Southwest Airlines** (☎ 800/435–9792, WEB www.southwest.com) serves Providence. **US Airways Express/Colgan Air** (☎ 800/428–4322, WEB www.usair. com) flies to Hyannis from Boston and New York (La Guardia Airport).

➤ CHARTERS: **Direct Flight** (☎ 508/693–6688). **Westchester Air** (☎ 914/761–3000 or 800/759–2929, WEB www. westchesterair.com).

CHECK-IN & BOARDING

Most carriers require you to check in 2 hours before your scheduled departure time for domestic flights and 2½ to 3 hours before international flights. Always **ask your carrier about its check-in policy.**

Assuming that not everyone with a ticket will show up, airlines routinely overbook planes. When everyone does, airlines ask for volunteers to give up their seats. In return, these volunteers usually get a certificate for a free flight and are rebooked on the next flight out. If there are not enough volunteers, the airline must choose who will be denied boarding. The first to get bumped are passengers who checked in late and those flying on discounted tickets, so **get to the gate and check in as early as possible,** especially during peak periods.

Always **bring a government-issued photo I.D. to the airport;** even when it's not required, a passport is best.

CUTTING COSTS

The least expensive airfares to Cape Cod are priced for round-trip travel and must usually be purchased in advance. Airlines generally allow you to change your return date for a fee; most low-fare tickets, however, are nonrefundable. It's smart to **call a number of airlines,** and when you are quoted a good price, **book it on the spot**—the same fare may not be available the next day. Always **check different routings** and look into using alternate airports. Also, price off-peak flights, which may be significantly less expensive than others. Travel agents, especially low-fare specialists (☞ Discounts & Deals), are helpful.

Consolidators are another good source. They buy tickets for scheduled international flights at reduced rates from the airlines, then sell them at prices that beat the best fare available directly from the airlines. Sometimes you can even get your money back if you need to return the ticket. Carefully read the fine print detailing penalties for changes and cancellations, purchase the ticket with a credit card, and **confirm your consolidator reservation with the airline.**

➤ CONSOLIDATORS: **Cheap Tickets** (☎ 800/377–1000 or 888/922–8849, WEB www.cheaptickets.com). **Discount Airline Ticket Service** (☎ 800/576–1600). **Unitravel** (☎ 800/325–2222, WEB www.unitravel.com). **Up & Away Travel** (☎ 212/889–2345). **World Travel Network** (☎ 800/409–6753).

➤ COURIER RESOURCES: **Air Courier Association** (☎ 800/282–1202, WEB www.aircourier.org). **Now Voyager** (☎ 212/431–1616).

ENJOYING THE FLIGHT

State your seat preference when purchasing your ticket, and then repeat it when you confirm and when you check-in. For more legroom, you can request one of the few emergency-aisle seats at check-in, if you are capable of lifting at least 50 pounds—a Federal Aviation Administration requirement of passengers in these seats. Seats behind a bulkhead also offer more legroom, but they don't have under-seat storage. Don't sit in the row in front of the emergency aisle or in front of a bulkhead, where seats may not recline.

If you have dietary concerns, **ask for special meals when booking.** These can be vegetarian, low-cholesterol, or kosher, for example. It's a good idea to pack some healthy snacks and a small bottle (plastic) of water in your carry-on bag. On long flights, try to maintain a normal routine, to help fight jet lag. At night, **get some sleep.** By day, **eat light meals, drink water** (not alcohol), and **move around the cabin** to stretch your legs. For additional jet-lag tips consult *Fodor's FYI: Travel Fit & Healthy* (available at bookstores everywhere).

Smoking policies vary from carrier to carrier. Many airlines prohibit smoking on all of their international flights; others allow smoking only on certain routes or certain departures. Ask your carrier about its policy.

FLYING TIMES

Flying time to Boston is 1 hour from New York, 2½ hours from Chicago, 6 hours from Los Angeles, and 3½ hours from Dallas.

HOW TO COMPLAIN

If your baggage goes astray or your flight goes awry, complain right away. Most carriers require that you **file a claim immediately.** The Aviation Consumer Protection Division of the Department of Transportation publishes *Fly-Rights,* which discusses airlines and consumer issues and is available on-line. At PassengerRights. com, a Web site, you can compose a letter of complaint and distribute it electronically.

➤ AIRLINE COMPLAINTS: **Aviation Consumer Protection Division** (✉ U.S. Department of Transportation, Room 4107, C-75, Washington, DC 20590, ☎ 202/366–2220, WEB www. dot.gov/airconsumer). **Federal Aviation Administration Consumer Hotline** (☎ 800/322–7873).

RECONFIRMING

Check the status of your flight before you leave for the airport. You can do this on your carrier's Web site, by linking to a flight-status checker (many Web booking services offer these), or by calling your carrier or travel agent.

AIRPORTS

The major gateway to Cape Cod is Boston's Logan International Airport

(BOS). The T. F. Green Airport (PVD) in Providence, Rhode Island, served by the low-cost carrier Southwest Airlines and other major carriers, is an alternative. Smaller airports include the Barnstable and Provincetown municipal airports.

➤ AIRPORT INFORMATION: Boston: **Logan International Airport** (☎ 617/561–1806 or 800/235–6426, WEB www.massport.com/logan). Providence: **T. F. Green Airport** (☎ 401/737–8222 or 888/268–7222, WEB www.pvd-ri.com). Hyannis: **Barnstable Municipal Airport** (☎ 508/775–2020). Provincetown: **Provincetown Municipal Airport** (☎ 508/487–0241).

BEACHES

In season you have to pay for parking at public beaches. Parking at "restricted" beaches is available only to residents and to visitors with permits. If you're renting a house, you can purchase a weekly beach permit; contact the town chamber of commerce for details (☞ Visitor Information *in* the A to Z sections of the appropriate chapters). Walkers and cyclists do not need permits to use restricted beaches. The official season generally begins the last weekend in June and ends on Labor Day. Note that even at resident beaches in season, the lots are often open to all early in the morning (before 8) and late in the afternoon (after 4 or 5).

BIKE TRAVEL

Biking is very popular on Cape Cod—some trails are as busy as the roads in summer. Note that Massachusetts law requires children under 13 to wear protective helmets while riding a bike, even as a passenger. For information on trails, maps, and rentals in your area, *see* listings for specific towns.

BOAT & FERRY TRAVEL

In season, ferries connect Boston and Plymouth with Provincetown.

Ferries are also a convenient way to get to Martha's Vineyard and Nantucket, two islands south of Cape Cod that have attractive, historic towns and lovely beaches well worth a day trip or a longer stay. For further information, *see* Close-Up: A Day on Martha's Vineyard *in* Chapter 3 and Close-Up: A Visit to the Gray Lady *in* Chapter 4; also *see* Guidebooks.

Ferries to Martha's Vineyard leave Woods Hole year-round. In summer you can also catch Vineyard ferries in Falmouth and Hyannis. All provide parking lots where you can leave your car overnight ($6–$10 per night). A number of parking lots in Falmouth hold the overflow of cars when the Woods Hole lot is filled, and free shuttle buses take passengers to the ferry, about 15 minutes away. Signs along Route 28 heading south from the Bourne Bridge direct you to open parking lots, as does AM radio station 1610, which you can pick up within 5 mi of Falmouth.

Ferries to Nantucket leave Hyannis year-round. In season, a passenger ferry connects Nantucket with Martha's Vineyard, and a cruise from Hyannis makes a day trip with stops at both islands.

From New Bedford you can take a ferry to Martha's Vineyard from mid-May to mid-October and to Cuttyhunk Island year-round (although between mid-October and mid-April, service is very limited).

FERRIES TO PROVINCETOWN

For details on ferries from Boston to Provincetown, *see* The Outer Cape A to Z *in* Chapter 6. For service from Plymouth to Provincetown, *see* Approaching the Cape A to Z *in* Chapter 2.

FERRIES TO MARTHA'S VINEYARD

The Steamship Authority runs the only car ferries, which make the 45-minute trip from Woods Hole to Vineyard Haven year-round and to Oak Bluffs from late May through September. During the summer and on autumn weekends, you *must* have a reservation if you want to bring your car (passenger reservations are never necessary). You should **make car reservations as far ahead as possible**; in season call weekdays from 5 AM to 9:55 PM for faster service. Standby car reservations to the Vineyard are only available Tuesday–Thursday. Those with confirmed car reservations must be at the terminal 30 minutes (45 minutes in season) before sailing time. One-way passenger fare year-round is $5.50, bicycles $3. Cost for a car traveling one-way in season (mid-May through mid-October) is $52 (not including passengers). Call for off-season rates.

Hy-Line makes the 1¾-hour run from Hyannis to Oak Bluffs May–October. From June to mid-September the Around the Sound cruise makes a one-day round-trip from Hyannis with stops at Nantucket and Martha's Vineyard ($37.50). The parking lot fills up in summer, so **call to reserve a parking space** in high season. One-way fare is $13.50; bicycles cost $5.

The *Island Queen* makes the 35-minute trip from Falmouth to Oak Bluffs from late May through Columbus Day. Ferries run multiple times a day from mid-June through early September, with less frequent service in the spring and fall; call for schedule. Round-trip fare is $10, bicycles $6; one-way $6, bicycles $3.

Patriot Boats runs a Falmouth Harbor to Oak Bluffs ferry year-round, with several trips Monday through Saturday; there's no service on Sundays or national holidays. The company also operates a year-round 24-hour water taxi and offers boat charters. The ferry costs $6 one-way.

The 600-passenger ferry *Schamonchi*, run by the Steamship Authority, travels several times a day from New Bedford to Oak Bluffs from mid-May through September. The trip takes about 1½ hours. One-way fare is $10, bicycles $5.

➤ BOAT & FERRY INFORMATION: **Hy-Line** (⊠ Ocean St. dock, ☎ 508/778–2600 or 888/778–1132; 508/778–2602 for reservations; 508/693–0112 in Oak Bluffs; WEB www.hy-linecruises.com). *Island Queen* (⊠ Falmouth Harbor, ☎ 508/548–4800, WEB www.islandqueen.com). **Patriot Boats** (⊠ 227 Clinton Ave., Falmouth Harbor, ☎ 508/548–2626 or 800/734–0088 in MA, WEB www.patriotpartyboats.com). *Schamonchi* (⊠ Billy Wood's Wharf, Rodney French Blvd., New Bedford, ☎ 508/997–1688, WEB www.mvferry.com). **Steamship Authority** (☎ 508/477–8600 for infor-

mation and car reservations; 508/693–9130 on the Vineyard; 508/540–1394 TTY for information and car reservations; 508/548–3788 for day-of-sailing information; WEB www.islandferry.com).

FERRIES TO NANTUCKET

For details on ferries from Harwich Port, *see* The Lower Cape A to Z *in* Chapter 5.

The Steamship Authority runs car-and-passenger ferries from Hyannis to Nantucket year-round, a 2¼-hour trip. A faster passenger ferry only takes an hour. All of the ferries have snack bars. For policies *see* Ferries to Martha's Vineyard. Note that there are no standby car reservations on ferries to Nantucket. One-way passenger fare is $13, bicycles $5. Cost for a car traveling one-way mid-May through mid-October is $160; mid-October through mid-May, $100. One-way high-speed passenger ferry fare is $24, bicycles $5.

Hy-Line's high-end, high-speed *Grey Lady II* ferries between Hyannis and Nantucket year-round in just under an hour. Such speed has its downside in rough seas—lots of bucking and rolling that some find literally nauseating. Seating ranges from benches on the upper deck to airlinelike seats in side rows of the cabin to café-style tables and chairs in the cabin front. There's a snack bar on board. One-way fare is $33, bicycles $5.

Hy-Line's slower ferry makes the roughly two-hour trip from Hyannis between early May and late October. The M.V. *Great Point* offers a first-class section ($22 one-way) with a private lounge, rest rooms, upholstered seats, carpeting, complimentary Continental breakfast or afternoon cheese and crackers, a bar, and a snack bar. Standard one-way fare is $13.50, bicycles $5.

➤ BOAT & FERRY INFORMATION: **Hy-Line** (⊠ Ocean St. dock, ☎ 508/778–0404 or 888/778–1132 for *Grey Lady II*; 508/778–2602 for *Great Point* ferry reservations; 508/778–2600 for ferry information; 888/778–1132; 508/228–3949 on Nantucket; WEB www.hy-linecruises.com). **Steamship Authority** (⊠ South St. dock,

☎ 508/477–8600; 508/228–3274 on Nantucket for reservations; 508/228–0262 for information; 508/540–1394 TTD; WEB www.islandferry.com).

FERRIES TO CUTTYHUNK ISLAND

The M/V *Alert II* travels between New Bedford and Cuttyhunk Island. The trip takes about one hour. The ferry runs daily mid-June through mid-September, several times a week from mid-April to mid-June and from mid-September to mid-October, and once a week the rest of the year. Same-day round-trip fare is $19, one-way $12.75, bicycles $3.50.

➤ BOAT & FERRY INFORMATION: **M/V Alert II** (✉ Fisherman's Wharf/Pier 3, New Bedford, ☎ 508/992–1432, WEB www.cuttyhunk.com).

BUSINESS HOURS

MUSEUMS & SIGHTS

Hours for sights on the Cape vary widely from place to place and from season to season. Some places are staffed by volunteers and have limited hours (open just a few hours a day several days a week), even in summer, although major museums and attractions will be open daily in summer. Always check the hours of a place you plan to visit, and if you'll be traveling some distance to a sight, call ahead to confirm that it will be open.

PHARMACIES

Many pharmacies on the Cape are open from 8 or 9 AM until 8 or 9 PM; some stay open later in the summer. *See* chapter A to Z sections for specific listings.

SHOPS

Shop hours are generally from 9 or 10 to 5, though in high season many tourist-oriented stores stay open until 9 PM or later. Except in the main tourist areas, shops are often closed on Sunday.

BUS TRAVEL

Greyhound serves Boston from all over the United States; from there you can connect to a local carrier, such as Bonanza Bus Lines, which serves Bourne, Falmouth, and Woods Hole on the Cape, plus nearby Fall River and New Bedford. The Plymouth &

Brockton Street Railway buses travel all the way to Provincetown from Boston and Logan Airport, with stops en route.

The Cape Cod Regional Transit Authority operates several buses within the Cape, all of them wheelchair-accessible and equipped with bike racks. The SeaLine runs along Route 28 Monday through Saturday between Hyannis and Woods Hole (one-way fare $3.50, from Hyannis to Woods Hole; shorter trips are less), with stops including Mashpee Commons, Falmouth, and the Woods Hole Steamship Authority docks. The SeaLine connects in Hyannis with the Plymouth & Brockton line as well as the Villager, another bus line that runs along Route 132 between Hyannis and Barnstable Harbor, serving the Cape Cod Mall. The driver will stop when signaled along the route.

The b-bus is composed of a fleet of minivans that will transport passengers door to door between any towns on the Cape. Service runs seven days a week, year-round, though reservations must be made in advance. The cost is $2 per ride plus 10¢ per mile.

The H2O Line offers daily regularly scheduled service year-round between Hyannis and Orleans along Route 28. The Hyannis–Orleans fare is $3.50; shorter trips are less. Buses connect in Hyannis with the SeaLine, the Villager, and Plymouth & Brockton lines.

➤ BUS INFORMATION: **Bonanza** (☎ 508/548–7588 or 800/556–3815, WEB www.bonanzabus.com). **Cape Cod Regional Transit Authority** (☎ 508/385–8326; 800/352–7155 in MA; WEB www.capecodtransit.org). **Greyhound** (☎ 800/231–2222, WEB www.greyhound.com). **Plymouth & Brockton Street Railway** (☎ 508/746–0378, WEB www.p-b.com).

CAMERAS & PHOTOGRAPHY

Early morning or early evening fog can present a photographic challenge on the Cape, but when it's not foggy, these are great times for pictures—beaches are less crowded and the light is especially magical. Shots of lighthouses or sand dunes are classics, as are photos of your dinner of lobster or fried clams.

The *Kodak Guide to Shooting Great Travel Pictures* (available at bookstores everywhere) is loaded with tips.

➤ PHOTO HELP: **Kodak Information Center** (☎ 800/242–2424, WEB www.kodak.com).

EQUIPMENT PRECAUTIONS

Don't pack film and equipment in checked luggage, where it is much more susceptible to damage. X-ray machines used to view checked luggage are becoming much more powerful and therefore are much more likely to ruin your film. Try to **ask for hand inspection of film,** which becomes clouded after repeated exposure to airport X-ray machines, and **keep videotapes and computer disks away from metal detectors.** Always **keep film, tape, and computer disks out of the sun.** Carry an extra supply of batteries, and **be prepared to turn on your camera, camcorder, or laptop** to prove to airport security personnel that the device is real.

CAR RENTAL

Rates in Boston begin at $30–$40 a day and $125–$185 a week for an economy car with air-conditioning, an automatic transmission, and unlimited mileage. Rates in Hyannis range from $30 to $45 a day and from $159 to $259 a week. These rates do not include tax on car rentals, which is 5%.

➤ MAJOR AGENCIES: **Alamo** (☎ 800/327–9633; 020/8759–6200 in the U.K., WEB www.alamo.com). **Avis** (☎ 800/331–1212; 800/879–2847 in Canada; 02/9353–9000 in Australia; 09/526–2847 in New Zealand; 0870/606–0100 in the U.K., WEB www.avis.com). **Budget** (☎ 800/527–0700; 0870/156–5656 in the U.K., WEB www.budget.com). **Dollar** (☎ 800/800–4000; 0124/622–0111 in the U.K., where it's affiliated with Sixt; 02/9223–1444 in Australia, WEB www.dollar.com). **Hertz** (☎ 800/654–3131; 800/263–0600 in Canada; 020/8897–2072 in the U.K.; 02/9669–2444 in Australia; 09/256–8690 in New Zealand, WEB www.hertz.com). **National Car Rental** (☎ 800/227–7368; 020/8680–4800 in the U.K., WEB www.nationalcar.com).

➤ LIMOUSINE AGENCIES: **Aristocrat Limousine** (☎ 508/420–5466 or 800/992–6163) for service from the Boston or Providence airports to the Cape. **Avlamar, Inc.** (☎ 508/778–0070 or 888/404–5663, WEB www.avlamar.com) for airport pick-up service from Boston and Providence, and limo service Cape-wide.

CUTTING COSTS

For a good deal, **book through a travel agent who will shop around.** Also, **price local car-rental companies**—whose prices may be lower still, although their service and maintenance may not be as good as those of major rental agencies—and **research rates on-line.** Remember to ask about required deposits, cancellation penalties, and drop-off charges if you're planning to pick up the car in one city and leave it in another. If you're traveling during a holiday period, also make sure that a confirmed reservation guarantees you a car.

INSURANCE

When driving a rented car you are generally responsible for any damage to or loss of the vehicle. You may also be liable for any property damage or personal injury that you may cause while driving. Before you rent, see what coverage you already have under the terms of your personal auto-insurance policy and credit cards.

For about $15 to $20 a day, rental companies sell protection, known as a collision- or loss-damage waiver (CDW or LDW), that eliminates your liability for damage to the car; it's always optional and should never be automatically added to your bill.

In Massachusetts the car-rental agency's insurance is primary; therefore, the company must pay for damage to third parties up to a preset legal limit, beyond which your own liability insurance kicks in. However, **make sure you have enough coverage to pay for the car.** If you do not have auto insurance or an umbrella policy that covers damage to third parties, purchasing liability insurance and a CDW or LDW is highly recommended.

REQUIREMENTS & RESTRICTIONS

In Massachusetts you must be 21 to rent a car, and rates may be higher if you're under 25. You'll pay extra for child seats (about $3 per day), which are compulsory for children under five, and for additional drivers (about $2 per day). When picking up a car, non–U.S. residents will need a reservation voucher (for prepaid reservations made in the traveler's home country), a passport, a driver's license, and a travel policy that covers each driver.

SURCHARGES

Before you pick up a car in one city and leave it in another, **ask about drop-off charges or one-way service fees,** which can be substantial. Note, too, that some rental agencies charge extra if you return the car before the time specified in your contract. To avoid a hefty refueling fee, **fill the tank just before you turn in the car,** but be aware that gas stations near the rental outlet may overcharge. It's almost never a deal to buy the tank of gas in the car when you rent it; the understanding is that you'll return it empty, but some fuel usually remains.

CAR TRAVEL

To reach Cape Cod from Boston (60 mi), take Route I–93 south, then Route 3 south, and cross the Sagamore Bridge. After finding your way out of a rotary, you'll be on U.S. 6, the Cape's main artery, leading toward Hyannis and Provincetown. From western Massachusetts, northern Connecticut, and northern New York State, take I–84 East to the Massachusetts Turnpike (I–90E) and take I–495 to the Bourne Bridge. From New York City, New Jersey, Philadelphia, Washington, D.C., and all other points south and west, take I–95 north toward Providence, where you'll pick up I–195 east (toward Fall River/New Bedford) to Route 25 east to the Bourne Bridge. From the Bourne Bridge you can take Route 28 south to Falmouth and Woods Hole (about 15 mi), or follow signs to U.S. 6 if you're headed east.

Driving times can vary widely depending on traffic. In good driving conditions you can reach the Sagamore Bridge from Boston in about 1¼ or 1½ hours, the Bourne Bridge from New York City in about 4½ or 5 hours.

On summer weekends, when more than 100,000 cars a day cross each bridge, **make every effort to avoid arriving in late afternoon,** especially on holidays. U.S. 6 and Route 28 are heavily congested eastbound on Friday evening, westbound on Sunday afternoon, and in both directions on Saturday (when rental homes change hands). On the north shore, the Old King's Highway—Route 6A—parallels U.S. 6 and is a scenic country road passing through occasional towns. When you're in no hurry, use back roads—you won't get there any faster, but they're less frustrating and much more rewarding.

RULES OF THE ROAD

Massachusetts permits a right turn on a red light (*after* a full stop) unless a sign says otherwise. Also, when you approach one of the Cape's numerous rotaries (traffic circles), note that the vehicles already in the rotary have the right of way and that those vehicles entering the rotary must yield. Be careful: some drivers forget (or ignore) this principle.

In Massachusetts highway speed limits are 55 mph near urban areas, 60 or 65 mph elsewhere. Speed limits on U.S. 6 on the Cape vary as it changes from four lanes to two lanes.

CHILDREN ON CAPE COD

Cape Cod, which has everything from miniature golf to beaches, is extremely family-oriented. Every imaginable diversion is available for children, including lodgings and restaurants that cater specifically to them and that are affordable for families on a budget. Cottages and condominiums are popular with families, offering privacy, room, kitchens, and sometimes laundry facilities. Often cottage or condo communities have play yards and pools, sometimes even a full range of children's programs. The Bristol County Convention & Visitors Bureau, which covers part of southeastern Massachusetts, publishes a booklet, *Especially For Kids in Bristol County.*

For some child-friendly events, *see* Festivals and Seasonal Events *in* When to Go.

If you are renting a car, don't forget to **arrange for a car seat** when you reserve. For general advice about traveling with children, consult *Fodor's FYI: Travel with Your Baby* (available in bookstores everywhere).

➤ LOCAL INFORMATION: The **Bristol County Convention & Visitors Bureau** (✉ 70 N. 2nd St., Box 976, New Bedford, MA 02741, ☎ 508/997–1250 or 800/288–6263, WEB www.southofboston.org).

FLYING

If your children are two or older, **ask about children's airfares.** As a general rule, infants under two not occupying a seat fly at greatly reduced fares or even for free. When booking, **confirm carry-on allowances** if you're traveling with infants. In general, for babies charged 10% of the adult fare you are allowed one carry-on bag and a collapsible stroller; if the flight is full, the stroller may have to be checked or you may be limited to less.

Experts agree that it's a good idea to use safety seats aloft for children weighing less than 40 pounds. Airlines set their own policies: U.S. carriers usually require that the child be ticketed, even if he or she is young enough to ride free, since the seats must be strapped into regular seats. Do **check your airline's policy about using safety seats during takeoff and landing.** Safety seats are not allowed everywhere in the plane, so get your seat assignments as early as possible.

When reserving, **request children's meals or a freestanding bassinet** (not available at all airlines) if you need them. But note that bulkhead seats, where you must sit to use the bassinet, may lack an overhead bin or storage space on the floor.

LODGING

Most hotels on Cape Cod allow children under a certain age to stay in their parents' room at no extra charge, but others will charge children as extra adults; be sure to **find out the cutoff age for children's discounts.**

If you're planning to stay at a bed-and-breakfast, be sure to **ask the owners in advance** whether the B&B welcomes children. Some establishments are filled with fragile antiques, and owners may not accept families with children below a certain age.

SIGHTS & ATTRACTIONS

Places that are especially appealing to children are indicated by a rubber-duckie icon (🐤) in the margin.

CONSUMER PROTECTION

Whether you're shopping for gifts or purchasing travel services, **pay with a major credit card** whenever possible, so you can cancel payment or get reimbursed if there's a problem (and you can provide documentation). If you're doing business with a particular company for the first time, **contact your local Better Business Bureau and the attorney general's offices** in your state and (for U.S. businesses) the company's home state as well. Have any complaints been filed? Finally, if you're buying a package or tour, always **consider travel insurance** that includes default coverage (☞ Insurance).

➤ BBBs: **Council of Better Business Bureaus** (✉ 4200 Wilson Blvd., Suite 800, Arlington, VA 22203, ☎ 703/276–0100, FAX 703/525–8277, WEB www.bbb.org).

CUSTOMS & DUTIES

IN AUSTRALIA

Australian residents who are 18 or older may bring home A$400 worth of souvenirs and gifts (including jewelry), 250 cigarettes or 250 grams of tobacco, and 1,125 ml of alcohol (including wine, beer, and spirits). Residents under 18 may bring back A$200 worth of goods. Prohibited items include meat products. Seeds, plants, and fruits need to be declared upon arrival.

➤ INFORMATION: **Australian Customs Service** (Regional Director, ✉ Box 8, Sydney, NSW 2001, ☎ 02/9213–2000, FAX 02/9213–4000, WEB www.customs.gov.au).

IN CANADA

Canadian residents who have been out of Canada for at least seven days may bring in C$750 worth of goods duty-free. If you've been away fewer than seven days but more than 48 hours, the duty-free allowance drops to C$200; if your trip lasts 24 to 48 hours, the allowance is C$50. You may not pool allowances with family members. Goods claimed under the C$750 exemption may follow you by mail; those claimed under the lesser exemptions must accompany you. Alcohol and tobacco products may be included in the seven-day and 48-hour exemptions, but not in the 24-hour exemption. If you meet the age requirements of the province or territory through which you reenter Canada, you may bring in, duty-free, 1.5 liters of wine *or* 1.14 liters (40 imperial ounces) of liquor *or* 24 12-ounce cans or bottles of beer or ale. If you are 19 or older you may bring in, duty-free, 200 cigarettes and 50 cigars. Check ahead of time with the Canada Customs and Revenue Agency or the Department of Agriculture for policies regarding meat products, seeds, plants, and fruits.

You may send an unlimited number of gifts (only one gift per recipient, however) worth up to C$60 each duty-free to Canada. Label the package UNSOLICITED GIFT—VALUE UNDER $60. Alcohol and tobacco are excluded.

➤ INFORMATION: **Canada Customs and Revenue Agency** (✉ 2265 St. Laurent Blvd. S, Ottawa, Ontario K1G 4K3, ☎ 204/983–3500 or 506/636–5064; 800/461–9999 in Canada, WEB www.ccra-adrc.gc.ca).

IN NEW ZEALAND

All homeward-bound residents may bring back NZ$700 worth of souvenirs and gifts; passengers may not pool their allowances, and children can claim only the concession on goods intended for their own use. For those 17 or older, the duty-free allowance also includes 4.5 liters of wine or beer; one 1,125-ml bottle of spirits; and either 200 cigarettes, 250 grams of tobacco, 50 cigars, *or* a combination of the three up to 250 grams. Meat products, seeds, plants, and fruits must be declared upon arrival to the Agricultural Services Department.

➤ INFORMATION: **New Zealand Customs** (✉ Head Office, The Customhouse, 17–21 Whitmore St., Box

2218, Wellington, ☎ 09/300–5399, WEB www.customs.govt.nz).

IN THE U.K.

From countries outside the European Union, including the United States, you may bring home, duty-free, 200 cigarettes or 50 cigars; 1 liter of spirits or 2 liters of fortified or sparkling wine or liqueurs; 2 liters of still table wine; 60 ml of perfume; 250 ml of toilet water; plus £145 worth of other goods, including gifts and souvenirs. Prohibited items include meat products, seeds, plants, and fruits.

➤ INFORMATION: **HM Customs and Excise** (✉ St. Christopher House, Southwark, London, SE1 OTE, ☎ 020/7928–3344, WEB www. hmce.gov.uk).

DINING

For additional dining information, *see* Pleasures and Pastimes *in* Chapter 1. There's a 5% sales tax on restaurant meals. The restaurants we list are the cream of the crop in each price category. Note that ordering a lobster dinner, which can be far more expensive than other menu items, may push your meal into a higher price category than the restaurant's price range shows. Properties indicated by a ✕☷ are lodging establishments whose restaurant warrants a special trip.

CATEGORY	COST*
$$$$	over $26
$$$	$19–$26
$$	$11–$18
$	under $11

per person for a main course at dinner

In general, when you order a regular coffee, you get coffee with milk and sugar.

RESERVATIONS & DRESS

Reservations are always a good idea; we mention them only when they're essential or not accepted. Book as far ahead as you can, and reconfirm as soon as you arrive. (Large parties should always call ahead to check the reservations policy.) We mention dress only when men are required to wear a jacket or a jacket and tie.

WINE, BEER & SPIRITS

Massachusetts is not a major wine-growing area, but Westport Rivers

Winery in Westport and the Cape Cod Winery in East Falmouth produce respectable vintages. The family that owns Westport Rivers also runs the local Buzards Bay Brewing Co.

In Massachusetts, you can generally buy alcoholic beverages (wine, beer, and spirits) in liquor stores, known locally as package stores. A few exceptions allow some grocery stores to sell wine and beer.

DISABILITIES & ACCESSIBILITY

The Cape Cod Disability Access Directory includes access information about ATMs, beaches, health care facilities, theaters, and other places on the Cape. It's available online, or you can request a copy from the Cape Cod Chamber of Commerce (☞ Visitor Information). The Cape Cod National Seashore visitor centers can provide information about accessible facilities at the park. The Cape Organization for Rights of the Disabled (CORD) will supply information on accessibility of restaurants, hotels, beaches, and other tourist facilities on Cape Cod. Sight Loss Services provides information on accessibility and other needs and referrals for people with vision impairments. For information about accessibility in Massachusetts state parks and beaches, contact the Massachusetts Department of Environmental Management.

➤ LOCAL RESOURCES: **Cape Cod Disability Access Directory** (WEB www. capecoddisability.org). **Cape Cod National Seashore** (✉ South Wellfleet 02663, ☎ 508/349–3785, WEB www. nps.gov/caco). **Cape Cod National Seashore visitor centers** (☎ 508/255–3421 in Eastham; 508/487–1256 in Provincetown, WEB www.nps. gov/caco). **Cape Organization for Rights of the Disabled** (CORD; ☎ 508/775–8300; 800/541–0282 in MA, WEB www.vse.cape.com/~bhcord/). **Massachusetts Department of Environmental Management** (☞ Visitor Information). **Sight Loss Services** (☎ 508/394–3904; 800/427–6842 in MA, WEB www.sightloss.org).

LODGING

Despite the Americans with Disabilities Act, the definition of accessibility seems to differ from hotel to hotel.

Some properties may be accessible by ADA standards for people with mobility problems but not for people with hearing or vision impairments, for example.

If you have mobility problems, ask for the lowest floor on which accessible services are offered. If you have a hearing impairment, check whether the hotel has devices to alert you visually to the ring of the telephone, a knock at the door, and a fire/emergency alarm. Some hotels provide these devices without charge. Discuss your needs with hotel personnel if this equipment isn't available, so that a staff member can personally alert you in the event of an emergency.

If you're bringing a guide dog, get authorization ahead of time and write down the name of the person you spoke with.

RESERVATIONS

When discussing accessibility with an operator or reservations agent, **ask hard questions.** Are there any stairs, inside *or* out? Are there grab bars next to the toilet *and* in the shower/tub? How wide is the doorway to the room? To the bathroom? For the most extensive facilities meeting the latest legal specifications, **opt for newer accommodations.** If you reserve through a toll-free number, consider also calling the hotel's local number to confirm the information from the central reservations office. Get confirmation in writing when you can.

➤ COMPLAINTS: **Aviation Consumer Protection Division** (☞ Air Travel) for airline-related problems. **Departmental Office of Civil Rights** (for general inquiries, ✉ U.S. Department of Transportation, S-30, 400 7th St. SW, Room 10215, Washington, DC 20590, ☎ 202/366–4648, FAX 202/366–9371, WEB www.dot.gov/ost/docr/index.htm). **Disability Rights Section** (✉ U.S. Department of Justice, Civil Rights Division, Box 66738, Washington, DC 20035-6738, ☎ 202/514–0301 or 800/514–0301; 800/514–0383 TTY, for ADA inquiries; WEB www.usdoj.gov/crt/ada/adahom1.htm).

TRAVEL AGENCIES

In the United States, the Americans with Disabilities Act requires that travel firms serve the needs of all travelers. Some agencies specialize in working with people with disabilities.

➤ TRAVELERS WITH MOBILITY PROBLEMS: **Access Adventures** (✉ 206 Chestnut Ridge Rd., Scottsville, NY 14624, ☎ 716/889–9096, dltravel@ prodigy.net), run by a former physical-rehabilitation counselor. **Accessible Vans of America** (✉ 9 Spielman Rd., Fairfield, NJ 07004, ☎ 877/ 282–8267; 888/282–8267 for reservations, FAX 973/808–9713, WEB www. accessiblevans.com). **CareVacations** (✉ No. 5, 5110–50 Ave., Leduc, Alberta T9E 6V4, Canada, ☎ 780/ 986–6404 or 877/478–7827, FAX 780/ 986–8332, WEB www.carevacations. com), for group tours and cruise vacations. **Flying Wheels Travel** (✉ 143 W. Bridge St., Box 382, Owatonna, MN 55060, ☎ 507/451–5005 or 800/535–6790, FAX 507/451–1685, WEB www.flyingwheelstravel.com).

➤ TRAVELERS WITH DEVELOPMENTAL DISABILITIES: **Sprout** (✉ 893 Amsterdam Ave., New York, NY 10025, ☎ 212/222–9575 or 888/222–9575, FAX 212/222–9768, WEB www. gosprout.org).

DISCOUNTS & DEALS

You can sometimes pick up discount coupons for various attractions at local Chamber of Commerce offices. Some places, from restaurants to amusement centers, also post discount coupons on their Web sites.

Be a smart shopper and **compare all your options** before making decisions. A plane ticket bought with a promotional coupon from travel clubs, coupon books, and direct-mail offers or on the Internet may not be cheaper than the least expensive fare from a discount ticket agency. And always keep in mind that what you get is just as important as what you save.

DISCOUNT RESERVATIONS

To save money, **look into discount reservations services** with Web sites and toll-free numbers, which use their buying power to get a better price on hotels, airline tickets, even car rentals.

When booking a room, always **call the hotel's local toll-free number** (if one is available) rather than the central reservations number—you'll often get a better price. Always ask about special packages or corporate rates.

➤ AIRLINE TICKETS: ☎ **800/AIR–4LESS**.

➤ HOTEL ROOMS: **RMC Travel** (☎ 800/ 245–5738, WEB www.rmcwebtravel. com). **Turbotrip.com** (☎ 800/473–7829, WEB www.turbotrip.com).

PACKAGE DEALS

Don't confuse packages and guided tours. When you buy a package, you travel on your own, just as though you had planned the trip yourself. Fly/drive packages, which combine airfare and car rental, are often a good deal.

ECOTOURISM

Throughout the Cape, including the Monomoy Islands, Sandy Neck in Barnstable, and the Cape Cod National Seashore, signs indicate (in season) the nesting areas of the endangered piping plover. Warning signs around the Cape urge you to protect fragile sand dunes by not walking or climbing on them.

Most towns have recycling protocols; if you're renting a house, ask your agent for information.

GAY & LESBIAN TRAVEL

Provincetown, at the tip of the Cape, is one of the East Coast's leading lesbian and gay seaside destinations and also has a large year-round lesbian and gay community. Dozens of P-town establishments, from B&Bs to bars, cater specifically to lesbian and gay visitors, and all of the town's restaurants are gay-friendly; several are gay-owned and -operated. Hyannis has Cape Cod's sole gay bar outside P-town.

For details about the gay and lesbian scene, consult *Fodor's Gay Guide to the USA* (available in bookstores everywhere).

➤ GAY- & LESBIAN-FRIENDLY TRAVEL AGENCIES: **Different Roads Travel** (✉ 8383 Wilshire Blvd., Suite 902, Beverly Hills, CA 90211, ☎ 323/ 651–5557 or 800/429–8747, FAX 323/

651–3678, lgernert@tzell.com). **Kennedy Travel** (✉ 314 Jericho Turnpike, Floral Park, NY 11001, ☎ 516/352–4888 or 800/237–7433, FAX 516/354–8849, WEB www.kennedytravel.com). **Now Voyager** (✉ 4406 18th St., San Francisco, CA 94114, ☎ 415/626–1169 or 800/255–6951, FAX 415/626–8626, WEB www.nowvoyager.com). **Skylink Travel and Tour** (✉ 1006 Mendocino Ave., Santa Rosa, CA 95401, ☎ 707/546–9888 or 800/225–5759, FAX 707/546–9891, WEB www.skylinktravel.com), serving lesbian travelers.

GUIDEBOOKS

Plan well and you won't be sorry. Guidebooks are excellent tools—and you can take them with you. You may want to check out color-photo-illustrated guides such as *Fodor's Exploring New England* and the Southern New England guide in the Compass American series—both thorough on culture and history. *Fodor's Road Guide USA: Connecticut, Massachusetts, and Rhode Island* is packed with hotel, restaurant, and attractions listings. Also see *Fodor's Pocket Martha's Vineyard* and *Fodor's Pocket Nantucket* if you're planning a trip to the islands as part of a Cape trip. All are available at on-line retailers and bookstores everywhere.

HEALTH

Most Cape Cod pharmacies will refill an out-of-town prescription if you provide the prescribing doctor's phone number for verification. Most pharmacies post emergency numbers on their doors.

A common problem on the East Coast is Lyme disease (named after Lyme, Connecticut, where it was first diagnosed). This bacterial infection is transmitted by deer ticks and can be very serious, leading to chronic arthritis and worse if left untreated. Pregnant women are advised to **avoid areas of possible deer tick infestation**; if contracted during early pregnancy, Lyme disease can harm a fetus.

Deer ticks are most prevalent April–October but can be found year-round. They are about the size of a pinhead. Wear light-color clothing, which makes it easier to spot any ticks that might have attached themselves to you. Anyone planning to explore wooded areas or places with tall grasses (including dunes) should **wear long pants, socks drawn up over pant cuffs, and a long-sleeve shirt with a close-fitting collar**; boots are also recommended. The National Centers for Disease Control recommends that DEET repellent be applied to skin (not face!) and that permethrin be applied to clothing directly before entering infested areas; **use repellents very carefully** and conservatively with small children. Ticks also attach themselves to pets.

Recent research suggests that if ticks are removed within 12 hours of attachment to the body, the infectious bacteria is not likely to enter the bloodstream. That makes evenings a good opportunity to check yourself for ticks—look at the warm spots and hairlines on the body that attract ticks.

To remove a tick, apply tweezers to where it is attached to the skin and pull on the mouth parts. Try not to squeeze the body of the tick, which can send the body fluids containing the bacteria into the bloodstream. (Heating the tip of the tweezers before grasping the tick will cause the bug to release its bite, allowing for removal of the entire tick, including the sometimes-embedded head.) Disinfect the bite with alcohol and save the tick in a closed jar in case symptoms of the disease develop.

The first symptom of Lyme disease may be a ringlike rash or flulike symptoms, such as general feelings of malaise, fever, chills, and joint or facial pains. If diagnosed early, it can be treated with antibiotics. If you suspect your symptoms may be due to a tick bite, inform your doctor and ask to be tested.

Also **ask your physician about Lymerix, the Lyme disease vaccine**; it takes three shots and 12 months to be 80% effective but is worth considering. Brochures on the disease are available at many tourist information areas.

Poison ivy is a pervasive vinelike plant, recognizable by its leaf pattern: three shiny green leaves together. In spring new poison ivy leaves are red; likewise, they can take on a reddish tint as fall approaches. The oil from these leaves produces an itchy skin rash that spreads with scratching. If you think you may have touched some leaves, **wash as soon as you can** with soap and cool water.

➤ LYME DISEASE INFO: **Centers for Disease Control** (☎ 404/332–4555, WEB www.cdc.gov). **Massachusetts Department of Public Health** (✉ Southeast Office, 109 Rhode Island Rd., Lakeville, MA 02347, ☎ 508/947–1231, WEB www.state.ma.us/dph).

HOLIDAYS

Major national holidays include New Year's Day (Jan. 1); Martin Luther King, Jr., Day (3rd Mon. in Jan.); President's Day (3rd Mon. in Feb.); Memorial Day (last Mon. in May); Independence Day (July 4); Labor Day (1st Mon. in Sept.); Thanksgiving Day (4th Thurs. in Nov.); Christmas Eve and Christmas Day (Dec. 24 and 25); and New Year's Eve (Dec. 31). Patriot's Day (3rd Mon. in Apr.) is a Massachusetts state holiday.

INSURANCE

The most useful travel-insurance plan is a comprehensive policy that includes coverage for trip cancellation and interruption, default, trip delay, and medical expenses (with a waiver for pre-existing conditions).

Without insurance you will lose all or most of your money if you cancel your trip, regardless of the reason. Default insurance covers you if your tour operator, airline, or cruise line goes out of business. Trip-delay covers expenses that arise because of bad weather or mechanical delays. Study the fine print when comparing policies.

U.K. residents can buy a travel-insurance policy valid for most vacations taken during the year in which it's purchased (but check pre-existing-condition coverage).

Always **buy travel policies directly from the insurance company**; if you buy them from a cruise line, airline, or tour operator that goes out of business you probably will not be covered for the agency or operator's

default, a major risk. Before making any purchase, **review your existing health and home-owner's policies** to find what they cover away from home.

➤ TRAVEL INSURERS: In the U.S.: **Access America** (✉ 6600 W. Broad St., Richmond, VA 23230, ☎ 800/284–8300, FAX 804/673–1491 or 800/346–9265, WEB www.etravelprotection.com). **Travel Guard International** (✉ 1145 Clark St., Stevens Point, WI 54481, ☎ 800/826–1300, 715/345–0505 for international callers, FAX 800/955–8785, WEB www.travelguard.com).

FOR INTERNATIONAL TRAVELERS

For information on customs restrictions, *see* Customs & Duties.

CAR RENTAL

When picking up a rental car, non-U.S. residents need a reservation voucher for any prepaid reservations that were made in the traveler's home country, a passport, a driver's license, and a travel policy that covers each driver.

CAR TRAVEL

In fall 2001, gasoline cost $1.49–$1.89 per gallon. Stations are plentiful. Most stay open late (24 hours along large highways and in big cities), except in rural areas, where Sunday hours are limited and where you may drive long stretches without a refueling opportunity. Highways are well paved. Interstate highways—limited-access, multilane highways whose numbers are prefixed by "I–"—are the fastest routes. Interstates with three-digit numbers encircle urban areas, which may have other limited-access expressways, freeways, and parkways as well. Tolls may be levied on limited-access highways. So-called U.S. highways and state highways are not necessarily limited-access but may have several lanes.

Along larger highways, roadside stops with rest rooms, fast-food restaurants, and sundries stores are well spaced. State police and tow trucks patrol major highways and lend assistance. If your car breaks down on an interstate, pull onto the shoulder and wait for help, or have your passengers wait while you walk to an emergency phone. If you carry a cell phone, dial *55, noting your location on the small green roadside mileage markers.

Driving in the United States is on the right. Do **obey speed limits** posted along roads and highways. Watch for lower limits in small towns and on back roads. Massachusetts requires front-seat passengers to wear seat belts. On weekdays between 6 and 10 AM and again between 4 and 7 PM **expect heavy traffic.** To encourage carpooling, some expressways have special lanes for so-called high-occupancy vehicles (HOV)—cars carrying more than one passenger.

Book stores, gas stations, convenience stores, and rest stops sell maps (about $3) and multiregion road atlases (about $10).

CONSULATES & EMBASSIES

The nearest consulates are in Boston. New Zealand doesn't have a consulate in Boston.

➤ AUSTRALIA: (✉ 15 School St., Boston, ☎ 617/227–3131).

➤ CANADA: (✉ 3 Copley Pl., Boston, ☎ 617/262–3760).

➤ UNITED KINGDOM: (✉ 600 Atlantic Ave., Boston, ☎ 617/248–9555).

CURRENCY

The dollar is the basic unit of U.S. currency. It has 100 cents. Coins include the copper penny (1¢); the silvery nickel (5¢), dime (10¢), quarter (25¢), and half-dollar (50¢); and the golden $1 coin, replacing a now-rare silver dollar. Bills, denominated $1, $5, $10, $20, $50, and $100, are all green and identical in size; designs vary. The exchange rate in fall 2001 was $1.43 per British pound, 64¢ per Canadian dollar, 51¢ per Australian dollar, and 42¢ per New Zealand dollar.

ELECTRICITY

The U.S. standard is AC, 110 volts/60 cycles. Plugs have two flat pins set parallel to each other.

EMERGENCIES

For police, fire, or ambulance, **dial 911** (0 in rural areas).

INSURANCE

Britons and Australians need extra medical coverage when traveling overseas.

➤ INSURANCE INFORMATION: In the U.K.: **Association of British Insurers** (✉ 51 Gresham St., London EC2V 7HQ, ☎ 020/7600–3333, FAX 020/7696–8999, WEB www.abi.org.uk). In Australia: **Insurance Council of Australia** (✉ Level 3, 56 Pitt St., Sydney NSW 2000, ☎ 02/9253–5100, FAX 02/9253–5111, WEB www.ica.com.au). In Canada: **RBC Insurance** (✉ 6880 Financial Dr., Mississauga, Ontario L5N 7Y5, ☎ 905/816–2400 or 800/668–4342, FAX 905/813–4704, WEB www.rbcinsurance.com). In New Zealand: **Insurance Council of New Zealand** (✉ Level 7, 111–115 Customhouse Quay, Box 474, Wellington, ☎ 04/472–5230, FAX 04/473–3011, WEB www.icnz.org.nz).

MAIL & SHIPPING

You can buy stamps and aerograms and send letters and parcels in post offices. Stamp-dispensing machines can occasionally be found in airports, bus and train stations, office buildings, drugstores, and the like. You can also deposit mail in the stout, dark blue, steel bins at strategic locations everywhere and in the mail chutes of large buildings; pickup schedules are posted.

For mail sent within the United States, you need a 34¢ stamp for first-class letters weighing up to 1 ounce (23¢ for each additional ounce) and 21¢ for domestic postcards. For overseas mail, you pay 80¢ for 1-ounce airmail letters, 70¢ for airmail postcards, and 35¢ for surface-rate postcards. For Canada and Mexico you need a 60¢ stamp for a 1-ounce letter and 50¢ for a postcard. For 70¢ you can buy an aerogram—a single sheet of lightweight blue paper that folds into its own envelope, stamped for overseas airmail.

To receive mail on the road, have it sent c/o General Delivery at your destination's main post office (use the correct five-digit zip code). You must pick up mail in person within 30 days and show a driver's license or passport.

PASSPORTS & VISAS

When traveling internationally, **carry your passport** even if you don't need one (it's always the best form of I.D.) and **make two photocopies of the data page** (one for someone at home and another for you, carried separately from your passport). If you lose your passport, promptly call the nearest embassy or consulate and the local police.

Visitor visas are not necessary for Canadian citizens, or for citizens of Australia and the United Kingdom who are staying fewer than 90 days.

➤ AUSTRALIAN CITIZENS: **Australian State Passport Office** (☎ 131–232, WEB www.dfat.gov.au/passports). **United States Consulate General** (✉ MLC Centre, 19-29 Martin Pl., 59th floor, Sydney NSW 2000, ☎ 1902/941–641 visa-inquiry line, WEB www.usis-australia.gov/consular/visas.html).

➤ CANADIAN CITIZENS: **Passport Office** (☎ 819/994–3500, 800/567–6868 in Canada).

➤ NEW ZEALAND CITIZENS: **New Zealand Passport Office** (☎ 04/494–0700 or 04/474–8100 for application procedures, WEB www.passports.govt.nz). **Embassy of the United States** (✉ 29 Fitzherbert Terr., Thorndon, Wellington, WEB usembassy.state.gov/wellington). **United States Consulate General** (✉ Citibank Center, 3rd Floor, 23 Customs St. East, Auckland, ☎ 09/303–2724, WEB www.usconsulateauckland.org.nz).

➤ U.K. CITIZENS: **London Passport Office** (☎ 0870/521–0410, WEB www.ukpa.gov.uk), for application procedures and emergency passports. **U.S. Consulate General** (✉ Queen's House, 14 Queen St., Belfast BTI 6E2, Northern Ireland). **U.S. Embassy Visa Branch** (✉ 5 Upper Grosvenor St., London W1A 2JB); send a self-addressed, stamped envelope. **U.S. Embassy Visa Information Line** (☎ 09068/200–290 or 020/7355–3335, WEB www.usembassy.org.uk).

TELEPHONES

All U.S. telephone numbers consist of a three-digit area code and a seven-digit local number. In many locations, you dial only the seven-digit number when calling locally. However, eastern Massachusetts implemented a 10-digit dialing system in 2001. You have to **dial the area code plus the seven-digit number for all local calls.** To call another region, as always, dial "1," then all 10 digits; the same goes for calls to numbers prefixed by "800," "888," and "877"—all toll-free. For calls to numbers preceded by "900" you must pay—usually dearly.

For international calls, dial "011" followed by the country code and the local number. For help, dial "0" and ask for an overseas operator. The country code is 61 for Australia, 64 for New Zealand, 44 for the United Kingdom. Calling Canada is the same as calling within the United States. Most local phone books list country codes and U.S. area codes. The country code for the United States is 1.

For operator assistance, dial "0". To obtain someone's phone number, call directory assistance, 555–1212 or occasionally 411 (free at public phones). To have the person you're calling foot the bill, phone collect; dial "0" instead of "1" before the 10-digit number.

At pay phones, instructions are usually posted. Usually you insert coins in a slot (10¢–35¢ for local calls) and wait for a steady tone before dialing. When you call long-distance, the operator tells you how much to insert; prepaid phone cards, widely available in various denominations, are easier. Call the number on the back, punch in the card's personal identification number when prompted, then dial your number.

LODGING

Accommodations on the Cape range from campsites to B&Bs to luxurious self-contained resorts offering all kinds of sporting facilities, restaurants, entertainment, services (including business services and children's programs), and all the assistance you'll ever need in making vacation arrangements.

Single-night lodgings for those just passing through can be found at countless tacky but cheap and conveniently located little roadside motels, as well as at others that are spotless and cheery yet still inexpensive, or at chain hotels at all price levels; these places often have a pool, TVs, or other amenities to keep children entertained in the evening.

Families may want to **consider condominiums, cottages, and efficiencies,** which offer more space; living areas; kitchens; and sometimes laundry facilities, children's play areas, or children's programs.

The lodgings we list are the cream of the crop in each price category. We always list the facilities that are available—but we don't specify whether they cost extra: when pricing accommodations, always ask what's included and what costs extra. Properties indicated by a ✕🖃 are lodging establishments whose restaurant warrants a special trip even if you are not staying at that establishment.

CATEGORY	COST*
$$$$	over $200
$$$	$150–$200
$$	$100–$150
$	under $100

All prices are for a standard double room in high season, excluding 5.7% state tax and gratuities. Some inns add a 15% service charge.

Assume that hotels operate on the **European Plan** (EP, with no meals included) unless we specify that they use the **Continental Plan** (CP, with a Continental breakfast), **Breakfast Plan** (BP, with a full breakfast), **Modified American Plan** (MAP, with breakfast and dinner), or the **Full American Plan** (FAP, with all meals).

CONDO & HOUSE RENTALS

If you want a home base that's roomy enough for a family and comes with cooking facilities, **consider a furnished rental.** These can save you money, especially if you're traveling with a group. Many visitors to the Cape rent a house if they are going to stay for a week or longer, rather than stay at a B&B or hotel. These can save you money; however, some rentals are luxury properties, economical only when your party is large. Many local real-estate agencies deal with rentals, and most specialize in a specific area. If you do decide to rent, be sure to book a property well in advance of

your trip, as many properties are rented out to the same families or groups year after year. Rental opportunities are often greater in the smaller, quieter towns, such as Yarmouth, Chatham, Wellfleet, and Truro. For the names of regional agencies, *see* the A to Z section of the appropriate chapter in this book, consult the local chamber of commerce guide, and if you can, get hold of the local yellow pages. *See* Home, Sweet Rental Home *in* Chapter 7 for tips on arranging a rental.

Home-exchange directories (☞ Home Exchanges) list rentals (often second homes owned by prospective house swappers), and some services search for a house or apartment for you (even a castle, if that's your fancy) and handle the paperwork. Some send an illustrated catalog; others send photographs only of specific properties, sometimes at a charge. Up-front registration fees may apply.

➤ CAPE-WIDE RENTAL AGENT: **Waterfront Rentals** (✉ 20 Pilgrim Rd., West Yarmouth 02673, ☎ 508/778–1818, 🖷 508/771–3563, 🆆ᴇᴮ www.waterfrontrentalsinc.com) covers Bourne to Truro.

B&BS

Bed-and-breakfast inns have long been very popular on Cape Cod. Many are in interesting old sea captains' homes and other 17th-, 18th-, and 19th-century buildings; others are in newer homes in which a few rooms and bathrooms have been set aside for rent. In many cases, B&Bs are not appropriate for families—noise travels easily, rooms are often small, and the furnishings are often fragile; so be sure to ask. Most B&Bs do not provide phones or TVs in guest rooms, many are not air-conditioned, and more and more prohibit smoking.

In summer you must reserve lodgings as far in advance as possible—several months for the most popular inns. Assistance with last-minute reservations is available at the Cape Cod Chamber of Commerce information booths and through the chamber of commerce's Web site (☞ Visitor Information). Off season, rates are much reduced, and service may be more personalized.

Numerous B&B reservation agencies can aid you in choosing an inn. One company, DestINNations (part of the TOURCO company), handles a limited number of upscale inns, resorts, and B&Bs on the Cape. For more information get a free B&B guide from the Massachusetts Office of Travel & Tourism (☞ Visitor Information). The Cape Cod Chamber of Commerce (☞ Visitor Information) also publishes a free B&B guide.

➤ RESERVATION SERVICES: **Bed and Breakfast Cape Cod** (⊠ Box 1312, Orleans 02653, ☎ 508/255–3824 or 800/541–6226, FAX 508/240–0599, WEB www.bedandbreakfastcapecod. com). **DestINNations** (⊠ 29 Bassett La., Hyannis 02601, ☎ 508/790–0577 or 800/333–4667, FAX 508/790–1115, WEB www.destinnations.com).

CAMPING

There are many private and state-park camping areas on Cape Cod. Write to the Massachusetts Office of Travel & Tourism and the Cape Cod Chamber of Commerce (☞ Visitor Information). For details on camping in specific areas, look for the ⚠ icon in that area's Dining and Lodging section and consult the A to Z section of that chapter.

HOME EXCHANGES

If you would like to exchange your home for someone else's, **join a home-exchange organization,** which will send you its updated listings of available exchanges for a year and will include your own listing in at least one of them. It's up to you to make specific arrangements.

➤ EXCHANGE CLUBS: **HomeLink International** (⊠ Box 47747, Tampa, FL 33647, ☎ 813/975–9825 or 800/638–3841, FAX 813/910–8144, WEB www.homelink.org; $106 per year). **Intervac U.S.** (⊠ Box 590504, San Francisco, CA 94159, ☎ 800/756–4663, FAX 415/435–7440, WEB www.intervacus.com; $93 yearly fee includes one catalogue and on-line access).

HOSTELS

No matter what your age, you can **save on lodging costs by staying at hostels.** In some 4,500 locations in more than 70 countries around the world, Hostelling International (HI), the umbrella group for a number of national youth-hostel associations, offers single-sex, dorm-style beds, and, at many hostels, rooms for couples and family accommodations. Membership in any HI national hostel association, open to travelers of all ages, allows you to stay in HI-affiliated hostels at member rates; one-year membership is about $25 for adults (C$35 for a two-year minimum membership in Canada, £12.50 in the U.K., A$52 in Australia, and NZ$40 in New Zealand); hostels run about $10–$25 per night. Members have priority if the hostel is full; they're also eligible for discounts around the world, even on rail and bus travel in some countries.

Cape Cod has some excellent hostels. In season, when all other rates are jacked up beyond belief, hostels are often the only budget-accommodation option, but you must plan ahead to reserve space. You may luck out on last-minute cancellations, but it would be unwise to rely on them. *See* the lodging listings *in* the appropriate chapters for specific information.

➤ ORGANIZATIONS: **Hostelling International—American Youth Hostels** (⊠ 733 15th St. NW, Suite 840, Washington, DC 20005, ☎ 202/783–6161, FAX 202/783–6171, WEB www. hiayh.org). **Hostelling International—Canada** (⊠ 400–205 Catherine St., Ottawa, Ontario K2P 1C3, ☎ 613/237–7884, 800/663–5777 in Canada, FAX 613/237–7868, WEB www.hihostels. ca). **Youth Hostel Association of England and Wales** (⊠ Trevelyan House, 8 St. Stephen's Hill, St. Albans, Hertfordshire AL1 2DY, U.K., ☎ 0870/870–8808, FAX 01727/844126, WEB www.yha.org.uk). **Youth Hostel Association Australia** (⊠ 10 Mallett St., Camperdown, NSW 2050, ☎ 02/9565–1699, FAX 02/9565–1325, WEB www.yha.com.au). **Youth Hostels Association of New Zealand** (⊠ Level 3, 193 Cashel St., Box 436, Christchurch, ☎ 03/379–9970, FAX 03/365–4476, WEB www. yha.org.nz).

HOTELS

All hotels listed have private bath unless otherwise noted.

➤ TOLL-FREE NUMBERS: **Best Western** (☎ 800/528–1234, WEB www.bestwestern.com). **Choice** (☎ 800/221–2222, WEB www.choicehotels.com). **Comfort Inn** (☎ 800/228–5150, WEB www.comfortinn.com). **Days Inn** (☎ 800/325–2525, WEB www.daysinn.com). **Holiday Inn** (☎ 800/465–4329, WEB www.basshotels.com). **Radisson** (☎ 800/333–3333, WEB www.radisson.com). **Ramada** (☎ 800/228–2828; 800/854–7854 for international reservations, WEB www.ramada.com or www.ramadahotels.com). **Sheraton** (☎ 800/325–3535, WEB www.starwood.com/sheraton).

MEDIA

NEWSPAPERS & MAGAZINES

Glossy regional magazines include *Cape Cod Life*, with feature articles about Cape people and places; *Provincetown Arts*, which focuses on Provincetown artists, performers, and writers, and also publishes essays, fiction, interviews, and poetry; and *CapeWomen*, in which articles feature profiles of Cape-based women and address issues of interest to women; the magazine also publishes the annual *P'TownWomen*.

The *Cape Cod Times* is a daily newspaper, with current news from the around the Cape and elsewhere. *A-Plus,* available free in galleries and as several newspaper supplements, has arts listings. In Provincetown look for the *Banner* and *Provincetown Magazine,* both weeklies, for art and entertainment listings.

RADIO & TELEVISION

You can generally get Boston and Providence TV stations on the Cape. There is also a community station, C3TV.

WBUR, a Boston-based National Public Radio station, broadcasts on the Cape with different frequencies in different towns: 1240 AM in West Yarmouth, WSDH 91.5 FM in Sandwich, and WCCT 90.3 FM in Harwich. A second public radio station operates at WCAI 90.1 FM from Woods Hole, with support from WGBH in Boston.

MONEY MATTERS

Prices throughout this guide are given for adults. Substantially reduced fees are almost always available for children, students, and senior citizens. For information on taxes, *see* Taxes.

ATMS

Cape Cod has many machines in all the towns.

CREDIT CARDS

Throughout this guide, the following abbreviations are used: **AE,** American Express; **D,** Discover; **DC,** Diners Club; **MC,** MasterCard; and **V,** Visa.

➤ REPORTING LOST CARDS: **American Express** (☎ 800/327–2177); **Discover Card** (☎ 800/347–2683); **Diners Club** (☎ 800/234–6377); **MasterCard** (☎ 800/307–7309); and **Visa** (☎ 800/847–2911).

NATIONAL PARKS

Look into discount passes to save money on park entrance fees. The National Parks Pass ($50) gets you and your companions free admission to all parks for one year. (Camping and parking are extra.) A percentage of the proceeds from sales of the pass will fund National Parks projects. Both the Golden Age Passport ($10), for those 62 and older, and the Golden Access Passport (free), for travelers with disabilities, entitle holders to free entry to all national parks, plus 50% off fees for the use of many park facilities and services. You must show proof of age and of U.S. citizenship or permanent residency (such as a U.S. passport, driver's license, or birth certificate) and, if requesting Golden Access, proof of disability. The Golden Age and Golden Access passes are available at all national parks wherever entrance fees are charged. The National Parks Pass is available by mail or through the Internet.

➤ PASSES BY MAIL: **National Park Service** (✉ National Park Service/Department of Interior, 1849 C St. NW, Washington, DC 20240, ☎ 202/208–4747, WEB www.nps.gov). **National Parks Pass** (✉ 27540 Ave. Mentry, Valencia, CA 91355, ☎ 888/GO–PARKS, WEB www.nationalparks.org).

OUTDOORS & SPORTS

For details on enjoying the outdoors in your chosen vacation spot, including water sports, *see* the appropriate regional chapter.

BASEBALL

The Cape Cod Baseball League, considered the country's best summer league, is scouted by all the major-league teams. Ten teams play a 44-game season from mid-June to mid-August; admission is free to games at all 10 fields, although donations are accepted. The teams also conduct baseball clinics for children and teens.

➤ CONTACTS: **Cape Cod Baseball League** (☎ 508/432–6909, WEB www.capecodbaseball.org).

BIKING

The Travel Center at the American Youth Hostels' Boston hostel sells a "Cape Ann & North Shore/Cape Cod & Islands" bike map that includes information on the Claire Saltonstall Bikeway between Boston and Provincetown (135 mi) or between Boston and Woods Hole (85 mi). Brochures about the bikeway, as well as other bike trails on the Cape, may also be available from the Cape Cod Chamber of Commerce (☞ Visitor Information).

➤ CONTACT: **Travel Center at the American Youth Hostels' Boston hostel** (✉ 12 Hemenway St., Boston 02115, ☎ 617/531–3523, WEB www.usahostels.org).

FISHING

Charter boats and party boats (per-head fees, rather than the charters' group rates) fish in season for bluefish, tuna, marlin, and mako and blue sharks. Throughout the year there's bottom fishing for flounder, tautog, scup, fluke, cod, and pollack.

The Cape Cod Chamber of Commerce's *Sportsman's Guide* provides fishing regulations, surf-fishing access locations, a map of boat-launching facilities, and more. The state Division of Fisheries and Wildlife has a book with dozens of maps of Cape ponds. Remember, you'll need a license for freshwater fishing, available for a nominal fee at bait-and-tackle shops. No licence is needed for saltwater fishing.

Molly Benjamin's fishing column in the Friday *Cape Cod Times* gives the latest information about fishing on the Cape—what's being caught and where.

GOLF

The Cape Cod Chamber of Commerce has a "Golf Map of Cape Cod," locating dozens of courses on the Cape. Summer greens fees range from $25 to $50.

PACKING

Only a few Cape Cod restaurants require formal dress, as do some dinner cruises. The area prides itself on informality. Do **pack a sweater or jacket, even in summer,** for nights can be cool. For suggested clothing to minimize bites from deer ticks and to prevent Lyme disease, *see* Health. Perhaps most important of all, **don't forget a swimsuit** (or two).

In your carry-on luggage, **pack an extra pair of eyeglasses or contact lenses and enough of any medication** you take to last the entire trip. You may also ask your doctor to write a spare prescription using the drug's generic name, since brand names may vary from country to country. In luggage to be checked, **never pack prescription drugs or valuables.** And don't forget to carry with you the addresses of offices that handle refunds of lost traveler's checks. Check *Fodor's How to Pack* (available in bookstores everywhere) for more tips.

To avoid customs and security delays, carry medications in their original packaging; don't pack any sharp objects, including knives of any size or material, scissors, manicure tools, and corkscrews, or anything else that might arouse suspicion. If you need such objects on your trip, consider shipping them to your destination or buying them there.

CHECKING LUGGAGE

You are allowed one carry-on bag and one personal article, such as a purse or a laptop computer. Make sure that everything you carry aboard will fit under your seat or in the overhead bin. Get to the gate early, so you can board as soon as possible, before the overhead bins fill up.

If you are flying internationally, note that baggage allowances may be determined not by piece but by weight—generally 88 pounds (40 kilograms) in first class, 66 pounds (30 kilograms) in business class, and 44 pounds (20 kilograms) in economy.

Airline liability for baggage is limited to $2,500 per person on flights within the United States. On international flights it amounts to $9.07 per pound or $20 per kilogram for checked baggage (roughly $640 per 70-pound bag) and $400 per passenger for unchecked baggage. You can buy additional coverage at check-in for about $10 per $1,000 of coverage, but it excludes a rather extensive list of items, shown on your airline ticket.

Before departure, **itemize your bags' contents** and their worth, and label the bags with your name, address, and phone number. (If you use your home address, cover it so potential thieves can't see it readily.) Inside each bag, **pack a copy of your itinerary.** At check-in, **make sure that each bag is correctly tagged** with the destination airport's three-letter code. If your bags arrive damaged or fail to arrive at all, file a written report with the airline before leaving the airport.

SENIOR-CITIZEN TRAVEL

To qualify for age-related discounts, **mention your senior-citizen status up front** when booking hotel reservations (not when checking out) and before you're seated in restaurants (not when paying the bill). Be sure to have identification on hand. When renting a car, ask about promotional car-rental discounts, which can be cheaper than senior-citizen rates.

➤ EDUCATIONAL PROGRAMS: **Elderhostel** (⊠ 11 Ave. de Lafayette, Boston, MA 02111-1746, ☎ 877/426–8056, FAX 877/426–2166, WEB www. elderhostel.org).

SHOPPING

For an overview of some of the local specialties, *see* Pleasures and Pastimes *in* Chapter 1. Because of the Cape's large year-round population, shops tend to remain open, though most

Provincetown and Wellfleet shops and galleries do close in winter.

Cape Cod Arts, published by *Cape Cod Life,* lists galleries Cape-wide. Provincetown and Wellfleet are the main centers for art, and their gallery associations have pamphlets on local galleries. For a directory of area antiques dealers and auctions, contact the Cape Cod Antique Dealers Association. For a listing of crafts shops on the Cape, write to the Artisans' Guild of Cape Cod, Cape Cod Potters, or the Society of Cape Cod Craftsmen.

Throughout the Cape, shop owners respond to both the flow of tourists and their own inclinations. Especially off season, it's best to **phone a shop before going out of your way to visit.**

➤ LOCAL RESOURCES: **Cape Cod Antique Dealers Association** (send business-size self-addressed, stamped envelope to ⊠ Box 191, Yarmouth Port 02675; WEB www.ccada.com). **Cape Cod Arts** (⊠ Box 1385, Pocasset 02559, WEB www.capecodlife.com/CCA). **Provincetown Gallery Guild** (⊠ Box 242, Provincetown 02657). **Wellfleet Art Galleries Association** (⊠ Box 916, Wellfleet 02667).

Artisans' Guild of Cape Cod (send business-size self-addressed, stamped envelope to ⊠ 46 Debs Hill Rd., Yarmouth 02675). **Cape Cod Potters** (⊠ Box 76, Chatham 02633, WEB www.capecodpotters.com). **Society of Cape Cod Craftsmen** (⊠ Box 1709, Wellfleet 02667-1709).

SMART SOUVENIRS

Local crafts, cranberry glass or a Pairpoint Crystal cup plate, and special-interest books about the Cape (purchased at one of the many fine bookstores) can make satisfying reminders of a visit.

STUDENTS ON CAPE COD

➤ I.D.s & SERVICES: **Council Travel** (CIEE; ⊠ 205 E. 42nd St., 15th floor, New York, NY 10017, ☎ 212/822–2700 or 888/268–6245, FAX 212/822–2699, WEB www.counciltravel.com). **Travel Cuts** (⊠ 187 College St., Toronto, Ontario M5T 1P7, Canada, ☎ 416/979–2406, 800/667–2887 in Canada, FAX 416/979–0956, WEB www.travelcuts.com).

TAXES

The state hotel tax rate is 5.7%.

SALES TAX

Massachusetts state sales tax is 5%.

TELEPHONES

Eastern Massachusetts implemented a 10-digit dialing system in 2001. You have to **dial the area code plus the seven-digit number for all local calls.** To call another region, as always, dial "1," then all 10 digits; the same goes for calls to numbers prefixed by "800," "888," and "877."

TIME

Cape Cod is in the Eastern Standard time zone.

TIPPING

At restaurants a 15% tip is standard for waiters; up to 20% may be expected at more expensive establishments. The same goes for taxi drivers, bartenders, and hairdressers. Coat-check operators usually expect $1 per coat; bellhops and porters should get 50¢ to $1 per bag; hotel maids in upscale hotels should get about $1.50 per day of your stay. On package tours, conductors and drivers usually get $10 per day from the group as a whole; check whether this has already been figured into your cost. For local sightseeing tours you may individually tip the driver-guide $1–$5, depending on the length of the tour and the number of people in your party, if he or she has been helpful or informative. Ushers in theaters do not expect tips.

TOURS & PACKAGES

Because everything is prearranged on a prepackaged tour or independent vacation, you spend less time planning—and often get it all at a good price.

BOOKING WITH AN AGENT

Travel agents are excellent resources. But it's a good idea to collect brochures from several agencies as some agents' suggestions may be influenced by relationships with tour and package firms that reward them for volume sales. If you have a special interest, **find an agent with expertise in that area**; the American Society of Travel Agents (ASTA; ☞ Travel Agencies) has a database of specialists worldwide.

Make sure your travel agent knows the accommodations and other services of the place being recommended. Ask about the hotel's location, room size, beds, and whether it has a pool, room service, or programs for children, if you care about these. Has your agent been there in person or sent others whom you can contact?

Do some homework on your own, too: local tourism boards can provide information about lesser-known and small-niche operators, some of which may sell only direct.

BUYER BEWARE

Each year consumers are stranded or lose their money when tour operators—even large ones with excellent reputations—go out of business. So **check out the operator.** Ask several travel agents about its reputation, and try to **book with a company that has a consumer-protection program.** (Look for information in the company's brochure.) In the United States, members of the National Tour Association and the United States Tour Operators Association are required to set aside funds to cover your payments and travel arrangements in the event that the company defaults. It's also a good idea to choose a company that participates in the American Society of Travel Agents' Tour Operator Program (TOP); ASTA will act as mediator in any disputes between you and your tour operator.

Remember that the more your package or tour includes the better you can predict the ultimate cost of your vacation. Make sure you know exactly what is covered, and **beware of hidden costs.** Are taxes, tips, and transfers included? Entertainment and excursions? These can add up.

➤ TOUR-OPERATOR RECOMMENDATIONS: **American Society of Travel Agents** (☞ Travel Agencies). **National Tour Association** (NTA; ✉ 546 E. Main St., Lexington, KY 40508, ☎ 859/226–4444 or 800/682–8886, WEB www.ntaonline.com). **United States Tour Operators Association**

(USTOA; ✉ 275 Madison Ave., Suite 2014, New York, NY 10016, ☎ 212/599–6599 or 800/468–7862, FAX 212/599–6744, WEB www.ustoa.com).

TRAIN TRAVEL

Because of continuing financial difficulties, Amtrak service to the Cape was suspended in 1998; it is not currently scheduled to resume, but call for an update.

➤ TRAIN INFORMATION: Amtrak (☎ 800/872–7245, WEB www.amtrak.com).

TRANSPORTATION
AROUND CAPE COD

A car is by far the most practical way to get around the Cape, although there is limited bus service. A good general resource for information about getting around the Cape is the free Smart Guide, published by the Cape Cod Chamber of Commerce; it's available from the Chamber (see Visitor Information) or online at WEB www.smartguide.org. Also see Getting Around in the A to Z sections of the appropriate chapters.

TRAVEL AGENCIES

A good travel agent puts your needs first. Look for an agency that has been in business at least five years, emphasizes customer service, and has someone on staff who specializes in your destination. In addition, **make sure the agency belongs to a professional trade organization.** The American Society of Travel Agents (ASTA)—the largest and most influential in the field with more than 26,000 members in some 170 countries—maintains and enforces a strict code of ethics and will step in to help mediate any agent-client disputes involving ASTA members if necessary. ASTA (whose motto is "Without a travel agent, you're on your own") also maintains a Web site that includes a directory of agents. (If a travel agency is also acting as your tour operator, see Buyer Beware in Tours & Packages.)

➤ LOCAL AGENT REFERRALS: American Society of Travel Agents (ASTA; ✉ 1101 King St., Suite 200, Alexandria, VA 22314, ☎ 800/965–2782 24-hr hot line, FAX 703/739–7642, WEB www.astanet.com). Association

of British Travel Agents (✉ 68–71 Newman St., London W1T 3AH, U.K., ☎ 020/7637–2444, FAX 020/7637–0713, WEB www.abtanet.com). Association of Canadian Travel Agents (✉ 130 Albert St., Suite 1705, Ottawa, Ontario K1P 5G4, Canada, ☎ 613/237–3657, FAX 613/237–7052, WEB www.acta.net). Australian Federation of Travel Agents (✉ Level 3, 309 Pitt St., Sydney NSW 2000, Australia, ☎ 02/9264–3299, FAX 02/9264–1085, WEB www.afta.com.au). Travel Agents' Association of New Zealand (✉ Level 5, Tourism and Travel House, 79 Boulcott St., Box 1888, Wellington 10033, New Zealand, ☎ 04/499–0104, FAX 04/499–0827, WEB www.taanz.org.nz).

VISITOR INFORMATION

Before you go, contact the state's office of tourism and the area's chambers of commerce for general information, seasonal events, and brochures. For specific information on Cape Cod's state forests and parks, the area's farmers' markets and fairs, or wildlife, contact the special-interest government offices below. You can also check Web sites on the Internet (☞ Web Sites). When you arrive, you can pay a visit to the local chamber of commerce for additional information. For a list of local Cape Cod and nearby chambers of commerce that can also provide information, see Visitor Information in the A to Z sections of the appropriate chapters.

The Army Corps of Engineers has a 24-hour recreation hot line for canal-area events, weather, and tidal and fishing information.

➤ LOCAL CONTACTS: Cape Cod Chamber of Commerce (✉ junction of Rtes. 6 and 132, Hyannis 02601, ☎ 508/862–0700 or 888/332–2732, FAX 508/862–0727, WEB www.capecodchamber.org). Bristol County Convention & Visitors Bureau (✉ 70 N. 2nd St., Box 976, New Bedford, MA 02741, ☎ 508/997–1250 or 800/288–6263, WEB www.southofboston.org). Cape Cod National Seashore (✉ South Wellfleet 02663, ☎ 508/349–3785, WEB www.nps.gov/caco). Destination Plymouth (WEB www.visit-plymouth.com).

➤ STATE: **Massachusetts Office of Travel & Tourism** (✉ 10 Park Plaza, Suite 4510, Boston 02116, ☎ 800/227–6277; 800/447–6277 for brochures, FAX 617/973–8525, WEB www.massvacation.com).

➤ SPECIAL INTERESTS: **Army Corps of Engineers** (☎ 508/759–5991). **Department of Environmental Management** (✉ Division of Forests and Parks, 251 Causeway St., Suite 600, Boston 02114, ☎ 617/626–1250). **Department of Food and Agriculture** (✉ 251 Causeway St., Suite 500, Boston 02114, ☎ 617/626–1700, FAX 617/626–1850). **Division of Fisheries and Wildlife** (✉ Field Headquarters, 1 Rabbit Hill Rd., Westborough 01581, ☎ 508/792–7270, FAX 508/792–7275).

WEB SITES

Do check out the World Wide Web when planning your trip. You'll find everything from weather forecasts to virtual tours of famous cities. Be sure to **visit Fodors.com** (www.fodors.com), a complete travel-planning site. You can research prices and book plane tickets, hotel rooms, rental cars, vacation packages, and more. In addition, you can post your pressing questions in the Travel Talk section. Other planning tools include a currency converter and weather reports, and there are loads of links to travel resources.

GENERAL INFORMATION

For general information, visit the Cape Cod Information Center (www.allcapecod.com) or Cape Cod Online (www.capecodonline.com); also *see* Visitor Information.

TRANSPORTATION

Smart Traveler (www.smartraveler.com) provides real-time updates on traffic conditions on Cape Cod. You can look at live Web cam pictures of the Bourne and Sagamore bridges at the Cape Cod USA site (www.capecodusa.com).

For Cape Cod bus and trolley schedules, check with the Cape Cod Regional Transit Authority (www.capecodtransit.org). The transportation information site of the Cape Cod Commission (www.gocapecod.org) has links to trans-

portation providers, updates on transportation-related construction projects, and information on bicycling and walking, including updates on the Cape Cod Rail Trail. The Massachusetts Bicycle Coalition (www.massbike.org) has information for bicyclists. Rails-to-Trails Conservancy (www.railtrails.org) provides general information about rail trails, such as the Cape Cod Rail Trail.

Island ferry information and schedules are available online from the Steamship Authority (www.islandferry.com) and from Hy-Line (www.hy-linecruises.com). From New Bedford you can travel to Vineyard Haven on the ferry *Schamonchi* (www.mvferry.com) and to Cuttyhunk Island on the M/V *Alert II* (www.cuttyhunk.com).

DISABILITY ACCESS

Directory of Accessible Facilities lists accessible recreational facilities in Massachusetts (www.state.ma.us/dem/access.htm). Cape Cod Disability Access Directory (www.capecoddisability.org) has useful information about facilities on Cape Cod.

WHEN TO GO

Memorial Day through Labor Day (or, in some cases, Columbus Day) is high season on Cape Cod. This is summer with a capital *S*, a time for barbecues, beach bumming, swimming, and water sports. During summer everything is open for business on the Cape, but you can also expect high-season evils: high prices, crowds, and traffic.

The Cape, however, is increasingly a year-round destination. *See* The Cape's Six Seasons *in* Chapter 7 for some highlights of the off-season.

CLIMATE

Although there are plenty of idyllic beach days to go around on the Cape, rain or fog is not an uncommon part of even an August vacation here. Visitors who do not learn to appreciate the beauty of the land and sea in mist and rain may find themselves mighty cranky.

Temperatures in winter and summer are milder on the Cape than on the mainland, due in part to the warming influence of the Gulf Stream and the moderating ocean breezes. As a rule, the Cape gets much less snow than the mainland, and what falls generally does not last. Still, winter can bring bone-chilling dampness.

The following are average daily maximum and minimum tempera-

tures for Hyannis; it's likely to be 2–3 degrees cooler on the coast.

➤ FORECASTS: **Weather Channel Connection** (☎ 900/932–8437), 95¢ per minute from a Touch-Tone phone.

For local Cape weather, coastal marine forecasts, and today's tide times, call the weather line of **WQRC** (☎ 508/771–5522) in Hyannis.

Climate

Jan.	40F	+4C	May	62F	17C	Sept.	70F	21C
	25	−4		48	+9		56	13
Feb.	41F	+5C	June	71F	22C	Oct.	59F	15C
	26	−3		56	13		47	8
Mar.	42F	+6C	July	78F	26C	Nov.	49F	9C
	28	−2		63	17		37	3
Apr.	53F	12C	Aug.	76F	24C	Dec.	40F	4C
	40	+4		61	16		26	−3

FESTIVALS AND SEASONAL EVENTS

The Massachusetts Office of Travel & Tourism offers events listings and a whale-watch guide for the entire state. Also see the events calendar in "Cape-Week," an arts-and-entertainment supplement published every Friday in the *Cape Cod Times*; it's available online at www.capeweek.com.

➤ LATE APR.: The weekend-long **Brewster in Bloom** (☎ 508/896–3500, WEB www.brewsterinbloom. com) greets the spring season with a daffodil fest each year during the last weekend in April. Geared to promote small-town life, the festival includes arts-and-crafts shows, a parade, tours of historic homes and inns, a golf tournament, and a giant antiques and collectibles market.

➤ MAY 17–19: The Green Briar Nature Center and Jam Kitchen in Sandwich holds its annual **Green Briar Herb Festival** (☎ 508/888–6870), where you can pick up perennials, wildflowers, and dozens of herb varieties.

➤ MID-MAY: **Cape Cod Maritime Week** (☎ 508/362–3828, WEB www. capecodcommission.org/hdn) celebrates the Cape's maritime history with lighthouse tours, guided shore-front walks, and special exhibits Cape-wide.

➤ JUNE–AUG.: **Summer theater, town-band concerts**, and **arts-and-crafts fairs** enliven most every Cape town.

➤ EARLY JUNE: The **Cape Cod Antique Dealers Association Annual Antiques Show** at Sandwich's Heritage Plantation (☎ 508/888–3300) is attended by 50 dealers of fine 18th- and 19th-century English and American furniture, folk art, Sandwich glass, jewelry, paintings, and quilts.

➤ MID-JUNE: **Cape Heritage '02** (☎ 508/362–0066) is a weeklong celebration of the Cape's history and culture hosted by museums, historical societies, visual and performing groups, libraries, and environmental organizations. The theme for 2002 is "Domestic Life: The Culinary, Gardening, Homemaking, and Family Traditions of Cape Cod."

➤ MID- TO LATE JUNE: The **Portuguese Festival** (☎ 508/487–3424) honors Provincetown's Portuguese heritage with a lively weekend of traditional foods, dances, concerts, games, fireworks, and other events.

The **Blessing of the Fleet** in Provincetown concludes the Portuguese Festival weekend. On Sunday, a parade ends at the wharf, where fishermen and their families and friends pile onto boats and form a procession. The bishop stands on the dock and blesses the boats with holy water as they pass by.

Falmouth welcomes the **Soundfest Chamber Music Festival** (☎ 508/548–2290, WEB www.coloradoquartet.com), including the Colorado Quartet and guest artists. Daily events during the two-week festival include student performances, concerts, master classes, and lectures.

➤ JULY 4 WEEKEND: The **Mashpee Powwow** (☎ 508/477–0208) brings together Wampanoags from North and South America for three days of dance contests, drumming, a fireball game, and a clambake, plus the crowning of the Mashpee Wampanoag Indian princess on the final night.

Fireworks displays are a part of July 4 celebrations in several Cape towns.

➤ MID-JULY: The **Barnstable County Fair** (☎ 508/563–3200, WEB www.barnstablecountyfair.org/) in East Falmouth, begun in 1844, is Cape Cod's biggest event. The nine-day affair includes livestock and food judging; horse, pony, and oxen pulls and shows; arts-and-crafts demonstrations; carnival rides; lots of food; and appearances by the formerly famous bent on comebacks.

➤ LATE JULY: The Cape Cod Symphony Orchestra sets up at the Mashpee Commons for the first of two annual **Sounds of Summer Pops Concerts** (☎ 508/362–1111).

➤ AUG.: The **Cape & Islands Chamber Music Festival** (☎ 508/945–8060 or 800/229–5739, WEB www.capecodchambermusic.org) is three weeks of top-caliber performances, including a jazz night, at various locations in August. The festival also sponsors an off-season concert series; call or check the Web site for the schedule.

➤ EARLY AUG.: The Boston Pops Esplanade Orchestra wows the crowds with its annual **Pops by the Sea** concert (☎ 508/362–0066, WEB www.artsfoundationcapecod.org/Fleet.html), held at the Hyannis Village Green at 5 PM. Each year a guest conductor strikes up the band.

New Bedford's **Feast of the Blessed Sacrament** (☎ 508/979–1745 or 800/508–5353, WEB www.portuguesefeast.com) is one of the largest celebrations of Portuguese culture in the country. Music, dance, a parade, carnival rides, and traditional foods—particularly the giant *carne de espeto* outdoor barbecue—are all part of the four-day event.

➤ MID-AUG.: The **Falmouth Road Race** (✉ Box 732, Falmouth 02541, ☎ 508/540–7000, WEB www.falmouthroadrace.com) is a world-class race covering the coast from Woods Hole to Falmouth Heights; to participate, apply by mail the fall or winter prior to the race.

➤ LATE AUG.: The Cape Cod Symphony Orchestra comes to Eldridge Field Park in Orleans for its **Sounds of Summer Pops Concert** (☎ 508/362–1111).

The annual **New England Jazz Festival** (☎ 508/477–2580, WEB www.bochcenterarts.com), produced by the Boch Center for the Performing Arts, takes place at Mashpee Commons.

The Osterville Historical Society holds its annual **antiques show** (☎ 508/428–5861) on the third or fourth Thursday in August.

➤ SEPT.: The **Annual Bourne Scallop Fest** (☎ 508/759–6000), the weekend after Labor Day, attracts thousands of people to Buzzards Bay for three days of music, parades, carnival rides, and, of course, fried scallops.

The **Harwich Cranberry Festival** (☎ 508/430–2811, WEB www.harwichcranberryfestival.com) includes an arts-and-crafts show, a carnival, fireworks, pancake breakfasts, an antique-car show, and much more.

➤ MID-OCT.: **Seafest,** an annual tribute to the maritime industry, marks one of the few times that Chatham Light (☎ 508/945–5199) is open to the public.

➤ LATE OCT.: **Fall foliage.** The leaf season usually peaks around the end of October. Colors might flame a few weeks earlier or later, however, depending on the weather in the preceding months.

➤ THANKSGIVING EVE: The **Lighting of the Monument** festivities (☎ 508/487–1310) commemorate the Pilgrims' landing, with the lighting of

5,000 white and gold bulbs draped over the Pilgrim Monument. The lighting occurs each night until just after the New Year. A musical performance accompanies the lighting, and the monument museum holds an open house and tours. Other events include dramatic readings of the Mayflower Compact (which was signed in Provincetown Harbor), fireworks, and numerous Thanksgiving dinner celebrations. Various arts and crafts events kick off around the same time and continue through the holiday season.

➤ EARLY DEC.: Many Cape towns do up the Christmas season in grand style. To take in the best-known celebration, plan an excursion to the nearby island of Nantucket for the annual **Christmas Stroll** (☎ 508/228–1700, WEB www.nantucket-stroll.com), which takes place the first weekend of the month. Activities include theatrical performances, art exhibitions, crafts sales, and a tour of historic homes. To avoid the throngs, visit on one of the surrounding weekends (festivities begin the day after Thanksgiving and last through New Year's Eve).

Various Cape towns also have **holiday strolls**; call the Cape Cod Chamber of Commerce for a free brochure (☎ 508/862–0700).

Falmouth's **Christmas by the Sea** (☎ 508/548–8500 or 800/526–8532), the first full weekend of December, includes lighting ceremonies at the Village Green, caroling at Nobska Light in Woods Hole, a house tour, church fairs, and a parade.

Provincetown's **HolidayFest** (☎ 800/882–7202, WEB www.provincetownholidayfest.com), begun in 2001, enhances holiday spirits with performances, tree walks, carol strolls, and parties.

➤ DEC.: Chatham's **Christmas by the Sea** weekend (☎ 508/945–5199), generally the first weekend of the month, includes caroling, other special events, and a dinner dance at the grand Chatham Bars Inn. The events are part of a monthlong celebration beginning just after Thanksgiving and ending with a lavish First Night celebration, with fireworks over Oyster Pond on New Year's Eve.

Smart Travel Tips A to Z

1 DESTINATION: CAPE COD

The Seasons of America Past and Present

New and Noteworthy

What's Where

Pleasures and Pastimes

Fodor's Choice

THE SEASONS OF AMERICA PAST AND PRESENT

"The world to-day is sick to its thin blood for lack of elemental things," wrote Henry Beston in his 1928 Cape Cod classic, *The Outermost House,* "for fire before the hands, for water welling from the earth, for air, for the dear earth itself underfoot." It is this that Cape Cod most has to offer an increasingly complex and artificial world: the chance to reconnect with elemental things. Walking along the shore poking at the washed-up sea life or watching birds fish in the surf, listening to the rhythm of the waves, experiencing the tranquillity of night on the beach or the power of a storm on water—all this is somehow life affirming and satisfyingly real.

Shaped continually by ocean currents, this windswept land of sandy beaches and dunes has an amazing natural beauty. Everyone comes for the seaside, yet Cape Cod's crimson cranberry bogs, birch and beech forests, grassy meadows, freshwater ponds, and marshlands are just as splendid. Local history is fascinating; whale-watching offers an exhilarating encounter with the natural world; bike trails lace the landscape; shops display everything from antiques to fashions to kitsch; and restaurants cook up seafood as fresh as it comes, as well as fine international cuisine.

Separated from the Massachusetts mainland by two heavily trafficked bridges over the Cape Cod Canal (17½ mi long and, at 480 ft wide, the world's widest sea-level canal), the Cape is always likened in shape to an outstretched human arm bent at the elbow, its Provincetown fist turned back toward the mainland. Writer Philip Hamburger, a Wellfleet habitué, has said the Cape "winds around to face itself"; Cape Cod Bay rests within the arm's embrace. The open Atlantic Ocean pounds the Cape's eastern coast, and Nantucket Sound washes the southern shore.

Cape Cod is only about 60 mi southeast of Boston and 70 mi from end to end, so you could make a cursory circuit of it in two or three days, but this is a place to relax—to swim and sun, to fish, boat,

and golf, to hunt for antiques and wander through art galleries, to attend summer theater, to buy lobster and fish fresh off the boat, or just to take leisurely walks, bike rides, and drives along pretty country roads that happily hold out against modernity.

THE CRAGGY ARM has modest geologic origins: it started as debris deposited by a retreating glacier in the last Ice Age. The peninsula's moderate coastal climate and diverse terrain foster an equally diverse assortment of plant and animal life, some of which exist nowhere else in northern climes. Barrier beaches (sandbars that protect an inner harbor from the battering of the ocean) such as Monomoy, near Chatham, are breeding and nesting grounds for a stunning variety of shore and sea birds, and the Cape's marshes and ponds are rich in waterfowl. Stellwagen Bank, just north of Provincetown, is a prime feeding ground for whales and dolphins, and shallow sandbars are favorite playgrounds for harbor and gray seals. Among the flotsam and jetsam along the shores, beachcombers find horseshoe crabs, starfish, sea urchins, sponges, jellyfish, and a plethora of shells—white quahogs, elegant scallops, blue mussels, long, straight razor clams, spiraling periwinkles, pointy turret shells, smooth, round moon snails, conical whelks, and rough-ridged oysters.

Life on Cape Cod has always been linked to the sea. The Cape got its current name from English explorer Bartholomew Gosnold, who first anchored off what is now Provincetown in 1602 and named the area for the "great store of codfish" his crew took aboard. The importance of whaling to the area—in the early to mid-19th century Nantucket was the world's premier whaling port, and mainland New Bedford was a prosperous whaling city—is reflected in local museums, where the travels of the area's whaling and packet-schooner seamen and captains are illustrated with antique nautical equipment, harpoons, charts, maps, journals, scrimshaw (created in the seamen's copious spare time), and gifts from faraway ports for wives who had waited so patiently. Of course, not all wives waited; some chose to go along with their husbands for the ride. For today's vacationer, the maritime environment also yields plenty of recreational activities, including water sports, fishing charters, and even Jeep safaris to isolated beaches for surf casting.

Happily, much of the Cape's land is protected from development. Nature preserves encompassing pine forests, marshes, swamps, cranberry bogs, and other topographical features are patterned with well-marked walking and cycling trails. Thanks to the establishment of the Cape Cod National Seashore in 1961, in low season you can walk for almost 30 mi along the Atlantic beach and rarely see a trace of human habitation, other than the lighthouses that stand watch over the Cape's dangerous shoals and a few old shacks in the dunes of Provincetown. Across dunes anchored by poverty grass sprawl beach plums, pink salt-spray roses, and purple beach peas.

Through the creation of National Historic districts, in which change is kept to a minimum to preserve the area's historic integrity, similar protection has been extended to the Cape's oldest and loveliest man-made additions. One of the most important and eye-pleasing districts is the Old King's Highway (Route 6A), on the Cape's north shore, where some of the Cape's first towns were incorporated in the mid-1600s. Lining this tree-shaded country road are simple saltboxes from the earliest days, fancier houses built later by prosperous sea captains, and traditional Cape cottages, shingles weathered to a silvery gray, with soft pink roses spilling across them. Here, too, are the Cape's windmills, as well as the white-steepled churches, the taverns, and the village greens so redolent of early New England. The city of Provincetown is a historic district as well, preserving for posterity its cheerful mix of tiny waterfront shops (former fish shacks) and captains' mansions, among them a 1746 Cape house and a mansarded French Second Empire building.

The Cape also preserves its past in a wealth of small museums—nearly every town has one—where exhibits often hark back to the days when Native Americans were the sole inhabitants (in 1620, when the Pilgrims first anchored at Provincetown before heading on to Plymouth, an estimated 30,000 Wampanoags lived on what is now Cape Cod). Often set in historic homes, these museums provide a visual history of the lives of the English settlers and their descendants, including their economic pursuits: from farming to harvesting salt, salt hay, and cranberries (first cultivated commercially in Dennis in the early 1800s and still an important local crop) to fishing and whaling to tourism, which first took hold in the late 19th century.

THE CAPE is rightly noted for its shopping, especially for art, crafts, and antiques. Although there's no shortage of touristy souvenirs, Cape Cod has a long tradition of serious galleries, most featuring the works of local artists. Provincetown, in particular, has been known as an art colony for more than 100 years. In 1899 Charles W. Hawthorne opened the Cape Cod School of Art, attracting students and fellow artists to the tip of the Cape in droves; by 1916 five additional art schools had been established, and more than 300 artists lived and worked in Provincetown. The prominence of artists and art schools continued through the 20th century, and the Cape Cod School of Art, Hawthorne School of Art, Provincetown Art Association and Museum School, and Provincetown Fine Arts Work Center still serve hundreds of students each year.

Theater groups, too, are well established. The oldest professional summer theater in the county is Dennis's Cape Playhouse, founded in 1927. Eugene O'Neill's first play was produced in Provincetown even earlier, in 1916. Both professional troupes and small community theaters carry on the tradition each summer.

If you come here in summer, you'll soon see that the Cape is highly family oriented. The endless child-friendly amusements range from miniature golf to nature walks, from canoe trips to the Cape Cod Baseball League and the ever-beckoning beach. Typical New England diversions include chowder suppers and clambakes, outdoor band concerts, and, of course, ice cream.

The "season" used to be strictly bounded by Memorial Day and Labor Day, but these lines have blurred; many properties now open as early as April and close as late as November, and a core remain open year-round. Unfortunately, most historic sites and museums, staffed mainly by volunteers, must adhere to the traditional dates, making them inaccessible in the off season. In summer you have your choice of plunking yourself down on or near a beach and never moving; filling your schedule with shopping, historic sites, and active exploration; or combining the two.

In fall the water might be warm enough for swimming as late as October—the crowds are gone, and prices are lower. Changing foliage, though no match for the dramatic displays farther north, is an enjoyable addition to a fall visit. The moors turn to purple and gold and rust; bushes along roadsides burn a brilliant red. Cranberries ripen to a bright burgundy hue and are harvested by a method fascinating to watch. The trees around freshwater marshes, ponds, and swamps tend to color brighter and earlier, particularly the red-maple swamps, Provincetown's Beech Forest, and all of Route 6A from Sandwich to Orleans. Fall and winter are oyster and scallop season, so those restaurants that remain open serve a wide selection of dishes made with these fresh delicacies. Winter is a quiet time, when many facilities and activities shut down, but prices are at their lowest, and you can often walk the beaches in total solitude. For quiet or romantic weekend getaways, country inns offer cozy rooms with canopy beds, where you can curl up before the fireplace after a leisurely candlelight dinner.

Spring is a wee bit wet. Once the daffodils burst up from the roadsides, everything starts to turn green. By April seasonal shops and restaurants begin to open their doors, and the locals open their arms to yet another summer.

NEW AND NOTEWORTHY

Exhibits and video presentations about the canal's history and about local flora and fauna fill the **Cape Cod Canal Visitor Center** in Sandwich, set to be fully open by mid-2002.

Provincetown's annual **Portuguese Festival** has evolved into quite an event, with ethnic foods and crafts, bands playing in the streets, a children's fishing derby, traditional dances, and a parade. Honoring the history of the Portuguese in Provincetown and their role in the fishing industry, the festival ends with a Sunday procession from St. Peter's Church to MacMillan Wharf, where the bishop blesses the town's fishing vessels.

Not reviewed this year but worth noting, the former Sheraton Four Points in Hyannis has been remade as the 261-room **Cape Codder Resort and Spa** (WEB www.capecodderresort.com)

The Cape Cod Chamber of Commerce has expanded its "Smart Map" of transportation into a more detailed **"Smart Guide,"** which includes bus, ferry, train, trolley, and flight services; bicycling and walking information; and sources for traffic reports. Pick up a copy at any chamber of commerce office, at many shops and attractions, or on the World Wide Web (WEB www.smartguide.org).

WHAT'S WHERE

Cape Cod has 15 towns, each broken up into villages. Things can get complicated: the "town" of Barnstable, for example, consists of Barnstable, West Barnstable, Cotuit, Marstons Mills, Osterville, Centerville, and Hyannis. Likewise, the terms *Upper Cape* and *Lower Cape,* derived from a sailing viewpoint, can be confusing; they were named based on their relations to the latitudes, which increase as you sail south. The Upper Cape—think "upper arm"—encompasses Bourne, Falmouth, Mashpee, and Sandwich. The Mid Cape includes Barnstable, Yarmouth, and Dennis. The Lower Cape covers Brewster, Harwich, Chatham, Orleans, Eastham, Wellfleet, Truro, and Provincetown. The Outer Cape, as in "outer reaches," is the end of the Lower Cape; technically it includes only Wellfleet, Truro, and Provincetown.

There are three major roads on the Cape. U.S. 6 is the fastest way to get from the mainland to Orleans or to most points along the way. Route 6A winds more slowly along the north shore through scenic towns, while Route 28 runs south through some overdeveloped areas. Past Orleans, on the way out to Provincetown, the roadside clutter of much of U.S. 6 belies the beauty of what actually surrounds it.

Approaching the Cape

Heading for the Cape from either Boston or Providence, you'll pass southeastern Massachusetts towns that range from intriguing historic villages to gritty industrial cities to bucolic seaside communities with as much charm—and far fewer crowds—than the Cape itself. Along Boston's South Shore, historic Plymouth takes you back to the 1600s and is well worth a stop, particularly if you're traveling with kids. If you're approaching from the south and west, Fall River and New Bedford provide a dose of history from the country's whaling days and early industrial era. Along the southeastern coast and onward to the Cape, the communities of Westport and South Dartmouth, among others, are seafront destinations that hark back to the old-time New England pleasures of seafood, summertime, and the shore.

The Upper Cape

The sprawling region nearest the bridges is perhaps the Cape's most historic area and its most contemporary area rolled into one. Along the northern bay side lie the Cape's oldest towns—Sandwich was settled back in 1637. Nearby Mashpee, where more than 600 residents are descended from the original Wampanoags, is one of two Massachusetts towns with Native American–governed areas. The west coast from Bourne through North and West Falmouth mixes residential suburbs with hidden coves and beaches lining the bay, while Falmouth proper is an established year-round community with all the suburban amenities you'd expect.

The Mid Cape

Like the Upper Cape, the Mid Cape region has a northern shore lined with quiet, historic villages, in this case, Barnstable, Yarmouth, and Dennis. There's more hubbub—some would say honky-tonk—along the southern coast. Hyannis, the Cape's geographic center and transportation hub, is popular with those who like to be in the thick of things; dining and entertainment options are many. Still, even amid the south-shore bustle, there are plenty of quiet attractions in the villages of Cotuit, Osterville, and West Dennis.

The Lower Cape

The Lower Cape towns of Brewster, Harwich, Chatham, Orleans, and Eastham make good bases for exploring the Cape. A fine area for nature lovers, the Lower Cape is home to the peaceful Monomoy National Wildlife Refuge, the popular Nickerson State Park, and a plentiful assortment of beaches and ponds. Cape Cod National Seashore, which stretches from Chatham to Provincetown, begins here; Salt Pond Visitor Center is in Eastham. The area also has plenty of fine restaurants and attractive shops.

The Outer Cape

The narrow "forearm" of the Cape, at spots less than 2 mi wide between Cape Cod Bay and the Atlantic Ocean, includes many of the Cape's least-developed areas, particularly in Wellfleet and Truro. This is the Cape of dunes and beach grasses, of crashing surf and scrubby pines—the Cape that most attracts seekers of solitude. But there's action here, too, at the Cape's "fist," in popular Provincetown, where the dunes give way to a summer scene packed with nightlife, art, food, and fun.

PLEASURES AND PASTIMES

Beaches

Cape Cod has more than 150 ocean and freshwater beaches, with something for just about every taste. Bay-side beaches generally have more temperate waters and gentle waves. South-side beaches, on Nantucket Sound, have rolling surf and, though still on the chilly side, are moderated by the Gulf Stream. The inland areas of the Cape are dotted with numerous freshwater ponds, many with warm water and sandy beaches that are ideal for young children. Ocean beaches on the Cape Cod National Seashore have cold water, serious surf, and are, by and large, superior—wide, long, sandy, and dune backed, with great views. They're also contiguous: you can walk from Eastham to Provincetown practically without leaving sand. This almost always ensures privacy, if you stroll far enough away from crowds. From late July through August, Outer Cape beaches are sometimes troubled with red algae in the water, which, while harmless, can be annoying; check with the Cape Cod National Seashore about conditions. To mitigate the crowd factor, arrive either early in the morning or later in the afternoon. Parking lots tend to fill up by 10 AM in summer.

In season you'll have to pay for parking at public beaches; parking at restricted beaches is open to residents and visitors with permits (☞ Beaches *in* Smart Travel Tips A to Z). Walkers and bicyclists can enter these restricted beaches without permits, however. From the last June weekend ending before July 1 through Labor Day is the latest official take on what constitutes the season's boundaries. Although parking is usually free in the off-season, you'll probably also find snack bars closed and lifeguards nowhere to be found.

Biking

Biking on the Cape will satisfy avid and occasional cyclists alike. There are plenty of flat back roads, as well as a number of well-developed bike trails. The Cape's top bike path, the Cape Cod Rail Trail, offers a scenic ride through the area. Following the paved right-of-way of the old Penn Central Railroad, it's about 25 mi long, stretching from South Dennis to South Wellfleet. The Cape Cod National Seashore maintains three bicycle trails. Head of the Meadow Trail is 2 mi of easy cycling between dunes and salt marshes from High Head Road, off Route 6A in North Truro, to the Head of the Meadow Beach parking lot. Province Lands Trail is a 5¼-mi loop off the Beech Forest parking lot on Race Point Road in Provincetown, with spurs to the Herring Cove and Race Point beaches and to Bennett Pond. The paths wind up and down hills amid dunes, marshes, woods, and ponds and offer spectacular views—on an exceptionally clear day, you can see the Boston skyline. There's a picnic grove at Pilgrim Spring. Nickerson State Park in Brewster has 8 mi of trails through forest.

Conservation Areas

Bustle and noise may seem unavoidable on a Cape vacation, but you'll find a sure-fire escape at one of the numerous nature refuges. There you can delight in seeing an osprey nest, the slow-motion stalking of a great blue heron, the head of a river otter coursing through the water, great shorebird colonies, a meadow in late summer, or that stray berry-studded blueberry bush. This is simply the best way to experience the vitality and diversity of the region.

Flora and fauna of local interest are beach-plum bushes, which bloom in late May and bear fruit in the fall; the spring-blooming, white-flowered shadbush and its red-purple June berries; shade- and moisture-loving cinnamon ferns; June-blooming pasture rose and the lovely Rugosa roses, which bloom throughout the summer; the brilliant orange butterfly weed, so named for the affinity monarch butterflies have for the nectar of its summer flowers; the fragrant midsummer blooms of the sweet pepper bush; blueberry and huckleberry bushes; the low-slung, waxy-leaved, dark-green teaberry, with its early fall red berries; fall-flowering seaside goldenrod and sea lavender; caribou moss, also near the sea; the plentiful beach grass (which you should avoid treading on in order to keep it plentiful); oval-leaf bayberry bushes, whose scent is a wintertime household delight; and tupelo, sassafras, pygmy beech, cottonwood, Norway spruce, red cedar, pitch pine, tamarack, and numerous other trees. Unfortunately, you need to watch out for poison ivy, that invasive spoiler of human comfort (its berries are a great boon to birds, however).

As for wildlife, there are hawks and harriers, ospreys, pheasants, quail, numerous ducks and geese, terns, bobwhites, meadowlarks, catbirds, towhees, swallows, orioles, goldfinches, yellowthroats, a great variety of warblers, and more spring and fall migrants than can be mentioned; a kingdom of mollusks and sea creatures—horseshoe, hermit, fiddler, and blue crabs; oysters; scallops; quahogs; and so on; and rabbits, raccoons, otter, muskrats, mice, and deer. From beach to marsh to meadow to salt-sprayed sand plains, the variety of habitats is tremendous.

Note: Along with the poison ivy alert, check yourself for deer ticks after a day's walk or hike in the outdoors.

Dining

Cape Cod received its name from the thickness of the schools of cod that early explorers found around its shores. These days the ominous local joke is that the peninsula should be renamed, except there is no alternative species certain to be around for the next few generations. But don't give up hope and expect to eat steaks. Plenty of great seafood can still be had, and here's one encouraging little secret: largely because of strict federal regulations, codfish have been making a quiet but remarkable comeback in the past few years. You'll see more and more cod on the menus, and it will be fresh.

Many Cape fisherfolk took a look at the offshore problems and decided to become less hunter and more farmer. Some have moved into aquaculture, staking grants along the tidal flats of Cape Cod Bay and planting quahogs or oysters. These shellfish are not fed any artificial food, and they aren't laced with any chemicals. They are simply planted in one area, protected from predators, and harvested when they reach market size. As a result, fresh shellfish is a great bet at restaurants and markets. If you buy some littlenecks or quahogs, turn the shell over and see if there are little rays or lines of lighter color radiating from the base of the shell. If so, you've gotten a cultured clam, known by scientists as a "notata." They're as sweet to eat as their wild cousins.

Traditionally, Cape restaurants have not favored fancy sauces or sophisticated cooking techniques. Now there is a younger generation of Cape Cod chefs who aren't afraid to bring more ingredients and international influence to the table, who know that if they keep everything else on the plate as fresh as the fish, the results can be truly memorable. This approach has tended to drive the price of dinner ever higher. Prices have not reached chic New York levels by a long shot, but good Cape restaurants are charging as much as many good Boston restaurants—and delivering equally impressive quality.

The other emerging trend at many Cape restaurants is toward a menu that runs up and down the price ladder. Except for at the most elegant spots, it is common to find both expensive full dinners and fancy burgers and eclectic pizzas side by side. This can help hold down the price of an evening out.

That said, there's a—you name it—Lobster Pot/Trap/Claw/Bowl/Net in every town. These restaurants are still authen-

tic and the best place to go with a family, although there is no place left where good seafood could be called inexpensive. And if you order lobster, you're likely to find its price to be easily the highest on the menu. You don't need to be a stodgy traditionalist to agree that the fry-o-lators in many home-style seafood restaurants and clam shacks impart the real lusciousness to classic Cape Cod cooking. For a quintessential summertime Cape experience, nothing beats simple standbys. The standard summer lunch is a lobster roll—a very light lobster salad with practically no mayonnaise on a plain white frankfurter roll.

At dinnertime dress is largely casual. According to legend, one older Cape Codder takes this edict so seriously that he chops off any ties he sees and adorns his cabin in Chatham with the remains. But in certain rooms—such as Chillingsworth or the Dan'l Webster Inn or Chatham Bars Inn—a sports coat is virtually mandatory. Another recent and important development: an increasing number of restaurants are remaining open year-round, even if they scale back in winter.

Finally, note that many towns on the Cape do not allow smoking inside any restaurant, and a few have also banned lighting up in bars. This is strictly enforced, so if you see some people standing outside your restaurant of choice in one of these towns, they may not be in line for a table but may be taking a puff in the open air.

For price ranges *see* Dining *in* Smart Travel Tips A to Z.

Lodging

With a tourism-based economy, the Cape naturally abounds in lodgings, including self-contained luxury resorts, grand old oceanfront hotels, chain hotels, mom-and-pop motels, antiques-filled bed-and-breakfasts, cottages, condominiums, and apartments. If you're planning to stay a week or longer, renting a house is another popular option.

Choosing where you want to stay will depend on the kind of vacation you have in mind. If you love the beach, think about whether you'd rather stay near the dune-backed National Seashore, where waters are coldest, or near the somewhat warmer south-shore waters. The National Seashore is less developed and great for walking, while the Mid Cape and Falmouth beaches most often are more circumscribed and more crowded with families.

Sandwich and other towns along the north-shore Route 6A Historic District have quiet, traditional villages with old-Cape atmosphere and charming B&Bs. If you want more action, head for the Mid Cape. Hyannis is the center of it all, with a busy Main Street, active nightlife, and some fine beaches.

For the austere Cape of dunes and sea, try the beach cottages of the sparsely developed Lower Cape between Wellfleet and Provincetown. P-town itself is something completely different: in summer a frantic wall-to-wall jumble of shops and houses bursting with a large contingent of lesbians and gay men, along with a hopping nighttime scene. Staying in town makes getting to everything by foot or bike possible.

For price ranges *see* Lodging *in* Smart Travel Tips A to Z.

Nightlife and the Arts

Since the early 1900s creative people have been drawn to Cape Cod summers, and their legacy and ongoing contribution is a thriving arts scene. In addition to professional theater, which offers top-name talent in season, almost every town has a community theater that provides quality entertainment—often mixing local players with visiting pros—throughout the year. The Cape also gets its share of music stars, from pop to classical, along with local groups ranging from barbershop quartets to Bach chorales to classical music or chamber ensembles, often playing at school auditoriums or town halls.

In 1999 Provincetown celebrated its centennial as America's oldest art colony, a tradition that still thrives today. Its many galleries exhibit Cape and non-Cape artists, and the Fine Arts Work Center has launched the careers of many well-known award-winning authors. Wellfleet and Orleans have emerged as vibrant art centers. Both towns have attracted craftspeople who sell through a number of unique and sophisticated shops.

Nighttime on Cape Cod can be very special in many ways. In less developed areas, the stars are amazingly bright and make beach walks even more wondrous. Light-

house beacons cutting shafts through the night sky have a fascination impossible to resist. If you're up *really* late, or really early, head for Chatham Light or a National Seashore beach to catch a terrific sunrise.

Another Cape twist on nightlife is that many daytime activities, such as fishing, take on a completely different aspect at night. Scuba enthusiasts might consider night diving: colors are more vivid by flashlight, much sea life is phosphorescent or bioluminescent, and nocturnal species come out to play. It's important to know the tides and safe locations—check with a dive shop.

Shopping

Art galleries and crafts shops abound on Cape Cod, a reflection of the long attraction the area has held for artists and craftspeople. Throughout the Cape you'll find weavers, candle makers, glassblowers, papermakers, and potters, as well as an inordinate number of shops specializing in country crafts from straw dolls to handmade Christmas ornaments—and, of course, plenty of tourist schlock. The region is also popular for antiquing, which means that both the genuine articles and the kitschy wanna-bes are in ready supply. Coastal environments and a seafaring past account for the proliferation of sea-related crafts (as well as marine-antiques dealers) on the Cape. A craft form that originated on the years-long voyages to whaling grounds is scrimshaw, the etching of finely detailed designs of sailing ships and sea creatures onto a hard surface. In the beginning, the bones or teeth of whales were used; today's ecologically minded (and legally constrained) scrimshanders use a synthetic substitute such as Corian, a Du Pont countertop material.

Cranberry glass, a light ruby glass made by fusing gold with glass or crystal, is sold in gift shops all over the Cape. It was once made by the Sandwich Glass company (among others) but now retains only the association with Cape Cod, as it is made elsewhere in the United States and in Europe.

For great vacation reading, the Cape has a number of highly browsable bookstores, some specializing in secondhand titles. Many have large selections of books about Cape Cod, from fiction to nautical matters to the great outdoors.

Auctions, held on the Cape all year long, range from country-barn types to the internationally known Eldred's Auctions. Though the high-end auctions deal in very fine antiques, they also include some lower-price merchandise and often yield interesting Cape pieces, such as old sea chests, at good prices.

Sports and the Outdoors

The Cape is a top American destination for swimming, surfing, windsurfing, sailing, and indulging in virtually all other water sports. Shipwrecks make for interesting dive sites, but don't expect a tropical underwater landscape. On the water, canoeing and sea kayaking are great around the bay's marshy inlets. The Cape is also one of the world's finest whale-watching spots; a whale breaching alongside your boat is an awe-inspiring sight.

Fishing on the Cape is both a profession and a pastime. Hundreds of freshwater ponds are good for perch, pickerel, and trout; surf casting off beaches and deep-sea fishing for blues, bass, and flounder is also popular. You'll need a license for freshwater fishing, available for a nominal fee at most most bait-and-tackle shops.

Golfers will find a number of excellent courses, including championship layouts; most stay open nearly year-round. Bicycling is a joy on the mostly level roads, along paved and scenic bike paths, and through the many nature preserves. Bird-watchers have many habitats from which to choose, often in a single nature preserve. The Cape Cod National Seashore has nine walking trails through varied terrain, and there are paths through conservation areas and nature preserves Cape-wide. In winter, ponds and shallow flooded cranberry bogs sometimes freeze hard enough for skating. Check conditions with the local fire department before venturing onto unfamiliar territory.

Spectators can choose from a plethora of bike and running races, golf competitions, horse shows, sailboat races, and the well-attended Cape Cod Baseball League games, breeding ground of champions.

Theater

In 1916 a young aspiring writer arrived in Provincetown to try his hand at writing plays. In July of that year, Eugene O'Neill's first play, *Bound East for Cardiff,* made its debut in a waterfront fish house to tremendous success. More than 80 years later theater continues to thrive on the Cape. The country's most renowned summer theater, the Cape Playhouse, in Dennis—where Bette Davis got her start, first as an usher, then as an actress (in 1928, in *Mr. Pim Passes By*)—tops the list for the best and brightest stage fare. The Wellfleet Harbor Actors Theater has staged many important New England and world premieres. The Cape Cod Theatre Project, in Falmouth and Woods Hole, presents staged readings of new works by leading playwrights, followed by an audience discussion with the author.

The Provincetown Repertory Theatre (PRT), founded in 1995 by Ken Hoyt, made an early splash when it brought legendary director Jose Quintero out of retirement in the summer of 1996 to direct two one-act O'Neill plays. More recently, a play developed at the PRT based on work by Edward Gorey moved to New York for several months. Although founder Hoyt left the theater in 2001, the PRT is still one to watch.

Community theater flourishes here as well, most notably at the Academy Playhouse in Orleans, the Cape Cod Repertory Theatre Co. in Brewster, and the Harwich Junior Theatre.

Town-Band Concerts

Traditional New England town-band concerts are held weekly each summer in many Cape towns—take along chairs, blankets, sweaters, and a picnic supper if you like and go early to get a good spot.

FODOR'S CHOICE

No two people will agree on what makes a perfect vacation, but it's fun and helpful to know what others think. We hope you'll have a chance to experience some of Fodor's Choices yourself while visiting Cape Cod. For detailed information about each, refer to the appropriate chapter.

Old New England

The town of **Sandwich,** with its salt marsh, cemetery, museums, abundance of old houses, and lovely setting on Shawme Pond, is unsurpassed for regional charm.

Bright crimson cranberries floating on flooded bogs just before the fall harvest are a perfect reminder of the handwork that was one of the joys of the seasonal roundup.

At **Hallet's century-old drugstore** in Yarmouth Port, life can be sweet, especially when you're sipping an ice cream soda while swiveling on a stool at a marble bar.

En route to the Cape, **Plimoth Plantation,** a living history museum that takes you back to the Pilgrims' 1627 settlement, makes a fascinating detour to the New England of centuries past.

Natural Phenomena

If you crave a little rejuvenation or just want to commune with nature, spend an afternoon observing life on the salt marsh at **Bass Hole Boardwalk** in Yarmouth Port or taking a walk onto the tidal flats when the water is out.

From Chatham Light, looking out at the **Chatham Break** in the sandbar is a reminder of the power of the sea and a fascinating display of the process of geological change.

Seeing harbor seals off Race Point in Provincetown in winter is one of the pleasures of the seaside Cape at a time when you feel like you have the place to yourself.

Sunset over Cape Cod Bay on any bay beach from Eastham to Provincetown is an unforgettable delight at any time of year.

Whales breaching alongside your whalewatch boat will fill you with a sense of wonder unlike any you've ever felt. It's also quite a treat to see dolphins jumping in and out of the boat's bow waves or in its wake.

Beaches and Conservation Areas

The **Massachusetts Audubon Wellfleet Bay Wildlife Sanctuary** in South Wellfleet, with its numerous adult and children's programs and its beautiful salt-marsh setting, is a favorite migration stop for Cape vacationers year-round.

Nauset Light, Coast Guard, Marconi, and Race Point beaches stretch majestically along the length of the Cape Cod National Seashore. Backed by dunes, they are *the* classic Cape beaches.

Walking along the beach, any beach, particularly in the peaceful early morning or late afternoon, is a great reminder of what the Cape is all about.

Shopping

Sandwich Auction House has been holding weekly auctions for more than two decades, with periodic theme sales of toys, silver, paperweights, and collectibles.

The **weekly flea market** (Wednesday, Thursday, and weekends in summer; weekends all other seasons) at the Wellfleet Drive-In Theater is one big browse, whether or not you take anything home with you.

Herridge Books in Wellfleet reflects the town's longtime appeal to vacationing writers, with an outstanding collection of interesting reading. A book lover could easily take a day or more to do justice to what's on the shelves in this store.

Farm stands (often roadside) throughout the Cape provide one of the best ways to get close to the land and the rhythm of rural life.

Dining

The Back Eddy, Westport. On your way to the Cape, stop by for superb seafood—from classic preparations to sophisticated contemporary variations—at this casual harborside treasure. $$–$$$

Front Street, Provincetown. In a town that consistently continues to raise the level of the Cape's cuisine, this small, unassuming venue serves nothing short of superb, original food, offered by a marvelous staff. You couldn't ask for much more at Cape's end. $$–$$$

Inaho, Yarmouth Port. Inaho uses the great Cape fresh seafood to maximum effect, and the setting and presentation, from lighting to service, perfectly celebrate a remarkably conscious kitchen. $$–$$$

Mojo's, Provincetown. If every hole-in-the-wall were as inventive and cared as much about its menu as this one, the world would be a cheaper, better place. You'll find everything from fried clams and steak subs to veggie burgers and salads here. $–$$

Sagamore Inn, Sagamore. Rustic, roomy, family run, not pretentious or expensive— this is the kind of place you might stop in for lunch on a rainy day and then for dinner the following night. *$–$$*

Lodging

Brass Key, Provincetown. This elegant complex encompasses several fully restored structures that unite Victorian splendor and modern luxury. *$$$$*

Captain's House Inn, Chatham. Friendly and professional service, colonial atmosphere, and wonderful old buildings make this one of the Cape's most pleasant B&Bs. *$$$–$$$$*

Augustus Snow House, Harwich Port. This elegant Victorian inn takes you back to another era, with a tearoom where you can savor afternoon tea on weekends. *$$$–$$$$*

La Maison Cappellari, Falmouth. A lushly landscaped yard and handsome wall murals in some rooms add a touch of Europe to Cape Cod at this Italianate villa. *$$$–$$$$*

Heaven on High, West Barnstable. Perfectly named, perfectly decorated, and perfectly comfortable, Heaven on High is such a blessed hilltop haven you might never want to leave to explore the town's nearby sights and sounds. *$$$*

Children's Activities

Sandwich has the **Thornton W. Burgess Museum,** namesake of the creator of Peter Cottontail and great for children; **Heritage Plantation,** with superb old cars, a working 1912 carousel, and grounds perfect for running around; and the **Green Briar Nature Center and Jam Kitchen,** with walking trails, the Smiling Pool pond, natural-history exhibits, and Peter Rabbit's great-great-grandchildren.

The **Cape Cod Museum of Natural History** in Brewster offers a great variety of bay, marsh, and estuary cruises with naturalists who haul up traps so children can observe aquatic creatures up close. There are also field walks, exhibits, and a pond- and sea-life room with live specimens.

Pirate's Cove in South Yarmouth far outdoes the average miniature golf course, architecturally speaking. Give in and pick up a putter at least once—you may have a good time even if your children aren't alongside you.

Whale watches out of Provincetown can be a tremendous thrill—genuinely exciting and pleasantly educational.

2 APPROACHING THE CAPE

PLYMOUTH, FALL RIVER, WESTPORT, SOUTH DARTMOUTH, NEW BEDFORD

If you're driving to the Cape, make the journey half the fun—explore a little *before* you reach the bridges. Southeastern Massachusetts is a time warp, and Plimoth Plantation meticulously re-creates New England's first settlement as it appeared in 1627. Approaching Cape Cod from the west, you'll pass through Fall River, with its bizarre history of Lizzie Borden, and New Bedford, a 19th-century whaling center. Along the way are some lovely seaside villages where a stop for fresh fish or a walk on the beach will help get you into that Cape state of mind.

Revised by
Carolyn Heller

MANY LESSER-KNOWN SITES in southeastern Massachusetts make enjoyable stops en route to Cape Cod. If you're a history buff or want to give your kids an educational experience they won't soon forget, don't miss Plymouth, the community locals proudly call America's Hometown: here you can see that monument you've heard about since childhood, Plymouth Rock, and walk the decks of the *Mayflower II*. A few miles down the road is Plimoth Plantation, a re-created 17th-century Puritan village where trained staff members vividly dramatize the everyday lives of the first English settlers. Watch them make cheese, forge nails, and explain where and when they bathe (hint: not often).

If you're coming from the south or west, consider stopping in the seafaring towns of New Bedford and Fall River. In Fall River, history took a macabre turn with the Trial of the Century—the 19th century, that is. Fall River was the hometown of Lizzie Borden, who was accused, and acquitted, of dispatching her parents with "40 whacks" of an axe. Borden history has become a cottage industry here, yet there's more to Fall River than the Borden saga; the town is also home to Battleship Cove, a floating museum complex.

Nearby New Bedford was a major whaling port in the 19th century and now holds the nation's largest museum on the history of whaling. Exhibits include the world's largest model ship and a rare skeleton of a 66-ft blue whale.

Along the coves of Buzzards Bay, southeastern Massachusetts is dotted with seaside towns and sandy beaches, the best known of which is Horseneck Beach in Westport. The pretty villages of South Dartmouth are also worth a stop. Last but not least, a sustained roll through this part of the state reveals some high-quality restaurants and charming bed-and-breakfasts.

Pleasures and Pastimes

The Sea
With a coastline that meanders in and out of Buzzards Bay, southeastern Massachusetts has plenty of choice seaside areas. Westport's Horseneck Beach is a long stretch of sand that's hugely popular on weekends. Plymouth, too, has several popular beaches, from Plymouth Beach near town to the long crescent of sand at White Horse Beach to the south. But there are smaller beaches and coves where you can enjoy the shore in relative quiet—in Fairhaven, for example, and other small towns that dot the area.

If you're more interested in being on the water than in it, try a cruise from Onset Harbor or take a whale-watching trip. Whale-watch excursions run from Plymouth daily between June and September and on a more limited basis April–May and in October; they usually last three to four hours.

Dining
Like other Massachusetts shorefront towns, the communities approaching the Cape have plenty of seafood restaurants, where you find everything from clam shacks to more upscale dining options. In New Bedford and Fall River, which have large Portuguese populations, you can sample dishes made with spicy *linguica* (sausage) or *bacalau* (salt cod), and pick up some soft, doughy Portuguese sweet bread to sustain you as you explore.

CATEGORY	COST*
$$$$	over $26
$$$	$19–$26
$$	$11–$18
$	under $11

per person for a main course at dinner

Lodging

Plymouth's numerous lodging options include quaint B&Bs and large motels. Choices on the coast are more limited, although the area does have several recommendable small inns and B&Bs. If you're traveling with kids, be sure to ask whether they are welcome at smaller properties; some are not set up for youngsters.

CATEGORY	COST*
$$$$	over $200
$$$	$150–$200
$$	$100–$150
$	under $100

All prices are for a standard double room in high season, excluding 5.7% state tax and gratuities. Some inns add a 15% service charge.

Numbers in the margin correspond to points of interest on the Approaching the Cape map.

Plymouth

❶ *40 mi southeast of Boston.*

On December 26, 1620, 102 weary British men, women, and children disembarked from the *Mayflower* to found the first permanent European settlement north of Virginia. (Virginia was their intended destination, but storms pushed the ship off course.) Of the settlers, now known as the Pilgrims, a third were members of a Puritan sect of religious reformers known as the Separatists, so called because they wanted to establish their own church separate from the national Church of England. This separation was considered treasonous, so the group first fled to the city of Leiden in the Netherlands seeking religious freedom. After more than 10 years there, the group joined with other emigrants to start a new life in the New World.

Before coming ashore, the expedition's leaders drew up the Mayflower Compact, a historic agreement binding the group to the law of the majority. This compact became the basis for the colony's government. After a rough start (half the original settlers died during the first winter), the colony stabilized and grew under the leadership of Governor William Bradford. Two other founding fathers—military leader Myles Standish and John Alden—acquired mythical status via a poem by Longfellow, *The Courtship of Miles Standish*.

Forty miles south of Boston, Plymouth today is characterized by narrow streets, clapboard mansions, shops, and antiques stores. Some commercial names would make the Pilgrims shudder: The John Alden Gift Shop, Mayflower Seafoods, and, incongruously, Pocahontas Gifts, Sportswear and Sundries (Pocahontas lived in Virginia). But it's easy to overlook these and admire the picturesque waterfront. The town also holds a parade, historic-house tours, and other activities to mark Thanksgiving.

Plymouth is dotted with historic statues, including depictions of William Bradford on Water Street, a Pilgrim maiden in Brewster Gardens, and Massasoit (chief of the local Wampanoag tribe) on Carver Street. The largest freestanding granite statue in the country, the **National Monu-**

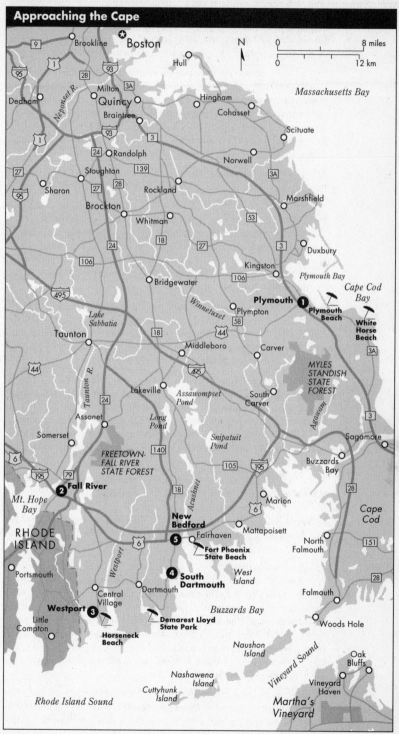

N

0 ———— 8 miles
0 ———— 12 km

Boston

Brookline

Hull

Massachusetts Bay

Dedham

Nepouset R.

Milton

Quincy

Braintree

Hingham

Cohasset

Scituate

Randolph

Stoughton

Norwell

Sharon

Brockton

Rockland

Marshfield

Whitman

Duxbury

Kingston

Plymouth Bay

Cape Cod Bay

Bridgewater

Winneluxet

Plymouth ❶ Plymouth Beach

Lake Sabbatia

Plympton

White Horse Beach

Taunton

Middleboro

Carver

MYLES STANDISH STATE FOREST

Assawompset Pond

Lakeville

South Carver

Agawam

Sagamore

Assonet

Long Pond

Snipatuit Pond

Somerset

FREETOWN-FALL RIVER STATE FOREST

Buzzards Bay

Fall River ❷

Marion

Cape Cod

Mt. Hope Bay

New Bedford

Mattapoisett

RHODE ISLAND

Fairhaven ❺ Fort Phoenix State Beach

North Falmouth

Portsmouth

Central Village

Dartmouth

❹ South Dartmouth

West Island

Falmouth

Westport ❸

Demarest Lloyd State Park

Buzzards Bay

Woods Hole

Little Compton

Horseneck Beach

Naushon Island

Oak Bluffs

Nashawena Island

Cuttyhunk Island

Vineyard Sound

Vineyard Haven

Rhode Island Sound

Martha's Vineyard

ment to the Forefathers, stands high on a grassy hill. Designed by Hammet Billings of Boston in 1854 and dedicated in 1889, it depicts Faith, surrounded by Liberty, Morality, Justice, Law, and Education and includes scenes from the Pilgrims' early days in Plymouth. ⊠ *Allerton St.*

Several historic houses are open for visits, including the 1640 **Sparrow House,** Plymouth's oldest structure. You can peek into several rooms furnished in the spartan style of the Pilgrims' era. A contemporary craft gallery also on the premises seems somewhat incongruous, but the works on view are high-quality. ⊠ *42 Summer St.,* ☏ *508/747–1240.* ⊟ *$2; gallery free.* ☉ *Apr.–June and Sept.–Dec., Thurs.–Tues. 10–5; July–Aug., Thurs.–Tues. 10–5, Sat. 10–8.*

The 1749 **Spooner House,** home to the same family for 200 years, has guided tours and a garden. ⊠ *27 North St.,* ☏ *508/746–0012.* ⊟ *$4.* ☉ *June–early Oct., Thurs.–Sat. 10–4.*

☾ Like Plimoth Plantation, the **Mayflower II,** a replica of the 1620 *Mayflower,* is manned by staff in period dress. The ship was built in England through research and a bit of guesswork, and then it sailed across the Atlantic in 1957. ⊠ *State Pier,* ☏ *508/746–1622,* WEB *www. plimoth.org.* ⊟ *$8; free with Plimoth Plantation combination ticket.* ☉ *Apr.–Nov., daily 9–5.*

A few dozen yards from the *Mayflower II* is **Plymouth Rock,** popularly believed to have been the Pilgrims' stepping-stone when they left the ship. Given the stone's unimpressive appearance—it's little more than a boulder—and dubious authenticity (as explained on a nearby plaque), the grand canopy overhead seems a trifle ostentatious.

Across the street from Plymouth Rock is **Cole's Hill,** where the company buried its dead—at night, so the local Native Americans could not count the dwindling numbers of survivors. Just past the hill, on what was once called 1st Street, is the site of the original settlement; in 1834 the street was renamed Leyden Street in honor of the Dutch city that sheltered the Pilgrims. Look for plaques designating the locations of the original lots.

☾ For a traditional view of the Pilgrims, visit the **Plymouth National Wax Museum,** on top of Cole's Hill. It contains 26 scenes with 180 life-size models that tell the settlers' story. Corny? Yes, but school-age kids love it. ⊠ *16 Carver St.,* ☏ *508/746–6468.* ⊟ *$6.* ☉ *Mar.–May and Nov., daily 9–5; June and Sept.–Oct., daily 9–7; July–Aug., daily 9–9.*

From the waterfront sights it's a short walk to one of the country's oldest public museums. The **Pilgrim Hall Museum,** established in 1824, transports you back to the time just before the Pilgrims' landing, with items carried by those weary travelers to the New World. Included are a carved chest, a remarkably well preserved wicker cradle, Myles Standish's sword, John Alden's Bible, Native American artifacts, and the remains of the *Sparrow Hawk,* a sailing ship that was wrecked in 1626. ⊠ *75 Court St. (Rte. 3A),* ☏ *508/746–1620,* WEB *www.pilgrimhall.org.* ⊟ *$5.* ☉ *Feb.–Dec., daily 9:30–4:30.*

Imagine an entire museum devoted to a Thanksgiving side dish. But the Ocean Spray–operated **Cranberry World** is amazingly popular. For one thing, you get free samples. After viewing details of how the state's local crop is grown, harvested, and processed, you can sip juices and sample products made from *Vaccinium macrocarpon* (the Latin name for cranberries). ⊠ *158 Water St.,* ☏ *508/747–2350.* ⊟ *$2.* ☉ *May–Nov., daily 9:30–5.*

NEED A
BREAK?

Sample some cranberry wine—it's oddly refreshing, and free—at the **Plymouth Bay Winery** (✉ 114 Water St., ☎ 508/746–2100), open March–December. For substantive fare, the **Lobster Hut** (☎ 508/746–2270), open year-round (except January) on Town Wharf at the waterfront, offers seafood in the classic breaded-and-fried style, plus sandwiches and luncheon specials.

★ ☕ Above the entrance of the **Plimoth Plantation** is the caution: you are now entering 1627. Believe it. Against the backdrop of the Atlantic Ocean, a Pilgrim village has been painstakingly re-created, from the thatch roofs, cramped quarters, and open fireplaces to the long-horned livestock. Throw away your preconceptions of white collars and funny hats; through ongoing research, the Plimoth staff has developed a portrait of the Pilgrims that's more complex than the dour folk pictured in elementary-school textbooks. Listen to the accents of the "residents," who never break out of character. You might see them plucking ducks, cooking rabbit stew, or tending garden. Feel free to engage them in conversation about their life, but expect only curious looks if you ask about anything that happened later than 1627.

Elsewhere on the plantation is **Hobbamock's Homestead,** where descendants of the Wampanoag Indians re-create the life of a Native American who chose to live near the newcomers. In the **Carriage House Craft Center** you'll see items created using the techniques of 17th-century English craftsmanship—that is, what the Pilgrims might have imported (you can also buy samples). At the **Nye Barn** you can see descendants of 17th-century goats, cows, pigs, and chickens, bred to represent animals raised in the original plantation. The visitor center has gift shops, a cafeteria, and multimedia presentations. Dress for the weather since many exhibits are outdoors. Admission tickets are good for two consecutive days; if you have time, you may want to spread out your plantation visit to take in all the sights. ✉ *Warren Ave. (Rte. 3A),* ☎ *508/746–1622,* WEB *www.plimoth.org.* 🎫 *$20; $22 including entry to Mayflower II.* ☉ *Apr.–Nov., daily 9–5.*

OFF THE
BEATEN PATH

JOHN ALDEN HOUSE MUSEUM – The only standing structure in which original Pilgrims are known to have lived is about 10 mi north of Plymouth in the town of Duxbury, settled in 1628 by Pilgrim colonists Myles Standish and John Alden, among others. Alden, who served as assistant governor of Plymouth colony, his wife, Priscilla, and eight or nine of their children occupied this house, which was built in 1653. One bedroom has a "seven-day dresser" with a drawer for each day of the week; the Sunday drawer, which held formal church wear, is the largest. ✉ *105 Alden St., Duxbury,* ☎ *781/934–9092,* WEB *www.alden.org.* 🎫 *Guided tours $4.* ☉ *Mid-May–mid-Oct., Mon.–Sat. noon–4.*

Dining and Lodging

$$–$$$ ✕ **Bert's Cove.** This local landmark, just off the entrance to Plymouth Beach, has great ocean views and a menu that includes veal medallions, sirloin steak, risotto, and fresh seafood, along with sandwiches and pizettas at lunch. The traditional fare has some contemporary touches, such as vegetable slaw with Asian flavors that replaces the standard coleslaw. ✉ *140 Warren Ave. (Rte. 3A),* ☎ *508/746–3330. AE, D, MC, V. Closed Mon. Nov.–Apr.*

$–$$ ✕ **Iguana's.** A good choice for both lunch and late-night dining, Iguana's serves fajitas, burritos, and other Mexican-Southwestern fare, plus burgers; sandwiches; and chicken, steak, and rib dishes. You'll find a bar, a patio, ocean views—and a live iguana. ✉ *Village Landing Marketplace, 170 Water St.,* ☎ *508/747–4000. AE, DC, MC, V.*

$ ✕ **The All-American Diner.** The look is nostalgia—red, white, and blue with movie posters. The specialty is beloved American foods—omelets and pancakes for breakfast; burgers, salads, and soups for lunch. ⊠ *60 Court St.,* ☎ *508/747–4763. AE, DC, MC, V. No dinner.*

$$–$$$ ✕⛉ **John Carver Inn.** This three-story Colonial-style redbrick building with a massive pillared facade is just a few steps from Plymouth's main attractions. The public rooms and dining rooms are lavish, with period furnishings and stylish drapes. The guest rooms are more matter-of-fact, but ask for one of the six environmentally sensitive rooms, which have filtered air and water and four-poster beds. The two-room suites have fireplaces and whirlpool baths. The indoor pool has a *Mayflower* ship model and a water slide. At its Hearth 'n Kettle Restaurant, a huge menu of American favorites, including hearty sandwiches and many types of seafood, is served by a staff dressed in Colonial attire. ⊠ *25 Summer St., 02360,* ☎ *508/746–7100 or 800/274–1620,* ᖴᗅᗊ *508/746–8299,* ᗯᗴᗊ *www.johncarverinn.com. 79 rooms, 6 suites. Restaurant, bar, pool, gym, meeting rooms. AE, D, DC, MC, V.*

$$–$$$ ⛉ **Governor Bradford on the Harbour.** The waterfront location here (directly across from the *Mayflower II*) is a big plus. Rooms are motel-basic, each with two double beds, a small refrigerator, and free HBO. ⊠ *98 Water St., 02360,* ☎ *508/746–6200 or 800/332–1620,* ᖴᗅᗊ *508/ 747–3032,* ᗯᗴᗊ *www.governorbradford.com. 94 rooms. No-smoking rooms, refrigerators, pool. AE, D, DC, MC, V.*

$$ ⛉ **Beach House Oceanfront B&B.** At the end of a long dirt road, this contemporary gray-shingle home overlooking the Atlantic makes a perfect hideaway. Although only about 10 minutes south of Plymouth center, the house feels a world apart. The deck, screened porch, and living room/dining room with floor-to-ceiling windows all face the wide expanse of the ocean, and steps lead down the cliff to a small private beach. Inside, the theme is white—from the leather sofas in the living room to the lace curtains and quilts in the bedrooms. ⊠ *45 Black Pond La. (mailing address: 429 Center Hill Rd., 02360),* ☎ *508/224–3517 or 888/262–2543,* ᗯᗴᗊ *www.beachhouseplymouth.com. 2 rooms, 1 suite. Beach. No smoking. MC, V. BP.*

Outdoor Activities and Sports

BEACHES

Plymouth Beach (⊠ Warren Ave. [Rte. 3A]), south of town next to Bert's Cove restaurant, has rest rooms, showers, and lifeguards (in season). Daily parking fees are $7 weekdays, $10 weekends.

White Horse Beach (⊠ Taylor Ave.) is a popular long, sandy beach in a neighborhood of summer cottages, off Route 3A south of Plimoth Plantation. Parking is very limited.

STATE PARKS

Myles Standish State Forest (⊠ Cranberry Rd., South Carver, Exit 5 off Rte. 3, ☎ 508/866–2526, ᗯᗴᗊ www.state.ma.us/dem/parks/mssf.htm) has more than 16,000 acres for hiking, biking, swimming, picnicking, and canoeing.

Fall River

❷ *54 mi southeast of Boston.*

It's a famous rhyme of woe: "Lizzie Borden took an axe / And gave her mother forty whacks. / When she saw what she had done, / She gave her father forty-one." And yet Lizzie, the maiden daughter of the town's prominent banker, was found innocent of the 1892 bludgeoning deaths of her father and stepmother in the most sensational trial of its time. She went on to spend the rest of her life quietly in Fall River, today a fading port and factory town.

In the 1800s Fall River became a major textile milling area, but by the 1920s much of the textile industry had moved to southern states. Many former mills housed factory outlets that attracted bargain hunters, although more recently, many of the outlets, too, have shut down or moved on. It's primarily the Borden tragedy—and the city's nautical attractions—that draw visitors today.

The best place to learn about the Borden case is the **Fall River Historical Society,** which has the world's largest collection of Borden artifacts, including courtroom evidence, photographs, and the handleless hatchet suspected of being the murder weapon. The 1835 Greek Revival–style mansion also has a wealth of information about the region, displaying memorabilia from the Fall River steamship line and artifacts related to Fall River's days as home of the world's largest cotton cloth manufacturer. Another exhibit illustrates 19th-century mourning practices, including elaborate decorations woven from human hair. One-hour tours are available on the hour (weekdays 9–3, no tour at noon; weekends 1–4). ⊠ *451 Rock St., at Maple St.,* ☎ *508/679–1071,* WEB *www.lizzieborden.org.* 🖼 *Guided tours $5.* ☯ *Apr.–May and Oct.–Nov., Tues.–Fri. 9–4:30; June–Sept. and Dec., Tues.–Fri. 9–4:30, weekends 1–5.*

If you're strong of heart and stomach, you may want to take in the **Lizzie Borden Bed & Breakfast Museum.** In 1996 the Borden home, the site of the murders, was transformed into a B&B. Even if you don't spend the night here, you can stop in to see the display of Lizzie-related items. ⊠ *92 2nd St.,* ☎ *508/675–7333,* WEB *www.lizzie-borden. com.* 🖼 *Guided tours $7.50.* ☯ *Late June–Labor Day, daily 11–2:30; Memorial Day–late June and Labor Day–Oct., weekends 11–2:30; tours every ½ hr, last tour at 2:30.*

Another Lizzie highlight is the **Borden burial plot** in the Oak Grove Cemetery on Prospect Street. Lizzie's home after her acquittal was at **306 French Street** (a private residence), where she lived until her death in 1927.

A visit to Fall River can skirt Lizzie Borden's sad saga entirely. The town's industrial docks and enormous factories recall the city's past as a major textile center in the 19th and early 20th centuries. In the past, Fall River served as a port; today the most interesting nautical site is **Battleship Cove,** a "floating" museum complex docked on the Taunton River. The cove is home to the 35,000-ton battleship USS *Massachusetts;* the destroyer USS *Joseph P. Kennedy, Jr.;* a World War II attack sub, the USS *Lionfish;* two PT boats from World War II; and a Cold War–era Russian-built warship. ⊠ *5 Water St., at Davol St., off Rte. 79,* ☎ *508/678–1100 or 800/533–3194,* WEB *www.battleshipcove.com.* 🖼 *$9.* ☯ *Apr.–June, daily 9–5; July–Labor Day, daily 9–5:30; Labor Day–Mar., daily 9–4:30.*

The **HMS** *Bounty,* built for the 1962 film *Mutiny on the Bounty,* docks periodically in the summer or fall adjacent to Battleship Cove. You can participate in sails organized by the Tall Ship Bounty Foundation; call for details. ☎ *631/588–7900,* WEB *www.tallshipbounty.org.* 🖼 *Admission varies.* ☯ *Call ahead for schedule, as ship is often on sail.*

♻ The **Fall River Carousel,** built in the 1920s, was rescued from the defunct Lincoln Amusement Park in 1992 and moved to Battleship Cove. The glorious restoration is now housed dockside. ⊠ *Battleship Cove,*

☎ *508/324–4300.* ☎ *Rides $.50.* ☉ *Generally June–Columbus Day, Tues.–Sun. 10–6; mid-Apr.–May, reduced hrs., call to confirm.*

The riverside **Fall River Heritage State Park** tells the story of Fall River's industrial past, focusing on the city's textile mills and their workers. The park has a visitor center, exhibits, and a summer concert series. ✉ *200 Davol St. W,* ☎ *508/675–5759,* WEB *www.state.ma.us/dem/parks/frhp.htm.* ☎ *Free.* ☉ *Daily 10–4.*

Two blocks from Battleship Cove, the **Marine Museum at Fall River** celebrates the age of sail and steamship travel, especially the lavishly fitted ships of the Old Fall River Line, which operated until 1937 between New England and New York City. The museum also contains the 28-ft-long, 1-ton model of the *Titanic* used in the 1952 movie. ✉ *70 Water St.,* ☎ *508/674–3533,* WEB *www.marinemuseum.org.* ☎ *$4.* ☉ *Mon.–Sat. 9–5, Sun. noon–4.*

Dining and Lodging

$$ ✕ **Waterstreet Café.** This casually sophisticated café, with exposed brick and sponge-painted walls, serves hummus and tabbouleh roll-ups, falafel, and other Middle Eastern–inspired salads and sandwiches. Other specialties are "something fresh in a shell over linguine" (pasta with clams or mussels) and Greek Island Shrimp, sautéed with artichoke hearts and feta cheese. It's across the street from the Marine Museum. ✉ *36 Water St.,* ☎ *508/672–8748. AE, MC, V. Closed Mon.–Tues.*

$$$ 🛏 **Lizzie Borden Bed & Breakfast Museum.** Could you stand to sleep in the same house where Lizzie Borden's father and stepmother met a bloody end? Choose from one of the four original bedrooms, two of which are suites, or two rooms converted from attic space. A full breakfast and a house tour are included, as well as a map of the "Lizzie Trail" (related sites in the Fall River area). You can also watch videos about the Borden case. Nonguests may tour the place between 11 and 3. Overnight guests must be 12 or older. ✉ *92 2nd St., 02721,* ☎ FAX *508/675–7333,* WEB *www.lizzie-borden.com. 4 rooms, 2 suites. No smoking. AE, D, MC, V. BP.*

Westport

③ *12 mi southeast of Fall River.*

As you venture south and east of Fall River, the urban landscape gives way to farm country. You'll pass rows of corn, old stone walls, and pastures of cows and horses. About 12 mi from Fall River, Westport has a mix of farmland and summer homes in a small village and scattered throughout the countryside, as well as one of the area's nicest beaches.

Although grapes may not come immediately to mind as a Massachusetts crop, the **Westport Rivers Vineyard and Winery** grows grapes and has been selling its wines since 1991. Its sparkling wines are particularly well regarded. Visitors can sample the wines, and there's a small art gallery above the store with changing exhibits. Free winery tours are offered on weekends. The winery also holds special food-and-wine events and festivals throughout the year; call or check the Web site for details. ✉ *417 Hixbridge Rd., off Rte. 88,* ☎ *508/636–3423,* WEB *www.westportrivers.com.* ☉ *Tasting room, shop, and gallery daily 11–5; tours weekends 11–4:30.*

Dining and Lodging

$$–$$$ ✕ **The Back Eddy.** Owner Chris Schlesinger has earned raves for his ★ East Coast Grill in Cambridge, and he's translated the same formula from Boston to the Westport waterfront. The menu emphasizes fish preparations ranging from straightforward (steamers, oysters on the half shell) to world beat (grilled peppered tuna with Asian spinach salad, roasted clams over linguine). The casual, wood-floor dining room is boisterous, with a lively bar scene, and most of the large windows overlook the harbor, ideal at sunset. Expect to wait for a table; reservations are accepted only for parties of six or more. ⊠ *1 Bridge Rd.,* ☎ *508/636–6500. AE, D, MC, V. Memorial Day–Labor Day, no lunch Mon.–Wed.; Labor Day–Memorial Day, hrs. vary, call ahead.*

$$ ⊞ **Paquachuck Inn.** Built in 1827 as a supply house for whaling ships, this wood-shingle building on Westport Point is now a modest, comfortable inn. The wood-floored rooms with exposed beams aren't large, but several have four-poster beds, and all offer at least a glimpse of the water. Unfortunately, none has a private bath, although one shared bath does have a whirlpool tub, and there's an outdoor shower, too. The large sunny breakfast room with comfy couches leads to a patio and yard—note the three whale vertebrae that are now a garden sculpture. ⊠ *2056 Main Rd., 02791,* ☎ FAX *508/636–4398,* WEB *www. paquachuck.com. 9 rooms share 3 baths. Breakfast room, dock. No smoking. MC, V. CP.*

Outdoor Activities and Sports

BEACHES

One of the nicest beaches in this part of the state, **Horseneck Beach State Reservation** (⊠ Rte. 88, ☎ 508/636–8816, WEB www.state.ma.us/ dem/parks/hbch.htm) draws summer crowds to its 2 mi of sand. There are rest rooms with showers, and lifeguards in season. Parking is $7 a day from Memorial Day through Labor Day.

South Dartmouth

❹ *4 mi east of Westport.*

As in nearby Westport, the South Dartmouth countryside is dotted with farms and summer homes, but since it's only a few miles south of New Bedford, residents who work in the New Bedford area also make their homes here year-round. One of the prettiest spots is Padanarum Village, where Gulf Road and Dartmouth Road meet—built around the sailboat-filled harbor, Padanarum is a little oasis of shops, galleries, and cafés. Nearby, the village of Russells Mills houses one of the region's oldest general stores and a pottery studio.

Lodging

$ ⊞ **Saltworks Bed & Breakfast.** This large 1840 Greek Revival house on the edge of Padanarum Village has only two guest rooms, but they're lovely. Both are suites, with a fireplace in the large bedroom—one has a striking brass bed—and a smaller bedroom/sitting room attached. The walls are decorated with artwork by owner Sandra Hall, who runs the inn with her husband, David. Downstairs are a comfortable common room and a wraparound porch, with views out to the harbor. ⊠ *115 Elm St., Padanarum Village 02748,* ☎ *508/991–5491,* FAX *508/979–8470. 2 suites. No smoking. AE, MC, V. Closed mid-Dec.–Mar. BP.*

Outdoor Activities and Sports

BEACHES

Demarest Lloyd State Park (⊠ Barney's Joy Rd., ☎ 508/636–8816, WEB www.state.ma.us/dem/parks/deml.htm) may be hard to find, but it's worth seeking out for its long beach of soft, white sand on a sheltered Buzzards Bay cove. Behind the beach is a wooded area with picnic tables and barbecue grills. The bathhouse has rest rooms and showers. In season (Memorial Day through Labor Day), there are lifeguards, and parking is $7 a day.

Shopping

Davoll's General Store (⊠ 1228 Russells Mills Rd., ☎ 508/636–4530), established in 1793, sells antiques and collectibles, as well as clothing, deli sandwiches, and a small selection of groceries.

Salt Marsh Pottery (⊠ 1167 Russells Mills Rd., ☎ 508/636–4813 or 800/859–5028) makes platters, bowls, and other unique ceramic pieces decorated with wildflowers.

New Bedford

❺ *15 mi east of Fall River, 50 mi south of Boston.*

In 1652 colonists from Plymouth settled in the area that now includes the city of New Bedford. The city has a long maritime tradition, beginning as a shipbuilding center and small whaling port in the late 1700s. By the mid-1800s the city had developed into a center of North American whaling.

Today New Bedford is home to the largest fishing fleet on the East Coast, and although much of the town is industrial, the restored historic district near the water is a pleasant stop. It was here that Herman Melville set his masterpiece, *Moby-Dick,* a novel ostensibly about whaling. New Bedford's whaling tradition is commemorated in the **New Bedford Whaling National Historical Park,** encompassing 13 blocks of the waterfront historic district. The park visitor center, housed in an 1853 Greek Revival former bank, provides maps and information about whaling-related sites. Beginning in spring 2002, you can view an orientation film about American whaling and the New Bedford historic sites. ⊠ *33 William St.,* ☎ *508/996–4095,* WEB *www.nps.gov/nebe.* ☉ *July–Labor Day, daily 9–5; Labor Day–June, daily 9–4.*

 The **New Bedford Whaling Museum,** established in 1903, is the world's largest museum devoted to the history of whaling. A highlight is the skeleton of a 66-ft blue whale, one of only three on view anywhere in the world. An interactive exhibit lets you listen to the underwater sounds of whales, dolphins, and other sea life, plus the sounds of a thunderstorm and a whale-watching boat—all as a whale might hear them. You can also peruse the collection of scrimshaw, visit exhibits on regional history, and climb aboard an 89-ft half-scale model of the 1826 whaling ship *Lagoda*—the world's largest ship model. ⊠ *18 Johnny Cake Hill,* ☎ *508/997–0046.* 🎟 *$6,* WEB *www.whalingmuseum.org.* ☉ *Daily 9–5; Memorial Day–Labor Day until 9 on Thurs.*

Seaman's Bethel, the small chapel described in *Moby-Dick,* is across the street from the whaling museum. ⊠ *15 Johnny Cake Hill,* ☎ *508/ 992–3295.* ☉ *Weekdays 10–5.*

The **New Bedford Art Museum,** a compact gallery space in the 1918 Vault Building (a former bank), showcases the work of area artists. Included are paintings by 19th- and early 20th-century New Bedford artists Albert Bierstadt, William Bradford, and Charles Henry Gifford. ⊠ *608 Pleasant St.,* ☎ *508/961–3072,* WEB *www.newbedfordartmuseum.org.* 🎟 *$3.* ☉ *June–Aug., Mon–Wed. and Fri.–Sun. 10–5, Thurs. 10–7; Sept.– May, Wed. and Fri.–Sun. noon–5, Thurs. noon–7.*

For a glimpse of upper-class life during New Bedford's whaling heyday, head ½ mi south of downtown to the **Rotch-Jones-Duff House and Garden Museum.** This 1834 Greek Revival mansion, set amid a full city block of gardens, was home to three prominent families in the 1800s and is filled with elegant furnishings from the era, including a mahogany piano, a massive marble-top sideboard, and portraits of the house's occupants. A self-guided audio tour is available. ⊠ *396 County St.,*

CUTTYHUNK ISLAND

IF CAPE COD AND OTHER Massachusetts seaside towns seem too crowded with sun-and-surf seekers, hop on the ferry from New Bedford to Cuttyhunk Island. One of the Elizabeth Islands, a chain that extends along Buzzards Bay 16 mi southwest of Woods Hole, Cuttyhunk has a year-round population of about 20 (although more people do turn up in the summer). It's a New England island the way New England islands used to be—with tall beach grass swaying in the breeze, rocky shores, a handful of sailboats cruising into the harbor, and few people.

There are some cars on Cuttyhunk, but not many. The island is only 2 mi long and 1 mi wide, and most people get around by foot or golf cart; you'll see lots of aging golf vehicles putt-putting around the island. There's a road that circles the island, although it withers to a dirt path as it heads out toward Gosnold Pond and the Cuttyhunk lighthouse. Near the center of the island, you can climb up Lookout Hill for views of the other Elizabeth Islands and across the sound to Martha's Vineyard. Nearby, there's a small village with a general store, a one-room schoolhouse, a church, a library, at least one seasonal café, and a B&B.

If you want to stay overnight, contact the **Cuttyhunk Fishing Club B&B** (☎ 508/992–5585, WEB www.cuttyhunkfishingclub.com), which rents eight rooms, plus a three-bedroom apartment; it's open mid-May through mid-October. **Pete's Place Rentals** (☎ 508/992–5131) has a small number of homes and apartments available for weekly rentals from mid-June to Labor Day; from Memorial Day to mid-June

and from Labor Day to Columbus Day, its properties can be rented with a two-night minimum.

English explorer Bartholomew Gosnold (1572–1607), who is credited with giving Cape Cod its name, landed on Cuttyhunk in 1602. He and his crew reportedly stayed for about three weeks on the island before continuing their journey and eventually returning to England.

Today Cuttyhunk is the only one of the Elizabeth Islands accessible by regular ferry service (you'll need a private boat to visit the others). The **M/V Alert II** ferry (☎ 508/992–1432, WEB www.cuttyhunk.com) makes the one-hour trip from New Bedford's Fisherman's Wharf (Pier 3) to Cuttyhunk daily mid-June–mid-September and several days a week in the spring and fall; between mid-October and mid-April regular service runs only once a week. The ferry generally leaves New Bedford in the morning and returns from Cuttyhunk in the midafternoon (with additional trips on Friday, Saturday, and Sunday); same-day round-trip fares are $19.

You can visit Cuttyhunk as a day trip from the Falmouth area. On Sunday from mid-July to mid-October, the Ashumet Holly and Wildlife Sanctuary runs a sailing trip from Woods Hole to Cuttyhunk.

If you're looking for nightlife, crowds, or organized activities, don't come to Cuttyhunk. There's not a lot to do here besides walk, swim, and stare out to sea. But after the hustle and bustle of mainland life, that's the way most visitors like it.

— By Carolyn Heller

☎ 508/997–1401, WEB *www.rjdmuseum.org.* 🎫 *$4.* 🕐 *June–Dec., Mon.–Sat. 10–4, Sun. noon–4; Jan.–May, Tues.–Sat. 10–4, Sun. noon–4.*

Dining and Lodging

$$–$$$ ✕ **Davy's Locker.** A huge seafood menu is the main draw at this spot overlooking Buzzards Bay. Choose from more than a dozen shrimp preparations or a Healthy Choice entrée—dishes prepared with olive oil, vegetables, garlic, and herbs. For landlubbers, chicken, steak, ribs, and the like are also served. ✉ *1480 E. Rodney French Blvd.,* ☎ *508/992–7359. AE, D, MC, V.*

$–$$ ✕ **Antonio's.** If you'd like to sample the traditional fare of New Bedford's large Portuguese population, friendly unadorned Antonio's serves up hearty portions of pork and shellfish stew, *bacalau* (salt cod), and grilled sardines, often on plates piled high with crispy fried potatoes and rice. ✉ *267 Coggeshall St., near intersection of I–195 and Rte. 18,* ☎ *508/990–3636. No credit cards.*

$–$$ ✕ **Freestone's City Grill.** In an 1877 former bank in the historic district, Freestone's serves soups and chowders, sandwiches and salads, plus fish, steaks, and vegetarian dishes. Traditional details—mahogany paneling, marble floors, brass rails—blend with contemporary art. ✉ *41 William St.,* ☎ *508/993–7477. AE, DC, MC, V. Closed Sun.*

$–$$ 🛏 **Edgewater Bed & Breakfast.** One of the most pleasant places to stay in New Bedford is just across the Acushnet River in Fairhaven, a residential suburb. The Edgewater's slogan is "So close to the water, you'll think you're on a boat," and it's true—this casual shingle house, built in 1760 and expanded in the 1880s, has water views from three sides. All the rooms are simply and traditionally furnished; the window-lined Captain's Suite, with a working fireplace and a king-size bed, has the best views. You can curl up by the fireplace on the living room's comfy couches or look out over the water from the deck. Owner Kathy Reed, who has run the B&B since the early 1980s, has plenty of ideas for things to see and do. ✉ *2 Oxford St., Fairhaven 02719,* ☎ *508/997–5512,* FAX *508/997–5784,* WEB *www.rixsan.com/edgewater. 3 rooms, 3 suites. Breakfast room. No smoking. AE, D, MC, V. CP.*

Nightlife and the Arts

On the second Thursday of every month from 5 to 9 PM, New Bedford hosts **AHA! nights** (☎ 508/264–8859), a downtown gallery night program to highlight the city's art, history, and architecture. Museums and galleries, including the Whaling Museum and the New Bedford Art Museum, have extended hours and offer free admission. Concerts, craft demonstrations, and other special events are often on the programs.

Outdoor Activities and Sports

BEACHES

Fort Phoenix State Beach Reservation (✉ Green St., Fairhaven, off Rte. 6, ☎ 508/992–4524, WEB www.state.ma.us/dem/parks/ftph.htm), the site of the Revolutionary War's first naval battle, has a small sandy beach. Parking is free, and there are rest rooms with showers.

En Route As you head east toward Cape Cod, a wet and wild adventure for the kids awaits at the **Water Wizz Water Park,** with a 50-ft-high water slide complete with tunnels and dips, a wave pool, a river ride, three tube rides, two enclosed water-mat slides, a children's slide, a pool, miniature golf, and food. The enclosed Black Wizard water slide descends 75 ft in darkness. ✉ *U.S. 6 and Rte. 28, Wareham, 2 mi west of Bourne Bridge,* ☎ *508/295–3255.* 🎫 *$26.* 🕐 *Mid-June–Labor Day, daily 10–6:30.*

APPROACHING THE CAPE A TO Z

To research prices, get advice from other travelers, and book travel arrangements, visit www.fodors.com.

AIR TRAVEL

Boston and Providence are the major air gateways for the region approaching Cape Cod (☞ Air Travel *and* Airports *in* Smart Travel Tips A to Z).

BOAT AND FERRY TRAVEL

Capt. John Boats runs a seasonal ferry between Plymouth and Provincetown, with daily service from mid-June through Labor Day, and less frequent service in the spring and fall. The boat departs from State Pier (near the *Mayflower II*) in Plymouth and docks at MacMillan Wharf in Provincetown. The trip takes approximately 90 minutes. A round-trip ticket costs $27, the one-way fare is $18, and bicycles can be transported for an additional $2. Ferry service is available Memorial Day through September.

➤ BOAT AND FERRY TRAVEL INFORMATION: **Capt. John Boats** (☎ 508/747–2400 or 800/242–2469, WEB www.provincetownferry.com).

BUS TRAVEL

American Eagle Motorcoach Inc. offers service from Boston to New Bedford. Bonanza Bus Lines runs frequent direct service between Boston and Fall River, as well as service to both Fall River and New Bedford from Providence. From Fall River and New Bedford to the Cape, Bonanza provides service to Bourne, Falmouth, Woods Hole, and Hyannis. Plymouth & Brockton Street Railway buses stop in Plymouth en route to the Cape from Boston. From the Plymouth stop take the Plymouth Area Link buses to the town center or to Plimoth Plantation.

➤ BUS INFORMATION: **American Eagle Motorcoach Inc.** (☎ 800/453–5040). **Bonanza Bus Lines** (☎ 508/548–7588 or 800/556–3815, WEB www.bonanzabus.com). **Plymouth & Brockton Street Railway** (☎ 508/746–0378, WEB www.p-b.com). **Plymouth Area Link** (☎ 508/746–0378, WEB www.gatra.org/pal.htm).

CAR TRAVEL

To get to Plymouth from Boston, take the Southeast Expressway I–93 south to Route 3 toward Cape Cod; Exits 6 and 4 lead to downtown Plymouth and Plimoth Plantation, respectively. To reach Fall River from Boston, take I–93 to Route 24 south; then take Route 79 south to reach the Battleship Cove area. From Providence to Fall River, follow I–195 east. To get to New Bedford from Fall River, go east on I–195, or if you're coming from Boston, follow I–93 to Route 24 south to Route 140 south, and continue to I–195 east; exit at Route 18 south for the historic district. Allow about one hour from Boston to Plymouth, Fall River, or New Bedford, about one hour from Plymouth to either Fall River or New Bedford, and about 15–20 minutes between New Bedford and Fall River. From Providence you can reach Fall River in about 20–25 minutes.

To reach Westport from Fall River, take I–195 east to Route 88 south, and continue on Route 88. For South Dartmouth take I–195 east to the Faunce Corner Mall Road exit, or take Dartmouth Road south from New Bedford, toward Padanarum Village.

EMERGENCIES

➤ EMERGENCY SERVICES: **Ambulance, fire, police** (☎ 911 or dial township station).

➤ HOSPITALS: **Jordan Hospital** (⊠ 275 Sandwich St., Plymouth, ☎ 508/746–2000, WEB www.jordan.org). **St. Luke's Hospital** (⊠ 101 Page St., New Bedford, ☎ 508/997–1515).

➤ 24-HOUR PHARMACIES: **CVS Pharmacy** (⊠ 1145 Kempton St. [Rte. 6, near Rte. 140], New Bedford, ☎ 508/999–3241; 8 Pilgrim Hill Rd. [off Rte. 44], Plymouth, ☎ 508/747–1465 WEB www.cvs.com).

TOURS

Cape Cod Canal Cruises (two or three hours, narrated) leave from Onset, just northwest of the Bourne Bridge. A Sunday jazz cruise, sunset cocktail cruises, and Friday and Saturday dance cruises are available. Children 12 and under cruise free on Family Discount Cruises, Monday through Saturday at 4; cruises cost between $10 and $14.

Colonial Lantern Tours offers guided evening walking tours April through November of the original Plymouth plantation site and historic district, as well as the nightly Blood, Gore, and Ghosts tour highlighting Plymouth's more macabre history.

Plymouth Amphibious Tours are one-hour tours of Plymouth and its waterfront, half on land and half in the water, in restored World War II amphibious "duck boats." The tours are available April through October for $17.

WHALE-WATCHING TOURS

Capt. John Boats offers several daily whale-watch cruises from Plymouth Town Wharf, June–Labor Day, and on a more limited schedule April–May and Labor Day–November. Andy Lynn Boats, at Plymouth Town Wharf, runs whale-watch trips June through September; call for schedule.

➤ FEES AND SCHEDULES: **Andy Lynn Boats** (☎ 508/746–7776). **Cape Cod Canal Cruises** (⊠ Onset Bay Town Pier, Onset, ☎ 508/295–3883, WEB www.hy-linecruises.com/canal.htm). **Capt. John Boats** (☎ 508/746–2643 or 800/242–2469, WEB www.whalewatchingplymouth.com). **Colonial Lantern Tours** (⊠ 35 North St., Plymouth, ☎ 508/747–4161 or 800/698–5636, WEB www.plimouth.com). **Plymouth Amphibious Tours** (⊠ Harbor Pl., off Water St., Plymouth, ☎ 508/747–7658 or 800/225–4000, WEB www.ducktoursplymouth.com).

TRAIN TRAVEL

With the exception of Plymouth, southeastern Massachusetts is not well served by trains. MBTA commuter rail service is available from Boston to Plymouth. Travel time is about one hour. From the station take the Plymouth Area Link buses (☞ Bus Travel) to the historic attractions.

➤ TRAIN INFORMATION: **MBTA** (☎ 617/222–3200, WEB www.mbta.com).

VISITOR INFORMATION

Plymouth Waterfront Visitor Information Center is generally open between April and November.

➤ TOURIST INFORMATION: **Bristol County Convention and Visitors Bureau** (⊠ 70 N. 2nd St., Box 976, New Bedford 02741, ☎ 508/997–1250 or 800/288–6263, WEB www.southofboston.org). **Destination Plymouth** (⊠ 170 Water St., Suite 10C, Plymouth 02360, ☎ 800/872–1620, WEB www.visit-plymouth.com). **Fall River Chamber of Commerce** (⊠ 200 Pocasset St., Fall River 02721, ☎ 508/676–8226, WEB www.fallriverchamber.com). **New Bedford Office of Tourism** (⊠ Waterfront Visitors Center, Pier 3, New Bedford 02740, ☎ 508/979–1745 or 800/508–5353, WEB www.ci.new-bedford.ma.us). **Plymouth Waterfront Visitor Information Center** (⊠ 130 Water St. [at Rte. 44], Plymouth 02360, ☎ 508/747–7525).

3 THE UPPER CAPE

As thick as a slab of its namesake fish, upper Cape Cod is the peninsula's most varied region and has its largest year-round population. Sandwich, the oldest town on the Cape, hugs the north shore, while the Buzzards Bay coast is a wooded mix of upscale vacation homes, small beaches, and inland countryside. Modern development surrounds the historic core of Falmouth; to the south, the lively village of Woods Hole gives way to the beaches of Nantucket Sound. Farther east, in Mashpee, Native American traditions are very much part of the present, as is one of the Cape's finest shopping centers.

T HE CLOSEST PART OF THE CAPE to the mainland, the Upper Cape has none of the briny, otherworldly breeziness of the Outer Cape and little of the resort feel of some Lower Cape towns such as Chatham. Instead, many year-round residents make their homes here, the beaches are intimate, and more attractions—freshwater ponds, conservation areas, and small museums—are inland. You'll discover plenty of history here: Sandwich is the oldest town on the Cape, and Bourne was the Pilgrims' first Cape Cod settlement and an important trading area. The first Native American reservation in the United States was established in Mashpee, which still includes a large Wampanoag population and a tribal council governing body.

Revised by
Carolyn Heller

Being able to find peace and quiet so close to the mainland and the traffic-clogged bridges is a nice Upper Cape surprise. Sandwich, its village streets lined with historic houses and museums, is preserved like a stage set. Heading east, Route 6A meanders past antiques shops, bed-and-breakfasts, and salt marshes. Falmouth, to the south, is an active year-round community, more suburban than seaside, though its easy-to-reach beaches are popular with families. In the villages of North and West Falmouth, along Buzzards Bay, tree-lined country lanes lead to sandy coves, while in East Falmouth and Waquoit, narrow spits of land jut into marshy inlets, and plenty of secluded sites for hiking and walking are yours for the taking. Woods Hole, a small but bustling village on the Cape's southwestern tip, is a center for international marine research; it's also the departure point for ferries to Martha's Vineyard.

To make the most of this convenient mix, take an early morning hike through a nature reserve or sit on a beach overlooking the sound and Martha's Vineyard. Pack a picnic, with fresh-from-the-farm-stand fruits or home-baked breads, and eat on the banks of a freshwater pond. Ride your bike along a shaded country road, or stretch out in the sand to watch the sailboats bobbing in the harbor and the sun sinking low over Buzzards Bay. You'll still have time to head back into town for that perfect lobster roll or plate of fried clams.

Pleasures and Pastimes

Beaches
Water surrounds the Upper Cape on three sides, giving beach lovers plenty of options. The south-side beaches, on Nantucket Sound, have rolling surf and are warmed by the Gulf Stream. Along Buzzards Bay, many small coves have sandy stretches (although most restrict parking to residents or permit holders in season). To the north, on Cape Cod Bay, the beaches generally have more temperate waters and gentle waves, but watch out for pebbles mixed in with the sand, particularly in the Sandwich area. Remember that you can also swim inland—the Upper Cape has many child-friendly freshwater ponds with sandy beaches and calm waters.

Biking
Several short bike trails, including the Shining Sea Trail between Falmouth and Woods Hole and the Cape Cod Canal Trail, which follows both sides of the canal, make the Upper Cape a good place for easy day rides. Many of the less-traveled roads in Bourne, West and North Falmouth, and in the interior between Sandwich and Falmouth are also good biking areas. The beaches of Buzzards Bay, their parking restricted to those with resident stickers, make excellent destinations for bike rides.

HOW TO
USE THIS GUIDE

Great trips begin with great planning, and this guide makes planning easy. It's packed with everything you need—insider advice on hotels and restaurants, cool tools, practical tips, essential maps, and much more.

COOL TOOLS

Fodor's Choice Top picks are marked throughout with a star.

Great Itineraries These tours, planned by Fodor's experts, give you the skinny on what you can see and do in the time you have.

Smart Travel Tips A to Z This special section is packed with important contacts and advice on everything from how to get around to what to pack.

Good Walks You won't miss a thing if you follow the numbered bullets on our maps.

Need a Break? Looking for a quick bite to eat or a spot to rest? These sure bets are along the way.

Off the Beaten Path Some lesser-known sights are worth a detour. We've marked those you should make time for.

POST-IT® FLAGS
Dog-ear no more!

"Post-it" is a registered trademark of 3M.

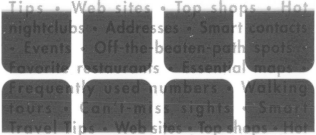

Favorite restaurants • Essential maps • Frequently used numbers • Walking tours • Can't-miss sights • Smart Travel Tips • Web sites • Top shops • Hot nightclubs • Addresses • Smart contacts • Events • Off-the-beaten-path spots • Favorite restaurants • Essential maps • Frequently used numbers • Walking tours • Can't-miss sights • Smart Travel Tips • Web sites • Top shops • Hot nightclubs • Addresses • Smart contacts • Events • Off-the-beaten-path spots • Favorite restaurants • Essential maps • Frequently used numbers • Walking tours •

ICONS AND SYMBOLS

Watch for these symbols throughout:

★	Our special recommendations
✕	Restaurant
🏠	Lodging establishment
✕🏠	Lodging establishment whose restaurant warrants a special trip
☺	Good for kids
☞	Sends you to another section of the guide for more information
✉	Address
☎	Telephone number
FAX	Fax number
WEB	Web site
🎟	Admission price
☺	Opening hours
$-$$$$	Lodging and dining price categories, keyed to strategically sited price charts. Check the index for locations.
①❶	Numbers in white and black circles on the maps, in the margins, and within tours correspond to one another.

ON THE WEB

Continue your planning with these useful tools found at **www.fodors.com**, the Web's best source for travel information.

"Rich with resources." —*New York Times*

"Navigation is a cinch." —*Forbes* "Best of the Web" list

"Put together by people bursting with know-how."
—*Sunday Times* (London)

Create a Miniguide Pinpoint hotels, restaurants, and attractions that have what you want at the price you want to pay.

Rants and Raves Find out what readers say about Fodor's picks—or write your own reviews of hotels and restaurants you've just visited.

Travel Talk Post your questions and get answers from fellow travelers, or share your own experiences.

On-Line Booking Find the best prices on airline tickets, rental cars, cruises, or vacations, and book them on the spot.

About our Books Learn about other Fodor's guides to your destination and many others.

Expert Advice and Trip Ideas From what to tip to how to take great photos, from the national parks to Nepal, Fodors.com has suggestions that'll make your trip a breeze. Log on and get informed and inspired.

Smart Resources Check the weather in your destination or convert your currency. Learn the local language or link to the latest event listings. Or consult hundreds of detailed maps—all in one place.

Dining

Like other parts of Cape Cod, the Upper Cape's dining scene includes basic seafood shacks, contemporary restaurants that draw inspiration from the far corners of the globe, and everything in between. Overall, the restaurant options tend toward the traditional, with fried clams, baked scrod, and boiled lobster gracing the most popular menus. Restaurants are more widely scattered in the Upper Cape towns—there are few "restaurant rows"—but if you like to wander and check out your dining options, try Mashpee Commons in Mashpee or Water Street in Woods Hole.

CATEGORY	COST*
$$$$	over $26
$$$	$19–$26
$$	$11–$18
$	under $11

*per person for a main course at dinner

Lodging

Sandwich and other towns along the north-shore Route 6A historic district have quiet, traditional villages with old-Cape atmosphere and charming B&Bs. Along Route 6A you can also find family-friendly motels, ranging from the modest to the better equipped. Historic B&Bs fill the center of Falmouth, while other small inns line the shore and neighboring streets of Falmouth Heights. Lodging options are fewer on the Buzzards Bay side (Bourne and West and North Falmouth), but several small B&Bs hidden away on country lanes provide glimpses of old New England. In Mashpee's New Seabury community, modern town houses and condominiums—with extensive resort amenities—are available as rentals.

CATEGORY	COST*
$$$$	over $200
$$$	$150–$200
$$	$100–$150
$	under $100

*All prices are for a standard double room in high season, excluding 5.7% state tax and gratuities. Some inns add a 15% service charge.

Nightlife and the Arts

There's plenty of entertainment on the Upper Cape, especially in season; choices range from the summer concerts at Sandwich's Heritage Plantation to the staged readings at the Cape Cod Theatre Project (in Falmouth and Woods Hole) to the year-round concerts sponsored by Mashpee's Boch Center for the Performing Arts. Bourne, Sandwich, and Falmouth all host summer town-band concerts, and festivals with entertainment take place throughout the year. If you're looking for art galleries and crafts shows, explore the Falmouth downtown area, Route 6A in East Sandwich, and Mashpee Commons.

Outdoor Activities and Sports

Hikers and walkers will find plenty of places to wander on the Upper Cape. Several recreation areas line the Cape Cod Canal, and trails crisscross the region's wildlife sanctuaries and nature reserves, including the Ashumet Holly sanctuary, Waquoit Bay National Estuarine Research Reserve, and the Mashpee River Woodlands. Canoeing and kayaking are great around the marshy inlets of both Cape Cod Bay and Buzzards Bay and on the Upper Cape's many freshwater ponds. In addition, the ponds, as well as the banks of the canal, are popular fishing sites.

Shopping

With its large year-round population, the Upper Cape houses many of the same shops you'd find anywhere in the suburban United States— the Gap, Starbucks, and Banana Republic are all here. Strip malls line Route 28 in Falmouth, although by far the nicest mall in this part of the Cape is the villagelike Mashpee Commons. Like any good tourist destination, the Upper Cape has plenty of T-shirt and souvenir shops almost everywhere you turn, and just over the bridges several outlet malls, including the Cape Cod Factory Outlet Mall and the Tanger Outlet Center, draw shoppers. The real charms of this part of the Cape are in its small boutiques and tucked-away galleries, where you can find that one-of-a-kind sweater or a watercolor inspired by the sun setting over the bay.

Exploring the Upper Cape

On the north shore, Sandwich, gracious and lovely, is the Cape's oldest town. Centered inland, Mashpee is a long-standing Native American township in which Native-owned land is governed by local Wampanoags. Falmouth, the Cape's second-most-populous town, is still green and historic, if seemingly overrun with strip malls. Woods Hole, one port from which to ferry over to Martha's Vineyard, is an international center of marine and biological research. Along the west coast, in parts of Bourne and West and North Falmouth, you'll find wooded areas ending in secluded coves; the south coast has long-established resort communities.

Numbers in the text correspond to numbers in the margin and on the Upper Cape map.

Great Itineraries

It's astonishing that, so close to the busy mainland, the lovely old town of **Sandwich** ① stands as one of the best examples of the Cape of yesteryear. Visit the Hoxie House, the Sandwich Glass Museum, or the beautiful grounds and collection of old cars at **Heritage Plantation** ②; have a picnic lunch on the banks of Shawme Pond; or spend the afternoon at the old-timey Green Briar Nature Center and Jam Kitchen walking the nature trails and picking out homemade jam to take with you. Here and all along the bay shore, you can explore salt marshes, so full of sea and bird life. If history's your thing, take a step back and start your Upper Cape trip at **Plimoth Plantation,** about 22 mi northwest of the Sagamore Bridge on Route 3A. The reconstructed settlement, where actors dress in period clothing and carry out the activities typical of earlier days, conveys a very tangible sense of the Cape's history.

To reach the Upper Cape's south shore, take Route 28A south through some lovely little towns, with detours to beautiful white-sand beaches. This is the way to Falmouth and to **Woods Hole** ⑥, the center for international marine research and the year-round ferry port for Martha's Vineyard. A small aquarium in town has regional sea-life exhibits, and there are several shops and museums. On the way out of town, the view from Nobska Light is breathtaking. In **Falmouth** ④ stroll around the village green, look into some of the historic houses, and stop at the Waquoit Bay National Estuarine Research Reserve for a walk along the estuary and barrier beach. Inland, on the eastern extent of the Upper Cape, the Wampanoag township of **Mashpee** ⑧ is one of the best places to learn about the Cape's Native American heritage.

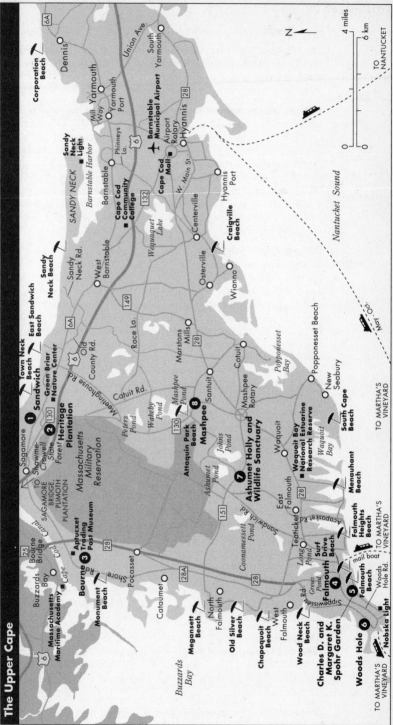

The Upper Cape

Sagamore

60 mi southeast of Boston and 30 mi northeast of New Bedford.

The village of Sagamore straddles the Cape Cod Canal and is perhaps best known for the bridge, completed in 1935, that bears its name. Primarily a small suburban community, the town has several stores for those interested in bargain hunting or gift shopping.

At **Pairpoint Crystal,** you can watch richly colored lead crystal being hand-blown in the factory as it has been since 1837. The shop sells candlesticks, vases, stemware, sun catchers, ornamental cup plates (used to hold the cup in the days when tea was poured into saucers to drink), and reproductions of original Boston and Sandwich glass pieces. ⊠ *851 Sandwich Rd. (Rte. 6A),* ☎ *508/888–2344 or 800/899–0953,* WEB *www.pairpoint.com.* ⌕ *Free.* ☉ *Showroom May–Dec., weekdays 9–6, Sat. 10–6, Sun. 11–6; Jan.–Apr., Mon.–Sat. 10–5, Sun. noon–5. Demonstrations May–Dec., weekdays 9–4; Jan.–Apr., call before visiting, since demonstration hrs are limited.*

Dining and Lodging

$–$$ ✕ **Sagamore Inn.** Old Cape Cod traditions are kept alive at this local
★   favorite, owned by the Pagliarani family since 1963. Pressed-tin walls and ceilings, fans, old wooden booths and tables, lace curtains, and white linen add up to a dining room so casual you almost overlook its elegance. All the food here is homemade (except the stuffed quahogs), very good yet traditional at the same time. The seafood platter is a knockout, the chicken potpie substantial, and the prime rib huge. Luncheon specials attract regulars from all over town, and the service is as friendly as family. A cozy, handsome old bar is under the same roof. ⊠ *1131 Rte. 6A,* ☎ *508/888–9707. Reservations not accepted. AE, MC, V. Closed Tues. and Nov.–Mar.*

$ △ **Scusset Beach State Reservation.** This park, which encompasses 490 acres near the Cape Cod Canal, with a cold-water beach on the bay, has 98 RV sites plus five tent sites, some wooded. There are cold showers on the beach and hot showers in the campground. ⊠ *140 Scusset Beach Rd., off Rte. 3 at Sagamore Bridge rotary, 02532,* ☎ *877/422–6762 for campsite reservations; 508/888–0859 for general information,* WEB *www.reserveamerica.com. 103 sites. Beach. MC, V.*

Outdoor Activities and Sports

The **Scusset Beach State Reservation** is a pleasant place for a swim, walk, or bike ride near the mainland side of the Sagamore Bridge. The beach sweeps along Cape Cod Bay, the nearby power plant mars the view inland. Its pier is popular for fishing; other activities include hiking, picnicking, and camping. There's a parking fee in season, generally Memorial Day to Labor Day. ⊠ *140 Scusset Beach Rd., off Rte. 3 at Sagamore Bridge rotary, 02532,* ☎ *508/888–0859.* ⌕ *Memorial Day–Labor Day, parking $7.* ☉ *Daily 8–8.*

Shopping

Cape Cod Factory Outlet Mall (⊠ Factory Outlet Rd., Exit 1 off U.S. 6, ☎ 508/888–8417) has more than 20 outlets, including Corning/Revere, Carter's, Bass, Bugle Boy, Van Heusen, Izod, London Fog, and Reebok.

Chocolate House Fudge and Gift Shop (⊠ 11 Cranberry Hwy. [Rte. 6A], ☎ 508/888–7065), just over the Sagamore Bridge on the Cape side, sells creamy fudge in 12 flavors, hand-dipped chocolates and truffles, saltwater taffy, and penny candy. The gift shop displays cranberry glass and other Cape items.

Christmas Tree Shops (✉ Cranberry Hwy. [Rte. 6A], Exit 1 off U.S. 6, ☎ 508/888–7010; other locations at Falmouth, Hyannis, Yarmouth Port, West Yarmouth, West Dennis, and Orleans) sell everything from furniture to clothes to kitchen goods.

Sandwich

★ ❶ *3 mi east of Sagamore Bridge, 11 mi west of Barnstable.*

A well-preserved, quintessential New England village, Sandwich wears its history proudly. The oldest town on Cape Cod was established in 1637 by some of the Plymouth Pilgrims and incorporated on March 6, 1638. Driving through town past the white-column town hall, the gristmill on Shawme Pond, the First Church of Christ with its spindle-like spire, and the 18th- and 19th-century homes that line the streets is like driving back in time—you may feel as if you should be holding a horse's reins rather than the steering wheel of a car. When you reach Main Street, park the car and get out for a stroll. Look at old houses on Main Street, stop at a museum or two, and work your way to the delightful Shawme Pond. While you walk, look for etched Sandwich glass from the old factory on front doors. There probably aren't two identical glass panels in town.

Unlike other Cape towns, whose deepwater ports opened the doors to prosperity in the whaling days, Sandwich was an industrial town for much of the 19th century. The main industry was the production of vividly colored glass, called Sandwich glass, which is now sought by collectors. The Boston and Sandwich Glass Company's factory here produced the glass from 1825 until 1888, when competition with glassmakers in the Midwest—and finally a union strike—closed it.

The **Sandwich Glass Museum** holds information about the history of the company, including a diorama showing how the factory looked in its heyday, and an outstanding collection of blown and pressed glass in many shapes and shimmering hues. Large glass lamps, vases, and pitchers are impressive, but so are the hundreds of small saucers on display. Glassmaking demonstrations are held in the summer. A few galleries contain relics of the town's early history. The gift shop sells some handsome reproductions, including some made by local artisans. ✉ *129 Main St.,* ☎ *508/888–0251,* WEB *www.sandwichglassmuseum.org.* 🖾 *$3.50.* ☉ *Apr.–Dec., daily 9:30–5; Feb.–Mar., Wed.–Sun. 9:30–4.*

A lovely place for a stroll or a picnic is the park around **Shawme Pond** (✉ Water and Grove Sts.), a favorite fishing site for children. The ducks and swans love to be fed, though posted signs warn you not to indulge them. Across the way—a perfect backdrop for this setting—stands the spired, white 1848 First Church of Christ, inspired by a design by British architect Christopher Wren.

Where Shawme Pond drains over its dam, a little wooden bridge leads over a watercourse to the waterwheel-powered **Dexter Gristmill,** built in 1654. In season the miller demonstrates and talks about the mill's operation and also sells its ground corn. ✉ *Water and Grove Sts.,* ☎ *508/888–4910.* 🖾 *$2; combination ticket with Hoxie House, $3.* ☉ *Late May, Labor Day–late Sept., Sat. 10–4:45; June–Labor Day, Mon.–Sat. 10–4:45.*

NEED A BREAK?

The delightful **Dunbar Tea Shop** (✉ 1 Water St. [Rte. 130], ☎ 508/833–2485) occupies a former billiards room–carriage house, now converted into a country cottage with paneled walls and assorted antiques and kitschy doodads. Lunch—from a smoked-fish platter with salad to quiche or a salmon tart—English cream tea, and tasty sweets are served

from 11 to 5 daily, July through October ('til 4:30 the rest of the year).
A gift shop sells British tea, specialty foods, and home decorating items.

The **Thornton W. Burgess Museum** is dedicated to the Sandwich native whose tales of Peter Cottontail, Reddy Fox, and a host of other creatures of the Old Briar Patch have been part of children's bedtimes for decades. Thornton Burgess (1874–1965), an avid conservationist, made his characters behave true to their species to educate children as he entertained them. Storytelling sessions, often featuring the live animal that the Burgess story is about, take place regularly in July and August. The many displays crowded into the small old house include some of Burgess's 170 books (although children are welcome, the exhibits are of the don't-touch variety). The small gift shop carries puppets, Burgess books, and Pairpoint Crystal cup plates decorated with Burgess characters. ✉ *4 Water St. [Rte. 130],* ☎ *508/888–4668,* WEB *www.thorntonburgess.org.* ✉ *$2 suggested donation.* ☉ *Apr.–Oct., Mon.–Sat. 10–4, Sun. 1–4; 1st 2 wks in Dec., Sat. 10–4, Sun. 1–4.*

Overlooking Shawme Pond is the **Hoxie House,** a remarkable old saltbox virtually unaltered since it was built in 1675. Even though people lived in it until the 1950s, the house was never modernized with electricity or plumbing. Furnishings reflect daily life in the colonial period, with some pieces on loan from the Museum of Fine Arts in Boston. Highlights are diamond-shape lead-glass windows and a collection of antique textile machines. ✉ *18 Water St. [Rte. 130],* ☎ *508/888–1173.* ✉ *$2; combination ticket with Dexter Gristmill $3.* ☉ *Memorial Day–mid-June, Sat. 10–5, Sun. 1–5; mid-June–mid-Oct., Mon.–Sat. 10–5, Sun. 1–5.*

The **Old Town Cemetery** (✉ Grove St.), on the opposite side of Shawme Pond from Hoxie House, is a classic, undulating New England graveyard. You can stop in for a peaceful moment and trace the genealogy of old Sandwich.

★ ☪ ❷ **Heritage Plantation,** on 76 beautifully landscaped acres overlooking the upper end of Shawme Pond, includes gardens and a café as well as an impressive complex of museum buildings with specialty collections from cars to toys. In 1967 pharmaceuticals magnate Josiah K. Lilly III purchased the estate and turned it into a nonprofit museum. The Shaker Round Barn showcases classic and historic cars—including a 1930 yellow-and-green Duesenberg built for Gary Cooper, a 1919 Pierce-Arrow, and a 1911 Stanley Steamer—as well as art exhibitions. The military museum houses antique firearms, a collection of 2,000 hand-painted miniature soldiers, military uniforms, and Native American arts. The art museum has an extensive Currier & Ives collection, Americana (including a mechanical-bank collection), antique toys such as a 1920 Hubley Royal Circus, and a working 1912 Coney Island–style carousel.

Paths crisscross the grounds, which include gardens planted with daylily, hosta, heather, herb, and fruit trees. Rhododendron enthusiasts will recognize the name of onetime estate owner and hybridizer Charles O. Dexter; the rhododendrons are in full glory from mid-May through mid-June. Daylilies reach their peak from mid-July through early August. Families visiting with youngsters should ask at the ticket office for the Family Funpacks with children's activities, or the Clue tours, scavenger-hunt games for exploring the grounds. In summer concerts are held in the gardens, often on Saturday evening and Sunday afternoon. The center of the complex is about ¾ mi on foot from the in-town end of Shawme Pond. ✉ *Grove and Pine Sts.,* ☎ *508/888–*

3300, WEB *www.heritageplantation.org.* ✉ *$12.* ☉ *Mid-May–Oct., Sat.–Wed. 9–6, Thurs.–Fri. 9–8; Nov.–Apr., Tues.–Sun. 10–4.*

At the **Cape Cod Canal Visitor Center,** run by the Army Corps of Engineers and slated to be fully operational by mid-2002, exhibits and video presentations describe the canal's history, area wildflowers, and local "critters." Among the special ranger-led programs are beach and dune walks, as well as evening star watches. The visitor center is opposite the Coast Guard Station, near Joe's Fish Market. ✉ *Ed Moffitt Dr.,* ☎ *508/759–4431.* ✉ *Free.* ☉ *Call for seasonal hours.*

For a view of the bay, you can walk to Town Neck Beach on the **Sandwich Boardwalk,** built over a salt marsh, creek, and low dunes. In 1991 Hurricane Bob and an October nor'easter destroyed the previous boardwalk. Individuals and businesses donated planks to rebuild it, which volunteers then installed. The donors' names; jokes (GET OFF OUR BOARD); thoughts (SIMPLIFY/THOREAU); and memorials to lovers, grandparents, and boats are inscribed on the planks. The long sweep of Cape Cod Bay stretches out around the beach at the end of the walk, where a platform provides fine views, especially at sunset. Stone jetties, dunes and waving grasses, and the entrance to the canal are in the foreground, and you can look out toward Sandy Neck, Wellfleet, and Provincetown or toward the white cliffs beyond Sagamore. The sandy strip on this mostly rocky beach is near the rugosa rose–patch dunes; the flowers have a delicious fragrance, and it's a good place for birding. The creeks running through the salt marsh make for great canoeing. From the town center it's about a mile to the boardwalk; cross Route 6A on Jarves Street and at its end turn left, then right, and continue to the boardwalk parking lot.

Ⓒ At the **Sandwich Fish Hatchery** you'll see more than 200,000 brook, brown, and rainbow trout at various stages of development; they are raised to stock the state's ponds. The mesh over the raceways keeps kingfishers and herons from a free lunch. You can buy feed for 25¢ and watch the fish jump for it. ✉ *164 Rte. 6A,* ☎ *508/888–0008.* ✉ *Free.* ☉ *Daily 9–3.*

OFF THE
BEATEN PATH

GREEN BRIAR NATURE CENTER AND JAM KITCHEN – Is it the soothing pond-side setting or its simple earthiness—who's to say? Whatever the reason, Green Briar Nature Center and Jam Kitchen, owned and operated by the Thornton Burgess Society, is a solid symbol of the old Cape. You'll pass a wildflower garden on your way in, and the Smiling Pool sparkles out back. Birds flit about the grounds, and great smells waft from vintage stoves in the Jam Kitchen, where you can watch as jams and pickles are made according to Ida Putnam's recipes, used here since 1903 (sun-cooked fruit preserves are especially superb). Come weekdays mid-April through mid-December to see jam being made in the Jam Kitchen; you can even take a jam-making class some evenings or Saturdays. The nature center has classes for adults and children, as well as walks, lectures, and a May herb festival, where herbs, wildflowers, and perennials are for sale. The Briar Patch Conservation Area behind the building has nature trails—take a walk and visit the real live animals that inspired Peter Cottontail, Grandfather Frog, and other beloved Thornton Burgess characters. ✉ *6 Discovery Hill Rd., off Rte. 6A east of Sandwich Center,* ☎ *508/888–6870,* WEB *www.thorntonburgess. org.* ✉ *$1 suggested donation.* ☉ *Apr.–Dec., Mon.–Sat. 10–4, Sun. 1–4; Jan.–Mar., Tues.–Sat. 10–4.*

Dining and Lodging

$–$$$ ✕ **Aqua Grille.** At this smart-casual bistro by the marina, offerings range from Cape basics (clam chowder, fried seafood, boiled lobsters) to more creative contemporary fare. The excellent lobster salad, for example, is a hearty serving of greens, tomatoes, avocados, baby green beans, and big meaty lobster chunks. The far-ranging menu and lively atmosphere make this a good spot to bring a crowd; sandwiches (salmon burgers, turkey wraps), grilled seafood, pastas, and steaks are all available. ⊠ *14 Gallo Rd.,* ☎ *508/888–8889. AE, MC, V. Closed mid-Oct.–Mar.*

$–$$ ✕ **Bee-Hive Tavern.** This informal and friendly colonial-style tavern hasn't been here since Revolutionary times (it opened in 1992), but the cozy dark-wood booths and wide-board floors look the part. The food is solid American fare such as burgers and sandwiches, fried seafood, Yankee pot roast, ribs, and steaks. A good selection of dinner-size salads has plenty of veggies, too. ⊠ *406 Rte. 6A, East Sandwich,* ☎ *508/ 833–1184. MC, V.*

$–$$ ✕ **Marshland Restaurant and Bakery.** Sandwich's version of down-home is this tiny coffee shop tucked onto a parking lot. For breakfast try an Italian omelet, a rich mix of Italian sausage, fresh vegetables, and cheese. The lunch specials—a grilled chicken club sandwich, lobster salad, a turkey Reuben, a daily quiche, and the like—are the best choices midday, and for dinner the prime rib does not quit. ⊠ *109 Rte. 6A,* ☎ *508/888–9824. No credit cards. No dinner Mon.*

$–$$ ✕ **Seafood Sam's.** Fried seafood is the name of the game at Sam's, across from the Coast Guard station, in the shadow of the canal power plant and a stone's throw from the Cape Cod Canal. You order from the counter, get a number, and sit in an airy dining room where the munch of fried clams accompanies the sound of lobsters cracking open. This very casual spot has a sign near the entrance to remind you that shirt and shoes are required. Sam's has gotten around, with branches in Harwich, Falmouth, and South Yarmouth. ⊠ *6 Coast Guard Rd.,* ☎ *508/ 888–4629. D, MC, V. Closed early Nov.–early Mar.*

$$$–$$$$ ✕🛏 **Dan'l Webster Inn.** Built in 1971 on the site of a 17th-century inn, the Dan'l Webster is essentially a contemporary hotel with old New England friendliness. The more formal restaurant's interesting menu is up-to-date, with contemporary dishes, such as Tuscan shrimp with white beans or horseradish-crusted salmon served over cucumber and jicama salad, taking their places beside veal Oscar, broiled scrod, and other classics. A casual tavern serves pizzas, burgers, and salads. You can include breakfast and dinner in the rate if you wish. Guest rooms, in the main inn and wings or in two nearby historic houses with four suites each, have floral fabrics and fine reproduction mahogany and cherry furnishings, including some canopy beds. The eight rooms on the second floor of the Jarves Wing are particularly spacious and have fireplaces and whirlpool tubs, as do some suites. Guests have access to nearby golf courses and a health club. ⊠ *149 Main St., 02563,* ☎ *508/888–3622 or 800/ 444–3566,* 𝖥𝖠𝖷 *508/888–5156,* 𝖶𝖤𝖡 *www.danlwebsterinn.com. 45 rooms, 9 suites. 2 restaurants, air-conditioning, no-smoking rooms, room service, pool. AE, D, DC, MC, V.*

$$–$$$ ✕🛏 **Belfry Inne & Bistro.** A 1902 former church and the adjacent "painted-lady" Victorian rectory house this one-of-a-kind inn. The six spacious rooms in the Abbey retain many original features of the church—an arch here, a massive stained-glass window there—along with a stylish mix of antique and more modern furnishings; the rooms have sitting areas, whirlpool tubs, and gas fireplaces, too. In the Drew House next door, the nine rooms are decorated with iron, spool, or sleigh beds and a whimsical blend of Laura Ashley prints and pastel-painted furnishings for a look that's fresh but traditional. The bistro, a dramatic space in the former sanctuary, serves contemporary fare:

pistachio-crusted salmon, filet mignon with marscapone mashed potatoes, or duck breast with wild mushroom risotto. ⊠ *8 Jarves St., 02563,* ☎ *508/888–8550 or 800/844–4542,* FAX *508/888–3922,* WEB *www.belfryinn.com. 14 rooms. Restaurant, bar. AE, D, DC, MC, V. No dinner Sun., Mon. No lunch. BP.*

$$$$ 🏠 **Bay Beach.** Waterfront accommodations are few in this part of the Cape, but you can wake to broad vistas of the bay at this B&B in a contemporary bayside house. Guest rooms are appointed like a well-turned-out suburban home, with lots of wicker, floral comforters, CD players, refrigerators, and, best of all, picture windows facing the water or the adjacent marshes. All have whirlpool tubs, gas fireplaces, and decks. Breakfast is a buffet in the casual dining room, with floor-to-ceiling windows for still more bay views; a boardwalk leads to a private beach. ⊠ *3 Bay Beach La., 02563,* ☎ *508/888–8813 or 800/ 475–6398,* FAX *508/888–5416,* WEB *www.baybeach.com. 3 rooms. Air-conditioning, beach. MC, V. Closed Nov.–Apr. BP.*

$$$ 🏠 **Wingscorton Farm.** This is, perhaps, the Upper Cape's best-kept se-
★ cret: an enchanting working farm with chickens, sheep, goats, horses, and other animals. Built in 1763, the main house, once a stop on the Underground Railroad, has a dining room with a fireplace with a 9-ft-long hearth. Oriental rugs, wing chairs, and a TV fill the paneled library-den. The main house has two second-floor suites, each with a fireplace, wide-plank floor, wainscoting, and, adjoining the main guest room, a smaller bedroom with twin beds. The property also includes a detached cottage, which rents by the week in season. A stone carriage house has a fully equipped kitchen, a living room with a pullout queen-size sofa, and a wood-burning stove; a spiral staircase leads to a loft with a bed and an oversize sundeck. A private bay beach is a five-minute walk. ⊠ *11 Wing Blvd., off Rte. 6A, about 4½ mi east of Sandwich Center, East Sandwich 02537,* ☎ *508/888–0534,* FAX *508/ 888–0545. 2 suites, 1 carriage house, 1 2-bedroom cottage. Beach, library. AE, MC, V. BP.*

$$–$$$ 🏠 **Sandwich Lodge & Resort.** A glorified motel—emphasis on glorified—on 10 rolling acres has a variety of rooms, all nicely decorated in soft mauve and navy. Suites (the deluxe are the newest), like efficiencies, are equipped with gleaming kitchens with refrigerators and two-burner stoves or microwave ovens; two even have two-person whirlpool tubs. The on-site restaurant serves lunch and dinner (ample portions, great prices) in a homey atmosphere. With advance notice, pets are allowed for a $15 fee. ⊠ *54 Rte. 6A, Box 1038, 02563,* ☎ *508/888–2275 or 800/ 282–5353,* FAX *508/888–8102,* WEB *www.sandwichlodge.com. 24 rooms, 36 suites, 4 efficiencies. Restaurant, bar, no-smoking rooms, indoor pool, outdoor pool, hot tub, Ping-Pong, shuffleboard, volleyball, laundry facilities. AE, D, MC, V. CP.*

$$ 🏠 **Captain Ezra Nye House.** Elaine and Harry Dickson's 1829 house in the heart of town once belonged to one of the old local families. The cozy, country-style rooms aren't crammed with period pieces, but the house brims with the Dicksons' hospitality—they cook a full breakfast and readily offer suggestions for day- or nighttime activities. ⊠ *152 Main St., 02563,* ☎ *508/888–6142 or 800/388–2278,* FAX *508/833–2897,* WEB *www.captainezranyehouse.com. 5 rooms, 1 suite. No smoking. Air-conditioning. AE, D, MC, V. BP.*

$$ 🏠 **Inn at Sandwich Center.** This 18th-century house (with 19th-century renovations) across from the Sandwich Glass Museum is listed on the National Register of Historic Places. The names of the Victorian-style rooms refer to a former owner or occupant of the house, although one, Miss Charlotte's Room, also takes its name from the house cat; a cat-pattern comforter tops the bed. The pretty Lottie Chipman Room has an antique four-poster bed and a rocker, while the spacious Robert

Morse Room has a nautical theme, as well as a private deck overlooking the gardens. Breakfast is served in the antiques-furnished keeping room, which has a fireplace and the original 1750 beehive oven. ⊠ *118 Tupper Rd., 02563,* ☏ *508/888–6958 or 800/249–6949,* FAX *508/ 888–2746,* WEB *www.innatsandwich.com. 5 rooms. Air-conditioning. No smoking. AE, MC, V. CP.*

$–$$ 🖭 **Earl of Sandwich Motor Manor.** Single-story Tudor-style buildings form a U around a duck pond and wooded lawn set with lawn chairs. Rooms in the main building (1966) and the newer buildings (1981–83) have rather somber decor, with dark exposed beams on white ceilings, dark paneled walls, quarry-tile floors with Oriental throw rugs, and chenille bedspreads, but they are of good size and have large windows. Pets are permitted with advance notice. ⊠ *378 Rte. 6A, East Sandwich 02537,* ☏ *508/888–1415 or 800/442–3275,* FAX *508/833–1039,* WEB *www.earlofsandwich.com. 24 rooms. Air-conditioning, no-smoking rooms, refrigerators, pool. AE, D, DC, MC, V. CP.*

$–$$ 🖭 **Spring Garden Inn Motel.** From the road the Spring Garden looks like yet another roadside motel, albeit a nice, well-maintained gray-shingle one. Out back, you'll step into another world—a wide green lawn overlooking a broad, peaceful expanse of marsh. Sink into a hammock, an Adirondack chair, or a swing, and relax. Grills and picnic tables are available for barbecues. Inside, the simple knotty-pine-wall rooms have two double beds topped with floral comforters. For the best marsh views, choose one of the second-floor rooms with a balcony. ⊠ *578 Rte. 6A, East Sandwich 02537,* ☏ *508/888–0710 or 800/ 303–1751,* FAX *508/833–2849,* WEB *www.springgarden.com. 8 rooms, 2 efficiencies, 1 suite. Picnic area, air-conditioning, refrigerators, pool. AE, D, MC, V. Closed Dec.–mid-Apr. CP.*

$ ⚠ **Shawme-Crowell State Forest.** Less than a mile from the Cape Cod Canal, this 742-acre state forest is a good base for local biking and hiking, and campers get free day use of Scusset Beach. Open-air campfires are allowed at the wooded tent and RV (no hookups) campsites. Heated bathroom and shower facilities are a blessing on chilly mornings. In 2001–02, the campground closed for the winter season, and at this writing had not confirmed their calendar for 2002–03; call for information. ⊠ *Rte. 130, 02563,* ☏ *508/888–0351; 877/422–6762 for reservations,* WEB *www.reserveamerica.com. 285 sites. MC, V. Closed Oct.–Mar.*

Nightlife and the Arts

THE ARTS

Heritage Plantation (⊠ Grove and Pine Sts., ☏ 508/888–3300) sponsors summer jazz and other concerts in its gardens from June to mid-September; bring chairs or blankets. Most concerts are free with admission to the complex.

Town-band concerts (⊠ Bandstand, Henry T. Wing Elementary School, Rte. 130 and Beale Ave., ☏ 508/888–5144) are held Thursday evening from July through late August starting at 7:30.

NIGHTLIFE

Bobby Byrne's Pub (⊠ 65 Rte. 6A, ☏ 508/888–6088), with other locations in Hyannis and Mashpee, has a comfortable pub atmosphere, a jukebox, and good light and full menus.

Outdoor Activities and Sports

BEACHES

Town Neck Beach, off Town Neck Road, is a long dune-backed bay beach with a mix of sand and pebbles. You'll need a resident parking sticker to leave your car in the large parking area between 8 AM and 4 PM in season. There are rest rooms and a snack bar.

East Sandwich Beach, on North Shore Road, lies behind the grass-covered dunes beyond a row of gray-shingle beach cottages. It's a long stretch of sand, but nearby parking is very limited (and restricted to residents between 8 AM and 4 PM in season). From Route 6A follow Ploughed Neck Road to North Shore Road.

Shopping

The sign in front of the **Bee-Hive General Store** (✉ 385 Rte. 6A, East Sandwich, ☎ 508/833–4907) boasts WICKED NEAT STUFF. Inside, the hodgepodge of clever and kitsch—candles, door knockers, lawn ornaments, jam, 5¢ candy, fish platters, toys—makes this an entertaining place to forage for gifts or souvenirs.

Brown Jug (✉ 155 Main St., at Jarves St., ☎ 508/833–1088) specializes in antique glass, such as Sandwich glass and Tiffany iridescent glassware, as well as Staffordshire china.

The **Giving Tree** (✉ 550 Rte. 6A, East Sandwich, ☎ 508/888–5446 or 888/246–3551), an art gallery and sculpture garden, shows contemporary crafts, jewelry, ceramics, and prints. It has walking paths through a peaceful bamboo grove, along the marsh, and over a narrow wooden suspension bridge.

Horsefeathers (✉ 454 Rte. 6A, East Sandwich, ☎ 508/888–5298) displays antique linens, lace, vintage baby and children's clothing, and Victoriana such as valentines.

Joe's Fish Market (✉ Cape Cod Canal, ☎ 508/888–2971), opposite Seafood Sam's and the Coast Guard station, sells fresh-from-the-tank lobsters. Call ahead, and they'll boil your crustaceans to order—a great idea for an easy dinner at your cottage or hotel or for a picnic overlooking the canal. Joe's also sells many varieties of fresh fish.

Sandwich Auction House (✉ 15 Tupper Rd., ☎ 508/888–1926), which auctions antiques, general merchandise, and Oriental rugs, is a great place to spend part of a Wednesday night (Saturday in the off-season); come after 2 to preview the items for sale. This local institution has weekly sales; in addition, specialty sales every four to six weeks present the cream of the crop of antiques received in that period. Specialty sales are also held for collections of modern rugs, silver, or toys.

Titcomb's Bookshop (✉ 432 Rte. 6A, East Sandwich, ☎ 508/888–2331) stocks used, rare, and new books, including a large collection of Cape and nautical titles and Americana, as well as an extensive selection of new children's books.

En Route **Route 6A** heads east from Sandwich, passing through the oldest settlements on the Cape. Part of the Old King's Highway historic district, the route is protected from development. Classic inns and enticing antiques shops alternate with traditional gray-shingle homes on this tree-lined road, and the woods periodically give way to broad vistas across the marshes. In autumn the foliage along the way is bright; maples with their feet wet in ponds and marshes put on a good display. Along Route 6A just east of Sandwich center, you can stop to watch cranberries being harvested in flooded bogs. If you're heading to Orleans and you're not in a hurry, this is a lovely route to take.

Bourne

❸ *6 mi southwest of Sandwich.*

The town of Bourne includes nine villages—Bourne Village, Bournedale, Buzzards Bay, Cataumet, Gray Gables, Monument Beach, Pocasset, Sagamore, and Sagamore Beach—along Buzzards Bay and both sides of the Cape Cod Canal. The villages range from honky-tonk commercial districts to bucolic waterfront suburbs. With a mix of year-round and summer residents, the area includes places for learning about the region's marine life and early commercial history, as well as several attractive recreation areas, established and maintained by the Army Corps of Engineers, for biking, hiking, and fishing along the canal.

The Pilgrims established their first Cape Cod settlement in Bourne in 1627, but back then it was still part of Sandwich; Bourne didn't become a separate town until 1884. By that time it had grown into a popular summer colony whose part-time residents included President Grover Cleveland and *Boston Globe* publisher Charles Taylor.

Present-day Bourne's maritime orientation was created by the Cape Cod Canal, which opened in 1914. The 17½-mi canal cut the distance for shipping traffic between Boston and New York by 75 mi and eliminated the often-treacherous journey around the Cape. The Army Corps of Engineers took over the canal's operation in the late 1920s and embarked on a project to widen it; the current Bourne and Sagamore bridges were built in the 1930s as part of this project.

The **National Marine Life Center,** on the mainland near the Chamber of Commerce office, has a small exhibit area devoted to whales, dolphins, seals, and other marine life. In summer there are weekly story hours for preschoolers, marine-life educational programs for older children, and evening lectures about the ocean environment for adults. The center hopes to break ground on an expanded facility for rehabilitating stranded marine animals that will include a marine animal hospital and nursery, rehabilitation pools, and additional exhibit space. ⊠ *120 Main St., Buzzards Bay,* ☎ *508/759–8722,* WEB *www.nmlc.org.* 🎫 *Free.* ☉ *Memorial Day–Labor Day, Mon.–Sat. 10–6, Sun. noon–6.*

On the mainland side, the **Massachusetts Maritime Academy,** founded in 1891, is the oldest such academy in the country. Future members of the Merchant Marines receive their training at its 55-acre campus in Buzzards Bay. The library has nautical paintings and scale models of ships from the 18th century to the present and is open to the public at no charge (hours are extensive but vary widely depending on whether school is in session; call ahead). For a 30- to 60-minute tour of the academy (weekdays only; times vary), call 48 hours in advance. The tours are designed for prospective students and their families but are open to all. ⊠ *Taylor's Point, Buzzards Bay,* ☎ *508/830–5000, Ext. 1201 for library; Ext. 1102 for tours,* WEB *www.mma.mass.edu.*

A monument to the birth of commerce in the New World, the **Aptucxet Trading Post Museum** was erected on the foundation of the original post archaeologically excavated in the 1920s. Here, in 1627, Plimoth Plantation leaders established a way station between the Native American encampment at Great Herring Pond, 3 mi to the northeast; Dutch colonists in New Amsterdam (New York), to the south; and English colonists on Cape Cod Bay. Before the canal was built, the Manomet River connected Herring Pond with Buzzards Bay (no, scavengers don't frequent it—it was misnamed for the migrating osprey that do), and a short portage connected the pond to Scusset River, which met Cape Cod Bay. The Native Americans traded furs; the Dutch traded linen cloth, metal tools, glass beads, sugar, and other staples; and the Pilgrims traded wool cloth, clay beads, sassafras, and tobacco (which they imported from Virginia). Wampum was the medium of exchange.

Inside the post, 17th-century cooking utensils hang from the original brick hearth; beaver and otter skins, furniture, and other artifacts such as arrowheads, tools, and tomahawks are displayed. Also on the grounds are a gift shop in a Dutch-style windmill, a saltworks (closed for renovation until sometime in 2002), herb and wildflower gardens, a picnic area overlooking the canal, and a small Victorian railroad station built for the sole use of President Grover Cleveland, who had a summer home in Bourne. To get here, cross the Bourne Bridge, then take the first right from the Bourne Bridge rotary onto Trowbridge Road and follow the signs. Note that the site is also open on holiday Mondays in season. ⊠ *24 Aptucxet Rd.,* ☎ *508/759–9487,* WEB *www.bournehistoricalsoc.org.* ⌨ *$3.50.* ☉ *May–June and Sept.–Columbus Day, Tues.–Sat. 10–5, Sun. 2–5; July–Aug., Mon.–Sat. 10–5, Sun. 2–5.*

☺ A break for energetic children pent up in a car for too many miles, **Adventure Isle** has minibikes, a giant slide, a Ferris wheel, children's rides, an arcade, bumper boats, batting cages, a double gyroscope (for those with strong stomachs), a miniature golf course, and laser tag. Check the web site for discount coupons. ⊠ *Rte. 28, 2 mi south of Bourne Bridge,* ☎ *508/759–2636 or 800/535–2787,* WEB *www.adventureisle. com.* ⌨ *$1.75–$4 per ride or $11.95 per day for unlimited rides.* ☉ *Mid-Apr.–May and Sept.–Oct., Fri.–Sun. 10 AM–8 PM; June–Aug., daily 10 AM–11 PM.*

Dining and Lodging

$$–$$$ ✕ **Chart Room.** Tucked away in the marina, in a former cargo barge, this traditional bay-side spot has been serving up seafood classics and fine harbor views since 1966. Clam chowder, broiled scrod, seafood Newburg, baked stuffed shrimp: they're all here, as are sirloin steak, broiled lamb chops, and even grilled cheese-and-tomato sandwiches. At lunch you can try the Chart Room's version of surf and turf—a stuffed quahog and a hot dog—but most people opt for the fresh (and overflowing) lobster salad sandwich. ⊠ *1 Shore Rd., at Kingman Marine, Cataumet,* ☎ *508/563–5350. AE, DC, MC, V. Closed Columbus Day– Memorial Day; weekdays Memorial Day–late June and Labor Day– Columbus Day.*

$–$$ ✕ **Stir Crazy.** One of a small but growing number of authentic Asian restaurants on the Cape—owner Bopha Samms hails from Cambodia— fits the bill when you reach your inevitable limit of seafood and Yankee cooking. Overlook the anonymous location (beside self-storage lockers, in a building that also houses a real estate office), because the real spice is where it belongs: in the food. Dishes blur the ethnic line with lively Cambodian, Thai, and Vietnamese influences. Look for *nhem shross* (an appetizer of vegetables and shrimp) and the refreshing *bar bong* (chilled noodles topped with pork, egg rolls, and coconut-peanut sauce). ⊠ *626 MacArthur Blvd. (Rte. 28 S), Pocasset,* ☎ *508/564–6464. Reservations not accepted. MC, V. No smoking. Closed Mon. No lunch Sat.–Thurs.*

$$ ⊡ **Wood Duck Inn.** Behind this cozy B&B in an 1848 house under the trees, a working cranberry bog and acres of conservation land spread out as far as you can see. The small but comfy Cottage Room has lace curtains and a brass bed with a floral comforter, while both suites have a bedroom plus a sitting room that doubles as extra sleeping space. The Garden Suite is done in romantic florals, and the Treetops Suite, up a spiral stair, resembles a contemporary apartment in forest green and white; it has a tiny but fully equipped kitchen and sweeping views of the land beyond. There's no common space for guests, but the innkeepers deliver breakfast to your door. ⊠ *1050 County Rd., Cataumet 02534,* ☎ FAX *508/564–6404,* WEB *www.woodduckinnbb.com. 1 room, 2 suites. Refrigerators. No smoking. No credit cards. CP.*

Nightlife and the Arts

The **Army Corps of Engineers** (☎ 508/759–4431), which maintains the Cape Cod Canal via a field office in Buzzards Bay, offers free daily programs in summer, including evening campfire programs on Canal-related topics (with marshmallow roasting). Call for program details and locations.

In Bourne, Thursday evening **town-band concerts** in July and August start at 7 in Buzzards Bay Park (✉ Main St., ☎ 508/759–6000).

Outdoor Activities and Sports

The **Army Corps of Engineers** (☎ 508/759–4431) sponsors guided walks, bike trips, and hikes, including canal and area natural history walks.

BASEBALL

The **Bourne Braves** of the collegiate Cape Cod Baseball League play home games at Coady School (✉ Trowbridge Rd., Bourne, ☎ 508/432–6909) from mid-June to mid-August.

BEACHES

Monument Beach off Shore Rd., a small but pretty crescent of sand adjacent to the town harbor, faces Buzzards Bay just south of Bourne Bridge. The beach has a snack bar, rest rooms, and a parking lot, restricted in season to those with resident permits. From Shore Road, turn right onto Emmons Road just past the old train depot.

BIKING

An easy, straight trail stretches on either side of the **Cape Cod Canal,** 6½ mi on the south side, 7 mi on the north, with views of the bridges and ship traffic on the canal. Contact the Army Corps of Engineers **Herring Run Visitor Center** (☎ 508/759–4431) for information about Canal trail access and parking. Directly across the street from the canal bike path on the mainland (near the Massachusetts Maritime Academy), **P & M Cycles** (✉ 29 Main St., Buzzards Bay, ☎ 508/759–2830) rents a large selection of mountain and hybrid bikes at reasonable rates.

FISHING

The Cape Cod Canal is a good place to fish—from the service road on either side—for blues, flounder, herring, mackerel, and striped bass seasonally making their way through the passage (April–November).

HIKING AND WALKING

Run by the Army Corps of Engineers, the **Herring Run Visitor Center** (✉ U.S. 6, Bournedale, ☎ 508/759–4431; 508/759–5991 for tides and weather and special events), on a bank of the canal with an excellent view, has picnic tables (close to noisy U.S. 6), access to the canal bike path, a herring run through which the fish travel on their spawning run in May, and short self-guided walking trails through woodland. The visitor center is on the mainland side of the canal, between the bridges.

On the Cape side of the canal, the Army Corps of Engineers manages the **Tidal Flats Recreation Area** (✉ Shore Rd., ☎ 508/759–4431), a small but peaceful canal-side park near the Cape railroad bridge. It's a pleasant site for picnicking or fishing, with a great view of the canal's ship traffic. There's access to the canal bike path, too, although reconstruction of the railroad bridge will limit access here through 2002. In the late afternoon, around 5 and again around 7, you can watch the bridge lower to allow a train to cross the canal; these times are approximate and can vary widely due to traffic and bridge work. To reach the recreation area, cross the Bourne Bridge and follow Trowbridge Road to Shore Road.

ICE-SKATING

John Gallo Ice Arena (⊠ 231 Sandwich Rd., ☎ 508/759–8904) is the place to go for ice-skating year-round (except May). Hours vary widely, and at this writing, the arena was planning a renovation that could affect its operation in 2002; call for details.

SCUBA DIVING

Rentals, instruction, group dives, and information are available through **Aquarius Diving Center** (⊠ 3239 Cranberry Hwy., Buzzards Bay, ☎ 508/759–3483), across the Bourne Bridge on the mainland.

Shopping

Tanger Outlet Center (⊠ U.S. 6 at Buzzards Bay rotary, Bourne, ☎ 800/406–8435) sells discounted women's, men's, and children's apparel at shops such as Izod, Nine West, Levi's, and Liz Claiborne.

North and West Falmouth

9 mi south of Bourne.

Wooded country lanes that lead to secluded coves, small harbors dotted with sailboats, and farm stands selling sweet corn and fresh berries—the villages along Route 28 between Bourne and Falmouth proper offer up a glimpse of the old Cape Cod. Native American names serve as reminders of the true first settlers here, and houses that date from the 18th century (as well as more modern summer retreats) line the roads.

Although Route 28 from the Bourne Bridge south to Falmouth is overly commercial in many areas, Route 28A between Pocasset and West Falmouth is more scenic, with side roads leading to attractive beaches, particularly Old Silver Beach, and small harbors. If you've brought your bicycle, the less-traveled lanes here make for good biking; many of the beaches along the bay restrict parking to residents, but bicyclists and walkers are free to explore.

NEED A BREAK? | **Peach Tree Circle Farm** (⊠ 881 Old Palmer Ave., West Falmouth, ☎ 508/548–4006) includes a bakery, a farm stand, and a cheery tearoom. Inexpensive lunches of soups, sandwiches, salads, and a few entrées such as quiche and chicken potpie are served year-round amid the smells of baking bread and herbs hung to dry.

Dining and Lodging

$–$$$ ✕ **Chapoquoit Grill.** Comfortable and always bustling, this unassuming local favorite has an Italian bent, starting with the creative pizzas and pastas. The long list of daily specials might include grilled salmon over greens with a lemon-basil vinaigrette or sirloin with a tamarind-mango glaze. A fireplace and coral-color walls make the front room intimate, while the larger rear dining room seems vaguely tropical (with a palm tree in the middle). Expect daunting waits for a table on summer weekends; come early or late. ⊠ 410 W. Falmouth Hwy. (Rte. 28A), West Falmouth, ☎ 508/540–7794. *Reservations not accepted. MC, V. No lunch.*

$$$$ ▦ **Inn at West Falmouth.** This luxurious 1898 estate-house inn is in a secluded area of an exclusive village. A mixture of contemporary and antique furnishings and polished hardwood floors sets an elegant but relaxed mood. Guest rooms have king- or queen-size beds (some with canopies), Italian marble bathrooms with whirlpool tubs, phones, hair dryers, and wall safes; some have fireplaces and private decks. Beyond the French doors, off the pale pink-and-green breakfast room, a patio

spilling over with potted plants and trees overlooks woods, gardens, and a tennis court and leads to the small pool and deck. ⊠ *Frazer Rd. off Blacksmith Shop Rd., Box 1208, West Falmouth 02574,* ☎ *508/540–7696,* FAX *508/540–9977,* WEB *www.innatwestfalmouth.com. 8 rooms. Pool, tennis court. No smoking. MC, V. CP.*

$$$–$$$$ 🏨 **Sea Crest Resort.** Location and amenities are strong draws at this modern conference center and resort, whose eight buildings sprawl along one end of beautiful Old Silver Beach. Rooms are crisp and clean, done in dark blues and pastels. Many rooms have ocean views, and some have gas-log fireplaces. A number of lodging packages are available. ⊠ *350 Quaker Rd., North Falmouth 02556,* ☎ *508/540–9400 or 800/225–3110,* FAX *508/548–0556,* WEB *www.seacrest-resort.com. 258 rooms, 8 suites. Restaurant, deli, piano bar, room service, indoor pool, outdoor pool, hot tub, sauna, putting green, 2 tennis courts, health club, shuffleboard, video games, children's programs (ages 3–12). AE, D, DC, MC, V.*

$$ 🏨 **Ideal Spot Motel.** Neat-as-a-pin, quiet, and a bit old-fashioned, this gray-shingle motel has simple, family-friendly rooms that are all good-size. Efficiencies have a queen-size bed or two doubles, plus a kitchen and a sitting area with a sofa bed; the large motel rooms have refrigerators. There's no pool, but it's only a mile to Chapoquoit Beach. ⊠ *Rte. 28A at Old Dock Rd., Box 465, West Falmouth 02574,* ☎ *508/548–2257 or 800/269–6910. 12 efficiencies, 2 rooms. Air-conditioning. D, MC, V. Closed Nov.–Mar.*

$–$$ 🏨 **Sjöholm Inn.** This rambling 1863 farmhouse on a country lane is comfortable and homey, like staying with a favorite aunt and uncle. The rooms—some in the main inn, some in the adjacent cottage house—are not fancy, but they're a pleasant mix of 1940s colonial-style furniture, hand-me-downs, and the occasional antique. One of the loveliest rooms (though it lacks a private bath) is the airy window-lined Sleeping Porch. There's also a cozy sunporch and a large yard with an outdoor shower. A separate two-bedroom cottage rents by the week. Unlike many B&Bs, the Sjöholm (pronounced *shewr*-holm) welcomes families. ⊠ *17 Chase Rd., off Rte. 28A, West Falmouth 02574,* ☎ *508/540–5706 or 800/498–5706,* WEB *www.sjoholminn.com. 15 rooms, 7 with bath; 1 cottage. Breakfast room, croquet, bicycles. No smoking. MC, V. BP.*

Nightlife and the Arts

Sea Crest Resort (⊠ 350 Quaker Rd., North Falmouth, ☎ 508/540–9400) has a summer and holiday-weekend schedule of nightly entertainment on the outdoor terrace, including dancing to country, Top 40, reggae, and jazz bands and a big-band DJ, as well as karaoke and comedy.

Outdoor Activities and Sports

BEACHES

Chapoquoit Beach (⊠ Chapoquoit Rd., West Falmouth), a narrow stretch of white sand, lines a peninsula that juts dramatically into the bay. Resident parking stickers are required at the beach lot in season, but the surrounding roads are popular with bicyclists. The beach has lifeguards and portable toilets.

Megansett Beach (⊠ County Rd., North Falmouth), hidden in a residential neighborhood, is a small, family-friendly location. Weathered gray-shingle homes line the cove, while boats moored at the adjacent yacht club bob in the bay. The beach has lifeguards and a portable toilet, but no other services. Resident parking stickers are required at the beach lot in season.

Old Silver Beach (⊠ off Quaker Rd., North Falmouth) is a long, beautiful crescent of soft white sand, with the Sea Crest Resort at one end.

It is especially good for small children because a sandbar keeps it shallow at one end and creates tidal pools full of crabs and minnows. The beach has lifeguards, rest rooms, showers, and a snack bar. There's a $10 fee for parking in summer.

Wood Neck Beach (✉ Wood Neck Rd., West Falmouth), in the Sippewisset area, is a sandy bayside beach backed by grass-covered dunes. At high tide the beach is very narrow, but sandbars and shallow tide pools make this a good place for children when the tide is out. Resident parking stickers are required in season.

HORSEBACK RIDING

Haland Stables (✉ 878 Rte. 28A, West Falmouth, ☎ 508/540–2552) offers lessons and trail rides by reservation Monday through Saturday.

TENNIS

Ballymeade Country Club (✉ 125 Falmouth Woods Rd., off Rte. 151, North Falmouth, ☎ 508/457–7620) has six Har-Tru and four hard courts, a grass tennis court, lessons, clinics, ball machines, and a pro shop that accepts court-time reservations from mid-June through mid-October.

Shopping

Open Door Gallery (✉ 544 W. Falmouth Hwy. [Rte. 28A], at Chapoquoit Rd., West Falmouth, ☎ 508/540–8484), a lovely place to browse, specializes in high-quality crafts. You may find intricately carved wooden bowls, humorous prints, creative sculpture, nature photographs, and handmade jewelry, as well as garden art. A nice collection of cards and moderately priced gift items round out the selection.

Summerhouse Gallery (✉ 646 W. Falmouth Hwy. [Rte. 28A], West Falmouth, ☎ 508/548–3593) is a tiny cottage-turned-gallery showing photographs and other works by Cape and New England artists. There's a small snack bar, too.

Falmouth

❹ *2 mi south of West Falmouth, 15 mi south of Bourne Bridge, 4 mi north of Woods Hole.*

The Cape's second-largest town, Falmouth was settled in 1660 by Congregationalists from Barnstable who had been ostracized by their church and deprived of voting privileges and other civil rights for being sympathizers with the Quakers (then the victims of severe repression). The town was incorporated in 1686 and named for Falmouth, England. The Falmouth area, sprawling over 44 square mi, includes eight villages: Falmouth, North Falmouth, West Falmouth, Hatchville, Teaticket, East Falmouth, Waquoit, and Woods Hole.

Much of Falmouth today is suburban, with a mix of old and new developments and a large year-round population. Many residents commute to other towns on the Cape, to southeastern Massachusetts, and even to Boston. The town has a quaint village center, with a typically old New England village green and a shop-lined Main Street. South of town center, Falmouth faces Nantucket Sound and has several often-crowded beaches popular with families. To the east, the Falmouth Heights neighborhood mixes inns, B&Bs, and private homes, nestled close together on residential streets leading to the sea. Bustling Grand Avenue, the main drag in Falmouth Heights, hugs the shore and the beach. Parks and ponds dot the town; one of the nicest, Grews Pond in Goodwill Park, is north of the town center—it's a lovely site for a picnic on a summer afternoon.

Today attractive old homes, some built by sea captains, flank the **Village Green,** which was added to the National Register of Historic Places in 1996. It served as a militia training field in the 18th century and a grazing ground for horses in the early 19th. Also on the green is the 1856 **Congregational Church,** built on the timbers of its 1796 predecessor, with a bell made by Paul Revere. The bell's cheery inscription reads: THE LIVING TO THE CHURCH I CALL, AND TO THE GRAVE I SUMMON ALL.

The **Falmouth Historical Society** maintains two museums that represent life in colonial Cape Cod. The 1790 **Julia Wood House** retains wonderful architectural details—a widow's walk, wide-board floors, lead-glass windows, and a colonial kitchen with wide hearth. Antique embroideries, baby shoes and clothes, toys and dolls, portraits, furniture, and the trappings of an authentically equipped doctor's office, all from the house's onetime owner, fill the house. Out back, a re-creation of the Hallett Barn, which was original to the property and was rebuilt in 2001, displays antique farm implements, a 19th-century horse-drawn sleigh, and other interesting items. The smaller **Conant House** next door, a 1794 half-Cape (an asymmetrical 1½-story building), holds military memorabilia, whaling items, scrimshaw, sailors' valentines, and a genealogical and historical research library. One collection includes books, portraits, and other items relating to Katharine Lee Bates, the native daughter who wrote "America the Beautiful." Guides give tours of the museums, and a pretty formal garden with a gazebo and flagstone paths is adjacent. You can take a break with "Tea in Julia's Garden," with tea sandwiches, scones, and other light refreshments, on Thursdays from 2 to 4, mid-June through August. Free walking tours of the town are available Tuesday at 4 in July and August, as are historical trolley tours; call for prices and times. ⊠ *Village Green, off Palmer Ave.,* ☎ *508/548–4857,* ⓦⒺⒷ *www.falmouthhistoricalsociety.org.* ⊡ *Museums $4, tea $6.* ⊙ *June–Aug., Tues.–Sat. 10–4; Sept.–Nov., weekends 1–4.*

The 1812 white Cape house at 16 Main Street marks the **birthplace of Katharine Lee Bates.** Now owned by the Falmouth Historical Society, it is no longer open to the public, but a plaque out front commemorates Bates's birth, in 1859.

❺ The **Charles D. and Margaret K. Spohr Garden,** 3 planted acres on Oyster Pond, is a pretty, peaceful, privately owned place. The springtime explosion of more than 700,000 daffodils gives way in turn to the tulips, azaleas, magnolias, flowering crabapples, rhododendrons, lilies, and climbing hydrangeas that inspire garden goers in summer. A collection of old millstones, bronze church bells, and ships' anchors decorates the landscape. ⊠ *Fells Rd. off Oyster Pond Rd.* ⊡ *Free.* ⊙ *Daily sunrise–sunset.*

☾ A good place for children on a rainy day, the **Leary Family Amusement Center** (⊠ 23 Town Hall Sq., off Rte. 28, ☎ 508/540–4877) has video-game rooms and candlepin bowling.

Dining and Lodging

$$–$$$ ✕ **Quarterdeck Restaurant.** Part bar, part restaurant—but all Cape Cod—this spot is across the street from Falmouth's town hall, so the lunch talk tends to focus on local politics. The stained glass is not old and authentic, but the huge whaling harpoons certainly are. Low ceilings and rough-hewn beams seem a good match for the menu, which includes hearty sandwiches such as Reubens and grilled chorizo at lunch and specials at night. The swordfish kebab, skewered with mushrooms, onion, and green pepper and served over jasmine rice, is especially good. ⊠ *164 Main St. (Rte. 28),* ☎ *508/548–9900. AE, D, DC, MC, V.*

$–$$$ ✕ **TraBiCa.** Part trattoria, part bistro, and part café (thus the unusual name), this appealing restaurant in a snug gray-shingle house mixes Italian classics, such as spaghetti and meatballs, sausage sandwiches, and eggplant parmigiana, with a changing menu of more sophisticated Mediterranean fare. The selection is fairly innovative for this part of the Cape, and the broad menu should please everyone from tots to Great Aunt Tillie. You could even dress up a bit; you'll see more khakis and polo shirts or sundresses than shorts and T-shirts here. ⊠ *327 Gifford St.,* ☎ *508/548–9861. MC, V. Closed Mon. Nov.–Apr. No lunch.*

$–$$ ✕ **Betsy's Diner.** An authentic-looking American treasure, Betsy's is a shiny, happy, busy place with a reassuring pink neon sign urging you to EAT HEAVY. The generous dining room, gleaming counter, and stools and booths by the big windows are all done in pretty pastel mauve-and-cream tones. Memorabilia and neon grace the walls. A classic diner menu with pancakes, waffles, and omelets is served all day, and typical dinner options are meat loaf and mashed potatoes, knockwurst and sauerkraut, and charbroiled pork chops. ⊠ *457 Main St. (Rte. 28),* ☎ *508/540–4446. Reservations not accepted. MC, V.*

$–$$ ✕ **The Clam Shack.** Fried clams—what else?—top the menu at this basic seafood joint right on Falmouth Harbor. The clams are crisp and fresh tasting; the meaty lobster roll and the fish-and-chips platter are good choices, too. Place your order at the counter and then take your tray to the picnic tables on the roof deck for the best views. More tables are on the dock in back, or you can squeeze into the tiny dining room. Just don't plan on a late night here—the Shack closes most evenings around 7:30. ⊠ *227 Clinton Ave., Falmouth Harbor,* ☎ *508/540–7758. No credit cards. Closed Labor Day–Memorial Day.*

$–$$ ✕ **McMenamy's.** For more than 25 years fried seafood has been the reason to eat here. The clams, scallops, and fish are all fried up good and crispy; the onion rings will delight lovers of the pungent bulb. There's no view—the otherwise pleasant outdoor deck faces the parking lot—and the dining room is done in basic Formica, but there's plenty of seating, so you can bring the family. ⊠ *70 Davis Straits (Rte. 28),* ☎ *508/540–2115. AE, D, MC, V.*

$ ✕ **Maryellen's Portuguese Bakery.** It's easy to drive right past this friendly, no-frills breakfast-and-lunch spot, hidden behind a Dairy Queen. Take a seat at the counter or at one of the few tables; call, "Good morning" to Maryellen, who will likely be bustling about the room; then order up breakfast with a Portuguese twist. You can get spicy *linguica* sausage with your eggs, or French toast made with Portuguese bread. Try the savory Portuguese omelet, filled with linguica, parsley, onions, and cheese. The lunch menu starts with BLTs and burgers but quickly moves on to kale soup and *cacoilha* (marinated pork). You can also pick up some Portuguese sweet bread or *malasadas* (fried dough) to go. ⊠ *829 Main St., near Falmouth Heights Rd.,* ☎ *508/540–9696. No credit cards. No dinner.*

$$–$$$ ✕🖻 **Coonamessett Inn.** One of the best—and oldest (since 1953)—of
★ the Cape's many quaint inn-restaurants remains delightfully sunk in the past. The main dining room is lovely, and the Cape Cod Room looks out over a pond and garden. The menu is on the traditional side; the many seafood choices include swordfish with grilled vegetable slaw, steamed or baked and stuffed lobster, and baked cod with corn and crab salad. Five buildings of one- or two-bedroom suites range around a broad landscaped lawn that spills down to a scenic wooded pond; several suites directly overlook the pond. Rooms are casually decorated, with bleached wood or pine paneling and New England antiques or reproductions. A large collection of Cape artist Ralph Cahoon's work

appears throughout the inn. ✉ *311 Gifford St., at Jones Rd., 02540,* ☎ *508/548–2300,* FAX *508/540–9831,* WEB *www.capecodrestaurants.org/ coonamessett. 28 suites, 1 cottage. Restaurant, bar, no-smoking rooms. AE, D, MC, V. CP.*

$$$–$$$$ 🏨 **Holiday Inn.** This chain link is a dependable option for families. A tried-and-true comfort formula has been applied here: large rooms with contemporary pastel decor, suites with king-size beds, and a large pool area surrounded by patio furniture and greenery. The restaurant is open for breakfast and dinner year-round. The hotel is across from a pond ½ mi outside Falmouth center. ✉ *291 Jones Rd., 02540,* ☎ *508/540– 2000 or 800/465–4329,* FAX *508/548–2712,* WEB *www.sixcontinentshotels. com. 93 rooms, 5 suites. Restaurant, no-smoking rooms, room service, indoor pool, gym, video games. AE, D, DC, MC, V.*

$$$–$$$$ 🏨 **Inn on the Sound.** Although far from secluded, this inn, perched on a bluff overlooking Vineyard Sound and offering glimpses of the island itself, is blissfully quiet. The living room and nine of the guest rooms (all named for various Falmouth area landmarks) face the water. Guest rooms have queen-size beds and unfussy contemporary furnishings such as natural oak tables, unbleached cottons, and ceiling fans; four have private decks. Common areas include the art-laden living room, with its boulder fireplace, oversize windows, and modern white couches; a bistrolike breakfast room; and a large porch with even more stunning water views. ✉ *313 Grand Ave., Falmouth Heights 02540,* ☎ *508/457– 9666 or 800/564–9668,* FAX *508/457–9631,* WEB *www.innonthesound. com. 10 rooms. Beach. No smoking. AE, D, MC, V. CP.*

$$$–$$$$ 🏨 **La Maison Cappellari at Mostly Hall.** With its deep, landscaped yard ★ and wrought-iron fence, this elegant inn with a wraparound porch looks very much like a private estate. (The house got its name when a young visitor is said to have exclaimed, "Look! It's mostly hall!") Owners Bogdan and Christina Simcic have given the imposing 1849 Italianate house an upscale European style. Christina painted wall murals in several bedrooms; the Tuscan Room's walls suggest an intimate Tuscan garden. Three rooms are more traditionally decorated, with floral wallpaper, canopy beds, and antique pieces. Breakfast is served in the living room with its marble fireplace or outside on the veranda. Although the inn is only steps from the town center, you can lounge in the lush gardens and feel a world away. ✉ *27 Main St. (Rte. 28), 02540,* ☎ *508/548– 3786 or 800/682–0565,* FAX *508/548–5778,* WEB *www.mostlyhall.com. 6 rooms. Air-conditioning, bicycles, library. No smoking. AE, D, MC, V. Closed mid-Dec.–mid-Apr. BP.*

$$$ 🏨 **Admiralty Inn.** This large roadside motel outside Falmouth center has a wide range of rooms and suites, and its child-friendly facilities make it a good bet for families. Standard rooms have two queen-size beds or one queen-size and one Murphy bed. King Jacuzzi rooms have king-size beds and whirlpool tubs in the bedroom. Town-house suites have cathedral ceilings with skylights, two baths (one with whirlpool), a loft with a king-size bed, a living room with a sofa bed, and a queen- or king-size bed. Children under 12 stay free. ✉ *51 Teaticket Hwy. (Rte. 28), 02540,* ☎ *508/548–4240 or 800/341–5700,* FAX *508/457– 0535,* WEB *www.vacationinnproperties.com. 70 rooms, 28 suites. Restaurant, bar, 2 pools, hot tub. AE, D, DC, MC, V.*

$$$ 🏨 **The Beach House.** If your idea of a perfect beach house is a rainbow of sunny colors, hand-painted furniture, and a deck that looks out toward the ocean—all just a two-block walk from the beach—the Beach House will fulfill your expectations. The walls of each guest room in this crisp and contemporary gray-shingle house reflect a theme: in the small but cheery Sunflower Room, a garden of flowers dances across the wall, while in the Fish Room the bed (with a headboard inspired by the waves) is surrounded by, yes, fish. Breakfast is served either in the kitchen, with

its walls painted like a summer garden, or next to the backyard pool. ⊠ *10 Worcester Ct., Falmouth Heights 02540,* ☎ *508/457–0310 or 800/ 351–3426,* FAX *508/548–7895,* WEB *www.capecodbeachhouse.com. 7 rooms, 1 suite. Pool. No smoking. MC, V. Closed Nov.–mid-Apr. CP.*

$$$ ⊡ **Capt. Tom Lawrence House.** A lawn shaded by old maple trees surrounds this pretty white house with a cupola, which is steps from downtown yet set back from the street enough to feel secluded. Built in 1861 for a whaling captain, the intimate B&B has romantic rooms with antique and painted furniture, French country wallpaper, soft colors, thick carpeting, cable TV, and refrigerators. The beds, all queen size (several with canopies) or king size, have firm mattresses, Laura Ashley or Ralph Lauren linens, and down comforters in winter. An efficiency apartment is bright and spacious, with a fully equipped eat-in kitchen and a private entrance. The large common room, the setting for breakfast and afternoon snacks, has a fireplace. ⊠ *75 Locust St., 02540,* ☎ *508/540– 1445 or 800/266–8139,* FAX *508/457–1790,* WEB *www.captaintomlawrence. com. 6 rooms, 1 efficiency. Air-conditioning, bicycles. No smoking. AE, MC, V. BP.*

$$$
★ ⊡ **Wildflower Inn.** You'll find many instances of what innkeepers Phil and Donna Stone call their "old made new again" decorating style: tables are constructed from early 1900s pedal-sewing-machine bases, and the sideboard in the living room/breakfast area was once a '20s Hotpoint electric stove. Each of the inn's five rooms (two with whirlpool tubs) is also innovatively decorated. The bed in the romantic Moonflower Room, tucked under the eaves, is draped in netting and has a skylight, while the bright and cheerful Geranium Room has a white-iron bed topped with a geranium-print comforter. Donna whips up delicious concoctions using edible wildflowers. The wraparound porch serves as the summer's breakfast nook; one morning the five-course breakfast might include sunflower crepes; the next, calendula corn muffins. ⊠ *167 Palmer Ave., 02540,* ☎ FAX *508/548–9524 or 800/294– 5459,* WEB *www.wildflower-inn.com. 5 rooms, 1 cottage. Air-conditioning. No smoking. AE, MC, V. Closed Jan.–Feb. BP.*

$$–$$$ ⊡ **Palmer House Inn.** This turn-of-the-20th-century Queen Anne home stands on a tree-lined street in the historic heart of Falmouth, just a short stroll past the village green. The Victorian interior may seem slightly suffocating—dark hardwoods, heavy period furniture, endless lace, and ornate stained-glass windows. Each room has an antique, wicker, or four-poster bed and a ceiling fan. One good bet is the third-floor Tower Room, with a view across the treetops. The large rooms in the 1910 carriage house are also airier, with more tailored appointments. The inn added four rooms, all with whirlpool baths, in 1999; three have king-size beds, and all have traditional but less ornate decor. A candlelight breakfast is served and afternoon refreshments are available. ⊠ *81 Palmer Ave., 02540,* ☎ *508/548–1230 or 800/472–2632,* FAX *508/540–1878,* WEB *www.palmerhouseinn.com. 16 rooms, 1 cottage. Air-conditioning, bicycles. No smoking. AE, D, DC, MC, V. BP.*

Nightlife and the Arts

THE ARTS

The **College Light Opera Company** (⊠ Highfield Theatre, off Depot Ave., ☎ 508/548–0668) presents nine musicals or operettas for one week each, the results of a summer program involving music and theater majors from Oberlin and other colleges. The company includes more than 30 singers and an 18-piece orchestra. Be forewarned: the quality can vary from show to show.

Established in 1994, the **Cape Cod Theatre Project** (☎ 508/457–4242) helps develop new American plays through a series of staged readings. Each summer the project presents three or four readings, which are followed by audience discussion with the playwright. Recent productions have included *One Under,* by Gloucester Stage Company director Israel Horovitz, and works by Pulitzer Prize winners Lanford Wilson and Paula Vogel. Performances take place in the Woods Hole Community Hall (⊠ Water St., Woods Hole) or at Falmouth Academy (⊠ 7 Highfield Dr., off Depot Ave., Falmouth).

Falmouth's summer **town-band concerts** are held in Marina Park (⊠ Scranton Ave., ☎ 508/548–8500 or 800/526–8532) on Thursday evening starting at 8.

NIGHTLIFE
Coonamessett Inn (⊠ 311 Gifford St., ☎ 508/548–2300) has dancing to soft piano, jazz trios, or other music in its lounge on weekends year-round.

Nimrod Inn (⊠ 100 Dillingham Ave., ☎ 508/540–4132) presents jazz and contemporary music at least six nights a week year-round.

Outdoor Activities and Sports

BASEBALL
The **Falmouth Commodores** (☎ 508/432–6909) of the collegiate Cape Cod Baseball League play home games at Guv Fuller Field (⊠ 790 E. Main St. [Rte. 28]) from mid-June to mid-August.

BEACHES
Some Falmouth hotels and motels will sell daily resident parking permits to guests, so do ask if you plan to drive to the beach.

A bit removed from the hubbub of town, with swaying beach grass and a salt pond behind, the narrow **Falmouth Beach,** on Surf Drive, faces Nantucket Sound and Martha's Vineyard. Lifeguards watch the beach in season, and there are portable toilets. You need a resident parking sticker to park in the beach lot in season.

Falmouth Heights Beach, on Grand Avenue, is an often-crowded crescent of sand on Nantucket Sound, backed by a row of inns and B&Bs. The beach has lifeguards (in summer) and portable toilets. There's a small strip of metered parking on Grand Avenue between Walden Avenue and Crescent Park Avenue.

Grews Pond, in Goodwill Park, a pretty tree-lined freshwater pond with a sandy beach and lifeguarded swimming area, is popular with local families. You'll find several sites for picnicking, along with rest rooms, and a volleyball net; there's also a playground nearby. You can enter the park from Route 28 just north of Jones Road or from Gifford Street opposite St. Joseph's Cemetery. Parking is free.

Surf Drive Beach, a family-friendly sandy cove on Surf Drive, faces Nantucket Sound with views out toward the Vineyard. The beach has rest rooms and showers, as well as lifeguards, and public parking is available; in summer the daily parking fee is $10.

BIKING
The **Shining Sea Trail** is an easy 3½-mi route between Locust Street, Falmouth, and the Woods Hole ferry parking lot. It follows the coast, providing views of Vineyard Sound and dipping into oak and pine woods; a detour onto Church Street takes you to Nobska Light. A brochure is available at the trailheads. If you're going to Martha's Vineyard with your bike, you can park your car in one of Falmouth's Steamship Authority lots and ride the Shining Sea Trail to the ferry. (The free shuttle buses between the Falmouth lots and the Woods Hole ferry docks also have bike carriers; ☞ Boat & Ferry Travel *in* Smart Travel Tips A to Z).

Corner Cycle (✉ 115 Palmer Ave., Falmouth, ☎ 508/540–4195) rents bikes, including tandems and children's bikes, by the hour, day, or week. It also rents Burley trailers for carrying small children and does on-site repairs. The shop is just two blocks from the Shining Sea Trail. **Holiday Cycles** (✉ 465 Grand Ave., Falmouth Heights, ☎ 508/540–3549) has surrey, tandem, and other unusual bikes.

FISHING

Freshwater ponds are good for perch, pickerel, trout, and more; you can obtain the required license (along with rental gear) at tackle shops, such as **Eastman's Sport & Tackle** (✉ 150 Main St. [Rte. 28], Falmouth, ☎ 508/548–6900).

Patriot Boats (✉ 227 Clinton Ave., Falmouth Harbor, ☎ 508/548–2626; 800/734–0088 in MA) has deep-sea fishing from party or charter boats. Advance bookings are recommended, particularly for weekend trips.

ICE-SKATING

Fall through spring, skaters take to the ice at the **Falmouth Ice Arena** (✉ 9 Skating La., off Palmer Ave., ☎ 508/548–7080; 508/548–6940 for pro shop). You can rent skates from the pro shop.

RUNNING

To run in the world-class **Falmouth Road Race** (✉ Box 732, Falmouth, 02541, ☎ 508/540–7000) in mid-August, send a stamped, self-addressed envelope to request an entry form. The race typically closes to entrants in early spring.

TENNIS AND RACQUETBALL

The huge **Falmouth Sports Center** (✉ 33 Highfield Dr., ☎ 508/548–7433) has three outdoor and six indoor tennis courts, and three racquetball-handball courts, as well as steam rooms and saunas, free weights, and physical and massage therapist services. Day and short-term rates are available.

Shopping

Bean & Cod (✉ 140 Main St. [Rte. 28], ☎ 508/548–8840 or 800/558–8840), a specialty food shop, sells cheeses, breads, and gourmet picnic fixings, along with pastas, coffees and teas, and unusual condiments. The store also packs and ships gift baskets.

Eight Cousins Children's Books (✉ 189 Main St. [Rte. 28], ☎ 508/548–5548) is the place to find reading material for toddlers through young adults. Besides nice sections on oceans and marine life, Native American peoples, and other Cape topics, the well-stocked shop carries audiotapes and games.

Howlingbird (✉ 91 Palmer Ave., ☎ 508/540–3787) stocks detailed hand-silk-screened marine-theme T-shirts and sweatshirts, plus hand-painted cards and silk-screened hats and handbags.

Maxwell & Co. (✉ 200 Main St. [Rte. 28], ☎ 508/540–8752) has traditional men's and women's clothing with flair from European and American designers, handmade French shoes and boots, and leather goods and accessories.

Rosie Cheeks (✉ 233 Main St. [Rte. 28], ☎ 508/548–4572), whose name was inspired by the owner's daughter, specializes in creative women's clothing and jewelry, with a particularly nice selection of hand-knit sweaters.

Woods Hole

6 *4 mi southwest of Falmouth, 19 mi south of the Bourne Bridge.*

The village of Woods Hole, which dangles at the Cape's southwestern tip, has a unique personality shaped by its substantial intellectual community. As a major departure point for ferries to Martha's Vineyard, it draws crowds of through traffic in season.

Well known as a center for international marine research, Woods Hole is home to several major scientific institutions. The National Marine Fisheries Service was here first, established in 1871 to study fish management and conservation. In 1888 the Marine Biological Laboratory (MBL), a center for research and education in marine biology, moved in across the street. Then in 1930 the Woods Hole Oceanographic Institution (WHOI) arrived, and the U.S. Geological Survey's Branch of Marine Geology followed suit in the 1960s.

Most of the year Woods Hole is a peaceful community of intellectuals quietly going about their work. In summer, however, the basically one-street village overflows with the thousands of scientists and graduate students who come from around the globe either to participate in summer studies at MBL, WHOI, or the National Academy of Sciences conference center or to work on independent research projects. A handful of waterside cafés and shops along Water Street compete for the most bicycles stacked up at the door. Parking, limited to a relatively small number of metered spots on the street, can be nearly impossible. If you're coming from Falmouth to wander here, either ride your bicycle down the straight and flat Shining Sea Trail or take the Cape Cod Regional Transit Authority's WHOOSH trolley (☞ Trolley Travel *in* The Upper Cape A to Z).

What accounts for this incredible concentration of scientific minds is, in part, the variety and abundance of marine life in Woods Hole's unpolluted waters, and the natural deepwater port. In addition, researchers have the opportunity for an easy interchange of ideas and information and the stimulation of daily lectures and discussions (many open to the public) by important scientists. The pooling of resources among the various institutions makes for economies of scale that benefit each while allowing all access to highly sophisticated equipment.

Scientific forces join together at the **Marine Biological Laboratory–Woods Hole Oceanographic Institution Library** (✉ 7 Marine Biological Laboratory St., off Water St., WEB www.mbl.edu), one of the best collections of biological, ecological, and oceanographic literature in the world. On top of its access to more than 200 computer databases and the Internet, the library subscribes to more than 5,000 scientific journals in 40 languages, with complete collections of most from their first issues. During World War II the librarian arranged with a German subscription agency to have German periodicals sent to neutral Switzerland to be stored until the end of the war. Thus the library's German collections are uninterrupted, where even those of many German institutions are incomplete. All journals are always accessible because they cannot be checked out and because the library is open 24 hours a day. The Rare Books Room contains photographs, monographs, and prints, as well as journal collections that date from 1665.

Unless you are a scientific researcher, the only way you'll get to see the library is by taking the **Marine Biological Laboratory tour** (☎ 508/289–7623; call for reservations and meeting instructions at least a week in advance if possible). The 1-hour tours (mid-June–August, weekdays at 1, 2, and 3), led by retired scientists, include an introductory slide show as well as stops at the library, the Marine Resources Center (where living sea creatures collected each day are kept), and one of the many working research labs.

The **Woods Hole Oceanographic Institution** is the largest independent, private oceanographic laboratory in the world. Several buildings in the village of Woods Hole house its shore-based facilities; others are on a 200-acre campus nearby. During World War II its research focused on underwater explosives, submarine detection, and the development of antifouling paint. Today its $93 million annual budget helps operate many specialized laboratories with state-of-the-art equipment. A graduate program is offered jointly with MIT. WHOI's research vessels roam the world's waters. Its staff led the successful U.S.–French search for the *Titanic* (found about 400 mi off Newfoundland) in 1985.

The Woods Hole Oceanographic Institution is open to the public only on guided tours, but you can learn about it at the small **WHOI Exhibit Center,** with videos and exhibits on the institution and its various projects, including research vessels. One-hour walking tours of the institution and its piers are offered in July and August, weekdays at 10:30 and 1:30; tours begin at the WHOI Information Office at 93 Water Street and are free, but reservations are required (☎ 508/289–2252). ✉ *15 School St.,* ☎ *508/289–2663,* WEB *www.whoi.edu.* ⊠ *$2 suggested donation.* ☉ *Memorial Day–Labor Day, Mon.–Sat. 10–4:30, Sun. noon–4:30; Apr. and Nov.–Dec., Fri.–Sat. 10–4:30, Sun. noon–4:30; early May–Memorial Day and Labor Day–Oct., Tues.–Sat. 10–4:30, Sun. noon–4:30.*

The **National Marine Fisheries Service Aquarium** displays 16 tanks of regional fish and shellfish. Magnifying glasses and a dissecting scope help you examine marine life, and several hands-on pools hold banded lobsters, crabs, snails, starfish, and other creatures. The top attraction is two harbor seals, on view in the outdoor pool near the entrance in summer; you can watch their feedings daily at 11 and 4. The exhibits aren't sophisticated, and the facility could be better maintained, but this popular place is definitely child-friendly. At press time the aquarium had closed to implement new security procedures; call to confirm hours before visiting. ⊠ *Albatross and Water Sts.,* ☎ *508/495–2267; 508/495–2001 for recorded information,* WEB *www.nefsc.nmfs.gov/ nefsc/aquarium.* ⊠ *Free.* ☉ *Mid-June–mid-Sept., daily 10–4; mid-Sept.–mid-June, weekdays 10–4.*

NEED A BREAK?
Pie in the Sky (⊠ 10 Water St., ☎ 508/540–5475), a small bakery with tables inside and out, sells cookies, pastries, and coffees, as well as a small selection of sandwiches.

A three-building complex, the **Woods Hole Historical Museum** (formerly known as the Bradley House Museum) displays paintings, a restored Woods Hole Spritsail boat, boat models, and a model of the town as it looked in the 1890s. One room is filled with elegant ladies' clothing from the late 1800s. The archives of the historical collection hold old ships' logs, postcards, newspaper articles, maps, diaries, and photographs; more than 200 tapes of oral history provided by local residents; and a 100-volume library on maritime history. Free guided walking tours of the village take place Tuesday at 4 in July and August; tours depart from the museum, which is across from the Martha's Vineyard ferry parking lot. ⊠ *573 Woods Hole Rd.,* ☎ *508/548–7270,* WEB *www.woodsholemuseum.org.* ⊠ *Donations accepted.* ☉ *Museum mid-June–late Sept., Tues.–Sat. 10–4. Archives year-round, Tues. and Thurs. 10–2.*

The 1888 **Episcopal Church of the Messiah,** a stone church with a conical steeple and a small medicinal herb garden in the shape of a Celtic cross, is a good place for some quiet time. The garden, enclosed by a holly hedge, has a bench for meditation. Inscriptions on either side of the carved gate read ENTER IN HOPE and DEPART IN PEACE. ⊠ *22 Church St.,* ☎ *508/548–2145,* WEB *www.messiahweb.org.* ☑ *Free.* ☉ *Daily sunrise–sunset.*

Impressive **Nobska Light** (⊠ Church St.) has spectacular views from its base of the nearby Elizabeth Islands and of Martha's Vineyard, across Vineyard Sound. The 42-ft cast-iron tower, lined with brick, was built in 1876 with a stationary light. It shines red to indicate dangerous waters or white for safe passage. Since the light was automated in 1985, the adjacent keeper's quarters have been the headquarters of the Coast Guard group commander—a fitting passing of the torch from one safeguarder of ships to another. The lighthouse is not open to the public except during special tours.

Dining and Lodging

$$–$$$ ✕ **Shuckers.** Some of the harborside tables at this casual, nautical-theme restaurant are so close to the dock that you almost feel as if you're sitting in the bobbing sailboats. The menu wanders from jerk chicken to pasta primavera to lobster ravioli, but it's best to stick with the grilled fish and other simple seafood dishes. The "world-famous" lobster boil—a boiled lobster, steamed clams and mussels, and an ear of corn—is justifiably popular. ⊠ *91-A Water St.,* ☎ *508/540–3850. AE, D, MC, V. Closed mid-Oct.–mid-May. Mid-May–Memorial Day and Labor Day–Columbus Day, closed Mon.–Thurs.*

$–$$$ ✕ **Fishmonger's Café.** To say this is the best restaurant in Woods Hole
★ sounds like faint praise in the scheme of Cape restaurants, but the menu is ambitious—particularly the inventive daily specials that take a new look at traditional seafood. The light, perfectly fried calamari is served with a hot pepper sauce, and the hearty *bruschetta* (broiled bread slices) with ricotta, fresh herbs, basil leaves, and olives is a treat. Many grilled seafood dishes come with tropical fruit sauces or glazes; mango and cilantro sauce over grilled salmon is particularly delectable. Vegetarians have lots of choices here, too. The main dining room overlooks the water, and there's a handsome wood bar. ⊠ *56 Water St.,* ☎ *508/540–5376. Reservations not accepted. AE, MC, V. Closed mid-Dec.–mid-Feb. and Tues. Labor Day–Mar.*

$$–$$$ 🏠 **Capeside Cottage.** This classic Cape house, built in 1942, has country-style rooms with the same basic touches: double beds, lace curtains, and fluffy quilts. A tiny one-room cottage out back, next to the kidney-shape in-ground pool, has a double bed and a sleep sofa but no kitchen. You can eat breakfast out by the pool or in the comfortable common room, which has a fireplace and lots of amenities for guests; there's a fridge and an assortment of teas, as well as a TV and VCR. ⊠ *320 Woods Hole Rd., 02543,* ☎ *508/548–6218 or 800/320–2322,* FAX *508/457–7519,* WEB *www.capesidecottage.com. 5 rooms, 1 cottage. Air conditioning, pool. No smoking. MC, V. BP.*

$$–$$$ 🏠 **Woods Hole Passage.** Here, a century-old carriage house and barn have been tastefully converted into a romantic showcase. The large rose-hued common room radiates comfort with its lace curtains, over-stuffed furniture, and a yellow pine floor. All rooms have queen-size beds; one (the smallest) is in the main house, the others in the restored barn, where the upstairs rooms have soaring ceilings. In good weather you can have breakfast on the flagstone patio in the lovely yard. The inn is near the Martha's Vineyard ferry stop, and gregarious and helpful owner Deb Pruitt sells ferry tickets at cost so you can avoid lines at the dock. Early risers can request "breakfast-in-a-bag" to take on

A DAY ON MARTHA'S VINEYARD

THE DOUBLE LIFE OF THIS ISLAND reveals itself in two seasons: from Memorial Day through Labor Day the quieter, some might say the real, Vineyard quickens into a vibrant, celebrity-studded place. Edgartown floods with people who come to wander narrow streets flanked with elegant boutiques, stately whaling captains' homes, and luxurious inns. The busy main port, Vineyard Haven, welcomes day-trippers fresh off ferries and private yachts to browse in its own array of shops carrying everything from wampum and sea-glass jewelry to chic fashions. Oak Bluffs, where pizza and ice-cream emporiums reign supreme, attracts diverse crowds with its boardwalk-town air and nightspots that cater to high-spirited, carefree youth. Around the island, pristine white-sand beaches beckon.

Most people know the Vineyard's summer persona, but in many ways its other self has even more appeal, for the off-season island is a place of peace and simple beauty. Drivers traversing country lanes through the agricultural center of the island find time to linger over pastoral and ocean vistas without being pushed along by a throng of other cars, bicycles, and mopeds. In nature reserves, the voices of summer are gone, leaving only the sounds of birdsong and the crackle of leaves underfoot. Private beaches are open to the public, and the water sparkles under crisp, blue skies. Whichever season you want to experience, you can make the trip by ferry to this island south of the western end of Cape Cod in 35 minutes to 1¾ hours from Woods Hole, Falmouth, or Hyannis.

The Vineyard is roughly triangular, with maximum distances of about 20 mi east to west and 10 mi north to south. The western end of the Vineyard, known as Up-Island—from the nautical expression of going "up" in degrees of longitude as you sail west—is more rural and wild than the eastern Down-Island end, which includes Vineyard Haven, Oak Bluffs, and Edgartown. Conservation land claims almost a quarter of the island, with preservationist organizations acquiring more all the time. The Land Bank, funded by a tax on real-estate transactions, is a leading group, set up to preserve as much of the island in its natural state as is possible and practical.

The many ways to spend a day here may tempt you to stay longer. You might want to spend a short time in Vineyard Haven (Tisbury is its official name) before getting rural Up-Island or heading for a beach. Or you can go straight to tony Edgartown to stroll past the antique white houses, pop into some of the museums that make up the excellent Vineyard Museum and Oral History Center, and shop. If you just want to have fun, Oak Bluffs, with its harbor scene, colorful Carpenter Gothic Victorian cottages, and nearby beaches, will be the place to go. You can bring over a car (reservations are essential in summer) or rent one. To get around without your own wheels, use the convenient year-round shuttle buses or the seasonal minibuses that run between Down-Island towns and Up-Island villages such as Chilmark and Menemsha and sights such as the lighthouse and red cliffs at Aquinnah. Taxis are another option, or you can choose pedal power and explore miles of bike trails at your own pace.

For visitor information, contact the **Martha's Vineyard Chamber of Commerce** (⊠ Beach Rd., Box 1698, Vineyard Haven 02568, ☎ 508/693–0085, WEB www.mvy.com), two blocks from the Vineyard Haven Ferry. For information on travel by ferry from Cape Cod, see Boat & Ferry Travel in Smart Travel Tips A to Z.

the road. ✉ *186 Woods Hole Rd., 02540,* ☎ *508/548–9575 or 800/*
790–8976, FAX *508/540–4771,* WEB *www.woodsholepassage.com. 5*
rooms. Air-conditioning, croquet, horseshoes, bicycles. No smoking.
AE, D, DC, MC, V. BP.

Nightlife and the Arts

The **Cape Cod Theatre Project** (☎ 508/457–4242; ☞ Falmouth) helps
develop new American plays through a series of staged readings each
summer. Performances are held in the Woods Hole Community Hall
(✉ Water St., Woods Hole) or at Falmouth Academy (✉ 7 Highfield
Dr., off Depot Ave., Falmouth).

The **Woods Hole Folk Music Society** (✉ Community Hall, Water St.,
☎ 508/540–0320) presents professional and local folk and blues in a
no-smoking, no-alcohol environment, with refreshments available during intermission. Concerts by nationally known performers take place
the first and third Sundays of the month from October to April, as well
as on the first Sunday of May.

Woods Hole Theater Company (✉ Community Hall, Water St., ☎ 508/
540–6525), the community's resident theater group since 1974, presents several productions each year, generally between late spring and
early fall.

Shopping

Handworks (✉ 68 Water St., ☎ 508/540–5291), tucked in the back
of the Community Hall building next to the drawbridge, is a cooperative arts and crafts gallery showcasing the work of local artists.

East Falmouth and Waquoit

5 mi northeast of Woods Hole.

These bucolic villages (well, bucolic once you leave Route 28 and its
strip malls) have much to offer nature lovers. Narrow fingers of land
poke out toward Nantucket Sound, so water is never far away, though
it's quiet inlets and marshy bays rather than the crashing surf of the
open ocean. The residential neighborhoods here, with both seasonal
and year-round homes, often end in dirt lanes that lead to the water.
Menauhant Beach, the nicest beach in these towns, sits on a thin sliver
of land with the sound on one side and a grass-lined cove on the other.
Inland, the land is more rural, with a number of farms (and farm stands)
still operating.

Note that as you head east from Falmouth center on Route 28, the street
signs change names as you travel through different areas. The road is
Main Street until you pass Falmouth Heights Road, when Route 28
becomes Davis Straits. Farther east it becomes Teaticket Highway,
then East Falmouth Highway, and then Waquoit Highway.

❼ Overseen by the Massachusetts Audubon Society, **Ashumet Holly and
Wildlife Sanctuary** is true to its name and its original plantsman, Wil-
fred Wheeler, with its 1,000-plus holly trees and shrubs composed of
65 American, Asian, and European varieties. Like Heritage Plantation
in Sandwich, this 45-acre tract of woodland, shady groves, meadows,
and hiking trails was purchased and donated by Josiah K. Lilly III to
preserve local land. Grassy Pond is home to numerous turtles and frogs,
and in summer 35 nesting pairs of barn swallows live in the open rafters
of the barn. Maps for self-guided tours cost $1. Tours to nearby Cut-
tyhunk Island (on a 50-ft sailing vessel) leave Woods Hole every Sunday from mid-July to mid-October; trips run from 9 to 5 and cost $45.
✉ *286 Ashumet Rd., East Falmouth,* ☎ *508/362–1426,* WEB *www.mas-
saudubon.org.* ▣ *$3.* ☉ *Trails daily sunrise–sunset.*

☺ **Waquoit Bay National Estuarine Research Reserve** encompasses 2,500 acres of estuary and barrier beach around the bay, making it a good birding site. **South Cape Beach** is part of the reserve; you can lie out on the sand or join one of the interpretive walks. **Flat Pond Trail** runs through a variety of habitats, including fresh- and saltwater marshes. **Washburn Island** is accessible by boat (your own) or by Saturday-morning tours (call to reserve); it offers 330 acres of pine barrens and trails, swimming, and 11 wilderness campsites (permit required; ☎ 877/422–6762). At the reserve headquarters, a 23-acre estate, an exhibit center includes displays about the bay's plants and animals, the Cape Cod watershed, and local Wampanoag culture. An interactive exhibit, outside on the lawn, allows you to trace the path of a raindrop; pick up a ball (the pseudo-raindrop) and follow its journey from cloud to land to river and on through the water cycle. In July and August the center offers nature programs for children and families, as well as a Tuesday-evening series (bring picnics) on environmental, historical, and artistic subjects. ⊠ *Rte. 28, 3 mi west of Mashpee rotary, Waquoit,* ☎ *508/457–0495,* ⓦⒺⒷ *www. waquoitbayreserve.org.* ☉ *Exhibit center: mid-June–Labor Day, Mon.– Sat. 10–4; Labor Day–mid-June, weekdays 10–4.*

Tony Andrews Farm and Produce Stand has pick-your-own strawberries (June), peas and beans (June–July), herbs (July–August), and tomatoes (August), as well as other produce on the stand. The farm schedules hayrides in summer and fall, and a haunted house is set up in October. You can pick your own pumpkins in fall and choose your Christmas tree in December. ⊠ *394 Old Meeting House Rd., East Falmouth,* ☎ *508/548–4717.* ☉ *June–Oct.; call for hrs. and for information about special events.*

Coonamessett Farm operates a farm store, where you can assemble your own gift baskets or purchase produce and specialty foods, as well as a small café serving soups, salads, baked goods, and beverages. You can tour the greenhouses and fields, learn about hydroponic growing systems, and examine a crayfish-culture research project. Members of the farm's Pick-Your-Own club ($15-per-year membership) can pick strawberries, lettuces, herbs, rhubarb, and other fruits and vegetables. The farm also rents canoes for use on the adjacent Coonamessett Pond. ⊠ *277 Hatchville Rd., East Falmouth,* ☎ *508/563–2560,* ⓦⒺⒷ *www.coonamessettfarm.com.* ☉ *Call for seasonal hrs.*

Rows and rows of grapevines—8,000 in all—line the fields of the **Cape Cod Winery,** established by Kristina and Antonio Lazzari in 1994. It now produces six wines, and in 1998 the Nobska red won a bronze medal at the International Eastern Wine Competition. ⊠ *681 Sandwich Rd., East Falmouth,* ☎ *508/457–5592,* ⓦⒺⒷ *www.capecodwinery.com.* ☉ *July–Aug., tastings Wed.–Sun. noon–5, tours weekends at 2; Memorial Day–June and Sept.–Thanksgiving, tastings weekends noon–4.*

Dining and Lodging

$–$$ ✕ **McGann's of Falmouth Pub and Restaurant.** A discovery to everyone but the local crowd, McGann's calls itself "a touch of Ireland on Cape Cod." The McGann family should know because they also have a pub in the town of Doolin, County Galway, Ireland. The place does have the slightly frayed grit of an Irish country tavern, with its worn floorboards and dusty ceramic poteen jugs lined up on a shelf. Typical bar food comes with an Irish twist here: Irish-style fish-and-chips; Gaelic chicken in an Irish whiskey and bacon sauce; and an Irish breakfast with eggs, sausage, and blood pudding, served all day. Though Guinness reigns, the bar has 20 beers on draft. In summer, there's music every night (several nights a week in the off-season), and Wednesday is karaoke night. ✉ *734 Teaticket Hwy. (Rte. 28), East Falmouth,* ☎ *508/540–6656. Reservations not accepted. AE, D, MC, V.*

$ ✕ **Moonakis Café.** Its popular breakfast gets high marks at this cheery café. You'll find all the standards and then some—eggs, pancakes, fruit salad—all nicely done. The chunky hash browns are fried with just the right amount of onions, and if the omelet with roasted tomatoes, olives, and goat cheese is on the menu, it's an excellent choice. Also recommended (if you're not on a diet) are the decadent Belgian waffles buried under strawberries, bananas, and whipped cream. ✉ *460 Waquoit Hwy. (Rte. 28), Waquoit,* ☎ *508/457–9630. No credit cards. No dinner.*

$$ ▥ **Green Harbor Waterfront Lodging.** Although the modest motel rooms here are clean and adequate, it's the friendly, summer camp–like setting that makes the Green Harbor great for families. There are old-fashioned lawn swings, a swimming pool, umbrella-topped picnic tables, barbecue grills, and the main attraction—the waterfront. It's not the open ocean here, but a peaceful tree-lined inlet, with rowboats and pedal boats for guests' use. Some of the no-frills rooms in the 1960s-vintage motel have microwaves and small refrigerators; others have kitchenettes. ✉ *134 Acapesket Rd., East Falmouth 02536,* ☎ *508/548–4747 or 800/548–5556,* FAX *508/540–1652,* WEB *www.gogreenharbor.com. 34 rooms, 1 cottage. Picnic area, kitchenettes, pool, wading pool, volleyball, boating, laundry facilities. No smoking. AE, D, DC, MC, V. Closed Nov.–Apr.*

$–$$ ▥ **Cape Wind.** If you're traveling with children who need space to run, the Cape Wind is a good choice. All the rooms in this gray-shingle motel face a broad green lawn that slopes down to the bay, and lawn chairs and picnic tables dot the grass. Rowboats and pedal boats are available, too. The rooms are decidedly basic, with standard motel furnishings and more hand-me-down pieces; some have been updated more recently than others—so ask before you reserve. All have refrigerators and coffeemakers, while some have microwaves and others have kitchenettes. The spacious one-bedroom apartment has a private terrace, but its half-basement location makes the interior rather dark. ✉ *34 Maravista Extension, Teaticket (East Falmouth) 02536,* ☎ *508/548–3400 or 800/ 267–3401,* FAX *508/495–0316,* WEB *www.capewind.com. 31 rooms, 1 apartment. No smoking, kitchenettes, pool, boating. D, MC, V. Closed Nov.–Feb.*

Outdoor Activities and Sports

BEACHES

Menauhant Beach, on Menauhant Road in East Falmouth, is a long, narrow stretch of sand, with a pond behind, in a quiet residential neighborhood. Its slightly more secluded location means it can be a bit less crowded than the beaches near Falmouth center. The beach has lifeguards, rest rooms, outdoor showers, and a small snack bar. Public parking is available; in season the fee is $10.

Mashpee

❽ *7 mi east of East Falmouth, 10 mi south of Sandwich.*

Mashpee is one of two Massachusetts towns (the other is Aquinnah, formerly known as Gay Head, on Martha's Vineyard) that have both municipally governed and Native American–governed areas. In 1660 the missionary Reverend Richard Bourne gave a 16-square-mi parcel of land to the Wampanoags (consider the irony—an outsider "giving" Native people their own land). Known as the Mashpee Plantation and governed by two local sachems, it was the first Native American reservation in the United States. In 1870 Mashpee was founded as a town. In 1974 the Mashpee Wampanoag Tribal Council was formed to continue its government with a chief, a supreme sachem, a medicine man, and clan mothers. More than 600 residents are descended from the original Wampanoags, and some continue to observe their ancient traditions.

More recently, several resort-residential communities have developed in the Mashpee area; the largest, New Seabury, is a full-fledged resort with apartment units available to visitors and one of the best golf courses on the Cape. Mashpee, with its villagelike Mashpee Commons mall, has also become a popular shopping destination. Yet away from the stores, the town retains a more rural character, with wooded roads, inland ponds, and reminders of the area's original settlers.

Housed in a 1793 half-Cape, the **Wampanoag Indian Museum** is a small museum on the history and culture of the tribe. Exhibits include baskets, weapons, hunting and fishing tools, clothing, arrowheads, and a small diorama depicting a scene from an early settlement. There is also a herring run on site, a small tidal stream that runs from the ocean into a pond. In spring, thick schools of herring swim to the calm safety of the pond to spawn. The tribe noticed this cycle and would net great numbers of herring as the fish made their way back to the sea. At this writing the museum was in the midst of a multi-year renovation but expected to be operational sometime in 2002; call before visiting. ⊠ *416 Rte. 130, near Great Neck Rd. N,* ☎ *508/477–1536 or 508/477–0208.* ⊠ *Donations accepted.* ☉ *Call for hrs.*

The **Old Indian Meeting House** was originally built on Santuit Pond in 1684 and was later moved to its present site on Route 28. The oldest standing church on Cape Cod, the meeting house is still used by the Mashpee tribe for worship and meetings. In summer, memorials and religious events are held, some incorporating traditional Wampanoag practices. Hours vary; call before visiting. ⊠ *Meeting House Rd. off Rte. 28,* ☎ *508/477–0208.* ☉ *Call for hrs.*

The **Old Indian Burial Ground,** near the meeting house on Meeting House Road, is an 18th-century cemetery with interesting headstones typical of the period carved with scenes and symbols and inscribed with witty sayings.

In a cavernous former church building, the **Cape Cod Children's Museum** welcomes children with interactive play, science exhibits, a 30-ft pirate play ship, a portable planetarium, and other playtime activities. The museum is best suited for preschoolers and children in the early elementary grades. ⊠ *577 Great Neck Rd. S,* ☎ *508/539–8788,* WEB *www.capecodchildrensmuseum.pair.com.* ⊠ *$4.* ☉ *Mon.–Sat. 10–5, Sun. noon–5.*

A perfect place for bird-watching, fishing, or canoeing, the **Mashpee River Woodlands** occupy 391 acres of conservation land along the Mashpee River. More than 8 mi of trails meander through the marshlands and pine forests. Park on Quinaquisset Avenue, River Road, or Mashpee Neck Road (where there's a public landing for canoe access). Trail maps are available at the Mashpee Chamber of Commerce (☞ *Visitor Information in* The Upper Cape A to Z). The trails are open daily, dawn to dusk.

Dining and Lodging

$$–$$$ ★ ✕ **The Flume.** The Cape belonged to the Wampanoags for centuries before the Pilgrims arrived, and the Flume, owned since the early 1970s by Wampanoag elder (and author) Earl Mills, pairs great food with reminders of that cultural tradition; Native American artifacts decorate the dining room. The food concentrates on a few New England

staples, including chowder considered to be among the best on the Cape. Traditional codfish cakes and beans, Yankee pot roast, soft-shell crabs in season, and Indian pudding are done to perfection. The Sunday roast turkey is a genuine treat, as are Aunt Jan's desserts. ⊠ *Lake Ave. off Rte. 130,* ☎ *508/477–1456. MC, V. Closed Thanksgiving–Easter. No lunch.*

$$–$$$ ✕ **Popponesset Inn.** The atmosphere, rather than the menu of traditional offerings such as lobster rolls, grilled swordfish, and steak, stands out as exceptional here. The site is a gem, with old Cape Cod saltbox houses, lovely Nantucket Sound in the background, and perfect evening light. The restaurant has a lounge, Poppy's, and a number of small dining rooms, some with skylights and others looking over the water through glass walls. Best of all is to sit outside, either under the tent or at one of the umbrella tables. You can dance to a band on some weekends. The Popponesset is in the New Seabury Resort. ⊠ *Shore Dr.,* ☎ *508/477–1100,* WEB *www.newseabury.com/poppy.html. AE, DC, MC, V. Closed Mon. and Nov.–late May. No lunch.*

$–$$$ ✕ **Contrast at the Commons.** The contemporary dinner menu runs from skate in brown butter, to *pappardelle* (broad noodles) with a wild mushroom sauce, to *achiote* (annatto-seed) roast chicken in this warm, sophisticated room with brightly painted walls, hand-painted tables, and modern sculpture. If you're looking for a lighter meal, choose from the simpler, but still innovative, bistro fare or fancy sandwiches. The tasty cod cakes are served over a hearty mix of potatoes, chorizo, and corn, and the individual grilled pizzas have a very thin, crisp Middle Eastern *lavash* crust; try the shrimp version with its good-size crustaceans. ⊠ *Market St., Mashpee Commons,* ☎ *508/477–1299. Reservations not accepted. AE, MC, V.*

$–$$ ✕ **Marketplace Raw Bar.** At this funky little seafood joint tucked away in Popponesset Marketplace, you can pull up a bar stool and chow down on littlenecks, cherrystones, oysters, steamers, and peel-your-own shrimp, all easily washed down with a local brew or a rum punch. Despite a few picnic tables out back, the casual atmosphere here is more "bar" than "seafood shack." There's live music some nights, too. ⊠ *Popponesset Marketplace, New Seabury,* ☎ *508/539–4858. AE, MC, V. Closed late Oct.–early Apr.*

$$$$ ✕🏨 **New Seabury Resort and Conference Center.** On a 2,000-acre point
★ surrounded by the waters of Nantucket Sound, this self-contained resort community rents apartments in some of its 13 "villages." For example, Maushop Village is a gray-shingle oceanfront complex of buildings set among narrow lanes of crushed seashells, with rugosa roses trailing over picket fences; the interiors attractively mix Cape-style and modern furnishings. Town-house units in Sea Quarters have solariums with whirlpool baths and gas-log fireplaces. All units have full kitchens and washer-dryers. Among the amenities (many of them seasonal) are fine oceanfront dining, a 3-mi private beach and an oceanfront pool, and the shops at Popponesset Marketplace. Golf and other packages are available. ⊠ *Off Great Neck Rd. S, Box 549, New Seabury 02649,* ☎ *508/477–9400 or 800/999–9033,* FAX *508/477–9790,* WEB *www. newseabury.com. 140 1- or 2-bedroom units. 2 restaurants, 2 pools, 2 18-hole golf courses, 16 tennis courts, health club, jogging, beach, boating, bicycles, shops. AE, DC, MC, V.*

Nightlife and the Arts

Bobby Byrne's Pub (⊠ Mashpee Commons, Rtes. 28 and 151, ☎ 508/477–0600) offers a comfortable pub atmosphere, an outdoor café, a jukebox, and good light and full menus.

The **Boch Center for the Performing Arts** (☎ 508/477–2580) presents top-name performers year-round and is home to the Annual New England Jazz Festival, held in late August. Plans are under way to construct a complex of buildings, including an amphitheater to accommodate 2,000 people, on an idyllic 10-acre tract of countryside in Mashpee. Until the complex is completed, performances are held at Mashpee Commons, in the Mashpee High School auditorium, or at other local venues.

The 90-member **Cape Symphony Orchestra** (☎ 508/362–1111) comes to Mashpee in July for its annual Sounds of Summer Pops Concert (it also performs an August concert in Orleans). The performance takes place at the Mashpee Commons.

Outdoor Activities and Sports

BEACHES

Attaquin Park Beach (✉ end of Lake Ave. off Rte. 130, near Great Neck Rd. N) is a pretty, sandy place, with a spectacular view of the interconnecting Mashpee and Wakeby ponds, the Cape's largest freshwater expanses. It's popular for swimming, fishing, and boating, but resident parking stickers are required in season.

South Cape Beach is a 2½-mi-long state and town beach on warm Nantucket and Vineyard sounds, accessible via Great Neck Road south from the Mashpee rotary. You can walk to get a bit of privacy on this beach, which is wide, sandy, and pebbly in parts, with low dunes and marshland. The only services are portable toilets, although lifeguards are on duty in season. A hiking trail loops through marsh areas and ponds, linking it to the Waquoit Bay National Estuarine Research Reserve. A $7 parking fee is charged from Memorial Day through Labor Day.

GOLF

New Seabury Country Club (✉ Shore Dr., New Seabury, ☎ 508/477–9111) has a superior 18-hole, par-72 championship layout on the water as well as an 18-hole, par-70 course. Both are open to the public September–May, depending on availability; reservations four days in advance are recommended, and proper attire is required.

HIKING AND WALKING

The 4 mi of walking trails at **Lowell Holly Reservation** (✉ S. Sandwich Rd. off Rte. 130, ☎ 781/821–2977), administered by the Trustees of Reservations, wend through American beeches, hollies, white pines, and rhododendrons on a peninsula between Mashpee and Wakeby ponds. The reservation has picnic tables and a little swimming beach. A small free parking area is open year-round, and an additional parking lot opens from Memorial Day to Labor Day ($6).

In summer, the **Mashpee Conservation Commission** (☎ 508/539–1400 Ext. 540 for schedules) has information about free naturalist-led guided walks of Mashpee's woods and conservation areas. Family nature walks, animal scavenger hunts, and "pond scoops" to explore aquatic life are among the choices for kids and their parents; sunrise walks on South Cape Beach and natural history tours of the Lowell Holly Reservation are also on the program.

Shopping

Mashpee Commons (✉ junction of Rtes. 28 and 151, ☎ 508/477–5400) has about 80 stores, including restaurants, art galleries, and a mix of local boutiques and national chains, in an attractive village square setting. There's also a multiscreen movie theater and free outdoor entertainment in summer. Some of the more unique shops include **M. Brann & Co.** (☎ 508/477–0299), a creative home-and-gift shop that carries everything from funky refrigerator magnets and unusual candlesticks to hand-crafted glassware, one-of-a-kind lamps, mirrors, and furniture, with many of the works by New England artists; **Signature Gallery** (☎ 508/539–0029), a high-end crafts gallery and store (with branches in Boston and in Westport, Connecticut) that stocks contemporary crafts, including textiles, ceramics, prints, and glass; and **Cape Cod Toys** (☎ 508/477–2221), crammed full of anything the children might possibly need (and then some!)—beach toys, board games, science projects, and more.

Popponesset Marketplace (✉ off Great Neck Rd. S, New Seabury, 2½ mi south of Rte. 28 from Mashpee rotary, ☎ 508/477–9111), open from late spring to early fall, has 20 shops (boutique clothing, antiques), eating places (a raw bar, pizza, ribs, Ben & Jerry's), miniature golf, and weekend entertainment (bands, fashion or puppet shows, sing-alongs).

THE UPPER CAPE A TO Z

To research prices, get advice from other travelers, and book travel arrangements, visit www.fodors.com.

AIRPORTS
Barnstable Municipal Airport is the main air gateway on the Cape.
➤ AIRPORT INFORMATION: **Barnstable Municipal Airport** (✉ 480 Barnstable Rd., Rte. 28 rotary, Hyannis, ☎ 508/775–2020).

BOAT AND FERRY TRAVEL
Year-round ferries to Martha's Vineyard leave from Woods Hole. Seasonal Vineyard ferries leave from Falmouth. For details *see* Boat & Ferry Travel *in* Smart Travel Tips A to Z.

BUS TRAVEL
Bonanza Bus Lines offers direct service to Bourne, Falmouth, and the Woods Hole steamship terminal from Boston's Logan Airport, downtown Boston, Providence (Rhode Island), Fall River, and New Bedford, as well as connecting service from New York, Connecticut, and Providence's T. F. Green Airport. Some of the buses from Boston also make stops in Wareham and Buzzards Bay. Bonanza runs a service between Bourne, Falmouth, and Woods Hole year-round.

Plymouth & Brockton Street Railway provides bus service to Provincetown from downtown Boston and Logan Airport, with stops en route. The Logan Direct airport express service bypasses downtown Boston and stops in Plymouth, Sagamore, Barnstable, and Hyannis.

For general information on Cape buses, *see* Bus Travel *in* Smart Travel Tips A to Z.
➤ BUS INFORMATION: **Bonanza Bus Lines** (☎ 508/548–7588 or 800/556–3815, WEB www.bonanzabus.com). **Plymouth & Brockton Street Railway** (☎ 508/746–0378, WEB www.p-b.com).

CAR TRAVEL
If your destination is Sagamore, Sandwich, or points east along Cape Cod Bay, cross the Sagamore Bridge to reach U.S. 6 or Route 6A. If you're headed for Bourne, Falmouth, Woods Hole, or Mashpee, take the Bourne Bridge instead and pick up Route 28 south. To reach East Falmouth or Mashpee, get off Route 28 at either Route 151 or Brick Kiln Road to bypass Falmouth center—both rejoin Route 28 east of Falmouth.

If you're not in a hurry, get off the main highways and seek out the Upper Cape's more scenic byways. Route 6A heading east from Sandwich is a heavily traveled but still scenic route that parallels Cape Cod Bay all the way to Orleans. Watch for cars turning suddenly, though, as there are shops and side roads along many stretches of 6A. Heading from the Bourne Bridge toward Falmouth, County Road and Route 28A are prettier alternatives to Route 28, and Sippewisset Road meanders near Buzzards Bay between West Falmouth and Woods Hole. Just remember that some of these roads travel through residential areas, so keep your speed down.

CHILDREN IN THE UPPER CAPE
SIGHTS AND ATTRACTIONS

Libraries usually offer regular children's story hours or other programs; check them out on a rainy day. Hours are listed in the newspapers each week.

The Army Corps of Engineers Junior Ranger Program for children ages 6–12 offers various summer activities that teach kids about the Cape Cod Canal and the area's natural history. Also good for families are star watches, beach and dune walks, and other nature programs.

The Cape Cod Baseball League has summer day camps and clinics, run by the individual teams, for children ages 5–13; most teams have six weeks of camp, typically weekday mornings.

The Green Briar Nature Center runs one-day and multiday nature programs, with classes geared to ages 4–5, 6–8, and 9 and up. Sample programs include a Cape Cod Safari, Canoe Adventures, and Night Nature.

At the Waquoit Bay National Estuarine Research Reserve, various summer programs for kids, including junior ranger activities that are generally one-hour programs at South Cape Beach for ages 6–12 (accompanied by an adult).

➤ LOCAL INFORMATION: **Army Corps of Engineers Junior Ranger Program** (☎ 508/759–4431). **Cape Cod Baseball League** (☎ 508/432–6909, WEB www.capecodbaseball.org). **Green Briar Nature Center** (☎ 508/888–6870, WEB www.thorntonburgess.org). **Waquoit Bay National Estuarine Research Reserve** (☎ 508/457–0495).

EMERGENCIES

Falmouth Hospital has a 24-hour emergency room. For rescues at sea call the Coast Guard. Boaters should use Channel 16 on their radios. The CVS pharmacy in Falmouth closes at 10 PM Monday–Saturday and 9 PM Sunday, with extended hours in the summer.

➤ DOCTORS AND DENTISTS: **Falmouth Walk-In Medical Center** (✉ 309 Teaticket Hwy. (Rte. 28), East Falmouth, ☎ 508/540–6790). **Mashpee Family Medicine** (✉ 5 Industrial Dr., off Rte. 28, Mashpee, ☎ 508/477–4282).

➤ EMERGENCY SERVICES: **Ambulance, fire, police** (☎ 911 or dial township station). **Coast Guard** (☎ 508/548–5151 in Woods Hole; 508/888–0335 in Sandwich and Cape Cod Canal).

➤ HOSPITALS: **Falmouth Hospital** (✉ 100 Ter Heun Dr., Falmouth, ☎ 508/548–5300).

➤ HOT LINES: **Massachusetts Poison Control Center** (☎ 800/682–9211).

➤ LATE-NIGHT PHARMACIES: **CVS** (✉ 105 Davis Straits, Falmouth, ☎ 508/540–4307, WEB www.cvs.com).

LODGING
APARTMENT AND HOUSE RENTALS

Donahue Real Estate lists both apartments and houses for summer rental in the Falmouth area. Real Estate Associates lists properties ranging from beach cottages to waterfront estates, with a focus on more expensive houses. It covers Falmouth, Bourne, and Mashpee, on the Upper Cape.

➤ LOCAL AGENTS: **Donahue Real Estate** (✉ 850 Main St., Falmouth 02540, ☎ 508/548–5412, FAX 508/548–5418, WEB www.falmouthhomes. com). **Real Estate Associates** (✉ Rtes. 151 and 28A, Box 738, North Falmouth 02556, ☎ 508/563–7173, FAX 508/563–6943, WEB www. realestateassc.com).

TAXIS

➤ TAXI COMPANIES: **All Village Taxi** (✉ Falmouth, ☎ 508/540–7200).

TOURS

Patriot Boats has two-hour day and sunset cruises from Falmouth Harbor on the 68-ft schooner *Liberté*. Another sunset cruise, which operates on Friday and Saturday evenings, passes six lighthouses in the Falmouth area. Rates and schedules vary.

➤ FEES AND SCHEDULES: **Patriot Boats** (✉ 227 Clinton Ave., Falmouth, ☎ 508/548–2626; 800/734–0088 in MA, WEB www.patriotpartyboats. com).

TROLLEY TRAVEL

The Cape Cod Regional Transit Authority runs seasonal trolleys in Falmouth, Mashpee, Hyannis, Yarmouth, and Dennis. Fares and times vary; call for more information.

➤ CONTACTS: **Cape Cod Regional Transit Authority** (☎ 508/385–8326; 800/352–7155 in MA, WEB www.capecodtransit.org).

VISITOR INFORMATION

The Cape Cod Chamber of Commerce is open year-round, Monday–Saturday 9–5 and Sunday 10–4. The year-round visitor information center on Route 25, in a rest area about 3 mi west of the Bourne Bridge, is open daily 9–5 (with extended hours 8 AM–10 PM from Memorial Day to Columbus Day).

The Cape Cod Canal Region, which includes Sandwich, Bourne and Wareham, has information centers at Sagamore rotary, at a train depot in Buzzards Bay, and on Rte. 130 in Sandwich (near the intersection with U.S. 6).

➤ TOURIST INFORMATION: **Cape Cod Chamber of Commerce** (✉ junction of U.S. 6 and 132, Hyannis, ☎ 508/862–0700 or 888/332–2732; 508/759–3814 for year-round visitor information center; WEB www. capecodchamber.org). **Cape Cod Canal Region** (✉ 70 Main St., Buzzards Bay 02532, ☎ 508/759–6000, WEB www.capecodcanalchamber. org). **Falmouth** (✉ 20 Academy La., Box 582, 02541, ☎ 508/548–8500 or 800/526–8532, WEB www.falmouth-capecod.com). **Mashpee** (✉ N. Market St., Mashpee Commons [Rte. 151], 02649, ☎ 508/477–0792 or 800/423–6274 outside MA, WEB www.mashpeechamber.com).

4 THE MID CAPE

Band concerts on village greens, peaceful beaches, and busy strips with saltwater taffy shacks and T-shirt shops reflect the diversity of the bustling Mid Cape. Staid Barnstable Village, with its 18th-century homes, is just minutes from Hyannis, the center of commerce for all Cape Cod. Languid Yarmouth Port vies for attention with motel-stacked South and West Yarmouth, and the pristine ponds and beaches of Dennis are colorfully adorned with umbrellas from South Dennis minimalls.

Revised by
Karl Luntta

M ORE A COLLOQUIALISM than a proper name, the designation *Mid Cape* refers to central Cape Cod, the most heavily populated—and touristed—part of the peninsula. To the north lies calm Cape Cod Bay, lined with wide beaches, inlets, creeks, and marshes. The tides on the bay are dramatic; at dead low some beaches double in size as the tidal flats stretch out for hundreds, even thousands, of feet.

The main thoroughfare through the north side of the Mid Cape is Route 6A, a scenic section that dates from 1684, making it one of the first major roads constructed on Cape Cod. Alternately called Old King's Highway, Main Street, and Hallet Street, the road winds through the villages of West Barnstable, Barnstable, Cummaquid, Yarmouth Port, and Dennis, with short side trips to north-side harbors and beaches. More residential than commercial, Route 6A is lined with antique captains' mansions and farmhouses that now serve as year-round private homes, bed-and-breakfasts, art galleries, restaurants, and antiques shops.

On the south side of the Mid Cape, the crowd pleaser is Nantucket Sound and its miles of long beaches. The main thoroughfare here, from Centerville to Osterville, through Hyannis and on to West Yarmouth, South Yarmouth, and Dennisport, is the busy—in every sense of the word—Route 28. This stretch, particularly between West Yarmouth and Dennisport, is the original vacationland of Cape Cod, a honky-tonk paradise filled with strip motels, clam shacks, miniature golf courses, ice cream parlors, and tacky T-shirt outlets. It's sort of a Cape Cod Disneyland, the archetype seaside vacation area that saw its boom time in the 1960s and hasn't changed much since.

Between routes 6A and 28 is the "mid" of the Mid Cape, a mostly residential area with some historic sections and a few quiet, freshwater ponds. Included here are the commercial sections of Hyannis, as well as tony Osterville and Hyannis Port, a well-groomed enclave and site of the Kennedy compound.

Pleasures and Pastimes

Beaches

Beach lovers will find numerous Shangri-Las throughout the Mid Cape. Sandy Neck, a peninsular strip of land that stretches across the north side of Barnstable Harbor, is one of the top 10 of Cape Cod, perfect for those who like (mostly) gentle surf and long shoreline walks. Also on the north side of the Mid Cape, Dennis's Corporation Beach and Mayflower Beach are great places for children, with wide tidal flats, snack huts, and rest rooms. South-side beaches, on Nantucket Sound, include the busy Craigville Beach in Centerville, popular with college students on break, and Kalmus Park Beach, in Hyannis, with a windy surf that attracts world-class wind-boarders. Yarmouth's best beaches lie along its Nantucket Sound side and include Seagull Beach and Smugglers Beach.

In and among Mid Cape towns are a number of freshwater kettle ponds, created by receding glaciers eons ago. Pond beaches are usually not as crowded as ocean beaches and have plenty of appeal for those who like cooling off in gentle water without the salt and sand. In Yarmouth Port, Dennis Pond attracts families to its shallow swimming area. Dennis's Scargo Lake has two public beaches, and Hathaway's Pond in Barnstable has a nice beach and rest rooms.

Biking

Bike enthusiasts are well placed on the Mid Cape: the scenic 25-mi Cape Cod Rail Trail begins in South Dennis, following the paved right-of-way of the old Penn Central Railroad, and ends in South Wellfleet.

Dining

The Mid Cape is chock-full of eateries, ranging from sedate, high-end haute cuisine houses such as Hyannis's Paddock, the Regatta of Cotuit, and Dennis's Red Pheasant to family places such as Barbyann's in Hyannis, or Jack's Outback in Yarmouth Port. Expect good fun and great eats at the area's dozens of clam shacks and other supercasual restaurants along Route 28 in Yarmouth and Dennis. If you simply want lots of choices, head to Barnstable and its villages, particularly Hyannis, where a stroll down Main Street will bring you to a dozen fine restaurants ranging from lunch joints to Thai, Italian, Cajun, and upscale American dining establishments.

CATEGORY	COST*
$$$$	over $26
$$$	$19–$26
$$	$11–$18
$	under $11

*per person for a main course at dinner

Lodging

On the northern (bay) side, Route 6A from Barnstable to Dennis has dozens of B&Bs, many in the elegant former homes of sea captains. In contrast, Route 28 on the south side has row after row of lodgings, from tacky roadside motels to medium-range family hotels, with larger seaside resorts along the side roads on Nantucket Sound. Main Street, Hyannis, is lined with motels, while several inns and B&Bs perch on side streets leading to Hyannis Harbor and Lewis Bay.

CATEGORY	COST*
$$$$	over $200
$$$	$150–$200
$$	$100–$150
$	under $100

*All prices are for a standard double room in high season, excluding 5.7% state tax and gratuities. Some inns add a 15% service charge.

Nightlife and the Arts

Since you'll pass an art gallery almost every minute on the drive along Route 6A between Barnstable and Dennis, you should stop in at some of these places, such as Cummaquid Fine Arts, which carries original contemporary art that's a decided improvement over the ubiquitous paintings of rowboats on beaches. Other gallery centers are on Main Street in Hyannis and on Main Street in Osterville.

As for summertime entertainment, the Mid Cape is ground zero. The Cape Cod Melody Tent, in Hyannis, has music, comedy, and even boxing matches, with internationally well-known performers ranging from Bill Cosby and George Carlin to singers Jimmy Cliff and Lyle Lovett. The Melody Tent—which really is a tent, albeit a large and comfortable one with a revolving stage—also produces children's matinee theater, with regular summer shows such as *Sleeping Beauty* and *The Frog Prince*. Your theater need can also be sated at the Cape Playhouse in Dennis, one of the country's oldest summer repertory theaters. Big stars who have come this way in the past include Henry Fonda, Gregory Peck, and Bette Davis. The Cape Playhouse also offers children's theater during the season. The Barnstable Comedy Club on Route 6A in Barnstable Village presents drama, sketches, and, yes, comedic works throughout the summer.

Nightlife is abundant in the Mid Cape, from bistros and bars that have regular entertainment—think Hyannis's Roadhouse Café for jazz to dance clubs like Pufferbellies in Hyannis, specializing in country line dancing. Special events such as the Boston Pops Esplanade Orchestra's Pops by the Sea concert, held on the Hyannis Village Green in August, are listed in local newspapers weekly.

Check out listings in the *Register,* the *Barnstable Patriot,* and the Tuesday and Friday editions of the *Cape Codder,* as well as the pullout section "Cape Week" in the Friday edition of the *Cape Cod Times.* You can pick up any of these publications at local supermarkets and convenience stores.

Outdoor Activities and Sports

Numerous fishing and tour boats depart Hyannis Harbor, Barnstable Harbor, and Dennis's Sesuit Harbor for trips ranging from deep-sea fishing excursions to harbor fishing, a favorite with the children. Barnstable Harbor is also the launch point for Hyannis Whale Watcher Cruises, which operates from spring through early fall. Canoeing and sea kayaking are excellent around the bay's marshy inlets, and windsurfing is popular at Hyannis's Kalmus Park Beach. Dennis's Swan River is great for kayaking and canoeing, and the Bass River, a border separating Yarmouth and Dennis, has river sightseeing excursions on a small boat, as well as fishing and, if you've got the permit, clamming.

Conservation-land walking trails are found in Yarmouth and Dennis, including a Dennis trail set up for hikers with vision impairments.

Shopping

Throughout the villages and towns of the Mid Cape, and particularly along Route 6A and the main streets of Hyannis, Centerville, Osterville, and Dennisport, are numerous boutiques, crafts shops, bookstores, antiques centers, candy shops (saltwater taffy, yes, but also exquisite chocolates and homemade fudge), and galleries. In general, look to the smaller towns and villages for specialty craft items such as Nantucket baskets, wicker furniture, and bird-watching esoterica. The Cape Cod Mall, between Routes 132 and 28 in Hyannis, has a range of clothing boutiques such as Ann Taylor Loft, the Gap, and Abercrombie and Fitch, as well as jewelry stores; specialty shops; and the anchor stores Macy's, Filene's, and Sears. Everyone is wild about Christmas Tree Shops, a local chain with stores in Yarmouth Port, West Yarmouth, West Dennis, and Hyannis that sells all sorts of amusing things at discount prices, including lava lamps, lanai furniture, candles, and cookies.

Exploring the Mid Cape

The Mid Cape includes the towns of Barnstable, Yarmouth, and Dennis, each divided into smaller townships and villages. The town of Barnstable, for example, consists of Barnstable Village, West Barnstable, Cotuit, Marstons Mills, Osterville, Centerville, and Hyannis, with the smaller quasi-villages (distinguished by their separate zip codes), of Craigville, Cummaquid, Hyannis Port, West Hyannis Port, and Wianno. Yarmouth contains Yarmouth Port, along on the north shore, and the mid and south villages of West Yarmouth and South Yarmouth. The town of Dennis's villages are easy to remember: Dennis, West Dennis, South Dennis, East Dennis, and Dennisport. Route 6A winds along the north shore through tree-shaded scenic towns and village centers,

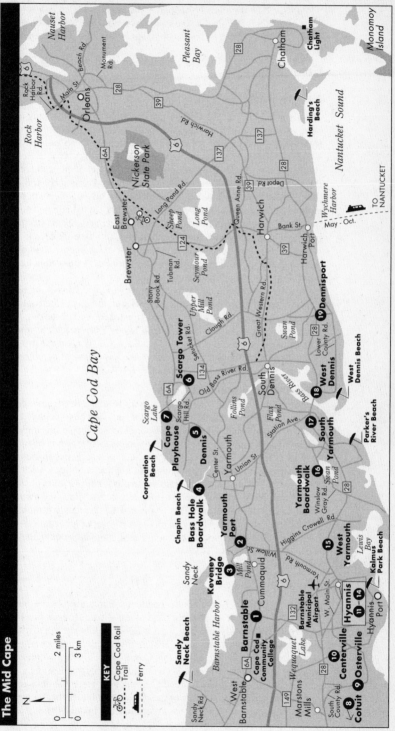

The Mid Cape

KEY

.... Cape Cod Rail Trail

---- Ferry

N

0   2 miles
0   3 km

Cape Cod Bay

Nantucket Sound

Monomoy Island

TO NANTUCKET

May - Oct.

Wychmere Harbor

Harding's Beach

Chatham Light

Chatham

Pleasant Bay

Nauset Harbor

Rock Harbor

Rock Harbor Rd.

Beach Rd.

Monument Rd.

Main St.

Orleans

Nickerson State Park

East Brewster

Brewster

Long Pond Rd.

Sheep Pond

Long Pond

Seymour Pond

Harwich

Queen Anne Rd.

Depot Rd.

Bank St.

Harwich Port

Dennisport

Swan Pond

West Dennis Beach

West Dennis

South Dennis

Bass River

Parker's River Beach

South Yarmouth

Yarmouth Boardwalk

Winslow Gray Rd.

Swan Pond

West Yarmouth

Lewis Bay

Kalmus Park Beach

Hyannis Port

Hyannis

Barnstable Municipal Airport

W. Main St.

Centerville

Osterville

Cotuit

Marstons Mills

Wequaquet Lake

South County Rd.

Cape Cod Community College

West Barnstable

Sandy Neck Rd.

Barnstable Harbor

Sandy Neck Beach

Sandy Neck

Barnstable

Cummaquid

Keveney Bridge

Mill Pond

Yarmouth Port

Bass Hole Boardwalk

Chapin Beach

Corporation Beach

Dennis

Cape Playhouse

Scargo Tower

Scargo Lake

Scargo Hill Rd.

Follins Pond

Flax Pond

Station Ave.

Old Bass River Rd.

Upper Mill Pond

Clough Rd.

Seuckel Rd.

Tubman Rd.

Stony Brook Rd.

Great Western Rd.

Higgins Crowell Rd.

Yarmouth Rd.

Willow St.

Center St.

Yarmouth

Union St.

Lower County Rd.

Harwich Rd.

6

6

6A

6A

28

28

28

28

39

39

39

137

137

124

134

149

132

6

① Barnstable
② Yarmouth Port
③ Keveney Bridge
④ Bass Hole Boardwalk
⑤ Dennis
⑥ Scargo Tower
⑦ Cape Playhouse
⑧ Cotuit
⑨ Osterville
⑩ Centerville
⑪–⑭ Hyannis
⑮ West Yarmouth
⑯ Yarmouth Boardwalk
⑰ South Yarmouth
⑱ West Dennis
⑲ Dennisport

while Route 28 dips south through some of the more overdeveloped parts of the Cape. Generally speaking, if you want to avoid malls, heavy traffic, and tacky motels, stay away from Route 28 from Falmouth to Chatham.

Great Itineraries

Numbers in the text correspond to numbers in the margin and on the Mid Cape map.

The crowded belly of the Cape is a center of activity unlike any other here, except perhaps Provincetown at the height of its summer crush. **Hyannis** ⑪–⑭ is the hub of Cape Cod, with plenty to do and see. Take a cruise around the harbor or go on a deep-sea fishing trip. There are shops and restaurants along Main Street and plenty of amusements for the youngsters. Kennedy fans might want to spend time at the JFK Museum. End the day with a concert at the Cape Cod Melody Tent. **Barnstable** ①, the county seat, has plenty of its own history and the wonderful Sandy Neck Beach to keep you occupied. Scenic Route 6A passes through **Yarmouth Port** ② and **Dennis** ⑤. There are beaches and salt marshes, museums, walking trails, and old graveyards all along this route if you feel like stopping. Yarmouth Port's **Bass Hole Boardwalk** ④ makes for a particularly beautiful stroll. In Dennis there are historic houses to tour, the Cape Museum of Fine Arts will introduce you to the work of Cape-associated artists, and the Cape Cod Rail Trail provides a premier path for bicyclists. Toward the end of the day, head for Scargo Hill and climb 30-ft **Scargo Tower** ⑥ to watch the sun set. At night you could catch a film at the Cape Cinema, on the grounds of the **Cape Playhouse** ⑦. The south shore has plenty of activities for children, from **Centerville** ⑩ to **Dennisport** ⑲.

When to Tour the Mid Cape

In the summer the Mid Cape bustles with tourists. But from Columbus Day weekend through April, the Mid Cape is a peaceful collection of towns and villages, with beaches (no fees) for strolling, trails for walking and biking, and a wealth of shopping and entertainment opportunities. Fall sees bursts of color in the easily accessed forests and marshes; winter brings a slower pace of life and a holiday spirit that locals love to celebrate with Christmas strolls featuring tours of shops, B&Bs, and old homes. Spring is also quiet, as the Mid Cape awakens to blooming trees, warmer days, reopened B&Bs, newly landscaped golf courses, and flower festivals. Boats come out of hibernation—the Hyannis Whale Watcher Cruises, for instance, starts its program in April.

Barnstable

❶ *11 mi east of Sandwich, 4 mi north of Hyannis.*

With nearly 50,000 year-round residents, Barnstable is the largest town on the Cape. It's also the second oldest—it was founded in 1639, two years after Sandwich. You'll get a feeling for its age in Barnstable Village, on and near Main Street (Route 6A), a lovely area of large old homes dominated by the Barnstable County Superior Courthouse. Behind the courthouse are the county lockup and a complex of government buildings, all best avoided. The Village Hall is home to the Barnstable Comedy Club, one of the oldest community theater groups in the country. Just north of the village are the marshes and beaches of Cape Cod Bay, including beautiful Sandy Neck Beach, as well as busy Barnstable Harbor. The Cape Cod Conservatory of Music and Arts and Cape Cod Community College are also in the vicinity.

The **Olde Colonial Courthouse,** built in 1772 as the colony's second courthouse, is the home of the historical society **Tales of Cape Cod** (✉ 3018

Main St. [Rte. 6A], ☎ 508/362–8927), which is restoring the courthouse to serve as a museum. A series of slide-illustrated lectures given by guest speakers is held Tuesday night in July and August. From the courthouse take a peek across the street at the old-fashioned English gardens at St. Mary's Episcopal Church.

The **Sturgis Library,** established in 1863, is in a 1644 building listed on the National Register of Historic Places. Its holdings date from the 17th century and include hundreds of maps and land charts, the definitive collection of Cape Cod genealogical material ($5 daily fee for non-residents), and an extensive maritime history collection. ✉ *3090 Main St. (Rte. 6A),* ☎ *508/362–6636,* WEB *www.capecod.net/sturgis.* ☉ *Mon., Wed., Fri. 10–5; Tues., Thurs. 1–8; Sat. 10–4; Sun. 1–5 (closed Sun. July–Aug.).*

Barnstable's maritime past is on display at the **Trayser Museum Complex.** On the National Register of Historic Places, the complex's red-painted brick main building houses a small collection of maritime exhibits—telescopes, captains' shaving boxes, items brought back from voyages, ship models, and paintings—as well as ivory, Sandwich glass, and arrowheads. The downstairs is a re-creation of the building as it looked in 1856, when it served as a customs house; don't miss the ornate bronze Corinthian columns. A restored customs-keeper's office with an original safe and a view of the harbor are on the second floor. Also on the grounds are a jail, circa 1690, with two cells bearing former inmates' graffiti, and a carriage house with early tools, fishing implements, and a 19th-century horse-drawn hearse. ✉ *3353 Main St. (Rte. 6A),* ☎ *508/362–2092.* ✏ *$2 suggested donation.* ☉ *Mid-June–Columbus Day, Tues.–Sun. 1:30–4:30.*

If you're interested in Cape history, the **Nickerson Memorial Room** at Cape Cod Community College has the largest collection of information on Cape Cod, including books, records, ships' logs, oral-history tapes, photographs, films, and more. It also has materials on the neighboring islands of Martha's Vineyard and Nantucket. ✉ *2240 Iyanough Rd., off Rte. 132, West Barnstable,* ☎ *508/362–2131 Ext. 4342,* WEB *www.capecod.mass.edu.* ☉ *Mon., Wed., Fri. 8:30–4:30; Tues. 9–12, 1–3.*

Dining and Lodging

$$–$$$ ✕ **Barnstable Tavern & Grille.** This handsome old building right in the village center, across from the courthouse, holds both a serious restaurant and a more relaxed tavern. The pasta Livorno (with jumbo shrimp, scallops, and lobster over linguine) and the Tavern Keeper's Special (a medley of seafood in a casserole) are local favorites. Lunch fare is lighter, and includes burgers, salads, and sandwiches. Look for live music on the patio Friday night. ✉ *3176 Main St. (Rte. 6A),* ☎ *508/362–2355. AE, MC, V.*

$$–$$$ ✕ **Dolphin Restaurant.** Want to know who's running for what local office, or what the next controversy is likely to be at the planning commission? Eavesdrop at the Dolphin. For decades this has been the place where opinions clash and deals are cut. There is a colonial feel inside, dark and inviting; the food clings to what might be called historically appropriate preparation. This is a place to go basic, ordering the baked stuffed haddock or the prime rib. The bar is small but welcoming, a good spot to chow down if you're dining solo. ✉ *3250 Main St. (Rte. 6A),* ☎ *508/362–6610. AE, MC, V.*

$–$$ ✕ **Mill Way Fish and Lobster.** This combination seafood market and ★ lunch place sits right on Barnstable Harbor, giving it access to the freshest seafood possible. It's tiny, with a fistful of outside picnic tables on a wooden deck and limited parking, but the fried clams and fish sandwiches are worth the inevitable wait. Arrive hungry and try the fat onion rings or the almost-too-big-for-lunch clambake, which comes with chowder, lobster, steamers, and an ear of corn. Mill Way is open until 7 for early dinners. ⊠ *275 Mill Way,* ☎ *508/362–2760. AE, D, MC, V. Closed Oct.–Mar.*

$–$$ ✕ **Whistleberries.** Most people settle for takeout from this tiny sandwich shop, but the lucky few who get a seat (two tables and three counter spots) are in for a treat. Breakfast is fresh muffins; "scrambled" eggs (they're actually steamed by the cappuccino machine); bagels; or burrito sandwiches stuffed with cheese, bacon, veggies, rice, beans, and sour cream. For lunch, try a wrap—there are many tempting choices, from barbecued chicken, turkey, or roast beef to specialties such as the Mediterranean, with red pepper, hummus, tabbouleh, tomato, onion, and feta cheese folded up in a spinach tortilla. ⊠ *3261 Main St. (Rte. 6A),* ☎ *508/362–6717. No credit cards. Closed Sun. No dinner.*

$$$ ▥ **Ashley Manor.** Set back from Old King's Highway behind private hedges and a wide lawn, this B&B is just a short walk from the village. The inn has preserved its antique wide-board floors and has open-hearth fireplaces, one with a beehive oven, in the living room, the dining room, and the keeping room. The rooms are toasty, too— all but one have a working fireplace or woodstove, and the four suites have whirlpool tubs. Antique and country furnishings, Oriental rugs, and glimmers of brass and crystal create an elegant atmosphere. Breakfast is served on the backyard terrace (overlooking fruit trees, a gazebo, and the tennis court) or in the formal dining room. Phones with data ports and TVs can be put in the rooms on request. ⊠ *3660 Main St. (Rte. 6A), Box 856, 02630,* ☎ *508/362–8044 or 888/535–2246,* 🖷 *508/362–9927,* 🕸 *www.ashleymanor.net. 2 rooms, 4 suites. Air-conditioning, tennis court, bicycles. No smoking. D, MC, V. BP.*

$$$ ▥ **Beechwood Inn.** Debbie and Ken Traugot's yellow and pale green
★ 1853 Queen Anne is trimmed with gingerbread, wrapped by a wide porch with wicker furniture and a glider swing, and shaded by old beech trees. Although the parlor is pure mahogany-and-red-velvet Victorian, guest rooms (all with queen- or king-size beds) have antiques in lighter Victorian styles, including Eastlake. Several rooms have fireplaces, and one room has a bay view. Bathrooms have pedestal sinks and antique lighting fixtures. Breakfast is served in the dining room, which has a pressed-tin ceiling, a fireplace, and lace-covered tables. Afternoon tea and homemade snacks are also available. ⊠ *2839 Main St. (Rte. 6A), 02630,* ☎ *508/362–6618 or 800/609–6618,* 🖷 *508/362–0298,* 🕸 *www.beechwoodinn.com. 6 rooms. Air-conditioning, refrigerators, bicycles. No smoking. AE, D, MC, V. BP.*

$$$ ▥ **Cobb's Cove.** Proprietors Henri-Jean and Evelyn Chester have created a rustic hideaway for guests who want both quiet and comfort. Lush, wild gardens filled with bird feeders and fountains surround the house. The interior has huge wood beams, rough burlap walls, and heavy wooden doors studded (just as they were in the olden days) with nail heads. Guest rooms are large; each has a dressing area and a private bath with whirlpool tub and robes. The two top-floor rooms have glass walls, and from the sitting areas you can enjoy the spectacular view of Cape Cod Bay. Breakfast is served in the rustic dining room, dominated by a Count Rumford–designed fireplace. Historic Barnstable village, beaches, and even whale-watching boats in the marina are only a short stroll away. ⊠ *31 Powder Hill Rd., Box 208, 02630,* ☎ *877/ 378–5172* 🖷 🖷 *or 508/362–9356,* 🕸 *www.cobbscove.com. 6 rooms. No smoking. AE, D, MC, V. BP.*

$$$ ▥ **Heaven on High.** There's no more appropriately named B&B on the
★ Cape. Deanna and Gib Katten's haven is indeed heaven, nestled high on a hill, on one of the Cape's oldest roads, overlooking dunes, Great Salt Marsh, and the Bay at Sandy Neck. The modern house's decor is a meld

of California beach house and Cape Cod comfort—light, airy, and breezy. The great room is filled with overstuffed chairs and couches, a fireplace, TV, and natural oak floors. Sliding glass doors lead to the living room and also to the deck, which runs the full length of the house, offering panoramic views of sand and surf. Deanna is an avid collector of, well, you name it, and she has filled every nook with her treasures. Each room is named for the expansive collection that it houses; the Silhouettes and Mirrors room, for instance, has both commodities in all shapes and sizes, as well as a queen-size bed, a fireplace, and a large private deck. Breakfast, served on fine china and Tiffany sterling, is heavenly. ✉ *70 High St., Box 346, West Barnstable, 02668,* ☎ *508/362–4441 or 800/362–4044,* ℻ *508/362–4465,* WEB *www.heavenonhigh. com. 3 rooms. Air-conditioning, refrigerators, putting green. No smoking, no kids under 16. D, MC, V. Closed Nov.–Dec. BP.*

$$$ 🏠 **Lamb and Lion Inn** More than a typical B&B, Lamb and Lion occupies a 1740 farmhouse and barn, as well as several additions, with rooms and suites gathered around a courtyard and large swimming pool. Several rooms open directly onto the courtyard, while others have private decks and entrances. Inside, decor ranges from summery cottage rooms, bright with blue-and-white-stripe wallpaper and wicker chairs, to more staid rooms adorned with antiques and dark woods. The Innkeeper's Pride Suite has a fireplace and sunken tub that opens to a private deck; the rustic but comfortable Barn-Stable, in the original barn, has three sleeping lofts that can accommodate six. Personal service includes pickups and drop-offs from local ferries and the Barnstable Municipal Airport. The Lamb and Lion accepts children (off-season) and pets (extra fee). ✉ *2504 Main St. (Rte. 6A), Box 511, Barnstable 02630,* ☎ *508/362–6823 or 800/909–6923,* ℻ *508/362–0227,* WEB *www. lambandlion.com. 4 rooms, 6 suites. Pool, hot tub, shop. MC, V. CP.*

$$ 🏠 **Acworth Inn.** This historic 1860 house has large rooms and a spa-
★ cious two-room suite. The rooms are decorated with soft pastels, lacy designer linens, and tasteful hand-painted furniture. The suite, with modern furnishings, also has a fireplace, whirlpool tub, TV/VCR, and refrigerator. Scrumptious breakfast is family-style and includes homemade granola; fresh muffins and fruit or chilled fruit soup; yogurt; and your choice of waffles, pancakes, or an omelet. The inn is 1 mi east of Barnstable Village. ✉ *4352 Main St. (Rte. 6A), Box 256, Cummaquid 02637,* ☎ *508/362–3330 or 800/362–6363,* ℻ *508/375–0304,* WEB *www.acworthinn.com. 4 rooms, 1 suite. Air-conditioning, bicycles. No smoking. AE, D, MC, V. BP.*

$$ 🏠 **Honeysuckle Hill.** Innkeepers Mary and Bill Kilburn ran an inn in Vermont before relocating to the Cape in 1998, and their experience and graciousness shine through in lots of little touches: a guest fridge stocked with sodas and water bottles, beach chairs with umbrellas (perfect for nearby Sandy Neck Beach), and an always-full cookie jar in the sunny dining room. The airy, country-style guest rooms in this expansive, gray-shingle 1810 Queen Anne–style cottage have lots of white wicker, featherbeds, checked curtains, and pastel-painted floors. The spacious second-floor Wisteria Room, overlooking the lush yard and flower gardens, is a particularly comfortable retreat, with its own entrance under a wisteria arbor. The screened-in porch is a peaceful place for early morning coffee. ✉ *591 Rte. 6A, West Barnstable 02668,* ☎ *508/362–8418 or 866/444–5522,* ℻ *508/362–8386,* WEB *www. honeysucklehill.com. 4 rooms, 1 suite. Air-conditioning. No smoking. AE, D, MC, V. BP.*

Nightlife and the Arts

The **Barnstable Comedy Club** (✉ Village Hall, Rte. 6A, ☎ 508/362–6333), the Cape's oldest amateur theater group (it celebrated its 75th anniversary in 1997), gives much-praised musical and dramatic performances throughout the year. Some folks who appeared here before they made it big are Geena Davis, Frances McDormand, and Kurt Vonnegut, a past president of the BCC.

Outdoor Activities and Sports

BEACH

Hovering above Barnstable Harbor and the 4,000-acre **Great Salt Marsh, Sandy Neck Beach** stretches some 6 mi across a peninsula that ends at **Sandy Neck Light.** The beach is one of the Cape's most beautiful—dunes, sand, and sea spread endlessly east, west, and north. The marsh used to be harvested for salt hay; now it's a haven for birds, which are out and about in the greatest numbers morning and evening, at low tide, and during spring and fall migration. The lighthouse, standing just a few feet from eroding shoreline at the tip of the neck, has been out of commission since 1952. It was built in 1857 to replace an 1827 light, and it used to run on acetylene gas. It is now privately owned and no longer accessible from the beach. If you like to hike, ask at the ranger station for a trail brochure. The main beach at Sandy Neck has lifeguards, a snack bar, rest rooms, and showers. As you travel east along Route 6A from Sandwich, Sandy Neck Road is just *before* the Barnstable line, although the beach itself is in West Barnstable. ⊠ *Sandy Neck Rd., West Barnstable,* ☎ *508/362–8300.* ⌦ *Parking $10 Memorial Day–Labor Day.* ☉ *Daily 9–9, but staffed only until 5 PM.*

FISHING

The **Barnstable Harbor Charter Fleet** (⊠ 186 Millway, ☎ 508/362–3908) has fishing trips on 10 sportfishing vessels from spring through fall. Reservations are recommended but not required.

WHALE-WATCHING

On **Hyannis Whale Watcher Cruises** out of Barnstable Harbor, a naturalist narrates and comments on whale sightings and the natural history of Cape Cod Bay. Trips last about four hours, there are concessions on board, and in July and August you can cruise at sunset, too. Reservations are required; book a day or two in advance. ⊠ *Mill Way, Millway Marina, off Phinney's La.,* ☎ *508/362–6088 or 800/287–0374,* WEB *www.whales.net.* ⌦ *$26.* ☉ *Apr.–Oct.*

Shopping

Black's Handweaving Shop (⊠ 597 Rte. 6A, West Barnstable, ☎ 508/362–3955), in a barnlike shop with working looms, makes beautiful handwoven goods in traditional and jacquard weaves. If you don't see what you want on display, you can commission it.

The **Crystal Pineapple** (⊠ 1540 Rte. 6A, West Barnstable, ☎ 508/362–3128 or 800/462–4009) has cranberry glass and many collectibles lines, including Dept. 56, Snowbabies, Swarovski crystal, and Disney Classics.

Maps of Antiquity (⊠ 1022 Rte. 6A, West Barnstable, ☎ 508/362–7169) sells original and reproduction maps of Cape Cod, New England, and other parts of the world. Some date to the 1700s.

West Barnstable Tables (⊠ Rte. 149, West Barnstable, ☎ 508/362–2676) has handcrafted tables, chairs, chests, and a range of furniture made from the finest woods.

Whippletree (⊠ 660 Rte. 6A, West Barnstable, ☎ 508/362–3320) is a large barn, decorated for each season and filled with country gift items and a year-round Christmas section. Goods include German nutcrackers, from Prussian soldiers to Casanovas.

Yarmouth Port

 4 mi northeast of Hyannis, 21 mi east of the Sagamore Bridge, 4 mi east of Barnstable.

Once known as Mattacheese, or "the planting lands," Yarmouth was settled in 1639 by farmers from the Plymouth Bay Colony. Yarmouth Port wasn't incorporated as a separate village until 1829. By then the Cape had begun a thriving maritime industry, and men turned to the sea to make their fortunes. Many impressive sea captains' houses—some now B&Bs and museums—still line the always-enchanting Route 6A, as well as side streets, and Yarmouth Port has some real old-time stores in town. Just a mile's drive north of Route 6A is the small but lovely Gray's Beach, where a boardwalk at the section called Bass Hole stretches hundreds of feet over the wide marsh and where the Callery-Darling conservation land trails loop through forest and marshland.

For a peek into the past, make a stop at **Hallet's,** a country drugstore preserved as it was in 1889, when the current owner's grandfather, Thacher Hallet, opened it. Hallet served not only as druggist but also as postmaster and justice of the peace. At the all-marble soda fountain with swivel stools, you can order the secret-recipe ice cream soda and, in season, an inexpensive breakfast or lunch. Above Hallet's Store, the **Thacher Taylor Hallet Museum** displays photographs and memorabilia of Yarmouth Port and the Hallet family. ⊠ *139 Hallet St. (Rte. 6A),* ☎ *508/362–3362.* ⊠ *Donations accepted for museum.* ☉ *Apr.–mid-Nov.; call for hrs.*

The 1886 **Village Pump,** (⊠ 220 Main St.) a black wrought-iron mechanism long used for drawing household water, is topped by a lantern and surrounded by ironwork with cutouts of birds and animals. In front is a stone trough that was used for watering horses. It's across from the Parnassus Book Service. The 1696 **Old Yarmouth Inn** (⊠ 223 Main St. [Rte. 6A], near Summer St., ☎ 508/362–9962), near the village pump, is the Cape's oldest inn and a onetime stagecoach stop.

The **Botanical Trails of the Historical Society of Old Yarmouth,** behind the post office (⊠ 231 Main St.), provide a good look at the area's flora in 50 acres of oak and pine woods and a pond, accented by blueberries, lady's slippers, Indian pipes, rhododendrons, hollies, and more. Stone markers and arrows point out the 2 mi of trails; you'll find trail maps in the gatehouse mailbox. Just beyond the historical society's trails, the little **Kelley Chapel** was built in 1873 by a father for a daughter grieving over the death of a child. An iron woodstove and a pump organ dominate the simple interior. ⊠ *Off Main St. (Rte. 6A).* ⊠ *$1 suggested donation.* ☉ *Gatehouse July–Aug., daily 1–4. Trails during daylight hrs year-round.*

The 1780 **Winslow Crocker House** is an elegantly symmetrical two-story Georgian with 12-over-12 small-pane windows and rich paneling in every room. After Crocker's death, his two sons built a wall dividing the house in half. The house was moved here from West Barnstable in 1936 by Mary Thacher, who donated it—along with her collection of 17th- to 19th-century furniture, pewter, hooked rugs, and ceramics—to the Society for the Preservation of New England Antiquities, which operates it as a museum. Tours are given every hour on the hour. ⊠ *250 Main St. (Rte. 6A),* ☎ *508/362–4385.* ⊠ *$5.* ☉ *June–mid-Oct., weekends 11–4.*

Built in 1840 onto an existing 1740 house for a sea captain in the China trade, then bought by another, who swapped it with a third captain, the **Captain Bangs Hallet House** is a white Greek Revival building with a hitching post out front and a weeping beech in back. The house and its contents typify a 19th-century sea captain's home, with pieces of pewter, china, nautical equipment, antique toys and clothing, and more on display. The kitchen has the original 1740 brick beehive oven and butter churns. ⊠ *11 Strawberry La., off Rte. 6A,* ☎ *508/362–3021.* ☞ *$3.* ⊙ *June–Oct., Sun. 1–3:30; tours at 1, 2, and 3.*

Purchased in 1640 and established as a prosperous farm in the late 1700s, the **Taylor-Bray Farm** (⊠ Bray Farm Rd., ☎ 508/385–6499) is listed on the National Register of Historic Places. The farm is occasionally open to the public by appointment through the caretaker/tenants. As of mid-2001, the farm was without a caretaker, but the town is searching. Call for information. The farm has picnic tables, walking trails, and a great view of the tidal marsh.

For a scenic loop with little traffic, turn north off Route 6A in town onto Church Street or Thacher Street, then left onto Thacher Shore Road. In fall this route is especially beautiful, with its impressive stands of blazing-red burning bush. Wooded segments alternate with open views of marsh. Keep bearing right, and at the WATER STREET sign, the dirt road on the right will bring you to a wide-open view of marshland as it meets the bay. Don't drive in too far, or you may get stuck. As you ❸ come out, a right turn will take you to **Keveney Bridge,** a one-lane wooden bridge over marshy Mill Pond, and back to Route 6A.

One of Yarmouth Port's most beautiful areas is Bass Hole, which ★ ☙ ❹ stretches from Homer's Dock Road to the salt marsh. **Bass Hole Boardwalk** (⊠ trail entrance on Center St. near Gray's Beach parking lot) extends over a marshy creek; amid the salt marshes, vegetated wetlands, and upland woods meander the 2½-mi **Callery-Darling nature trails.** Gray's Beach is a little crescent of sand with still water good for children—but don't go beyond the roped-in swimming area, the only section where the current isn't strong. At the end of the boardwalk, benches provide a place to relax and look out over abundant marsh life and, across the creek, the beautiful, sandy shores of Dennis's Chapin Beach. At low tide you can walk out on the flats for almost a mile. It's a far cry from the days when an 18th-century harbor here was the site of a schooner shipyard.

Dining and Lodging

$$–$$$$ ✕ **Abbicci.** Unassuming to a fault from the outside, Abbicci tells an entirely different story on the inside, with stunning modern decor, explosions of color, and a handsome black-slate bar. One of the first to bring northern Italian cooking to Cape Cod, chef-owner Marietta Hickey has remained true to the tradition and ahead of the crowd. She prepares rich and full-tasting yet heart-healthy fare, thanks to a light touch with olive oil and a watchful eye over the fat content of her dishes. One of the most pleasing is braised rabbit with fresh green beans and tiny onions over garlic mashed potatoes. In summer, fish and a dozen elegant pasta dishes take over. ⊠ *43 Main St. (Rte. 6A),* ☎ *508/362–3501. AE, D, DC, MC, V.*

$$–$$$ ✕ **Howes Cottage.** The main dining area of this pretty 1849 Gothic Revival house contains knickknacks and antiques, and a striking maple bar dominates the lounge. You'll find wide-plank pine floors and antique hutches throughout, as well as a hearth in the back room. The menu concentrates on regional American cuisine and includes rack of lamb, seared beef tenderloin with red-chili chutney, and a variety of pastas and seafood. The restaurant is perhaps overly ambitious, serving breakfast, lunch, and dinner in season, plus an all-day tavern menu, and service doesn't always meet the standard of the food.

⊠ *134 Main St. (Rte. 6A),* ☎ *508/362–9866. Reservations essential. AE, D, MC, V. Closed Mon. in off-season; no breakfast.*

$$–$$$ ✕ **Inaho.** Yuji Watanabe, the chef-owner of the Cape's best Japanese
★ restaurant, makes early morning journeys to Boston's fish markets to shop for the freshest local catch. His selection of sushi and sashimi is vast and artful, and vegetable and seafood tempura come out of the kitchen fluffy and light. If you're a teriyaki lover, you can't do any better than the chicken's beautiful blend of sweet and sour. One remarkable element of the restaurant is its artful lighting: small pinpoint lights on the food accentuate the presentation in a dramatic way. The serene and simple Japanese garden out back has a traditional goldfish pond. ⊠ *157 Main St. (Rte. 6A),* ☎ *508/362–5522. MC, V. Closed Mon. No lunch.*

$–$$ ✕ **Jack's Outback.** Tough to find, tough to forget, this eccentric little
★ serve-yourself-pretty-much-anything-you-want joint is right down the driveway from Inaho and goes by the motto "Good food, lousy service." The quintessential local hangout, it lives up to its motto in every way. Solid breakfasts give way by midday to thick burgers, freshly concocted sandwiches, pasta salads, homemade soups, and traditional home-cooked favorites such as Yankee pot roast and fried chicken. One of the owners, Jack Braginton-Smith, is a local historian of note. (As far as locals are concerned, if he *doesn't* insult you on the way in and out, you've been insulted.) Jack's has no liquor license, and you may not BYOB. ⊠ *161 Main St. (Rte. 6A),* ☎ *508/362–6690. Reservations not accepted. No credit cards. No dinner.*

$$$ ⊞ **Wedgewood Inn.** This handsome 1812 Greek Revival building,
★ white with black shutters and a fanlight, is on the National Register of Historic Places. The interior is sophisticated but welcoming, with a mix of fine colonial antiques, upholstered wing chairs, sporting prints, and maritime paintings. In the guest rooms, antique quilts top handcrafted cherry pencil-post beds. Two spacious suites in the main building have canopy beds, fireplaces, and porches; one has a separate sitting room. Three additional suites are in the restored barn behind the house and have king-size beds, TVs, and large bathrooms. Innkeeper Gerrie Graham cooks elegant breakfasts such as Belgian waffles with whipped cream and strawberries or eggs with hollandaise sauce. Her husband, Milt, serves breakfast and helps you make plans for the day. ⊠ *83 Main St. (Rte. 6A), 02675,* ☎ *508/362–5157 or 508/362–9178,* FAX *508/362–5851,* WEB *www.wedgewood-inn.com. 4 rooms, 5 suites. Air-conditioning. No smoking. AE, MC, V. BP.*

$$–$$$ ⊞ **Blueberry Manor.** The living room of this quiet, early 19th-century Greek Revival pairs Victorian furnishings and a marble fireplace with modern amenities, including a TV/VCR, a stereo, and a stash of puzzles, games, and books. Guest room furnishings are traditional, but there are no fussy lace treatments or curio shelves. The Lavender Room has a queen-size four-poster bed with a handmade quilt, an antique armoire, and a modern bath under the eaves with a skylight. The Rose Room has an exquisitely painted queen-size bed and cheery pink walls. The Willow Garden Suite, with a loft, fireplace, and private entrance, accommodates as many as four. The fruit from the blueberry bushes in the lush backyard and garden turns up at breakfast in homemade coffee cakes and other baked goods. ⊠ *438 Main St. (Rte. 6A), 02675,* ☎ *508/362–7620,* FAX *508/362–0053,* WEB *www.blueberrymanor.com. 3 rooms, 1 suite. Air-conditioning. No smoking. AE, MC, V. BP.*

$$–$$$ ⊞ **The Inn at Cape Cod.** A stately white Greek Revival building with imposing columns, the inn sits back from Route 6A in a parklike lawn adjacent to the Botanical Trails. The interior is eclectic. On the first floor, the large Joshua Sears Room, with a mahogany king four-poster bed, Oriental rug, and antique furnishings, is a traditional Victorian chamber, while the Far East Room—iron-and-wicker bed, Chinese curio chest, and wicker wing chairs—would feel at home in Beijing's Forbidden City. Upstairs, the romantic Village Suite with its Italian armoire and cherry writing desk opens to the front porch, and the frilly Victorian Room has its own fireplace. Some smaller rooms, particularly the basic pine Guest Room, are pint-size. Innkeepers Doug and Mary Heywood serve a hearty buffet breakfast and can accommodate children age 8 and older with a rollaway bed. ⊠ *4 Summer St., 02675,* ☎ *508/375–0590 or 800/850–7301,* FAX *508/362–9520,* WEB *www. capecodtravel.com/innatcapecod. 7 rooms, 1 suite. Air-conditioning. No smoking. AE, D, DC, MC, V. BP.*

$$ 🏠 **Lane's End Cottage.** Owner-innkeeper Valerie Butler's house indeed
★ sits at the end of a dirt lane, moved here in 1860 by oxen to make room for the neighboring church. And what a magical setting it is: a white picket fence, an English cottage garden, an English antiques–filled common room–library with a fireplace. Each guest room has tasteful appointments and beds with firm mattresses, feather comforters, and white spreads. The sun-drenched first-floor Terrace Room has a fireplace and French doors that lead to a cobblestone patio overlooking a flower-rimmed garden. There's no air-conditioning, but the rooms have fans, and the cottage is shaded by trees. Pets are allowed with prior notice—but only in the off-season. ⊠ *268 Main St. (Rte. 6A), 02675,* ☎ *508/362–5298. 3 rooms. Library. No smoking. No credit cards. BP.*

$–$$ 🏠 **Village Inn.** Guest rooms, with wide pine floorboards, are snug in this old-fashioned (some might say faded) 1795 sea captain's house. The Provincetown Room once served as the house's schoolroom; the original (but no longer used) light fixtures are still in place. Room sizes and amenities fluctuate; the tiny Wellfleet Room, which has a half-size tub, may be too small for some, but it's a bargain. Families should note that the Brewster, Truro, and Hyannis rooms connect and that the first-floor Yarmouth Room is the most spacious, with its own library, bathroom with fireplace, and private entrance. The common rooms have as many books as some public libraries. Children of all ages are welcome. Despite being closed in the off-season, Village Inn is open for Thanksgiving weekend and the Christmas holidays. ⊠ *92 Main St. (Rte. 6A), Box 1, 02675,* ☎ *508/362–3182,* WEB *www.thevillageinncapecod.com. 10 rooms, 8 with bath. No smoking. MC, V. BP. Closed mid-Oct.–Apr.*

Nightlife and the Arts

Oliver's (⊠ 6 Bray Farm Rd., off Rte. 6A, ☎ 508/362–6062) has live acoustic music in its tavern on weekends year-round.

Shopping

Cummaquid Fine Arts (⊠ 4275 Rte. 6A, Cummaquid, ☎ 508/362–2593) has works by contemporary resident Cape Cod artists, beautifully displayed in an old home.

Parnassus Book Service (⊠ 220 Main St. [Rte. 6A], ☎ 508/362–6420), occupying a three-story 1840 former general store, has a huge selection of old and new books—Cape Cod, maritime, Americana, antiquarian, and others—and is a great place to browse. Its book stall, outside on the building's side, is open 24 hours a day and works on the honor system—tally up your purchases and leave the money in the mail slot.) Parnassus also carries Robert Bateman's nature prints.

Peach Tree Designs (⊠ 173 Main St. [Rte. 6A], ☎ 508/362–8317) carries home furnishings and decorative accessories, some from local craftspeople, all beautifully made.

Pewter Crafters of Cape Cod (⊠ 933 Main St. [Rte. 6A], ☎ 508/362–3407) handcrafts traditional and contemporary pewter objects, from baby cups to tea services.

Dennis

❺ *4½ mi north of South Yarmouth, 4 mi east of Yarmouth Port, 5 mi north of Dennisport.*

The backstreets of Dennis still retain the colonial charm of seafaring days. The town was named for Reverend Josiah Dennis and incorporated in 1793. There were 379 sea captains living in Dennis when fishing, salt making, and shipbuilding were the main industries, and the elegant houses they constructed—now museums and B&Bs—still line the streets. In 1816 Dennis resident Henry Hall discovered that adding sand to his cranberry fields' soil improved the quality and quantity of the fruit. The decades after saw cranberry farming and tourism become the Cape's main commercial enterprises. Dennis has a number of conservation areas and nature trails and numerous freshwater ponds for swimming. The village center has antiques shops, general stores, a post office, and ice cream shops. There's also a village green with a bandstand, home to occasional summer concerts.

West Dennis and Dennisport, off Route 28 on the south shore of the Cape (the triceps, if you will), are covered separately below.

The **Josiah Dennis Manse,** a saltbox house with add-ons, was built in 1736 for Reverend Josiah Dennis. Inside, the home reflects life in Reverend Dennis's day. A child's room includes antique furniture and toys, the keeping room has a fireplace and cooking utensils, and the attic exhibits spinning and weaving equipment. Throughout you'll see china, pewter, and portraits of sea captains. The Maritime Wing has ship models, paintings, nautical artifacts, and more. On the grounds is a 1770 one-room schoolhouse, furnished with wood-and-wrought-iron desks and chairs. ⊠ *77 Nobscussett Rd., at Whig St.,* ☎ *508/385-2232.* ☞ *Donations accepted.* ☉ *Late June–Sept., Tues. 10–noon, Thurs. 2–4.*

❻ On a clear day, from the top of **Scargo Tower,** you'll have unbeatable panoramic views of Scargo Lake, the village's scattered houses below, Cape Cod Bay, and distant Provincetown. A wooden tower built on this site in 1874 was one of the Cape's first tourist attractions; visitors would pay 5¢ to climb to the top for the views. That tower burned down, and the present all-stone 30-ft tower was built in 1901 to replace it. Winding stairs bring you to the top; don't forget to read the unsightly, but amusing, graffiti on the way up. Expect crowds at sunrise and sunset. ⊠ *Scargo Hill Rd., off Rte. 6A or Old Bass River Rd.* ☞ *Free.* ☉ *Daily sunrise–sunset.*

| NEED A BREAK? | Dip into homemade ice cream and frozen yogurt at the **Ice Cream Smuggler** (⊠ 716 Main St. [Rte. 6A], across the street from the town green and cemetery, ☎ 508/385–5307). |

For Broadway-style dramas, comedies, and musicals, as well as children's plays, you can attend a production at the **Cape Playhouse,** the oldest professional summer theater in the country. In 1927 Raymond Moore, who had been working with a theatrical troupe in Provincetown, bought an 1838 former Unitarian Meeting House and converted it into a theater. The original pews still serve as seats. The opening performance was *The Guardsman,* starring Basil Rathbone; other stars who performed here in the early days, some in their professional stage debuts, include Bette Davis (who first worked here as an usher), Gregory Peck, Lana Turner, Ginger Rogers, Humphrey Bogart, Tallulah Bankhead, and Henry Fonda, who appeared with his then-unknown 20-year-old daughter, Jane. Cape resident Shirley Booth was such an admirer of the theater she donated her Oscar (for *Come Back Little Sheba*) and her Emmy (for *Hazel*) to the theater; both are on display in the lobby during the season. Behind-the-scene tours are also given in season; call for a schedule. The Playhouse offers children's theater on Friday morning during July and August. Also on the 26-acre property, now known as the Cape Playhouse Center for the Arts, are a restaurant, the **Cape Museum of Fine Arts,** and the **Cape Cinema,** whose exterior was designed in the style of the Congregational church in Centerville. Inside, a 6,400-square-ft mural of heavenly skies—designed by Massachusetts artist Rockwell Kent, who also designed the gold-sunburst curtain—covers the ceiling. ⊠ *820 Main St. (Rte. 6A),* ☎ *508/385–3911 or 877/385–3911,* WEB *www.capecodtravel.com/capeplayhouse.* ⊙ *Call for tour schedule.*

The **Cape Museum of Fine Arts** exhibits a permanent collection of more than 850 works by Cape-associated artists. Important pieces include a portrait of a fisherman's wife by Charles Hawthorne, the father of the Provincetown art colony; a 1924 portrait of a Portuguese fisherman's daughter by William Paxton, one of the first artists to summer in Provincetown; a collection of wood-block prints by Varujan Boghosian, a member of Provincetown's Long Point Gallery cooperative; an oil sketch by Karl Knaths, who painted in Provincetown from 1919 until his death in 1971; and works by abstract expressionist Hans Hoffman and many of his students. The museum also hosts film festivals, lectures, art classes, and trips. ⊠ *60 Hope La. (on the grounds of the Cape Playhouse), off Rte. 6A,* ☎ *508/385–4477,* WEB *www.cmfa.org.* ⊡ *$5.* ⊙ *Mid-May–mid-Oct., Mon.–Sat. 10–5, Sun. 1–5; mid-Oct.–mid-May, Tues.–Sat. 10–5, Sun. 1–5.*

Dining and Lodging

$$–$$$ ✕ **Gina's by the Sea.** Some places are less than the sum of their parts; Gina's is more. The funky old building is tucked into a sand dune, so that the aroma of fine northern Italian cooking blends with a fresh breeze off the bay. The dining room is tasteful, cozy, and especially wonderful in the fall when the fireplace is blazing. Blackboard specials could include angel-hair pasta or linguine with clams. If you don't want a long wait, come early or late. ⊠ *134 Taunton Ave.,* ☎ *508/385–3213. Reservations not accepted. AE, MC, V. Closed Dec.–Mar. and Mon–Wed. Oct.–Nov. No lunch Apr.–June and Sept.–Nov.*

$$–$$$ ✕ **Red Pheasant.** This is one of the Cape's best cozy country inns, with
★ a consistently good kitchen, where hearty American food is prepared with elaborate sauces and herb combinations. For instance, rack of lamb is served with an intense port-and-rosemary reduction, and exquisitely grilled veal chops come with a dense red wine and Portobello mushroom sauce. In fall look for the specialty game dishes, including venison and quail. Deep-fried goat cheese ravioli is another winner. Try to reserve a table in the more intimate Garden Room. The expansive wine list is excellent. Men may want to wear a jacket. ⊠ *905 Main St. (Rte. 6A),* ☎ *508/385–2133 or 800/480–2133. Reservations essential. D, MC, V. No lunch.*

$$–$$$ ✕ **Scargo Café.** Because the Cape Playhouse is right across the street, this café is a favorite before- and after-show haunt. Excellent early bird specials for the show crowd include scallops cooked in Harpoon beer (a Boston brew) and fettuccine Alfredo. The menu focuses on lighter fare for summer, but there's still plenty of richness, as well as a rather good wine cellar to complement it. Mussels Ferdinand features farm-

raised mussels with a buttery Pernod sauce over pasta. An added plus: the kitchen stays open until midnight in summer. ⊠ *799 Main St. (Rte. 6A),* ☎ *508/385–8200. AE, D, MC, V.*

$–$$ ✕ **Cap'n Frosty's.** This locally much-acclaimed though very modest fried-seafood-and-ice-cream joint has a regular menu, a small specials board, and a counter where you order and take a number written on a french fries box. The staff is young and hard working, pumping out fresh fried clams and fish-and-chips on paper plates. All frying is done in 100% canola oil, and rice pilaf is offered as a substitute for fries. There's seating inside as well as outside on a shady brick patio. ⊠ *219 Main St. (Rte. 6A),* ☎ *508/385–8548. Reservations not accepted. No credit cards. Closed Labor Day–Mar.*

$–$$ ✕ **Red Cottage Restaurant.** Up Old Bass River Road just ½ mi north of the town hall, the Red Cottage is indeed a red cottage that serves breakfast and lunch year-round. This friendly place has a long counter with swivel stools, and the grill is in plain view. The breakfasts are better than the lunches, but both are no-nonsense and just plain reliably good. The menu has something of an emphasis on "health," meaning egg-white omelets are available alongside the usuals, and "lite" cheese is used. ⊠ *36 Old Bass River Rd.,* ☎ *508/394–2923. Reservations not accepted. No credit cards. No dinner.*

$$ ⊡ **Four Chimneys Inn.** This three-story, four-chimney 1881 Queen Anne Victorian gem, once home to the town doctor, is now a relaxing getaway. Rooms vary in size and decor, but all have cherry four-poster, wicker, or antique pine or oak beds; chenille comforters; and hand-stenciled trim. Three rooms have fireplaces, and all have views of either Scargo Lake (across the street) or of the surrounding woods and flowering gardens. Owners Kelly and Barry Steele, who bought the inn in 2001, whip up a breakfast that might include egg casserole or pancakes, which you can enjoy in the high-ceiling dining room; the screened-in summer porch, with its lovely garden views, is an even more soothing place to start the day. Having afternoon tea under the wisteria-draped arbor is a wonderful way to wind down. ⊠ *946 Main St. (Rte. 6A), 02638,* ☎ *508/385–6317 or 800/874–5502,* FAX *508/385–6285,* WEB *www.fourchimneysinn.com. 7 rooms. No smoking. AE, MC, V. BP.*

$$ ⊡ **Isaiah Hall B&B Inn.** Lilacs and pink roses trail along the white picket ★ fence outside this 1857 Greek Revival farmhouse on a residential road on the bay side of town. Guest rooms have country antiques, floral-print wallpapers, and TVs, and are adorned with such homey touches as quilts and Priscilla curtains. In the attached carriage house, rooms have three walls stenciled white and one knotty pine, and some have small balconies overlooking a wooded lawn with gardens, grape arbors, and berry bushes. The carriage-house suite has a king-size bed, a separate sitting area with a pullout couch, and a refrigerator. Make-it-yourself popcorn, tea, coffee, and soft drinks are always available. ⊠ *152 Whig St., Box 1007, 02638,* ☎ *508/385–9928 or 800/736–0160,* FAX *508/385–5879,* WEB *www.isaiahhallinn.com. 9 rooms, 1 suite. Picnic area, air-conditioning, badminton, croquet. No smoking. AE, D, MC, V. Closed mid-Oct.–early May. CP.*

$$ ⊡ **Scargo Manor.** This 1895 sea captain's home has a prime location on Scargo Lake. Inside, there's plenty of room to spread out on the big screened porch with green wicker chairs, in the sitting room (with TV and fireplace), in the more formal living room, or in a red wicker chair in the cozy third-floor reading room (also with a TV). If you want a lake view, choose the all-blue Hydrangea Room, with a pineapple-top, queen-size four-poster bed; you can watch the stars through the skylight overhead. If you need lots of space, the Captain Howe's Suite has a king-size canopy bed, plus a separate sitting room with a fire-place that's bigger than the guest rooms at many B&Bs. Take a walk down to the inn's private beach and dock, where you'll find a gazebo. Don't miss innkeeper Jane MacMillin's yummy cinnamon bread. Kids are welcome. ⊠ *909 Main St. (Rte. 6A), 02638,* ☎ *508/385–5534 or 800/595–0034,* WEB *www.scargomanor.com,* FAX *508/385–3992. 4 rooms, 2 suites. Breakfast room, beach. No smoking. AE, D, DC, MC, V. Closed Jan.–Mar. CP.*

Nightlife and the Arts

The oldest professional summer theater in the country is the **Cape Playhouse** (⊠ 820 Main St. [Rte. 6A], ☎ 508/385–3911 or 877/385–3911), an 1838 former Unitarian Meeting House, where top stars appear each summer. The playhouse also mounts children's shows on Friday morning during July and August. On the grounds of the Cape Playhouse is the artsy **Cape Cinema** (☎ 508/362–2503), which shows foreign and first-run films throughout the summer.

The **Nau-Sets** (⊠ Dennis Senior Center, Rte. 134, ☎ 508/255–5079 or 508/385–9841) holds weekly square dances on Tuesday.

The **Reel Art Cinema** at the Cape Museum of Fine Arts (⊠ 60 Hope La., ☎ 508/385–4477) shows avant-garde, classic, art, and independent films on weekends. Call for a schedule.

Outdoor Activities and Sports

BEACHES

Parking at all Dennis beaches is $10 a day in season for nonresidents.

Chapin Beach (⊠ Chapin Beach Rd.) is a lovely dune-backed bay beach with long tidal flats so you can walk far out at low tide. It has no lifeguards or services.

Corporation Beach (⊠ Corporation Rd.) has lifeguards, showers, rest rooms, and a food stand. At one time a packet landing owned by a corporation of the townsfolk, the beautiful crescent of white sand backed by low dunes now serves a decidedly noncorporate use as a public beach.

Mayflower Beach (⊠ Dunes Rd. off Bayview Rd.) at low tide reveals hundreds of feet of tidal flats. The beach has rest rooms, showers, lifeguards, and a food stand.

For freshwater swimming, **Scargo Lake** (⊠ access off Rte. 6A or Scargo Hill Rd.) has two beaches with rest rooms, playgrounds, and a picnic area. The sandy-bottom lake is shallow along the shore, which is good for kids. It's surrounded by woods and is stocked for fishing.

BIKING

A guidebook published by the Dennis Chamber of Commerce includes bike tours and maps. You can rent bikes from a number of places along the 25-mi Cape Cod Rail Trail. **Barbara's Bike Shop** (⊠ Rte. 134, ☎ 508/760–4723) is at the Rail Trail entrance. **Brewster Bike** (⊠ Underpass Rd., Brewster, ☎ 508/896–8149) carries a large selection of bikes. **Idle Times** (⊠ Rte. 6A, ☎ 508/896–9242), at the Brewster section of the trail near Nickerson State Park, has bikes and accessories for transporting children.

You can pick up the Cape Cod Rail Trail at several points along its path. In fact, riding the entire trail in one day doesn't do justice to its sights and side trips (though it certainly can be done). Many bicyclists, especially those with small children, prefer the piecemeal method since they can relax and enjoy the sights—and not turn their legs into jelly.

The ride in Dennis starts as a flat, straight spin through a small pine forest, a good warming-up exercise. Your first road crossing is at busy

RIDING THE RAIL TRAIL

IN THE LATE 1800S visitors to Cape Cod could take the train from Boston all the way to Provincetown. But with the construction of the Sagamore and Bourne bridges in the mid-1930s, the age of the automobile truly arrived on the Cape. Today, although passenger trains no longer serve Cape Cod, the former train paths provide another, more leisurely way to explore the Cape—by bicycle. For many people, riding the trail through the fragrant woods is as quintessential a Cape experience as leaping into the cold Atlantic on a dune-backed beach.

The Cape's premier bike path, the Cape Cod Rail Trail was constructed in 1978 and extended in the mid-1990s and now offers a scenic ride from South Dennis to South Wellfleet. Following the paved right-of-way of the old Penn Central Railroad, it is 25 mi long, passing salt marshes, cranberry bogs, ponds, and Nickerson State Park, which has its own path.

Some serious bikers whiz along at top speed, but that's not the only way to travel. Along the way there are plenty of tempting places to veer off to spend an hour or two on the beach, to stop for lunch or ice cream, or just to smell the pine trees and imagine what the Cape looked like years ago. The terrain is easy to moderate and is generally quite flat, making it great for youngsters.

The trail starts at the parking lot off busy Route 134 south of U.S. 6, near Theophilus Smith Road in South Dennis, a far-from-scenic place that will make you appreciate the trail even more. It ends at the post office in South Wellfleet. The Dennis Chamber of Commerce will give you a free rail trail map, with distance markings to various points along the trail. It also notes the location of parking lots en route if you want to cover only a segment: in Harwich (across from Pleasant Lake Store on Pleasant Lake Avenue), in Brewster (at Nickerson State Park), and in Eastham (at the Salt Pond Visitor Center). Several bike shops near the trail in Dennis, Brewster, and Eastham can also provide information as well as convenient rentals.

If you want to ride the entire length and back in one day, you're in for a long ride. Experienced rail-trailers suggest doing the trail in segments, perhaps starting in the middle near Nickerson State Park and looping to one end and back. If you want to return to your starting point by public transportation, the easiest way is to start in Dennis, ride to Orleans, and catch the bike-rack-equipped H20 line bus back to Dennis; contact the Cape Cod Regional Transit Authority for schedule and route information.

The Cape Cod Rail Trail is popular with in-line skaters and pedestrians as well as bicyclists. Remember that wheels yield to heels, so cyclists should give walkers the right of way. Pass slower traffic on the left, and call out a warning before you pass. Children under 13 must wear helmets. As you ride through Orleans, a stretch of the trail is on busy town streets rather than on a dedicated bike thoroughfare, so use extra caution. And at one point in Harwich, you will cross a major highway. The trail can get crowded at times, especially in summer; if you prefer solitude (or cooler temperatures), set out earlier in the morning or later in the afternoon.

Busy bike trails share the same fate as roads: maintenance projects and expansion. A 3-mi spur leads from the rail trail through Harwich to the Chatham line; eventually this spur will go into Chatham center. Also in the works are plans to extend the trail westward into Yarmouth. **Nickerson State Park** (☎ 508/896–3491) maintains the rail trail; to view a map of the route before you leave home, go to WEB www.state.ma.us/mhd/paths/webrt.htm.

— By Carolyn Heller

Great Western Road, one of the town's major thoroughfares, after which you'll pass Sand Pond and Flax Pond in Harwich. The Dennis part of the trail is short, but it's worth starting here for the ample parking at the trail's entrance and for the several bike-rental places that set up shop on Route 134.

FISHING

Sesuit Harbor, on the bay side of Dennis off Route 6A, is busy with fishing and pleasure boats. Several are available for fishing charters. The **Bluefish** (⊠ Sesuit Harbor, Box 113, Dennis 02638, ☎ 508/385–7265) makes four-, six-, and eight-hour trips. The **LAD-NAV** (⊠ Sesuit Harbor, Box 2002, East Dennis 02641, ☎ 508/385–8150) takes as many as six anglers per trip on a 36-ft fishing vessel.

Shopping

Armchair Bookstore (⊠ 619 Rte. 6A, ☎ 508/385–0900) carries a surprisingly large selection of current releases, plus numerous books about Cape lore, history, and sights. Also on hand are cards and knickknacks and a children's section with books, games, and toys.

Emily's Beach Barn (⊠ 708 Rte. 6A, ☎ 508/385–8328) has fashionable women's beachwear, from bathing suits and wraps to sun hats and summer dresses and tops.

Robert C. Eldred Co. (⊠ 1483 Main St. [Rte. 6A], East Dennis, ☎ 508/385–3116) holds more than two dozen auctions per year, dealing in Americana; estate jewelry; top-quality antiques; marine, Asian, American, and European art; tools; and dolls. Its "general antiques and accessories" auctions put less expensive wares on the block.

Scargo Pottery (⊠ 30 Dr. Lord's Rd. S, off Rte. 6A, ☎ 508/385–3894) is set in a pine forest, where potter Harry Holl's unusual wares—such as his signature castle birdhouses—sit on tree stumps and hang from branches. Inside are the workshop and kiln, plus work by Holl's four daughters. With luck you'll catch a potter at the wheel; viewing is, in fact, encouraged.

Cotuit

❽ *9 mi southwest of Barnstable, 2½ mi southeast of Mashpee.*

Once called Cotuit Port, this charming little town was formed around seven Crocker family homesteads. Much of the town lies along and just south of Route 28, west of Osterville and east of Mashpee, and its center is not much more than a crossroads with a post office, old-time coffee shop, local pizza parlor, and general store, which all seem unchanged since the 1940s. Large waterfront estates line sections of Main Street and Ocean View Drive, where small coves hide the uncrowded Loop Beach and Ropes Beach. It's best to get to the beaches by bike, since traffic is light and beach parking is for residents only.

The **Cahoon Museum of American Art** is in one of the old Crocker family buildings, a 1775 Georgian colonial farmhouse that was once a tavern and an overnight way station for travelers on the Hyannis–Sandwich stagecoach line. Its several rooms display selections from the permanent collection of American primitive paintings by Ralph and Martha Cahoon along with other 19th- and early 20th-century artists. Special exhibitions, classes, talks, and demonstrations are held throughout the summer. ⊠ *4676 Falmouth Rd. (Rte. 28),* ☎ *508/428–7581,* WEB *www.cahoonmuseum.org.* 🎟 *$3 suggested donation.* ☉ *Feb.–Dec., Tues.–Sat. 10–4.*

The first motor-driven fire-fighting apparatus on Cape Cod, a 1916 Model T chemical fire engine, is housed in the **Santuit-Cotuit Historical Society Museum,** behind the Samuel Dottridge Homestead, which itself dates from the early 1800s. ⊠ *1148 Main St.,* ☎ *508/428–0461.* ▣ *Free.* ☉ *Mid-June–mid-Oct., Thurs.–Sun. 2:30–5.*

Cotuit Library (⊠ 871 Main St., ☎ 508/428–8141) holds a noncirculating set of luxurious leather-bound classics.

Dining and Lodging

$$$–$$$$ ✕ **Regatta of Cotuit.** This restaurant is in a restored colonial stagecoach inn filled with wood, brass, and Oriental carpets. The classic yet original fare includes pâtés of rabbit, veal, and venison and a signature seared loin of lamb with cabernet sauce, surrounded by chèvre, spinach, and pine nuts. Chef Heather Allen's signature premium fillet of buffalo tederloin is prepared differently each night, with seasonal starches and vegetables. The cozy taproom has its own bar menu. ⊠ *4631 Falmouth Rd. (Rte. 28),* ☎ *508/428–5715. AE, MC, V. Reservations essential. No lunch.*

$–$$ ✕ **The Mills.** With just 20 tables and a six-seat lunch counter, this busy breakfast and lunch spot has local and imported fans lining up to sample *linguica* (sausage) and cheese omelets, blueberry or cranberry pancakes, and thick cut (and intriguingly named) Texas French toast. The Mills also serves up fresh baked muffins, scones, and breads. Lunch is homemade soups and sandwiches, including burgers and veggie burgers. You can (and must) make reservations for the popular Friday-night fish dinners, the only dinner offered. ⊠ *Rte. 149, just north of Cotuit, Marstons Mills,* ☎ *508/428–9814. No credit cards.*

$$ ▣ **Josiah Sampson House.** Guest rooms in this 1793 Federal-style home have canopy beds, needlepoint rugs, antiques, and air-conditioning. Hannah's Room, the most spacious, has a queen-size four-poster bed, built-in window seats, and a massive working fireplace. Upstairs, the Sampson Room has an extra-large bathroom and a view of the backyard. Tennis privileges ($10 for 1½ hours) are available at the Kings Grant Racquet Club next door. ⊠ *40 Old Kings Rd., off Main St., Box 226, 02635,* ☎ *508/428–8383 or 877/574–6873,* ℻ *508/428–0116,* ⱲⒺⒷ *www.josiahsampson.com. 6 rooms, 1 suite. Air-conditioning, outdoor hot tub, bicycles. AE, MC, V. CP.*

Outdoor Activities and Sports

The **Cotuit Kettleers** of the collegiate Cape Cod Baseball League play home games at Lowell Park (⊠ Lowell St., 2 mi south of Rte. 28, ☎ 508/428–3358) from mid-June to mid-August.

Shopping

The **Sow's Ear Antique Company** (⊠ 4698 Rte. 28, ☎ 508/428–4931), in a house that dates from the late 1600s next to the Cahoon Museum, specializes in folk art—dolls, ship's models, wood carvings, antique quilts, and paintings.

Osterville

❾ *3 mi east of Cotuit, 7 mi southwest of Barnstable.*

A wealthy Barnstable enclave southwest of the town center, Osterville is lined with elegant waterfront houses, some of which are large "cottages" built in the 19th century, when the area became popular with a monied set. You'll find most beaches in the village, including the impressive **Dowses Beach,** are restricted to residents-only parking. If you want to swim locally, make sure your hotel or inn issues parking permits.

Despite its haute homes, the village of Osterville retains the small-town charm that permeates the Cape; its Main Street and Wianno Avenue area is a collection of trendy boutiques and jewelry shops mixed with a library, a post office, and country stores. The village's festivals of Daff O'ville Day (late April) and Christmas Stroll (mid-December) are heavily attended.

An 1824 sea captain's house is the setting for the **Osterville Historical Society Museum,** which displays antiques, dolls, and exhibits on Osterville's history. Two wooden boat museums, each showcasing various sailing vessels, as well as the Cammett House (dating from the late 18th century) are also on the property. ⊠ *155 W. Bay Rd.,* ☎ *508/428–5861.* ⊡ *$2.* ☉ *Mid-June–Sept., Thurs.–Sun. 1:30–4:30.*

NEED A
BREAK?
Gone Chocolate (⊠ 858 Main St., ☎ 508/420–0202) will tempt you with old-fashioned chocolate-pecan turtles, saltwater taffy, ice cream, and other confections.

Dining

$–$$$ ✕ **Wimpy's.** No, this is not a fast-food hamburger joint but a Cape standby with an extensive menu that favors Italian food and fried fish, from chicken picatta to a seafood platter. Wimpy's numerous and loyal clientele fills a big family dining room, a sunny atrium, and a dark traditional tavern that has cozy booths and a fine old bar. The frying batter and fish selections are on the bland side, so opt for the more inventive specials such as tortilla-crusted salmon topped in a caper sauce or a simple prime rib (when available). You can get takeout here, too. This is just about the only choice in town, so make the most of it. ⊠ *752 Main St.,* ☎ *580/428–6300; 508/428–3474 for takeout. AE, DC, MC, V.*

Outdoor Activities and Sports

Holly Hill Farm (⊠ 240 Flint St., Marstons Mills, ☎ 508/428–2621) offers horseback-riding instruction and day camp but no trail rides.

Shopping

Oak & Ivory (⊠ 1112 Main St., ☎ 508/428–9425) specializes in Nantucket lightship baskets made on the premises, as well as gold miniature baskets and scrimshaw. China, gold jewelry, and other gifts round out the selection.

Centerville

⑩ *2½ mi northeast of Osterville, 4 mi southwest of Barnstable.*

Centerville was once a busy seafaring town, a history evident in the 50 or so shipbuilders' and sea captains' houses along its quiet, tree-shaded streets. Offering the pleasures of both sheltered ocean beaches on Nantucket Sound, such as **Craigville Beach,** and freshwater swimming in Lake Wequaquet, it has been a popular vacation area since the mid-19th century. Shoot Flying Hill Road, named by Native Americans, is the highest point of land on the Cape, with panoramic views to Plymouth and Provincetown to the north and to Falmouth and Hyannis to the south.

Set in a 19th-century house, the **Centerville Historical Society Museum** exhibits furnished period rooms, Sandwich glass, miniature carvings of birds by Anthony Elmer Crowell, models of ships, marine artifacts, military uniforms and artifacts, antique tools, perfume bottles (dating from 1760 to 1920), 300 costumes (from 1650 to 1950), and quilts, and it has a research library. Each summer there are special costume exhibits or other shows. ⊠ *513 Main St.,* ☎ *508/775–0331.* ⊡ *$3.* ☉ *June–Sept., Wed.–Sat. 1:30–4:30.*

The **1856 Country Store** (⊠ 555 Main St., ☎ 508/775–1856) still sells penny candy, except that these days each candy costs at least 25 pennies. The store also carries newspapers, coffee, crafts, jams, and all kinds of gadgets and toys. You can sip your coffee—and take a political stance—by choosing a wooden bench out front, one marked DEMO-CRAT and the other REPUBLICAN.

NEED A
BREAK?

Sample the homemade goods at **Four Seas Ice Cream** (⊠ 360 S. Main St., ☎ 508/775–1394), a tradition for generations (67 years in 2001) of summer visitors. It's open Memorial Day–Labor Day until 10 PM.

The **Centerville Library** (⊠ 585 Main St., ☎ 508/790–6220) has a 42-volume noncirculating set of transcripts of the Nuremberg Trials.

Lodging

$$–$$$ 🏠 **Tradewinds Inn.** The 6-acre property, overlooking the Atlantic Ocean, Lake Elizabeth, and the pretty village of Craigville, has large, family-friendly ocean-view rooms, each with a balcony or patio. There are also three efficiencies with fully equipped kitchenettes, but skip the less attractive non-water-view rooms in the detached buildings. The furnishings are simple but appealing: whitewashed furniture, floral quilts, and tasteful if somewhat unspectacular prints dotting the walls. All rooms have TV and phones. A small, sandy beach just for guests is down the path from the main lodge. The wicker-festooned, knotty-pine-paneled lobby has a fireplace and a cocktail bar. ⊠ *780 Craigville Beach Rd., Box 477, 02632,* ☎ *508/775–0365 or 877/444–7966,* FAX *508/790–1404,* WEB *www.twicapecod.com. 28 rooms, 4 suites, 3 efficiencies. Air-conditioning, lobby lounge, putting green, beach. AE, MC, V. Closed Nov.–Apr. CP.*

Outdoor Activities and Sports

Craigville Beach, on Craigville Beach Road, is a long, wide strand that is extremely popular with the collegiate crowd (it's also known by its nickname, Muscle Beach). The beach has lifeguards, showers, and rest rooms, and there is food nearby. A $10 parking fee is charged in summer.

Many road races are held in season, and the **Hyannis Sprint I Triathlon** (☎ 508/477–6311) takes place at Craigville Beach in early summer.

Hyannis

⑪–⑭ *3½ mi east of Centerville, 23 mi east of the Bourne Bridge.*

Hyannis was named for the Native American Sachem Iyanno, who sold the area for £20 and two pairs of pants. Perhaps he would have sold it for far more had there been any indication that Hyannis would become known as the "home port of Cape Cod" or that the Kennedys would have pitched so many tents here. Hyannis is effectively the transportation center of the Cape; it's near the airport, and ferries depart here for Nantucket and (in season) Martha's Vineyard. The busy roads feeding into the town are lined with big-box stores you'll find anywhere.

A bustling year-round hub of activity, Hyannis has the Cape's largest concentration of businesses, shops, malls, hotels and motels, restaurants, and entertainment venues. Main Street is lined with used-book and gift shops, jewelers, clothing stores, summer-wear and T-shirt shops, and ice cream and candy stores, but the street can have a somewhat forlorn, down-at-the-heels feeling, as the malls outside downtown have taken their toll on business. There are, however, plenty of good eateries, both fun and fancy.

Perhaps best known for its association with the Kennedy clan, the Hyannis area was also a vacation site for President Ulysses S. Grant in 1874

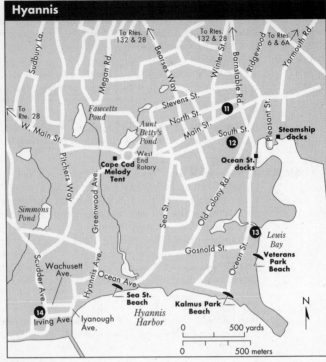

Hyannis

and later for President Grover Cleveland. Hyannis is making an effort to preserve its historical connection with the sea. By 1840 more than 200 shipmasters had established homes in the Hyannis–Hyannis Port area. Aselton Park (at the intersection of South and Ocean streets) and the Village Green on Main Street are the sites of events celebrating this history, and Aselton Park marks the starting point of the scenic Walkway to the Sea, which extends to the dock area.

Three parallel streets run through the heart of town. Busy, shop-filled Main Street runs one-way from east to west; South Street runs from west to east; and North Street is open to two-way traffic. The airport rotary connects with heavily trafficked Routes 132 and 28, and with U.S. 6. Off Ocean Street and Sea Street lie several excellent beaches, including Kalmus Park Beach, renowned for its stiff winds and hordes of windsurfers, and the smaller Veterans Park Beach, next to the Kennedy Memorial.

⓫ In Main Street's Old Town Hall, the surprisingly sparse **John F. Kennedy Hyannis Museum** explores JFK's Cape years (1934–63) through enlarged and annotated photographs culled from the archives of the JFK Library near Boston, as well as a seven-minute video narrated by Walter Cronkite. The gift shop sells mugs, T-shirts, and presidential memorabilia. ✉ *397 Main St.,* ☎ *508/790-3077.* 💳 *$3.* ☉ *Mid-Apr.–Oct., Mon.–Sat. 10–4, Sun. 1–4; last admission at 3:30. Nov.–mid-Dec. and mid-Feb.–mid-Apr., Wed.–Sat. 10–4.*

⓬ The **St. Francis Xavier Church** (✉ 347 South St., ☎ 508/775-0818) is where Rose Kennedy and her family worshiped during their summers on the Cape; the pew that John F. Kennedy used regularly is marked by a plaque.

Beyond the bustling docks where waterfront restaurants draw crowds, and ferries, harbor tour boats, and deep-sea fishing vessels come and

(13) go, the quiet esplanade by the **John F. Kennedy Memorial** (⊠ off Ocean St. south of Channel Point) overlooks boat-filled Lewis Bay. JFK loved to sail these waters, and in 1966 the people of Barnstable erected a plaque and fountain pool here in his memory. Adjacent to the memorial is **Veterans Park,** with a beach, a tree-shaded picnic and barbecue area, and a playground.

(14) Hyannis Port was a mecca for Americans during the Kennedy presidency, when the **Kennedy Compound** became the summer White House. The days of hordes of Secret Service men and swarms of tourists trampling down the bushes are gone, and the area is once again a community of quietly posh estates, though the Kennedy mystique is such that tourists still seek it out. The best way to get a glimpse of the compound is from the water on one of the many harbor tours or cruises.

Joseph P. and Rose Kennedy bought their house here—the largest one, closest to the water—in 1929 as a healthful place to summer with their soon-to-be-nine children. (Son Ted bought the house before his mother's death in 1995.) Sons Jack and Bobby bought neighboring houses in the 1950s. Jack's is the one at the corner of Scudder and Irving, with the 6-ft-high stockade fence on two sides. Bobby's is next to it, with the white fieldstone chimney. Ted bought a home on Squaw Island, a private island connected to the area by a causeway at the end of Scudder Avenue. It now belongs to his ex-wife, Joan. Eunice (Kennedy) and Sargent Shriver have a house near Squaw Island, on Atlantic Avenue.

The compound is relatively self-sufficient in terms of entertainment: Rose Kennedy's former abode (with 14 rooms and nine baths) has a movie theater, a private beach, a boat dock, a swimming pool, a tennis court, and a sports field that was the scene of the famous Kennedy touch-football matches. More recently, Maria Shriver, Caroline Kennedy Schlossberg, and other family members have had their wedding receptions here. In the summer of 1999 family members waited here for confirmation of John Kennedy Jr.'s death in a plane crash off Martha's Vineyard. He and his wife were flying her sister to the Vineyard before continuing on to a cousin's wedding in Hyannis; all three were killed.

Hyannis Public Library (⊠ 401 Main St., ☎ 508/775–2280) has a case full of books on JFK.

☺ Perfect for a rainy day, **Smith Family Amusement** is replete with bowling lanes, video-game rooms, and that old seaside favorite, Skee-ball. ⊠ *441 Main St.,* ☎ *508/775–3411.* ☉ *Daily; hrs vary.*

OFF THE BEATEN PATH | **CAPE COD POTATO CHIPS FACTORY** – There's a standing invitation on the back of the bag: come for a free factory tour and get free samples of the crunchy all-natural chips hand-cooked in kettles in small batches. ⊠ *Independence Dr. to Breeds Hill Rd., off Rte. 132,* ☎ *508/775–7253,* 𝚆𝙴𝙱 *www.capecodchips.com.* ☉ *Weekdays 9–5. Call for off-season hours.*

Dining and Lodging

$$–$$$$ ★ ✕ **The Paddock.** The Paddock is synonymous with excellent formal dining on the Cape. Its authentic Victorian style includes sumptuous upholstery in the main dining room and old-style wicker on the breezy summer porch. The menu is traditional yet deceptively innovative, combining fresh ingredients in novel ways. A salad of duck, apple, sharp Vermont cheddar, and walnuts on baby greens with cider-mustard vinaigrette is but one example. Steak au poivre, with the promise of five varieties of crushed peppercorns, is masterful; the superb Pacific Rim chicken is a grilled breast topped with oranges and mangoes, served on mixed greens and Asian noodles. Terrific brawny reds are on the

A VISIT TO THE GRAY LADY

THE ISLAND OF NANTUCKET lies one to two hours south of Hyannis or Harwich Port by ferry, with historic homes, stunning beaches, and rolling moors that make it an aesthetic world unto itself. In summer, the 14-by-3-mi island brims with activity as people descend to explore the well-preserved streets of Nantucket Town. Greek Revival houses and museums such as the Whaling Museum carry echoes of the mid-19th century, when this was the world's foremost whaling port. Nantucket was a busy place, dubbed the Gray Lady of the Sea by sailors because of fogs that swept in quickly. Today Nantucket's increasing chicness is matched by a dedication to preserving the island's natural beauty—no billboards or neon here—as well as an array of sophisticated pleasures: superlative resaurants, sumptuous B&Bs, and fine boutiques and antiques shops.

More than a few people debark from the ferries to find themselves mildly disoriented. While the journey from the Cape is pretty much southward, by the time the boat rounds Brant Point to enter the harbor, it's facing due west. Main Street of Nantucket Town, at the core of the historic district, has an east–west orientation, stemming from Straight Wharf out to Madaket Road, which proceeds 6 mi west to Madaket Beach. Milestone Road, accessed from a rotary at the end of Orange Street off Main Street, is a straight, 8-mi shot to the easternmost town of 'Sconset (formally, Siasconset), a tranquil village with tiny cottages and driveways of crushed white shells. 'Sconset makes a lovely day trip from Nantucket Town; you can stroll in the village and continue on to nearby beaches, bogs, and conservation areas.

To find your way to the south-shore beaches or among the hillocks of Polpis—Altar Rock is the island's highest point, at a mere 100 ft—you'll want to use a map. Renting a bike is a great way to explore the island at a leisurely pace, and the bike shops along the piers of Nantucket Town and the Nantucket Visitor Services and Information Bureau in the center of town offer a useful assortment of maps for free.

All Nantucket beaches (the island has more than 100 mi of sandy shoreline) are open to the public, a point of local pride. A half-dozen or so town-supervised beaches have amenities such as snack bars and lifeguard stations; the rest are the purview of solitary strollers. The northerly, Nantucket Sound–side beaches are nearly always placid, while the oceanside beaches are known for big round waves that will lift you off your feet. Outer beaches, such as Madaket and 'Sconset, present further challenges with strong sidelong currents. But even if you don't swim, you can still savor walking along the beach.

Like the original settlers and the early tourists, most people who visit Nantucket today come to escape—from cities, from stress. Nantucket has a bit of nightlife, including two raucous year-round dance clubs, but that's not what the island is about. It's about gray-shingle cottages, covered with pink roses in summer, about daffodil-lined roads in spring. It's about moors swept with salt breezes and scented with bayberry. Perhaps most of all, it's about rediscovering a quiet place within yourself and within the world, getting back in touch with the elemental and taking it home with you when you go.

For visitor information, contact the **Nantucket Chamber of Commerce** (⊠ 48 Main St., 02554, ☎ 508/228–1700, WEB www.nantucketchamber.org). The **Nantucket Visitor Services and Information Bureau** (⊠ 25 Federal St., 02554, ☎ 508/228–0925) provides information on activities, museums, restaurants, and accommodations. For information on travel by ferry from Cape Cod, see Boat & Ferry Travel in Smart Travel Tips A to Z.

award-winning wine list. An older crowd enjoys live music in the evening at the bar, where a Manhattan is still the drink of choice. ✉ *W. Main St. rotary, next to Melody Tent,* ☎ *508/775–7677. AE, DC, MC, V. Closed mid-Nov.–Mar.*

$$–$$$ ✕ **Fazio's.** Set in an old Italian bakery building, Fazio's looks like the
★ trattoria it is, with wood floors, high ceilings, and a deli case full of fresh pasta, breads, and cheeses (not for sale). There's also an espresso and cappuccino bar. Chef Tom Fazio's menu leans on simple, fresh ingredients and herbed pastas, such as thick, rough-cut black pepper tagliatelle with sausage and eggplant chunks in a garlicky tomato sauce. All ravioli, pastas, and breads are homemade. Take home some fresh cannoli for dessert. ✉ *294 Main St.,* ☎ *508/775–9400. Reservations not accepted. AE, MC, V. No lunch.*

$$–$$$ ✕ **Penguins Seagrill.** Owner-chef Bobby Gold experiments carefully, and never loses sight of the fresh grilled seafood he prepares so well. Baked stuffed lobster (from 1 to 3 pounds) is outstanding, served with crabmeat stuffing topped with fresh sea scallops. There are a number of excellent pasta dishes, again with seafood, such as pasta *Fiore* (shrimp, scallops, and lobster with mushrooms, scallions, sherry, and cream sauce on angel-hair pasta). All the breads and desserts are homemade. The bi-level dining room has wood and brick and carvings of sea life galore. ✉ *331 Main St.,* ☎ *508/775–2023. AE, DC, MC, V. No lunch weekends.*

$$–$$$ ✕ **Roadhouse Café.** This is one of the smartest choices for a night out
★ in Hyannis. Candlelight flickers off the white-linen tablecloths and dark-wood wainscoting. Popular menu items include the pepper-and-goat-cheese appetizer and shrimp and basil pesto over linguine with sun-dried tomatoes and whole roasted garlic cloves. All desserts are made on the premises, so do indulge in the rich tiramisu. In the more casual bistro and the mahogany bar, you can order from a separate menu, which includes thin-crust pizza as well as burgers, sandwiches, and other lighter fare. On Monday night year-round in the bistro is the best straight-ahead jazz on Cape Cod, with such regulars as pianist Dave McKenna and Lou Colombo (the trumpet-playing father of Dave). There's a piano bar every other night of the week between July 4 and Labor Day; it continues on Friday and Saturday in the off-season. ✉ *488 South St.,* ☎ *508/775–2386. Reservations essential. AE, D, MC, V. No lunch.*

$$–$$$ ✕ **RooBar.** A bit of Manhattan on Main Street, RooBar has a dark, sophisticated feel, with good music, low light, and a crowded, hip bar scene at night. A flickering wood-fired oven in the back wall produces "hand-spun to order" pizzas such as scallop and prosciutto with asparagus and goat cheese. The lunch menu is fresh and inventive and not to be overlooked. Try the Big-Ass Grilled Shrimp appetizer, three enormous grilled shrimp in a red curry and coconut sauce, and the fire-roasted half chicken entrée, rubbed with toasted fennel and cumin seeds. The owner is a member of actor Christopher Reeve's family, and a portion of all profits goes to the Christopher Reeve Foundation for Spinal Cord Research. ✉ *586 Main St.,* ☎ *508/778–6515. Reservations essential. AE, MC, V.*

$–$$$ ✕ **Baxter's Fish N' Chips.** Fried seafood being the Cape staple that it is, you may want to plan ahead for a trip to pay homage to one of the best fry-o-lators around. Fried clams are delicious and generous, cooked up hot to order with french fries and homemade tartar sauce. Outside, a number of picnic tables, some set up on an old floating ferry outside the main restaurant, allow you to lose no time in the sun while eating, with lobster, burgers, or something from the excellent raw bar. Indoors, Baxter's Boat House Club, slightly more upscale, serves the same menu but with a number of very good specials as well; no one under 21 is allowed here, however. The restaurant is right on Hyannis Harbor, and since 1955 it's been a favorite of boaters and bathers alike. ✉ *Pleasant St.*, ☎ *508/775–4490. Reservations not accepted. AE, MC, V. Closed Columbus Day–Apr. and weekdays Labor Day–Columbus Day.*

$–$$$ ✕ **Harry's.** This place serves up sizable portions of Cajun and creole
★   dishes with great spices. The menu includes a number of meal-size sandwiches and blackened local fish that's done to perfection, with a jambalaya that makes you wonder if there isn't a bayou nearby. It's also a prime location for music: you can hear blues, zydeco, and folk music Tuesday through Sunday in summer, weekends in the slower months. ✉ *700 Main St.,* ☎ *508/778–4188. Reservations not accepted. AE, DC, MC, V.*

$–$$ ✕ **Barbyann's.** For a reasonably priced family meal, try the steak, seafood, pizza, burgers, or one of the hardly authentic but child-pleasing Mexican dishes here. Best of all are the Buffalo chicken wings, hot and spicy and filling. There's an outdoor patio with umbrella tables, and "night bird" specials are offered all evening Monday–Thursday. ✉ *120 Airport Rd.,* ☎ *508/775–9795. Reservations not accepted. AE, D, DC, MC, V.*

$–$$ ✕ **Sam Diego's.** The bar is busy with people seeing and being seen, and the menu has satisfyingly authentic Mexican tortillas, burritos, and delicious *mole poblano* (chicken with a spicy, bittersweet cocoa sauce). The prop-shop decor may be a little cheesy—sombreros, Aztec birds, and the like—but the atmosphere is fun and friendly. Especially in the early evening, this place is popular with families, thanks in part to the all-you-can-eat chili and taco bar. An interesting dessert, crusty deep-fried ice cream, is served in a giant goblet. Later on, the bar scene picks up steam; dinner is served until midnight. ✉ *950 Iyanough Rd. (Rte. 132),* ☎ *508/771–8816. AE, D, MC, V.*

$–$$ ✕ **Starbuck's.** No, it's not another branch of the Seattle-based coffee company but something more like a T. G. I. Friday's with an edge. Walls and rafters are hung with doodads and hoo-has of every description, but there's no theme: a tuba here, a couple of mannequins there, a miniature World War I fighter plane from out of nowhere. The menu matches the decor, with selections yanked from all over the planet: ostensibly Asian shrimp deep-fried in a coconut-tempura batter, Buck's beef burrito from the Tex-Mex column, and Italian standards such as spaghetti and meatballs. There's also an assortment of burgers and Buckwiches. This might not be for everyone, but it's good if you're in the mood for something raucous. Reservations are essential on weekends. ✉ *624 Iyannough Rd. (Rte. 132),* ☎ *508/778–6767. AE, D, DC, MC, V.*

$–$$ ✕ **Ying's.** The huge menu at this little pan-Asian place combines the best of Thai, Korean, and Japanese cuisines. Ying's sushi and sashimi combos are artful, and its wealth of curried Thai seafood, noodles, and fried rice dishes range from spicy to, well, really spicy. For something different try the Korean *bibimbap* (vegetables, beef, and egg on rice with hot sauce). Tables are set up by the windows, and there's a sushi bar as well as a small lounge area with a selection of Asian beers. Avoiding alcohol? Try the sweet and thick Thai iced tea—you won't need dessert. But if you do, the fried ice cream is a treat. ✉ *59 Center St.,* ☎ *508/790–2432. AE, MC, V. No lunch weekends.*

$$$$ 🏨 **Sheraton Hyannis Hotel.** It's hard to beat the Sheraton, with its beautifully landscaped grounds, extensive services and pampering, and superior resort facilities. The lobby area is elegant, but the rooms, each with a private balcony, are admittedly a bit dull. ✉ *Scudder La., West End rotary, 02601,* ☎ *508/775–7775; 800/325–3535 (reservations center off Cape Cod),* FAX *508/778–6423,* WEB *www.sheraton.com. 230 rooms. Restaurant, pub, room service, air-conditioning, 1 indoor and 1 outdoor pool, hair salon, 18-hole golf course, putting green, 2 tennis courts, health club, business services. AE, D, DC, MC, V.*

Find America
WITH A COMPASS

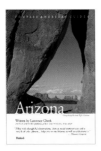
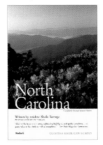
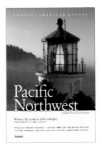

Written by local authors and illustrated throughout with spectacular color images from regional photographers, these companion guides reveal the character and culture of more than 35 of America's most spectacular destinations. Perfect for residents who want to explore their own backyards, and visitors who want an insider's perspective on the history, heritage, and all there is to see and do.

Fodor's COMPASS AMERICAN GUIDES

At bookstores everywhere.

$$$–$$$$ ☑ **Simmons Homestead Inn.** This 1820 former sea captain's country
★ estate is only two minutes from downtown Hyannis. Each room in the
main house or the detached barn is named for an animal. They have
antique, wicker, or canopied four-poster beds topped with brightly col-
ored quilts; some have fireplaces and private decks. The Bird Room,
the largest and cheeriest, has an old-fashioned cast-iron tub and a pri-
vate deck. You can borrow the 10-speed mountain bikes to explore
the town, and Simmons Pond is a short jaunt on the property's trail.
Gregarious innkeeper Bill Putman encourages you to return around 6
each evening for a wine-and-socializing hour. If you can't stand smoke,
beware: although the bedrooms are no-smoking, Putman—a smoker
himself—allows smoking in some public spaces. Kids are welcome; dogs
are permitted with advance notice for an additional $25. ☒ *288 Scud-
der Ave., Box 578, Hyannis Port 02647,* ☎ *508/778–4999 or 800/637–
1649,* FAX *508/790–1342,* WEB *www.simmonshomesteadinn.com. 12
rooms, 2 suites. No-smoking rooms, hot tub, bicycles, billiards. AE,
D, MC, V. BP.*

$$$ ☑ **Comfort Inn Cape Cod.** All the rooms at this cinder-block motel just
off the highway have white-oak-veneer furnishings and include one
king-size or two double beds, a table and chairs or a desk and chair, and
a wardrobe. Some king rooms have sofa beds. The quietest rooms are
those on the top floor that face the pond and woods; all have free HBO
movies and Nintendo, and pets are allowed. You'll have free use of the
nearby Barnstable Athletic Club, and kids under 18 stay free. Although
the location is convenient to the highway, keep in mind that Route 132
is extremely busy during the summer months. ☒ *1470 Iyanough Rd.
(Rte. 132), 02601,* ☎ *508/771–4804 or 800/228–5150 (national reservations number),* FAX *508/790–2336,* WEB *www.comfortinn-hyannis.com.
103 rooms, 1 suite. Indoor pool, sauna, hot tub, gym. AE, D, DC, MC,
V. CP.*

$$ ☑ **Anchor-In.** All rooms have harbor views at this inviting hotel on the
★ north end of Lewis Bay and Hyannis Harbor. Its simple street-side ap-
pearance belies its spacious accommodations and fairly extensive
grounds—and the rates are hard to beat. Most rooms have small bal-
conies overlooking the water and standard amenities such as air-con-
ditioning, cable TV, and phones. The deluxe and executive rooms'
wraparound porches make them worth the extra money. The Arnett
family owns this hotel, delivering the warm, personal service of a small
B&B. Main Street restaurants are minutes away, and ferries for Nan-
tucket and Martha's Vineyard are just around the corner. ☒ *1 South
St. 02601,* ☎ *508/775–0357,* FAX *508/775–1313,* WEB *www.anchorin.com.
43 rooms. Air-conditioning, pool. AE, D, MC, V.*

$$ ☑ **Breakwaters.** If these weathered gray-shingle cottages were any
closer to Nantucket Sound, they'd be in it. Privately owned condos rented
as cottages by the week (or day if vacancies occur), the one-, two-, and
three-bedroom units offer all the comforts of home. Each unit has one
or two full baths; kitchens with microwave, coffeemaker, refrigerator,
toaster, and stove; TV and phone (local calls are free); and a deck or
patio with grill and picnic table. Most have water views. An in-ground
heated pool is less than 200 ft from the lifeguarded town beach. Excluding Sunday, there is daily maid service. The laundromat at the end
of the street (at the corner of North Street) will wash and fold your
dirty duds for a nominal fee. From June through August you must rent
by the week: $925 (1 bedroom)–$2,200 (3 bedroom) per week. ☒ *432
Sea St., Box 118, 02601,* ☎ FAX *508/775–6831,* WEB *www.capecod.com/
breakwaters. 19 cottages. Refrigerators, pool, beach, baby-sitting. No
credit cards. No smoking. Closed mid-Oct.–Apr.*

$$ 🏨 **Capt. Gosnold Village.** An easy walk from the beach and town, this colony of motel rooms and pink-shutter cottages is ideal for families. Kids can ride their bikes around the quiet street, and the pool is fenced in and watched by a lifeguard. In some rooms walls are attractively paneled with painted pine; floors are carpeted, and simple furnishings are colonial or modern. All cottages have decks and gas grills and receive maid service (except Sunday). The cottages are divided into rooms, efficiencies, and 1- to 3-bedroom cottages. ⊠ *230 Gosnold St., 02601,* ☎ *508/775–9111,* WEB *www.captaingosnold.com. 18 cottages. Picnic area, pool, basketball. MC, V. Closed Nov.–mid-Apr.*

$$ 🏨 **Hyannis Inn Motel.** The second-oldest motel in Hyannis, the main building of this modest two-story spot served as press headquarters during JFK's presidential campaign. The main building's immaculate rooms have double, queen-size, or king-size beds, cable TV, and direct-dial phones; some have whirlpool tubs. The newer deluxe rooms—built in 1981 in a separate wing out back—are larger, sunnier, and quieter (they don't face Main Street) and have queen- or king-size beds, sleeper sofas, walk-in closets, and refrigerators. The restaurant serves breakfast only. Kids under 12 stay free. ⊠ *473 Main St., 02601,* ☎ *508/775–0255 or 800/922–8993,* FAX *508/771–0456,* WEB *www.hyannisinn. com. 77 rooms. Restaurant, pub, air-conditioning, indoor pool, sauna. AE, D, MC, V. Closed Dec.–Jan.*

$–$$ 🏨 **Cape Cod Inn.** This centrally located inn (formerly a HoJo hotel)—squarely placed on downtown Main Street—is within walking distance of all of Hyannis's major sights. The no-frills rooms have large double beds; most, unfortunately, have views of the drab parking lot. The inn is attached to the Duck Inn Pub, a popular local hangout, where breakfast is served. ⊠ *447 Main St., 02601,* ☎ *508/775–3000,* FAX *508/ 771–1457,* WEB *capecodtravel.com/capecodinn. 39 rooms, 1 suite. Restaurant, bar, indoor pool. AE, D, MC, V. CP.*

$–$$ 🏨 **Inn on Sea Street.** Charming and relaxed, this B&B is just a short walk from the beach and downtown Hyannis. Guest rooms, in the 1849 main house or the mansard-roof Victorian across the street, have canopy beds, antique furnishings, and claw-foot tubs. The across-the-street rooms are generally larger; all have queen-size beds, one has a private porch, and there's also a common living room and shared kitchen. Innkeepers Sylvia and Fred LaSelva are gracious and welcoming hosts. Breakfasts are served on china, silver, and crystal in the antiques-and-lace dining room of the main house or in the glassed-in sunporch. Out back, the small one-bedroom Honeymoon Cottage, all in white, has its own kitchen. You'll have privileges at the nearby Twin Brooks 18-hole golf course at the Sheraton Hyannis Hotel. Fred or Sylvia will pick you up from the local bus station or the airport. ⊠ *358 Sea St., 02601,* ☎ *508/775–8030,* FAX *508/771–0878,* WEB *www.innonseastreet. com. 9 rooms, 7 with bath; 1 cottage. Air-conditioning. No smoking. AE, D, MC, V. Closed Nov.–late-Apr. BP.*

$–$$ 🏨 **Sea Breeze Inn.** Each room in this cedar-shingle B&B two blocks
★ from the beach has antique or canopied beds and is simply decorated with well-chosen antiques. Larger families may want to stay in one of the three detached cottages; the nicest is the Rose Garden, with three bedrooms (two on the second level), two baths, a TV room, a fireplace, even a washer and dryer. If that's booked, try the Honeymoon Cottage, which has a canopy bed and an inviting double Jacuzzi (the cottage is fenced in for total privacy). Owner-innkeeper Patricia Gibney's breakfasts are worth getting up early for; you can eat in the dining room or in the outdoor gazebo, surrounded by winsome gardens. ⊠ *270 Ocean Ave., at Sea St., 02601,* ☎ *508/771–7213,* FAX *508/862–0663,* WEB *www.seabreezeinn.com. 14 rooms, 3 cottages. Air-conditioning. No smoking. AE, D, MC, V. CP.*

Nightlife and the Arts

THE ARTS

The **Boston Pops Esplanade Orchestra** (☎ 508/362–0066) wows a crowd with its annual Pops by the Sea concert, held in August at the Hyannis Village Green. Each year a celebrity guest conductor strikes up the band for a few selected numbers; past baton bouncers have included Olympia Dukakis, Joan Kennedy, Mike Wallace, and Art Buchwald.

In 1950 the actress Gertrude Lawrence and her husband, producer-manager Richard Aldrich, opened the **Cape Cod Melody Tent** (✉ 21 W. Main St., at West End rotary, ☎ 508/775–9100) to showcase Broadway musicals and concerts. Today it's the Cape's top venue for pop concerts and comedy shows; performers who have played here, in the round, include Aretha Franklin, Willie Nelson, Tom Jones, Ziggy Marley, KC and the Sunshine Band, Anne Murray, and Tony Bennett. The Tent also hosts a Wednesday-morning children's theater series in July and August.

The 90-member **Cape Symphony Orchestra,** under former D'Oyly Carte Opera conductor Royston Nash, gives regular classical and children's concerts with guest artists October through May. Performances are held at the Barnstable Performing Arts Center at Barnstable High School (✉ 744 W. Main St., Hyannis, ☎ 508/362–1111).

Opera New England of Cape Cod (☎ 508/771–3600 for schedules and locations and reservations) has two or three performances a year, in spring and fall, by the National Lyric Opera Company.

In July and August **town-band concerts** (☎ 508/362–5230 or 800/449–6647) are held on Wednesday evening starting at 7:30 on the Town Green on Main Street.

NIGHTLIFE

Bobby Byrne's Pub (✉ Rte. 28 at Bearses Way, ☎ 508/775–1425) is a branch of this local chain; it's comfortable and unpretentious.

Bud's Country Lounge (✉ Bearses Way and Rte. 132, ☎ 508/771–2505) has pool tables and provides live country music, dancing, and line-dancing lessons year-round.

Club 477 (✉ 477 Yarmouth Rd., ☎ 508/771–7511), in the old Hyannis train station, is the Upper and Mid Cape's only gay club. There's a piano bar on the lower level and a dance bar on the upper floor with music almost as hot as the crowd.

The **Prodigal Son** (✉ 10 Ocean St., ☎ 508/771–1337) showcases some of the best up-and-coming bands and musicians in New England. The lineup includes acoustic, blues, jazz, and rock, and even spoken-word performers. The high-octane java keeps the joint jumpin'. Call for schedule.

Pufferbellies (✉ 183 Iyanough Rd. [Rte. 28], ☎ 508/790–4300 or 800/233–4301), in an old railroad roundhouse by the Hyannis tracks, is the Mid Cape's largest dance club, with four dance floors of swing, country line dancing, and DJ tunes, as well as eats, Internet terminals, and even volleyball courts.

The **Roadhouse Café** (✉ 488 South St., ☎ 508/775–2386) has great jazz year-round.

Starbuck's (✉ 645 Iyanough Rd., ☎ 508/778–6767) presents live acoustic entertainment in its bar many nights year-round.

Outdoor Activities and Sports

BASEBALL

The **Hyannis Mets** (☎ 508/420–0962), of the collegiate Cape Cod Baseball League, play home games at McKeon Field (✉ High School Rd.) from mid-June to mid-August.

BEACHES

Kalmus Park Beach, at the south end of Ocean Street, is a fine, wide sandy beach with an area set aside for windsurfers and a sheltered area that's good for kids. It has a snack bar, rest rooms, showers, and lifeguards. The parking fee is $10 in season.

Veterans Park, next to the John F. Kennedy Memorial on Ocean Street, has a small beach that's especially good for kids; it's sheltered from waves and fairly shallow. There are picnic tables, barbecue facilities, showers, rest rooms, and a playground. The parking fee is $10 in season.

BIKING

Cascade Motor Lodge (✉ 201 Main St., ☎ 508/775–9717), near the bus and train station, rents three-speed and mountain bikes by the half day, full day, and week.

BOATING

Eastern Mountain Sports (✉ 1513 Iyanough Rd. [Rte. 132], ☎ 508/362–8690) rents kayaks and camping gear.

Sailing tours aboard the catboat *Eventide* (✉ Ocean St. Dock, ☎ 508/775–0222) include a variety of 1½-hour cruises through Hyannis Harbor and out into Nantucket Sound, such as a nature tour and a sunset cruise.

Hy-Line (✉ Ocean St. Dock, ☎ 508/778–2600) offers cruises on replicas of old-time Maine coastal steamers. The one-hour tours of Hyannis Harbor and Lewis Bay include a view of the Kennedy compound and other points of interest.

FISHING

Hy-Line (✉ Ocean St. Dock, ☎ 508/790–0696) leads fishing trips on a walk-on basis in spring and fall, but reservations are mandatory in summer.

GOLF

Sheraton Hyannis Hotel (✉ West End rotary, ☎ 508/775–7775) has a beautifully landscaped, challenging 18-hole, par-3 course, called Twin Brooks, open to nonguests. You may bump into some famous faces; many performers from the Cape Cod Melody Tent tee off here while in town.

HEALTH AND FITNESS CLUBS

Barnstable Athletic Club (✉ 55 Attucks La., Independence Park, off Rte. 132, ☎ 508/771–7734) has four racquetball-wallyball courts (wallyball is volleyball played on a racquetball court), a squash court, basketball, an aerobics room, whirlpools, sauna and steam rooms, and cardiovascular and free-weight equipment. Day care and day and short-term memberships are available.

Hyannis Athletic Club (✉ Sheraton Hyannis Hotel, West End rotary, ☎ 508/862–2535) has two outdoor tennis courts, a fitness club, and indoor and outdoor pools. Day and short-term memberships are available.

ICE-SKATING

The **Joseph P. Kennedy Jr. Memorial Skating Rink** (✉ 141 Bassett La., ☎ 508/790–6345), named after the late Kennedy scion and war hero, offers skating October through March, with special times reserved for teenagers, youngsters, and families; skate rentals are available.

MINIATURE GOLF

Cape Cod Storyland Golf is a 2-acre miniature golf course set up as a mini–Cape Cod, with each of the 18 holes a Cape town. The course winds around small ponds and waterfalls, a full-size working gristmill, and reproductions of historic Cape buildings. There's an additional charge of $5 for the bumper boats. ⊠ *70 Center St., by railroad depot,* ☎ *508/778–4339.* ⊐ *$7.* ⊙ *Mid-Apr.–Oct., daily 9 AM–midnight.*

Shopping

Cape Cod Mall (⊠ between Rtes. 132 and 28, ☎ 508/771–0200), the Cape's largest, has 120 shops, including department stores from Macy's to Marshall's, and a 12-screen movie complex.

A mix of Disney-esque fantasy and Victorian excess, the Hyannis branch of the **Christmas Tree Shops** (⊠ 655 Iyanough Rd. [Rte. 132], ☎ 508/778–5521) is the largest on the Cape. Many people come just to gawk at the glass-enclosed clock out front, made in the 1920s in Cincinnati.

Colonial Candle of Cape Cod (⊠ 388 Main St., ☎ 508/771–2790 or 508/771–3916) is touristy, but the candles are top-notch.

Hyannis Antique Co-op (⊠ 500 Main St., ☎ 508/778–0512) has a large selection of jewelry, glassware, porcelain, furniture, dolls, prints, and collectibles at good prices.

Nantucket Trading Company (⊠ 354 Main St., ☎ 508/790–3933), sort of a local version of Pier 1, sells an incredible array of neat necessities for your home, including edibles, table linens, cooking gadgets, and kitchen accessories.

The handsome flagship **Puritan** (⊠ 408 Main St., ☎ 508/775–2400) store carries upscale clothing brands from North Face to Eileen Fisher and Ralph Lauren and also sells outdoor gear. Service is great here; there are five other stores around the Cape.

If you're tired of wearing T-shirts and beach cover-ups, duck into **12 West** (⊠ 558 Main St., ☎ 508/771–7000) for upscale-casual women's clothing and accessories.

West Yarmouth

🕧 *4 mi south of Yarmouth Port, 3 mi east of Hyannis.*

There's no getting around it—the part of the Cape people love to hate is Route 28. Passing through the area, it's one motel, strip mall, nightclub, and miniature golf course after another. In 1989, as *Cape Cod Life* magazine put it, "the town [began] to plant 350 trees in hopes that eventually the trees' leaves, like the fig leaf of Biblical lore, [would] cover the shame of unkempt overdevelopment." Regardless of the glut of tacky tourist traps, there are some interesting sights in the little villages along the way. So take Route 28 if you want to intersperse amusements with your sightseeing, because you really can amuse yourself to no end on this section of 28. A sensible option if you want to avoid this road entirely: take speedy U.S. 6 to the exit nearest what you want to visit and then cut south across the interior. If you must travel the Route 28 area, take Buck Island Road, which runs north of and parallel to much of the busy route in West and South Yarmouth.

The village of West Yarmouth was settled in 1643 by Yelverton Crowe, who acquired his land from a Native American sachem. The deal they struck was that Crowe could have as much land as he could traverse in an hour in exchange for an "ox-chain, a copper kettle. . . and a few trinkets." The first settlers were farmers; in the 1830s, when Central Wharf near Mill Creek was built, the town turned to more commercial ventures as it became headquarters for the growing packet service that ferried passengers from the Cape to Boston.

Listed on the National Register of Historic Places, the 1710 **Baxter Grist Mill,** by the shore of Mill Pond, is the only mill on Cape Cod powered by an inside water turbine; the others use either wind or paddle wheels. The mill was converted to the indoor metal turbine in 1860 because of the pond's low water level and the damage done to the wooden paddle wheel by winter freezes. The original metal turbine is displayed on the grounds, and a replica powers the restored mill. A videotape tells the mill's history. ⊠ *Rte. 28,* ☎ *508/398–2231 Ext. 292.* ☞ *Free.* ☉ *Early June–Labor Day, weekends 1–5; also open Mon. or Fri. 1–5 on some holiday weekends.*

❶❻ A unique and lovely walking trail, the **Yarmouth Boardwalk** (⊠ off Meadowbrook La.) stretches through swamp and marsh and leads to the edge of Swan Pond, a pretty pond ringed with woods. To get here, take Winslow Gray Road northeast from Route 28, turn right on Meadowbrook Lane, and take it to the end.

An entertaining, educational, and occasionally hokey stop for kids, **ZooQuarium** has sea-lion shows, a petting zoo with native wildlife, wandering peacocks, pony rides in summer, aquariums, and educational programs. The Children's Discovery Center presents changing exhibits such as *Bone Up on Bones* (all about skeletons), *Zoo Nutrition* (in which kids prepare meals), and the self-explanatory *Scoop on Poop*. ⊠ *674 Main St. (Rte. 28),* ☎ *508/775–8883.* ☞ *$9.* ☉ *Mid-Feb.–June and Sept.–late Nov., daily 9:30–5; July–Aug., daily 9:30–6.*

NEED A   **Jerry's Seafood and Dairy Freeze** (⊠ 654 Main St. [Rte. 28], ☎ 508/
BREAK?   775–9752), open year-round, serves fried clams and onion rings, along with thick frappes (milk shakes), frozen yogurt, and soft ice cream at good prices.

Dining and Lodging

$$–$$$ ✕ **Red Rose Inn.** The breakfast and lunch menus are solid and the ocean views are hard to beat at this small inn and restaurant next to Englewood Beach. Red Rosbrough, with his wife, Rose—get it?—opened the inn, and it's now in the hands of grandson Rick Wilkey, the third-generation chef and innkeeper. Rose was fond of the classic women's dress hats of the flapper days and collected them, apparently with a passion—they hang, delicate but by the hundreds on hooks and shelves throughout the small, sunlighted dining room. Rick's breakfast menu is simple and hearty, with a few gems—eggs Oscar combines the classic Benedict recipe with crabmeat and asparagus, while Titanic French toast, a house favorite, flies off the griddle. The hearty Innkeeper's Special includes two eggs, two pancakes, and ham or sausage. ⊠ *6 New Hampshire Ave.,* ☎ *508/775–2944. No credit cards. Closed Mon.–Wed., off-season. No dinner.*

$–$$ ⊡ **Inn at Lewis Bay.** This 1920s Dutch Colonial overlooks Lewis Bay and is steps from the beach. Each room is furnished in country-antiques style, with Laura Ashley linens, fresh flowers, claw-foot tubs, and antique or canopy beds. The rooms also have a name and a theme, such as Secret Garden (ivy-print linens and wallpaper) and Sea Grass. Whalewatch, with its distinctive navys and maroons, is one of two rooms with water views. Bountiful breakfasts are served in the dining room, where the hand-stenciled strawberries on the ceiling match the wall-paper. At 4 PM, innkeeper Liz Latshaw serves tea and home-baked cookies. ⊠ *57 Maine Ave., 02673,* ☎ *508/771–3433 or 800/962–6679,* FAX *508/790–1186,* WEB *www.innatlewisbay.com. 7 rooms. Air-conditioning, beach. No smoking. AE, MC, V. BP.*

$–$$ 🖭 **Mariner Motor Lodge.** Although Route 28 is crowded and cheesy, there's no shortage of action, and there are several value-packed hotels. The Mariner, near the Hyannis–West Yarmouth line, is a good family lodging and a bargain, to boot. Although the rooms are standard-issue motel—think basic furnishings like floral bedcovers, carpets that can take a direct hit from a spilled soft drink, and long balcony windows (but no step-out balconies)—they all have a small refrigerator, TV, and phone. The outdoor pool is heated and large, and a heated indoor pool, with an oversize whirlpool hot tub, is great for rainy days. Also on site is a miniature golf course and vending machines for snacks. Kids stay free, and rates on weekdays are reduced. ⊠ *573 Rte. 28, 02673,* ☎ *508/771–7887 or 800/445–4050,* FAX *508/771–2811,* WEB *www.mariner-capecod. com. 100 rooms. Coffee shop, air-conditioning, in-room safes, no-smoking rooms. AE, D, MC, V.*

$ 🖭 **Americana Holiday Motel.** If you want the convenience of staying on Route 28, this family-owned and -operated strip motel is a good choice. All rooms have cable TV and a phone; those in the rear Pine Grove section overlook serene sea pines and one of the motel's three pools rather than traffic snarls. In the off-season the rates simply can't be beat. ⊠ *99 Main St. (Rte. 28), 02673,* ☎ *508/775–5511 or 800/ 445–4497,* FAX *508/790–0597,* WEB *www.americanaholiday.com. 149 rooms, 4 suites. Coffee shop, air-conditioning, refrigerators, 1 indoor and 2 outdoor pools, hot tub, sauna, putting green, shuffleboard, video games, playground. AE, D, DC, MC, V. Closed Nov.–Mar. CP.*

Nightlife and the Arts

Cape Cod Irish Village (⊠ 512 Main St. [Rte. 28], ☎ 508/771–0100) has dancing to two- or three-piece bands performing traditional and popular Irish music year-round. The crowd is mostly couples and people over 35.

Clancy's (⊠ 175 Main St. [Rte. 28], ☎ 508/775–3332) offers live entertainment, typically a mix of Irish, folk, and soft rock performed by acoustic guitarist and vocalist Terry Brennan, on weekends year-round.

Mill Hill Club (⊠ 164 Rte. 28, ☎ 508/775–2580) provides something for everyone, from more than 20 TVs to live music, hypnotist's acts, and the occasional men's and women's bikini contests—it's a young, and loud, crowd.

West Yarmouth's summertime **town-band concerts** are held on Monday in July and August at 7 PM at Mattacheese Middle School (⊠ off Higgins Crowell Rd., ☎ 508/778–1008).

Outdoor Activities and Sports

BIKE RENTAL

All Right Bike & Mower (⊠ 627 Main St. [Rte. 28], ☎ 508/790–3191) rents bikes and mopeds and does on-site repairs.

FISHING

Truman's (⊠ 608 Main St. [Rte. 28], ☎ 508/771–3470) can supply you with a required freshwater license and rental gear.

Shopping

The **Cranberry Bog Outlet Stores** (⊠ Rte. 28, ☎ no phone) are on the edge of a working cranberry bog. Bass, Van Heusen, and Izod are a few of the shops here.

South Yarmouth

⑰ *3 mi east of West Yarmouth, 6 mi east of Hyannis.*

The Bass River divides the southern portions of the towns of Yarmouth and Dennis. People also generally refer to the area of South Yarmouth as Bass River. Here you'll find charter boats and boat rentals, as well as a river cruise, plus seafood restaurants and markets. Like West Yarmouth, the town has its stretch of blight and overdevelopment on Route 28, but it also has some nice beaches that are good for families. For a good indication of what the town looked like in the late nineteenth century, take a drive down Pleasant Street and the Main Street section south of Route 28 to view old homes in the Federal and Greek Revival style. This section, along Bass River, was home to the elite businessmen, bankers, and sea merchants.

South Yarmouth was once called Quaker Village for the large numbers of Quakers who settled the area in the 1770s after a smallpox epidemic wiped out the local Native American population.

The 1809 **Quaker Meeting House** is still open for meetings. Two separate entrance doors and the partition down the center were meant to divide the sexes. The adjacent cemetery has simple markers with no epitaphs, an expression of the Friends' belief that all are equal in God's eyes. Behind the cemetery is a circa-1830 one-room Quaker schoolhouse. ⊠ *58 N. Main St.,* ☏ *508/398–3773.* ☉ *Services Sun. at 10.*

☾ **Pirate's Cove** is the most elaborate of the Cape's many miniature golf setups, with a hill, a waterfall, a stream, and the 18-hole Blackbeard's Challenge course. ⊠ *728 Main St. (Rte. 28),* ☏ *508/394–6200.* ▨ *$7.* ☉ *July–Aug., daily 9 AM–11 PM; Apr.–June and Sept.–Oct., most days 10–8, but call.*

☾ For rainy-day fun, the **Ryan Family Amusement Center** offers videogame rooms, Skee-Ball, and bowling. ⊠ *1067 Main St. (Rte. 28),* ☏ *508/394–5644.* ☉ *Daily; hrs vary.*

Dining and Lodging

$$–$$$ ✕ **The Skipper.** With expanded seating, a longer menu, and terrific ocean views, this classic Cape restaurant has been getting better and better since its inception in 1936. Sit downstairs in the nautical-theme main room or upstairs on the outside deck with views of Nantucket Sound. The menu is an odd but compelling mix of classic New England seafood, Italian favorites, and international dishes, from Thai pasta to Jamaican jerk chicken. The Skipper is open in season for breakfast, lunch, and dinner. ⊠ *152 South Shore Dr.,* ☏ *508/394–7406. Reservations not accepted. AE, D, MC, V. Closed Nov.–March.*

$$$ ▦ **Ocean Mist.** This three-story, upscale motel-style resort sits on its own private (but tiny) beach on Nantucket Sound. The rooms have modern furnishings, cable TV, and either wet bars or fully stocked kitchenettes. The duplex loft suites are a step above, with cathedral ceilings, a sitting area with pullout sofa, skylights, and one or two private balconies. ⊠ *97 S. Shore Dr., 02664,* ☏ *508/398–2633 or 800/248–6478,* ▣ *508/760–3151,* ▥ *capecodtravel.com/oceanmist. 32 rooms, 31 suites. Coffee shop, air-conditioning, indoor pool, hot tub, beach, laundry facilities. AE, D, MC, V.*

$$–$$$ ▦ **Capt. Farris House.** Steps from the Bass River Bridge dividing South Yarmouth and West Dennis and a short spin away from congested Route 28 sits this imposing 1845 Greek Revival home, built by the sea captain for whom it's named. The large rooms and suites have either antique or canopied queen- or king-size beds, extra pillows, plush comforters, fancy drapes, TVs, and tile baths (all but one with a whirlpool tub). Some have fireplaces and sundecks. Breakfast is served in the formal dining room or in the interior glassed-in brick courtyard, and might include quiche with pumpkin-pecan scones or thick French toast. Fresh baked goods and sherry are available for later-in-the-day nourishment. ⊠ *308 Old Main St., 02664,* ☎ *508/760–2818 or 800/ 350–9477,* FAX *508/398–1262,* WEB *www.captainfarris.com. 5 rooms, 4 suites. Air-conditioning. No smoking. AE, D, MC, V. BP.*

$$ 🖼 **Belvedere B&B.** Elisha Baker, a local sea captain, built this quaint Federal home around 1820. The Hamilton Room is the most spacious, with some frilly touches: lace curtains, a lacy bedspread, green floral wallpaper, and old pink-velvet chairs. Romantics may prefer the first-floor Boston Room, with green wicker chairs, a two-person whirlpool tub, and a queen-size bed topped with a rose quilt. The Virginia Anthony Room (with pink-and-white quilts on the twin four-poster beds) and the Florilla Room (with a queen-size bed, white wicker furnishings, and a pink wide-board floor) are both small but cozy and sunny; they share a bath across the hall. Those who want privacy might consider the Coach House, an efficiency unit behind the main house. Breakfast is served in the formal dining room or on the screened-in porch. ⊠ *167 Old Main St., 02664,* ☎ *508/398–6674 or 800/288–4080,* FAX *508/398–6674,* WEB *www.belvederebb.com. 4 rooms, 2 with bath; 1 efficiency. Air-conditioning. No smoking. AE, D, MC, V. BP.*

$$ 🖼 **Seaside.** Right on a Nantucket Sound beach, this 5-acre village of Cape-style cottages (studios and one- or two-bedroom units) has a view of scalloped beaches in both directions. Seaside was built in the 1940s, and the decor varies from cottage to cottage, as each is individually owned. All have kitchens or kitchenettes, and many have wood-burning fireplaces. The oceanfront cottages, right off a strip of grass set with lounge and Adirondack chairs, have the best view and decor. Cottages in the adjacent pine grove are generally very pleasant, and most have been updated within the past two years. Shoulder-season rates are very attractive. ⊠ *135 S. Shore Dr., 02664,* ☎ *508/398–2533,* FAX *508/398–2523. 43 cottages. Kitchenettes, picnic area, beach. D, MC, V. Closed mid-Oct.–Apr.*

Nightlife and the Arts

Feel like it's been too long since you last fox-trotted? **Betsy's Ballroom** (⊠ 528 Forest Rd., ☎ 508/362–9538) has Saturday-night ballroom dancing year-round to live bands on the Cape's largest dance floor. The bands deliver swing, waltzes, and fox-trot 8 PM–11 PM; it's BYO for drinks and snacks, and Betsy will provide the ice and cups. Admission is $7.50.

Outdoor Activities and Sports

BASEBALL

The **Yarmouth-Dennis Red Sox** of the collegiate Cape Cod Baseball League play home games at Red Wilson Field (⊠ Station Ave., ☎ 508/ 394–9466) from mid-June to mid-August.

SOCCER

The **Cape Cod Crusaders,** of the D-3 League, play action-packed home matches at the Alan Carlsen Field at Dennis-Yarmouth Regional High School (⊠ Station Ave., ☎ 508/790–4782) from April to mid-August.

BEACHES

The **Flax Pond** (⊠ N. Main St. between High Bank and Great Western Rds.) recreation area offers freshwater swimming, a lifeguard, and ducks, but no sand beach, just pine needle–covered ground. There's a pine-shaded picnic area with grills, as well as tennis and basketball courts and plenty of parking.

Parker's River Beach (⊠ S. Shore Dr.), a flat stretch of sand on warm Nantucket Sound, is perfect for families. It has a lifeguard, a concession stand, a gazebo and picnic area, a playground, outdoor showers, and rest rooms. There's a $10 parking fee in season.

BIKE RENTAL
Outdoor Shop (⊠ 50 Long Pond Dr., ☎ 508/394–3819) rents bikes and mopeds and does repairs.

GOLF
Blue Rock Golf Course (⊠ off Great Western Rd., ☎ 508/398–9295) is a highly regarded, easy-to-walk 18-hole, par-3, 3,000-yard public course crossed by a pond. The pro shop rents clubs; reservations are mandatory in season.

HEALTH AND FITNESS CLUBS
Mid Cape Racquet Club (⊠ 193 White's Path, ☎ 508/394–3511) has one racquetball, one squash, and nine indoor tennis courts; indoor basketball; a sauna, steam room, and whirlpools; massage services; and a free-weight and cardiovascular room—plus day care. It also offers spinning, kick boxing, and body pump classes. Daily rates are available.

West Dennis

⑱ *6 mi south of Dennis, 1 mi east of South Yarmouth.*

In another one of those tricks of Cape geography, the village of West Dennis is actually south of South Dennis on the east side of the Bass River. Dennisport is farther east, near the Harwich town line. If you're driving between West Dennis and Harwich, Lower County Road, with occasional glimpses of the sea between the cottages and beach-front hotels, is a more scenic alternative to overdeveloped Route 28.

Dining and Lodging

$$–$$$ ✕ **Christine's.** This family-run restaurant is sprawling, spacious, and a little generic—the type that attracts bus tours—with a big bar in its own room, a private function room, and a separate show club with a glittering stage offering cabaret acts, comedians, impersonators, and bands from all over the country. The menu here is mostly typical American restaurant fare, with basic Italian dishes and some seafood and steak. A nice touch is Lebanese specials such as a pine-nut and almond-crusted haddock with tahini sauce, and *kafta* (fresh ground lamb and beef blended with onions, mint, and Lebanese spices) grilled and served with almond rice and hummus. To help work off dinner, there's dancing year-round. ⊠ *581 Main St. (Rte. 28),* ☎ *508/394–7333. AE, D, MC, V.*

$$$$ 🏠 **Lighthouse Inn.** On a small private beach adjacent to West Dennis Beach, this traditional Cape resort has been in family hands since 1938. The main inn was built around a still-operational 1855 lighthouse and has five guest rooms. Scattered along a landscaped lawn are 23 individual weathered, shingle Cape cottages (one room to three bedrooms, no kitchens) and five multiroom buildings. Cottages have decks, knotty-pine and some painted walls, and generally nice, cabiny bedrooms. The oceanfront Guest House has a common room with a fireplace. In the main inn are a living room, a library, and a restaurant in three waterfront rooms that serves New England cuisine and seafood. In summer supervised activities and dinners for kids give parents some private time. ⊠ *1 Lighthouse Rd., Box 128, 02670,* ☎ *508/398–2244,* FAX *508/398–5658,* WEB *www.lighthouseinn.com. 40 rooms, 23 cottages. Restaurant, bar, room service, pool, miniature golf, tennis court, shuffleboard, beach, fishing, billiards, nightclub, recreation room, library, children's programs (ages 3–12), playground. MC, V. Closed mid-Oct.–mid-May. BP; MAP available.*

$-$$ ★ 🖼 **Beach House Inn.** This is the kind of house you'd expect when Nantucket Sound is your backyard: shingles weathered gray from the salt air; white wicker and natural oak furniture that's practical yet comfortable; walls of glass that frame the beauty—and sometimes ferocity—of Mother Nature. Some rooms have brass or four-poster beds, and all have TVs, ceiling fans, and decks, some of which overlook the front yard. The best room is undoubtedly Room 2, with its second-story waterfront deck and a private staircase leading to the inn's beach. The common room has a TV and wide assortment of hit movies on video. You can cook meals on the barbecue grills or in the fully equipped kitchen, which has a microwave. At the height of the season (mid-June–Labor Day), rooms must be rented by the week; in the off-season the inn must be rented as a whole, and is not run as a B&B. ✉ *61 Uncle Stephen's Rd., Box 494, 02670,* ☎ *508/398–4575; 617/489–4144 Columbus Day–Memorial Day,* WEB *www.innsandlodging.com/beachhouseinn. 7 rooms. Beach, playground. No smoking. No credit cards. CP.*

Nightlife and the Arts

Christine's (✉ 581 Main St. [Rte. 28], ☎ 508/394–7333) stages nightly entertainment in season in its 300-seat showroom. Concerts, sometimes with dancing, feature name bands from the 1950s to 1970s, Top 40 bands, or jazz. There are also stand-up comedy nights. Off-season the schedule includes live entertainment and dancing to a DJ on weekends, as well as special events.

The **Sand Bar** (✉ Lighthouse Rd., ☎ 508/398–7586) presents the boogie-woogie piano playing of local legend Rock King, who's been tickling the ivories—and people's funny bones—since the 1960s. The club is closed from mid-October to mid-May.

In season, you can dance to a DJ and live bands at **Sundancer's** (✉ 116 Main St. [Rte. 28], ☎ 508/394–1600). It's closed December and January.

Outdoor Activities and Sports
BEACHES

The **West Dennis Beach** (✉ Lighthouse Rd. off Lower County Rd.) is one of the best on the south shore. A breakwater was started here in 1837 in an effort to protect the mouth of Bass River but was abandoned when a sandbar formed on the shore side. It is a long, wide, and popular sandy beach, stretching for 1½ mi, with marshland and the Bass River across from it. Popular with windsurfers, the beach also has bathhouses, lifeguards, a playground, concessions, and parking for 1,000 cars. Nonresidents pay a $10 parking fee per day in season.

ICE-SKATING

Fall through spring, plus summer Saturdays and some evenings (call for schedule), ice-skating is available at the **Tony Kent Arena** (✉ 8 Gages Way, South Dennis, ☎ 508/760–2400). Keep your eyes peeled: this is where Nancy Kerrigan and Paul Wylie train. Rental skates are available.

JOGGING

Lifecourse (✉ Bob Crowell Rd. and Old Bass River Rd., South Dennis) is a 1½-mi jogging trail through woods, with 20 exercise stations along the way. It's part of a recreation area that includes basketball and handball courts, ball fields, a playground, and a picnic area.

Dennisport

🔵 *1 mi east of West Dennis, 10 mi west of Chatham.*

The Mid Cape's last southern village is Dennisport, a prime summer-resort area, with gray-shingle cottages, summer houses and condominiums, and lots of white picket fences covered with rambling roses. The Union Wharf Packing Company operated here in the 1850s, and sail makers and ship chandlers lined the shore. The beach where sea clams were once packed in the sands is now packed with sunbathers.

NEED A
BREAK?
Set in a rustic mid-19th-century barn decorated with such memorabilia as a working nickelodeon, the **Sundae School Ice Cream Parlor** (⊠ 387 Lower County Rd., ☎ 508/394–9122), open mid-April–mid-October, serves great homemade ice cream and frozen yogurt with lots of toppings, sugar-free ice cream, real whipped cream, and old-fashioned sarsaparilla and cream soda from an antique marble soda fountain.

Dining and Lodging

$$–$$$ ✕ **Clancy's.** A local landmark set on the bucolic Swan River, Clancy's is popular, with a parking lot that's often jammed by 5 PM. Calling itself a county (not country) tavern, this is an enormous operation, with long family tables, round tables, bar tables, booths, a deck overlooking the river, two bars, and many, many servers. On the seemingly endless menu are several variations of nachos, salads, and chili. Clancy's likes to be creative with the names of its dishes, so you'll find items such as steak Lucifer (sirloin topped with lobster, asparagus, and béarnaise sauce) and a Sunday-brunch menu with the like of crab, steak, or eggs Benny. ⊠ *8 Upper County Rd.,* ☎ *508/394–6661. Reservations not accepted. AE, DC, MC, V.*

$$–$$$ ✕ **Swan River Seafood Restaurant.** From the right table you can have a beautiful view of the Swan River marsh and Nantucket Sound beyond at this informal little eatery, which turns out great fresh fish, both traditional and creative. Besides the usual fried and broiled choices, try mako shark au poivre or scrod San Sebastian, simmered in garlic broth with littleneck clams. ⊠ *5 Lower County Rd.,* ☎ *508/394–4466. AE, MC, V. Closed mid-Sept.–late May. No lunch late May–mid-June.*

$–$$ ✕ **Bob Briggs' Wee Packet.** Cute as can be—maybe a little too cute—
★   this tiny dinette is decorated in classic Cape kitsch, with screaming-yellow tables, seascapes on the walls, and driftwood, seashells, and little bits of moss everywhere. The food is very good, very traditional, and very simple: plenty of local seafood (broiled swordfish and fish-and-chips are quite reliable) as well as sandwiches and salads. Try bread pudding with lemon sauce for dessert. You can pick up homemade freshly baked goods at the adjoining bakery and doughnut shop. Bob Briggs himself will greet you at the door, no doubt wearing his signature suspenders. ⊠ *79 Depot St., at Lower County Rd.,* ☎ *508/398–2181. Reservations not accepted. MC, V. Closed Oct.–Apr.*

$–$$ ✕ **Kream 'N Kone.** This is how it's been since 1953: order up some fried clams and a shake or a soda, get a number, wait five minutes, and sit down to some of the best fast food anywhere. The fried food will overflow your paper plate onto a plastic tray, but it's so good that what you thought you'd never be able to finish somehow vanishes. The onion rings in particular are a knockout. At times the prices seem surprisingly high, but not for what you get. A sister restaurant of the same name serves up the same great stuff down Route 28 a few miles into Chatham. ⊠ *Main St. (Rte. 28),* ☎ *508/394–0808. No credit cards. Closed Nov.–Apr.*

$ ✕ **Bob's Best Sandwiches.** Bob Theobald is a hands-on owner in the best sense; he makes his own bread, roasts his own turkey, opens every day at 7 AM, and doesn't close until around dinnertime. The result is one of the better breakfast and lunch spots around, as well as a busy catering business. The French toast for breakfast is a real treat, even better than the excellent omelets. For lunch try the big roast beef sandwich. ⊠ *613 Main St. (Rte. 28),* ☎ *508/394–8450. Reservations not accepted. No credit cards. No dinner.*

$$$ 🏠 **Pelham House.** The ocean-side Pelham House, south of Route 28, is a modern, if not particularly exciting, collection of spacious rooms, strategically angled to maximize ocean views. All are equipped with phones, cable TV, a small refrigerator, and a fan (no air-conditioning). Atop the property's ocean-facing section are several "penthouse" rooms with sitting areas, excellent views of Nantucket Sound, and more upscale furniture. But the location really generates a buzz—with about 400 ft of private beachfront, it's a great place to spend all day in the sun and sand. A complimentary full breakfast is served in season, a Continental breakfast in the cooler months. ⊠ *14 Sea St., Box 38 02639,* ☎ *508/398–6076 or 800/497–3542,* FAX *508/760–3999,* WEB *www.capecodtravel.com/pelhamhouse. 39 rooms. Breakfast room, pool, tennis, beach. AE, D, MC, V. Closed mid-Oct.–Mar. BP.*

$$ 🏠 **The Garlands.** There are innumerable strip motels and cottage colonies lining Old Wharf Road in Dennisport, but few places provide comfort and views to match this bi-level motel-style complex. There are 20 units in all—18 are two-bedroom suites. Each unit has a fully equipped kitchen, cable TV, private sundeck or patio, and daily maid service. The oceanfront VIP suites, simply named A and B (two bedrooms) and C and D (one bedroom), are the best picks here—the nearly floor-to-ceiling windows offer unobstructed water views; at high tide you're almost in the surf. ⊠ *117 Old Wharf Rd., Box 506, 02639,* ☎ *508/398–6987. 20 suites. Beach. No credit cards. Closed mid-Oct.–mid-Apr.*

Nightlife and the Arts
Clancy's (⊠ 8 Upper County Rd., ☎ 508/394–6661) has contemporary piano music year-round.

Improper Bostonian (⊠ Rte. 28, ☎ 508/394–7416), open only in summer, has a mix of live music and DJ-spun dance tunes Wednesday–Saturday and attracts a youngish crowd.

Outdoor Activities and Sports
Cape Cod Waterways (⊠ 16 Main St. [Rte. 28], ☎ 508/398–0080) rents canoes, kayaks, and electric paddleboats for leisurely travel on the Swan River.

Shopping
Factory Shoe Mart (⊠ 271 Main St. [Rte. 28], ☎ 508/398–6000) has such brand names as Capezio, Dexter, Clark, Esprit, Nike, Reebok, L. A. Gear, and Rockport.

THE MID CAPE A TO Z

To research prices, get advice from other travelers, and book travel arrangements, visit www.fodors.com.

AIR TRAVEL
Airline service is extremely unpredictable because of the seasonal nature of Cape travel—carriers come and go, while others juggle their routes.

CARRIERS
Cape Air/Nantucket Airlines flies direct from Boston to Hyannis and Provincetown year-round and from New Bedford to Martha's Vineyard and Nantucket. Cape Air has joint fares with Continental, Delta, Midwest Express, and US Airways and ticketing and baggage agreements with eight major U.S. airlines and with KLM. For charters, contact Cape Air.

US Airways Express flies nonstop from Boston and New York to Hyannis year-round. Connect in Boston with the airline's other routes. Westchester Air offers charter service from White Plains, New York, to from Hyannis, Martha's Vineyard, and Nantucket.

➤ AIRLINES AND CONTACTS: **Cape Air/Nantucket Airlines** (☎ 508/771–6944 or 800/352–0714, WEB www.flycapeair.com). **US Airways Express** (☎ 800/428–4322). **Westchester Air** (☎ 800/759–2929).

AIRPORTS

Barnstable Municipal Airport is in Hyannis, minutes from Barnstable village.

➤ AIRPORT INFORMATION: **Barnstable Municipal Airport** (✉ 480 Barnstable Rd., Rte. 28 rotary, ☎ 508/775–2020).

BUS TRAVEL

The Cape Cod Regional Transit Authority operates several bus services that link Cape towns. All buses are wheelchair-accessible and equipped with bike racks. The SeaLine operates along Route 28 Monday–Saturday between Hyannis and Woods Hole (average fare is $3.50 one-way from Hyannis to Woods Hole). Its many stops include Mashpee Commons, Falmouth, and the Woods Hole Steamship Authority docks. The SeaLine connects in Hyannis with the Plymouth & Brockton line, as well as the Villager, another bus line that runs along Route 132 between Hyannis and Barnstable Harbor. The driver will stop when signaled along the route.

The b-Bus is a fleet of minivans that will transport passengers door to door between any towns on the Cape. Service runs seven days a week, year-round, though reservations must be made in advance. The cost is $2 per ride, plus 10¢ per mi, half that for seniors.

The H2O Line offers daily regularly scheduled service year-round between Hyannis and Orleans along Route 28. The Hyannis–Orleans fare is $3.50; shorter trips cost less. Buses connect in Hyannis with the SeaLine, Villager, and Plymouth & Brockton lines.

Plymouth & Brockton Street Railway has service between Boston and Provincetown, with stops at many towns in between.

➤ BUS INFORMATION: **Cape Cod Regional Transit Authority** (☎ 508/385–8326; 800/352–7155 in MA, WEB www.capecodtransit.org).**Plymouth & Brockton Street Railway** (☎ 508/746–0378, WEB www.p-b.com).

CAR RENTAL

You can rent wheels at Barnstable Municipal Airport (☞ Airports, *above*).

➤ MAJOR AGENCIES: **Avis** (☎ 508/775–2888 or 800/831–2847, WEB www.avis.com). **Budget** (☎ 508/790–1614 or 800/527–0700, WEB www.budgetrentacar.com). **Hertz** (☎ 508/775–5825 or 800/654–3131, WEB www.hertz.com). **National** (☎ 508/771–4353 or 800/227–7368, WEB www.nationalcar.com).

CAR TRAVEL

U.S. 6 and Routes 6A and 28 are heavily congested eastbound Friday evening, westbound Sunday afternoon, and in both directions on Saturday in summer.

EMERGENCIES

Cape Cod Hospital has a 24-hour emergency room. Health Stop takes walk-in patients weekdays 8–8, Saturday 9–5, and Sunday 11–5. Mid Cape Medical Center is open every day 8–7:30 in summer, 8–6:30 after Labor Day. Dental Associates of Cape Cod accepts emergency walk-ins.

For rescues at sea, call the Coast Guard. Boaters should use Channel 16 on their radios.

➤ DOCTORS AND DENTISTS: **Dental Associates of Cape Cod** (✉ 262 Barnstable Rd., Hyannis, ☎ 508/778–1200). **Health Stop** (✉ Cape Town Plaza, Rte. 132, Hyannis, ☎ 508/771–7520). **Mid Cape Medical Center** (✉ 489 Bearses Way, at Rte. 28, Unit A-4, Hyannis, ☎ 508/771–4092).

➤ EMERGENCY SERVICES: **Ambulance, fire, police** (☎ 911 or dial township station).**Coast Guard** (☎ 508/888–0335 in Sandwich and Cape Cod Canal; 508/945–0164 in Chatham; WEB www.uscg.mil).

➤ HOSPITALS: **Cape Cod Hospital** (✉ 27 Park St., Hyannis, ☎ 508/771–1800, WEB www.capecodhealth.org).

➤ HOT LINES: **Massachusetts Poison Control Center** (☎ 800/682–9211, WEB www.mapoison.org).

➤ 24-HOUR PHARMACIES: **CVS** (✉ 176–182 North St., Hyannis, ☎ 508/775–8346).

LODGING

APARTMENT AND HOUSE RENTALS

Rentals throughout the Mid Cape are handled by Century 21, Sam Ingram Real Estate. Great Vacations Inc. specializes in locating vacation rentals in Brewster, Dennis, and Orleans. Peter McDowell Associates offers a wide selection of properties for rent by the week, month, or season; the company also rents larger homes for family reunions and other gatherings. Most places are in Dennis. Waterfront Rentals covers Bourne to Truro, listing everything from condos to estates.

➤ LOCAL AGENTS: **Century 21, Sam Ingram Real Estate** (✉ 938 Rte. 6A, Yarmouth 02675, ☎ 508/362–8844 or 800/676–3340, FAX 508/362–7889, WEB www.century21samingram.com). **Great Vacations Inc.** (✉ 2660 Rte. 6A, Brewster 02631, ☎ 508/896–2090). **Peter McDowell Associates** (✉ 585 Main St. [Rte. 6A], Dennis 02638, ☎ 508/385–9114 or 888/385–9114; ✉ 11 Main St. [Rte. 28], Dennisport 02639, ☎ 508/394–5400 or 800/870–5401, WEB www.capecodproperties.com). **Waterfront Rentals** (✉ 20 Pilgrim Rd., West Yarmouth 02673, ☎ 508/778–1818, FAX 508/771–3563, WEB www.waterfrontrentalsinc.com).

CAMPING

Eastern Mountain Sports rents tents and sleeping bags. Sandy Terraces is a seasonal family nudist campground.

➤ CONTACTS: **Eastern Mountain Sports** (✉ 1513 Rte. 132, Hyannis, ☎ 508/362–8690, WEB www.emsonline.com). **Sandy Terraces** (✉ Box 98, Marstons Mills 02648, ☎ 508/428–9209).

TAXIS

There are taxi stands at the Hyannis airport, the Hyannis bus station, and the Capetown Mall, across the street from the Cape Cod Mall. In Hyannis call Checker Taxi for pickups. Dick's Taxi will pick you up, and has a stand at the airport. John's Taxi & Limousine picks up in Dennis and Harwich only but will take passengers all over the Cape. Town Taxi is found at several locations around Hyannis, including Capetown Mall, the bus station, and on West Main Street.

➤ TAXI COMPANIES: **Checker Taxi** (☎ 508/771–8294). **Dick's Taxi** (☎ 508/428-4918). **John's Taxi & Limousine** (☎ 508/394–3209). **Town Taxi** (☎ 508/771–5555 or 888/771–8696).

TOURS

Cape Cod Duck Mobile takes you on a land-and-sea tour of downtown Hyannis and the harbor in a restored U.S. military amphibious vehicle. These 45-minute narrated tours depart on the hour, roll through downtown, then splash into Lewis Bay to cruise past the Kennedy compound and other sights. Tickets go on sale daily at 9:30 and in summer often sell out by noon. Tours run on the hour 10–4. Call for details about where to purchase tickets; admission for the tour is $14.

Hy-Line runs one-hour narrated boat tours of Hyannis Harbor, including a view of the Kennedy compound. Sunset and evening cocktail cruises are available; ticket prices for all tours range between $10 and $17. Starfish River Cruise offers 1½-hour water safari tours of the Bass River, past windmills, marshlands, and old captains' houses, all seen from a 32-ft aluminum boat with an awning. Trips cost $12.50 and run at 11, 1, 4, and 6, and there's a snack bar on board.

Sightsee from above with the Cape Cod Flying Service, or Cape Flight LTD. Cape Cod Soaring Adventures offers glider flights and lessons out of Marstons Mills.

The Cape Cod Central Railroad offers two-hour, 42-mi narrated rail tours from Hyannis to the Cape Cod Canal (admission $13), as well as a three-hour dinner train where you can settle back and watch the scenery as you nosh. The summer dinner train runs Tuesday through Sunday, and the cost is $50 per person. Another dinner train, created for families, with a children's menu and activities, runs on Tuesday evening. Trains run late May through October, Tuesday to Sunday; during the off-season, call for a schedule.

➤ FEES AND SCHEDULES: **Cape Cod Central Railroad** (✉ Hyannis Train Depot, 252 Main St., Hyannis, ☎ 508/771–3800 or 888/797–7245, WEB www.capetrain.com). **Cape Cod Duck Mobile** (✉ 447 Main St., Hyannis, ☎ 508/362–1117). **Cape Cod Flying Service** (✉ Cape Cod Airport, 1000 Race La., Marstons Mills, ☎ 508/428–8732 or 800/247–5263). **Cape Cod Soaring Adventures** (☎ 508/420–4201). **Cape Flight LTD** (Barnstable Municipal Airport, ✉ 480 Barnstable Rd., Rte. 28 rotary, Hyannis, ☎ 508/775–8171). **Hy-Line** (✉ Ocean St. dock, Pier 1, ☎ 508/778–2600, WEB www.hy-linecruises.com). **Starfish River Cruise** (✉ Rte. 28, West Dennis, just east of Bass River Bridge, ☎ 508/362–5555).

TROLLEY TRAVEL

The Cape Cod Regional Transit Authority runs seasonal trolleys in Falmouth, Mashpee, Hyannis, Yarmouth, and Dennis. Fares and times vary; call for more information.

➤ CONTACTS: **Cape Cod Regional Transit Authority** (☎ 508/385–8326; 800/352–7155 in MA, WEB www.capecodtransit.org).

VISITOR INFORMATION

The Cape Cod Chamber of Commerce is open year-round, Monday–Saturday 9–5 and Sunday 10–4.

➤ TOURIST INFORMATION: **Cape Cod Chamber of Commerce** (✉ junction of U.S. 6 and 132, Box 790, Hyannis 02601, ☎ 508/862–0700 or 888/332–2732, WEB www.capecodchamber.org). **Dennis** (✉ junction of Rtes. 28 and 134, West Dennis; ✉ Box 275, South Dennis 02660, ☎ 508/398–3568 or 800/243–9920, WEB www.dennischamber.com). **Hyannis** (✉ 1481 Rte. 132, 02601, ☎ 508/362–5230 or 877/492–6647, WEB www.hyannis.com). **Yarmouth** (✉ 657 Rte. 28, West Yarmouth 02673; ✉ Box 479, South Yarmouth 02664, ☎ 508/778–1008 or 800/732–1008, WEB www.yarmouthcapecod.com; information center, ✉ U.S. 6 heading east between Exits 6 and 7, ☎ 508/362–9796).

5 THE LOWER CAPE

This quieter, gentler part of the Cape holds some of the peninsula's most breathtaking natural scenery and gives a glimpse of the region's rich history. Brewster holds on to the past with aged oak trees and 19th-century sea captains' homes. Harwich and Harwich Port combine rural beauty with the bustle of boats and beachgoers. Elegant Chatham has a lively downtown, and Eastham is all about the sea, with splendid Atlantic and bay beaches.

S PECKLED with still-active cranberry bogs, sturdy trees, and pasture, the Lower Cape exudes a peaceful, residential aura. You won't find roadways cluttered with mini-golf complexes, trampolines, or bumper boats here. Although the building boom of the late 1990s filled many once-vacant expanses with sparkling new homes, the region is still marked by a quiet sense of history and simple purpose.

Revised by
Laura V. Scheel

Rich in history and Cape flavor, Brewster and Harwich stand opposite one another in the area just shy of the elbow. Harwich, inland, has antique homes; rambling old burial grounds; and a modest town center with shops, restaurants, museums, churches, and public parks. Brewster is similarly historic; examples of Victorian, Greek Revival, and colonial architecture abound, most of it meticulously preserved. Many homes have been converted to welcoming guest houses and bed-and-breakfasts, while others are privately owned.

The traditional, elegant town of Chatham perches dramatically at the end of the peninsular elbow. It's here the Atlantic begins to wet the shores of the Cape, sometimes with frightening strength. Chatham has shown vulnerability to the forces of nature over the years, as little by little its shores have succumbed to the insatiable sea.

North of Chatham is Orleans, supply center of the Lower and Outer Capes, replete with large grocery chains and shopping plazas. The famed Nauset Beach is here, its dune-backed shores crammed with sunseeking revelers in summer. Orleans does have a rich history; you just have to leave the maze of industry to find it. Continuing north, you'll reach Eastham, a town often overlooked because of its position on busy U.S. 6 but perfectly charming if you know where to look.

The Lower Cape is blessed with large tracts of open space, set aside for conservation. South of Chatham, the Monomoy National Wildlife Refuge is a twin-island bird sanctuary. Here dozens of species of birds are free to feed, nest, and expand their numbers without human meddling. Recreation seekers should head straight to Nickerson State Park in Brewster to frolic in freshwater ponds or enjoy a serene bike ride under the shade of trees. In Eastham, where the Cape Cod National Seashore officially begins, the Salt Pond Visitor Center has a wealth of area information, educational programs, and guided tours.

Pleasures and Pastimes

Beaches

The Lower Cape is straddled by four major bodies of water: the bracing and grand Atlantic Ocean and three more mild-mannered bays—Nantucket Sound, Pleasant Bay, and Cape Cod Bay. Those who prefer freshwater swimming can try the many ponds—some left over from the ancient glacial carving of the peninsula—sprinkled throughout the entire area.

On the south side, Harwich Port, Harwich, and Chatham dip into the shallower and warmer Nantucket Sound. The beaches here, which tend to be divided into smallish partitions designated according to public or private ownership, are popular with families, ice cream trucks, jet skiers, and windsurfers. Harwich and Chatham swimmers can also find a spot along Pleasant Bay. The waters here are very shallow, which makes it ideal for kayaks, canoes, and swimmers.

Brewster's glory is Cape Cod Bay, and dozens of beaches (public and private) extend for acres at low tide. Although swimmers won't have much luck at this time, treasure hunters can stroll the sands, keeping an eye out for shells and creatures left behind by the retreating waters. There's plenty of room to wander on the bayside, and you won't find a better spot to catch the nightly sunset.

The Lower Cape's ocean beaches are unbroken by dictates of ownership or man-made barriers from Chatham onward, so you're free to roam. Note that Chatham's ocean beaches are easily accessible by bike or foot, but there's no parking for cars. Orleans has Nauset Beach, a Cape Cod favorite. In Eastham the National Seashore and the town maintain several beaches that provide exhilarating ocean swimming.

Biking

The Cape's top bike route, the 25-mi Cape Cod Rail Trail, follows the paved right-of-way of the old Penn Central Railroad, from South Dennis to South Wellfleet. You can pick up the trail in Harwich, Brewster, Orleans, and Eastham. Nickerson State Park, in Brewster, has 8 mi of its own forested trails, some with access to the rail trail. From the Salt Pond Visitor Center in Eastham, take a jaunt off the rail trail for meandering paths leading to Nauset Beach, Coast Guard Beach, and beautiful Nauset Marsh. Cyclists in Chatham can follow the little green signs that denote the Chatham Bike Route; but use caution, as the roadway is shared with folks in cars who are just as eagerly taking in the view as you are. The trail runs beside the ocean and all the stunningly majestic homes that dominate the waterfront.

Dining

In a highly controversial policy change, many Cape towns—including Chatham, Orleans, Eastham, Brewster, and Harwich—have banished smoking from restaurants and bars. Despite the law, which has enraged many a business owner, dining out still remains one of the region's most popular pastimes, and seekers of fine food will not be disappointed.

Each town has its own batch of treasured and traditional restaurants, and all will be crowded in the summer. A significant number of restaurants close their doors once the crowds thin in October—including the beloved fried-seafood shacks—but plenty remain open throughout the year. Seafood is, not surprisingly, a major staple in these parts.

If you're in the mood for fine dining, a couple of good choices are Brewster's Chillingsworth for French cuisine in a European country-inspired setting, and Chatham Bars Inn for an elegant waterfront meal. Not sure what you want? In Chatham you can just stroll down Main Street and see what tickles your palate; diners in Orleans, Brewster, Harwich, and Eastham will have to do some driving if unsure of their eating desire, as restaurants are more spread out.

CATEGORY	COST*
$$$$	over $26
$$$	$19–$26
$$	$11–$18
$	under $11

*per person for a main course at dinner

Lodging

Money made in early maritime fortunes helped build exquisite historic homes, many of which are now unique and lovely inns. Chatham is blessed with dozens of these aged beauties, most with all the modern conveniences. B&Bs and intimate guest houses are the primary lodging choices, but there are several larger hotels such as Chatham Bars Inn and the Chatham Wayside Inn. Even these giants specialize in carefully designed decor and comfort. Outside town are roadside or waterfront hotel complexes, usually a bit softer on the budget and welcoming to families with small children.

Brewster is essentially a B&B kind of town, offering lodging in former sea captains' homes. Harwich and Orleans have a mixture of both family-friendly hotel complexes and lovingly restored inns. Eastham has quite a few large-scale hotels along U.S. 6, including Sheraton. Don't expect to find bargains in the summertime.

Other options include camping or weekly cottage rentals; all towns have the ubiquitous cottage colonies. Note that in summer these must be secured well in advance, usually through a local real estate agent.

CATEGORY	COST*
$$$$	over $200
$$$	$150–$200
$$	$100–$150
$	under $100

All prices are for a standard double room in high season, excluding 5.7% state tax and gratuities. Some inns add a 15% service charge.

Nightlife and the Arts

Chatham's Main Street is lined with galleries and studios showcasing local and national artists. In Orleans weekly outdoor art shows sell the works of local painters and craftspeople, and offer free demonstrations. Eastham and Harwich also host outdoor arts and crafts forays. Harwich's biggie is the Professional Arts and Crafts Festival, held in July and August.

The theater tradition remains strong throughout the Lower Cape. In Harwich the Harwich Junior Theatre stages a variety of performances year-round and offers children's classes in the summer. Community theater dominates the scene in Orleans and Chatham. Off-season, Eastham shines with the First Encounter Coffee House, a lively place for local music and poetry readings in an alcohol-free setting. Brewster is home to the professional Cape Cod Repertory Theatre, where performances are staged both indoors and out under the stars.

Popular and free town-band concerts are held all over the Cape, and other concerts are presented by various church groups and community organizations. There's a continuous, lively schedule of events throughout the summer in each town; pick up a free guide at information centers and stores.

Nightlife on the Lower Cape is never wild, but it's certainly not dull. Many bars in Orleans, Chatham, and Harwich feature live local bands, including the Chatham Squire, the Land Ho! in Orleans, Brewster's rustic Woodshed, and the spirited Irish Pub in West Harwich. More peaceful nighttime diversions include solitary beach walking by moonlight, and stargazing (watch for the extraordinary Perseid meteor shower display in August). The National Seashore schedules storytelling nights around a beach bonfire.

Outdoor Activities and Sports

Cape Cod, especially the Lower and Outer regions, is an outdoor playground. From Eastham to Provincetown, the Cape Cod National Seashore offers miles of hiking and biking trails, several historic sites, and many beautiful, natural places to explore.

The Cape's rivers, ponds, inlets, and harbors are great for canoeing or kayaking. Whether on your own or as part of a guided tour (the Cape Cod Museum of Natural History, in Brewster, has a full schedule of

The Lower Cape

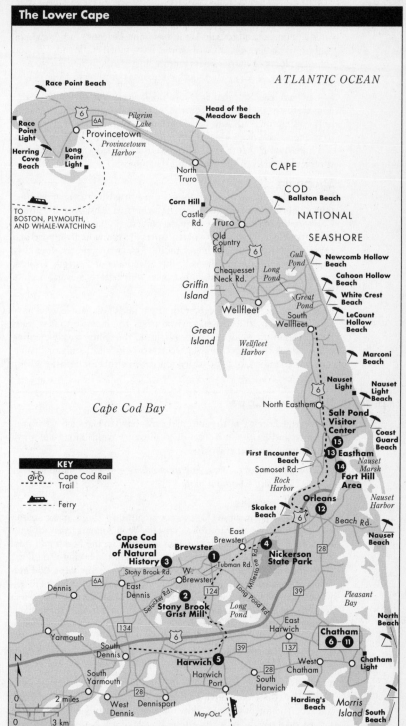

ATLANTIC OCEAN

Race Point Beach

Race Point Light

Herring Cove Beach

Long Point Light

Provincetown

Provincetown Harbor

Pilgrim Lake

Head of the Meadow Beach

North Truro

CAPE

COD

Corn Hill

Castle Rd.

Truro

Old Country Rd.

Ballston Beach

NATIONAL

SEASHORE

Gull Pond

Newcomb Hollow Beach

Cahoon Hollow Beach

Chequesset Neck Rd.

Griffin Island

Long Pond

White Crest Beach

Wellfleet

Great Pond

South Wellfleet

LeCount Hollow Beach

Great Island

Wellfleet Harbor

Marconi Beach

Nauset Light

Nauset Light Beach

North Eastham

Salt Pond Visitor Center

Coast Guard Beach

Cape Cod Bay

KEY

🚲 Cape Cod Rail Trail

⛴ Ferry

First Encounter Beach

Samoset Rd.

Rock Harbor

15

13 Eastham

Nauset Marsh

14 Fort Hill Area

Skaket Beach

12 Orleans

Nauset Harbor

Beach Rd.

Nauset Beach

Cape Cod Museum of Natural History

Brewster

East Brewster

1

Tubman Rd.

4

Nickerson State Park

Stony Brook Rd.

W. Brewster

Dennis

East Dennis

Setucket Rd.

3

2

Stony Brook Grist Mill

Pleasant Bay

North Beach

East Harwich

Chatham

6–**11**

Yarmouth

South Dennis

5 Harwich

Harwich Port

West Chatham

Chatham Light

South Yarmouth

West Dennis

Dennisport

South Harwich

Harding's Beach

Morris Island

South Beach

N

0   2 miles

0   3 km

May-Oct.

TO BOSTON, PLYMOUTH, AND WHALE-WATCHING

such trips), these peaceful ventures provide a break from the crowds and an up-close look at the local flora and fauna. Several rental shops offer equipment and instruction in Eastham, Orleans, and elsewhere. Ambitious anglers in search of striped bass, bluefish, flounder, or cod will find plenty of charter boats for hire. In general, fishing is a tremendous industry on Cape Cod, both commercial and recreational.

In Eastham, the National Seashore's Salt Pond Visitor Center maintains walking and biking trails in the woods and around Nauset Marsh. In Brewster, the Punkhorn Parklands include nearly 2,000 acres open to walkers, horseback riders, and mountain bikers. Chatham visitors can hike over to Morris Island (mindful of the tides), which affords spectacular views of the ocean and the dunes.

Shopping

In Cape Cod you can buy everything from a sweatshirt to a handcrafted reproduction of an early American brass lantern. Absent on the Lower Cape are the national chain stores so popular on the mainland and on the upper Cape. Out in these parts, stores are individually owned and carry a selection of unique merchandise. The area, however, does have its fill of kitsch-laden gift shops, selling all manner of magnets, T-shirts, mugs, and beach towels—all emblazoned with local themes such as lobsters and lighthouses.

Cape Cod has long been a center for artists and craftspeople, who have been inspired by the natural environment. The massive tourist trade helps sustain them, as most artisans spend the winter busily creating and replacing stock of ceramics, jewelry, works in fabric, sculpture, paintings, photography, or glass wiped out with visitors' dollars the season before.

Exploring the Lower Cape

U.S. 6 is the fastest way to get from the mainland to Harwich, Chatham, Orleans, and Eastham. Route 6A to Brewster winds along the north shore through scenic towns.

Numbers in the text correspond to numbers in the margin and on the Lower Cape and Chatham maps.

Great Itineraries

Brewster ① has something for everyone—antiques shops, museums, an old gristmill open to the public, Bassett's Wild Animal Farm for children, freshwater ponds for swimming or fishing, the beach and tidal flats to explore when the water is low, and miles of biking and hiking trails through **Nickerson State Park** ④. Don't miss the **Cape Cod Museum of Natural History** ③, which will take a couple of hours to explore. Main Street in the handsome town of **Chatham** ⑥–⑪ is perfect for strolling, shopping, and dining. A trip to the Monomoy Islands is a must for bird-watchers. Back in town, you can watch glassblowing in process at the Chatham Glass Company, visit the Old Atwood House and Railroad Museums, and drive over to take in the view from Chatham Light.

On the way north from Chatham, take the less commercial end of Route 28 to **Orleans** ⑫, driving alongside sailboat-speckled views of Pleasant Bay. You might want to allow time for a good long bike ride on the Cape Cod Rail Trail or for an afternoon relaxing at Nauset Beach. **Eastham** ⑬ is the next stop on the way up the arm, where the **Fort Hill Area** ⑭ has the historic Penniman House Museum and some wonderful walks along the adjacent trails. Stop at the National Seashore's **Salt Pond Visitor Center** ⑮ for some interesting information about the area; then take the bike trails to Coast Guard Beach and Nauset Light, with a view of the Three Sisters Lighthouses, now settled in a small park area.

When to Tour the Lower Cape

Although the crowds of summer are testament to the appeal of the lower Cape—its spectacular beaches, outdoor pursuits, crafts and art shows, concerts, and special events—more and more visitors are beginning to appreciate the surrounding seasons. Because of the ocean-side climate, spring and fall are simply lesser shades of full-blown summer. In late May and early June businesses closed in the winter months open their doors, lodging rates are lower, and the agonies of summertime traffic, long waits at restaurants, and parking restrictions at area beaches can all be avoided. September, October, and even November are the same. The waters usually remain warm enough to swim well into October, and seasonal businesses do their best to rid their stocks of merchandise by having generous sales.

You won't get the expected splendors of New England foliage on the Lower Cape, because the landscape changes more subtly. Swaying salt-marsh grasses turn golden, cranberry bogs explode in a vividness of ruby harvest, and the ocean relaxes into a deep, deep blue. The light becomes softer and its patterns more dramatic on both land and sea. In the towns of Harwich, Brewster, and Orleans, where the soil is substantial enough to support mighty oaks and maples, the colors of autumn do come through. A drive along Route 6A under the canopy of changing leaves is just as breathtaking as a summer jaunt past blooming gardens.

Brewster

❶ *6 mi north of Chatham, 5 mi west of Orleans, 20 mi east of Sandwich.*

Calling itself "the Sea Captains' Town," Brewster retains a firm and appreciative grip on its past. The town flourished under the boon of maritime-related profit, giving it an essence of old-world elegance that still lingers. Historic Route 6A, the Old King's Highway, winds through the center of town. This road, the old stagecoach route, was once nearly the only one at this end of the Cape, and both residents and legislators are determined to keep it well preserved. Homes and businesses must adhere to historic detail—there are no neon signs, no strip malls— only the gentle accoutrements of a more graceful era.

Named for Plymouth leader William Brewster, the area was settled in 1659 but was not incorporated as a separate town until 1803. In the early 1800s Brewster was the terminus of a packet cargo service from Boston. In 1849 Thoreau wrote that "this town has more mates and masters of vessels than any other town in the country." A large number of mansions built for sea captains remain today, and quite a few have been turned into handsome B&Bs. In the 18th and 19th centuries the bay side of Brewster was the site of a major salt-making industry. Of the 450 saltworks operating on the Cape in the 1830s, more than 60 were here.

Brewster's location on Cape Cod Bay makes it a perfect place to learn about the natural history of the Cape. The Cape Cod Museum of Natural History is here, and the area is rich in conservation lands, state parks, forests, freshwater ponds, and brackish marshes. When the tide is low in Cape Cod Bay, you can stroll the beaches and explore tidal pools up to 2 mi from the shore on the Brewster flats. When it's high tide, the water is relatively warm and very calm for swimming. Both Nickerson State Park and the Punkhorn Parklands offer up thousands of acres through which to wander.

Windmills used to be prominent in Cape Cod towns; the Brewster area once had four. The 1795 **Higgins Farm Windmill** (⊠ off Rte. 6A, just west of the Cape Cod Museum of Natural History)—an octagonal type mill shingled in weathered pine with a roof like an upturned boat—was moved here in 1974 and has been restored. The millstones are original. At night the mill is often spotlighted and makes quite a sight.

On the grounds of the Higgins Farm Windmill is a one-room house from 1795, the **Harris-Black House.** Once, amazingly enough, home to a family of 13, the restored building is today partially furnished and dominated by a brick hearth and original woodwork. ⊠ *Off Rte. 6A, just west of Cape Cod Museum of Natural History,* ☎ *508/896–9521.* ▭ *Free.* ☉ *June and Sept. weekends 1–4; July–Aug. Tues.–Fri. 1–4.*

② A short drive outside Brewster is the **Stony Brook Grist Mill,** a restored, operating, 19th-century fulling mill (a mill that shrinks and thickens cloth), now also a museum. The old mill's waterwheel slowly turns in a small, tree-lined brook. Inside, exhibits include old mill equipment and looms; you can watch cornmeal being stone-ground and get a lesson in weaving on a 100-year-old loom. Out back, across wooden bridges, a bench has a view of the pond and of the sluices leading into the mill area.

Early each spring, in April and early May, Stony Brook's **Herring Run** boils with alewives (herring) making their way to spawning waters; it is an amazing sight. The fish swim in from Cape Cod Bay up Paine's Creek to Stony Brook and the ponds beyond it. The rushing stream is across the street from the mill. The herring run consists of ladders that help the fish climb the rocky waters. Farther down the path to the stream, there is an ivy-covered stone wishing well and a wooden bridge with a bench. ⊠ *Setucket Rd. off Rte. 6A,* ☎ *no phone.* ▭ *Donations accepted.* ☉ *May–Aug., Thurs.–Sat. 2–5.*

☞ ③ For nature enthusiasts, a visit to the **Cape Cod Museum of Natural History** is a must; it's just a short drive west from the heart of Brewster along Route 6A. The museum and grounds include guided field walks; a shop; a natural history library; lectures; classes; nature and marine exhibits such as a working beehive and a pond- and sea-life room with live specimens; and self-guided trails (one goes out to a tranquil setting by the bay) through 80 acres of forest, marshland, and ponds, all rich in birds and other wildlife. The exhibit hall upstairs has a wall display of aerial photographs documenting the process by which the famous Chatham sandbar was split in two.

Combining art and nature, the monthly exhibitions in the Personal Response to the Earth gallery display artists' interpretations of the environment; most of the multimedia works are for sale. The museum also offers guided canoe and kayak trips from May through September and several cruises that explore different Cape waterways: Nantucket Sound, Pleasant Bay, and Nauset Marsh. Onboard naturalists point out the wildlife and relay historical information unique to each habitat. Call for tour times and fees, and sign up as early as you can. The museum has wildlife movies and slide lectures on Wednesday at 7:30, early July through August, in the auditorium. There's a full program of children's and family activities in summer, including one-day workshops and one- and two-week day camps of art and nature classes for preschoolers through grade 9. ⊠ *869 Main St. (Rte. 6A),* ☎ *508/896–3867; 800/479–3867 in MA,* 🅆🅔🅑 *www.ccmnh.org.* ▭ *$5.* ☉ *Mon.–Sat. 9:30–4:30, Sun. 11–4:30.*

☞ Set on a re-created 19th-century common with a picnic area, the **New England Fire & History Museum** exhibits 35 antique vehicles, including the only surviving 1929 Mercedes-Benz fire engine. Other highlights are the late Boston Pops conductor Arthur Fiedler's private collection of fire-fighting memorabilia, 14 mannequins in historical uniforms depicting firefighters through the centuries, a Victorian apothecary shop, an animated diorama of the Chicago Fire of 1871 complete with smoke and fire, a historic working forge, and medicinal herb gardens. Guided tours are given. ⊠ *1439 Main St. (Rte. 6A),* ☎ *508/896–5711.* ⊇ *$6.* ⊙ *Mid-May–Labor Day, weekdays 10–4; Labor Day–Columbus Day, weekends noon–4.*

The **Brewster Ladies' Library** (⊠ 1822 Main St. [Rte. 6A], ☎ 508/896–3913) occupies a restored Victorian building and a 1997 addition.

At the junction of Route 124, the **Brewster Store** (⊠ 1935 Main St. [Rte. 6A], ☎ 508/896–3744, WEB www.brewsterstore.com) is a local landmark. Built in 1852 as a church, it is a typical New England general store providing such essentials as the daily papers, penny candy, and benches out front for conversation. There's a selection of Cape books to add to your collection. The Brewster Scoop out back serves ice cream mid-June through Labor Day. Upstairs, the old front of the store has been re-created, and memorabilia from antique toys to World War II bond posters are displayed. Downstairs there is an antique nickelodeon that you can play.

Known as the Church of the Sea Captains, the handsome **First Parish Church** (⊠ 1969 Main St. [Rte. 6A], ☎ 508/896–5577), with Gothic windows and a capped bell tower, is full of pews marked with the names of famous Brewster seamen. Out back is an old graveyard where militiamen, clergy, farmers, and sea captains rest side by side.

The **Brewster Historical Society Museum,** in an 1830s house, is made up of a sea captain's room with paintings and artifacts, an 1890 barbershop, a child's room with antique toys and clothing, a room of women's period gowns and accessories, and other exhibits on local history and architecture. Out back, a ¼-mi nature trail over dunes leads to the bay. ⊠ *3371 Main St. [Rte. 6A],* ☎ *508/896–9521.* ⊇ *Free.* ⊙ *June and Sept., weekends 1–4; July–Aug., Tues.–Fri. 1–4.*

For a lovely hike or run through the local wilds, try the **Punkhorn Parklands,** studded with freshwater kettle-hole ponds, which has 45 mi of scenic trails meandering through 800 acres of meadows, marshes, and pine forests. ⊠ *End of Run Hill Rd., off Stony Brook Rd.*

Although today they are open to the public for recreation, the 1,961 acres encompassed by **Nickerson State Park** were once part of a vast estate belonging to Roland C. Nickerson, son of Samuel Nickerson, a Chatham native who became a multimillionaire and founder of the First National Bank of Chicago. At their long, private beach or their hunting lodge, Roland and his wife, Addie, lavishly entertained such visitors as President Grover Cleveland in English country-house style, with coachmen dressed in tails and top hats and a bugler announcing carriages entering the front gates.

The estate was like a village unto itself. Its gardens provided much of the household's food, supplemented by game from its woods and fish from its ponds. It also had its own electric plant and a nine-hole golf course by the water. The enormous mansion Samuel built for his son in 1886 burned to the ground 20 years later, and Roland died two weeks after the event. The even grander stone mansion built to replace it in 1908 is now part of the Ocean Edge resort. In 1934 Addie donated the land for the state park in memory of Roland and their son, who died during the 1918 flu epidemic.

The park consists of acres of oak, pitch pine, hemlock, and spruce forest dotted with seven freshwater kettle ponds formed by glacial action. Some ponds are stocked with trout for fishing. You can swim in the ponds, canoe, sail, motorboat, bike along 8 mi of paved trails that have access to the Cape Cod Rail Trail, picnic, and cross-country ski in winter. Bird-watchers seek out the thrushes, wrens, warblers, woodpeckers, finches, larks, Canada geese, cormorants, great blue herons, hawks, owls, ospreys, and other species that frequent the park. Occasionally, red foxes and white-tailed deer are spotted in the woods. Tent and RV camping is extremely popular here, and visitor programs are offered in season. A map of the park is available on-site. ⊠ *3488 Rte. 6A,* ☎ *508/896–3491,* WEB *www.state.ma.us/dem/parks/nick.htm.* ⌨ *Free.* ☉ *Daily dawn–dusk.*

NEED A
BREAK?   **Box Lunch** (⊠ Underpass Rd. near Cape Cod Rail Trail crossing, Brewster, ☎ 508/896–1234), famous for its unique "rollwiches," is quickly spreading around the Cape. This location has the same tasty selection of breakfast and lunch roll-ups, perfect for a break and a bite while on the Cape Cod Rail Trail or just touring around. In summer the Box Lunch stays open until 9 PM; it closes at 4 PM when the weather turns cooler.

Dining and Lodging

$$$$ ✕ **Chillingsworth.** Although generally regarded as the crown jewel of
★   Cape restaurants for many years, Chillingsworth's extremely formal and somewhat stiff presentation seems a less essential experience as other dining has become more sophisticated here. Even so, the excellent, terribly pricey classic French menu and wine cellar continue to win award after award. Every night the seven-course table d'hôte menu rotates through an assortment of appetizers, entrées, and "amusements." Favorites have been a super-rich risotto, roast lobster, and grilled venison. The Garden Room, a sort of patio in the front of the restaurant, has a more modest bistro menu for lunch, dinner, and Sunday brunch. If you want to linger, there are some guest rooms here, too. ⊠ *2449 Main St. (Rte. 6A),* ☎ *508/896–3640. AE, DC, MC, V. Closed Thanksgiving–Memorial Day; closed Mon. mid-June–Thanksgiving; closed some weekdays Memorial Day–mid-June and mid-Oct.–Thanksgiving.*

$$–$$$ ✕ **Brewster Fish House.** Long overshadowed by its pricier neighbors, the Fish House finally has carved a niche for itself: Old Cape standards are starting to take a backseat to new ideas, and there's an expanded menu. Classic scrod and boiled dinners still play backup to evolving experimentations with duck, rack of lamb, Cornish game hen, and tenderloin of beef in the classic style. The wine list offers a half-dozen whites and a half-dozen reds that you don't often see by the glass. ⊠ *2208 Rte. 6A,* ☎ *508/896–7867. Reservations not accepted. MC, V. Call for information about off-season closing.*

$$–$$$ ✕ **Spark Fish.** "Spark" refers to a wood-fire grill, which the kitchen uses often. Owner Steven Parrott's menu emphasizes simple ingredients—fresh herbs, garlic, and fruit salsas—and lets the flavors of local seafood, quality meats, and good vegetables shine through without complicated sauces. The inside is as unfussy as the menu and, like the food, is more about elegant understatement than elaborate decoration. A full wine list is available. In the off-season, there's comfortable fireside dining. ⊠ *2671 Rte. 6A,* ☎ *508/896–1067. MC, V.*

$$ ✕ **Brewster Inn and Chowder House.** This local-flavor-infused institution has been around for a long, long time. Home cooking in the traditional New England style is the rule; you'll find no fancy or fussy fusion recipes here—just comfort food in a casual setting. Look for simple but tasty meat and seafood standards, and don't miss the rich and full-bodied New England clam chowder. The service is friendly, the prices are kind, and you won't leave hungry. The restaurant serves lunch and dinner daily year-round. ⊠ *1993 Rte. 6A,* ☎ *508/896–7771. MC, V.*

$–$$ ✕ **Laurino's Cape Cod Tavern.** There's something timeless about this eatery with warm wood paneling, generous booth-style seating, and red-and-white-check tablecloths. It's an easy place to feed the whole family lunch and dinner but not a place for Cape Cod fish, so steer yourself instead to the burgers or the specialty pizzas that come in two sizes. Try a Buffalo Chicken Pizza or the Kitchen Sink, which, as you might expect, has plenty of toppings. At the long, friendly bar you can sit with a buddy over a beer and a big plate of Macho Nachos. In summer live music serenades the late-night crowd of revelers. ⊠ *3668 Main St. (Rte. 6A),* ☎ *508/896–6135. Reservations not accepted. AE, MC, V.*

$$$$ 🏨 **Ocean Edge.** This huge, self-contained resort is almost like a town. Sports facilities are superior, and activities such as concerts, tournaments, and clambakes are scheduled throughout the summer. The championship 18-hole golf course and numerous tennis courts attract both the advanced player and the novice looking to sharpen skills in the on-site instructional programs. Accommodations range from oversize hotel rooms in the conference center, with sitting areas and direct access to the health club and tennis courts, to luxurious one- to three-bedroom condominiums in the woods. Two- to three-bedroom beachfront villas offer immediate access to the resort's private beach. Each condominium has a washer-dryer; some units have fireplaces, and many have ocean views. The resort is so spread out you may need a car to get from your condo to the pool. MAP plans are subject to availability. ⊠ *2907 Main St. (Rte. 6A), 02631,* ☎ *508/896–9000 or 800/ 343–6074,* 𝐅𝐀𝐗 *508/896–9123,* 𝐖𝐄𝐁 *www.oceanedge.com. 197 condominium units, 90 rooms. 4 restaurants, pub, room service, 2 indoor and 4 outdoor pools, ponds, saunas, driving range, golf privileges, putting greens, 11 tennis courts, basketball, gym, beach, bicycles, children's programs (ages 4–17), concierge. AE, D, DC, MC, V.*

$$–$$$$ 🏨 **Brewster Farmhouse.** This restored 1846 farmhouse on historic Route 6A has several comforting touches, from the goose-down pillows in the guest rooms to the turndown service with bedside sherry and chocolates. One room has a fireplace, another a king-size canopy bed and sliders out to a private deck. In keeping with the historic theme, a combination barn–carriage house was built several years back, adding three luxury-size rooms with antiques and reproduction pieces, including a white wrought-iron canopy bed. These rooms all have fireplaces and whirlpool baths. In good weather a breakfast prepared by the inn's owners, Carol and Gary Concors, is served on a patio looking onto the 2-acre backyard, which has apple trees and gardens on its edges and a heated pool and whirlpool in its center. ⊠ *716 Main St. (Rte. 6A), 02631,* ☎ *508/896–3910 or 800/892–3910,* 𝐅𝐀𝐗 *508/896–4232,* 𝐖𝐄𝐁 *www. brewsterfarmhouseinn.com. 8 rooms, 1 suite. Pool, bicycles. No smoking. AE, D, DC, MC, V. BP.*

$$–$$$$ 🏨 **Captain Freeman Inn.** A splendid 1866 Victorian built for a packet-
★ schooner-fleet owner continues to show off its original opulence with a marble fireplace, herringbone-inlay flooring, ornate Italian plaster ceiling medallions, tall windows, and 12-ft ceilings. Guest rooms have hardwood floors, antiques and Victorian reproductions, and beds with eyelet spreads and fishnet or lace canopies. The eight "luxury rooms" are truly indulgent, with queen-size canopy beds, sofas, fireplaces, TVs with VCRs, mini-refrigerators, and French doors leading to small enclosed porches with private whirlpool spas. Winter weekend cooking schools allow you to learn from the innkeeper's skills in the off-season. ⊠ *15 Breakwater Rd., 02631,* ☎ *508/896–7481 or 800/843– 4664,* 𝐅𝐀𝐗 *508/896–5618,* 𝐖𝐄𝐁 *www.captainfreemaninn.com. 12 rooms. Pool, badminton, croquet, bicycles. No smoking. AE, MC, V. BP.*

$$–$$$ 🏠 **The Ruddy Turnstone.** Built in the early 1800s, this beautifully preserved Cape homestead is set on 3 acres that gently slope to a marsh at the edge of the property. Modern amenities make life easy while antiques, quilts, and pine-board floors with braided rugs (in the main house) or original barn-board walls (in the Carriage House) take you back in time. Rooms have queen-size beds and large baths, most with shower-tub combos. An upstairs common sitting room provides an incredible vista of the marsh and the bay beyond; another common room has a fireplace and small library. One spectacular upstairs room has fine bay views through generous windows (no need to lift your head from the pillow). A delicious country breakfast is served at little tables on the porch or in the dining room. ⊠ *463 Main St. (Rte. 6A), 02631,* ☎ *508/385–9871 or 800/654–1995,* FAX *508/385–5696,* WEB *www.sunsol.com/ruddyturnstone. 5 rooms. Air-conditioning. No smoking. MC, V. Closed Nov.–Apr. BP.*

$–$$$ 🏠 **Old Sea Pines Inn.** Fronted by a white-column portico and
★ wraparound veranda overlooking a broad lawn, the Old Sea Pines evokes the atmosphere of a summer estate from an earlier time. A sweeping staircase leads to guest rooms decorated with reproduction wallpaper, antiques, and framed old photographs. Many rooms are very large; some have fireplaces, including the inn's best room, which also has a sitting area in an enclosed sunporch. Rooms in a newer building are sparsely but well decorated, with bright white modern baths, and have cast-iron queen-size beds. The shared-bath rooms are *very* small but sweetly done, and a steal in summer. There's a Sunday dinner theater, also open to the public, in season. ⊠ *2553 Main St. (Rte. 6A), Box 1070, 02631,* ☎ *508/896–6114,* FAX *508/896–7387. 24 rooms, 19 with bath; 3 suites and 2 family-size rooms. Restaurant. No smoking. AE, D, DC, MC, V. Closed Jan.–Mar. BP.*

$$ 🏠 **Isaiah Clark House.** This former 18th-century sea captain's residence, just west of the town proper, retains its wide-plank flooring and low, sloping ceilings and has a varied selection of antiques. The original inhabitants are not forgotten here, from the scrawled signature of 13-year-old son Jeremiah in a closet and framed historic documents and photographs to the namesake of each of the rooms (all Clark family women). Most rooms have queen-size four-poster or canopy beds, braided rugs, and fireplaces. The extensive gardens yield some of the fruit used in the homemade pies, muffins, and breads. ⊠ *1187 Main St. (Rte. 6A), 02631,* ☎ *508/896–2223 or 800/822–4001,* WEB *www.isaiahclark.com. 7 rooms. AE, D, DC, MC, V. BP.*

$–$$ 🏠 **Poore House Inn.** Indeed, this 5-room, 1837 home was once the town's actual poor house, a shelter for widows and orphans. Today, you can dwell alongside painted antiques and sleep beneath floral quilts and 19th century coverlets. The rooms are on the smaller side, but their prettiness and lack of clutter make them comfortable. Each has a private bath, though the one for room 3 is a quick scamper across the hall. A single room has a twin bed for solo travelers or an extra body (the inn is not suitable for those under 8) and there is even a larger, pet-friendly room. Outside a beautiful yard and brick patio overlook the gardens and greenhouse. ⊠ *2511 Main St. (Rte. 6A), 02631,* ☎ *508/896–0004 or 800/233–6662,* WEB *www.capecodtravel.com/poore. 5 rooms. AE, D, DC, MC, V. Closed Nov.–mid-Apr. CP.*

$ ⛺ **Nickerson State Park.** The Cape's largest and most popular camping site is on almost 2,000 acres teeming with wildlife, white pine, hemlock, and spruce forest. The area is jammed with opportunities for trout fishing, walking, or biking along 8 mi of paved trails and for canoeing, sailing, motorboating, and bird-watching. State park regulations have increased both rates and services; basic sites cost $15 from June to October and $5 from October to December 31; the park is closed to campers the rest of the year. Yurts are also available for rental ($25 for a small one and $30 for a large; both sizes include electricity and water). RVs must be self-contained. Facilities include showers, bathrooms, picnic tables, barbecue areas, and a store. Maps and schedules of park programs are available at the park entrance. ⊠ *3488 Main St. (Rte. 6A), 02631,* ☎ *508/896–3491; 877/422–6762 for reservations,* FAX *508/896–3103,* WEB *www.state.ma.us/dem/parks/nick.htm. 418 sites. No credit cards.*

Nightlife and the Arts

The **Cape Cod Repertory Theatre Co.** (⊠ 3379 Main St. [Rte. 6A], ☎ 508/896–1888) performs several impressive productions each summer, from original works to classics, in its indoor Arts and Crafts–style theater way back in the woods. Mesmerizing entertainment for children, in the form of lively outdoor (and often interactive) theater, is provided here, too. Performances of fairy tales, music, and folktales are given on Tuesday and Friday mornings at 10 in June, July, and August. The theater is just west of Nickerson State Park.

Sunday evenings by the bay are filled with the sounds of the **town-band concerts,** held in the gazebo on the grounds of Drummer Boy Park (⊠ Rte. 6A). The park is about ½ mi west of the Cape Cod Museum of Natural History, on the western side of Brewster. Families with little ones will delight in the park's playground with its ornate wood facilities.

The **Woodshed** (⊠ 1993 Main St. [Rte. 6A], ☎ 508/896–7771), the rustic bar at the Brewster Inn, is a good place to soak up local color and listen to pop duos or bands that perform nightly. It's open May through October.

Outdoor Activities and Sports

BASEBALL

The **Brewster Whitecaps** (☎ 508/896–9284 in summer; 781/784–7409 in winter) of the collegiate Cape Cod Baseball League play home games at Cape Cod Regional Tech High School (⊠ Rte. 124, Harwich) from mid-June to mid-August.

BEACHES

Flax Pond in Nickerson State Park (3488 Main St. [Rte. 6A], ☎ 508/896–3491), surrounded by pines, has picnic areas, a bathhouse, and water-sports rentals.

Brewster's bay beaches all have access to the flats that at low tide make for very interesting tidal-pool exploration. Eponymous roads to each beach branch off Route 6A; there's limited parking. All of the bay beaches require a daily, weekly, or seasonal parking pass which can be purchased at the town hall (☎ 508/896–3701); a proof-of-stay form may be required. **Breakwater Landing** is one of the most popular beaches in town and has an ample parking area. **Linnell Landing** has a smaller lot and tends to fill up quickly. A favorite among the toddler crowd and the sunset seekers, **Paine's Creek** also lacks a large lot, but if you get there early enough, you can find a spot. Harder to find down a dead-end street but worth it, **Robin's Hill** is known for its intriguing tidal pools. Further east off Route 6A is **Crosby Beach,** ideal for beach walkers who can trek straightway to Orleans if they so desire.

BIKING

The **Cape Cod Rail Trail** has many access points in Brewster, among them Long Pond Road, Underpass Road, and Millstone Road.

Open during summer only but located right alongside the Cape Cod Rail Trail is the tiny **Idle Times Bike Shop** (⊠ Rte. 6A, just west of Nickerson State Park, ☎ 508/896–9242), with bikes both big and small for rent. You can't beat the proximity to the trail and the easy parking.

The **Rail Trail Bike Shop** (✉ 302 Underpass Rd., ☎ 508/896–8200) rents bikes, including children's bikes, and in-line skates. Parking is free, and there's a picnic area with easy access to the Rail Trail.

FISHING

Many of Brewster's freshwater ponds are good for catching perch, pickerel, and more; five ponds are well stocked with trout. Especially good for fishing is Cliff Pond in Nickerson State Park. You'll need a **fishing license,** available from the town hall (✉ 3918 Main St. [Rte. 6A], ☎ 508/896–3701).

When fishing guidance is in order, you can sign up with **Brewster Flats Fishing & Outfitters** (✉ 2655 Main St. [Rte. 6A], ☎ 508/896–2719) for custom sport-fishing trips that include bait, tackle, and all-weather gear.

GOLF

The par-72, 18-hole **Captain's Golf Course** (✉ 1000 Freeman's Way, ☎ 508/896–5100) is an excellent public course.

Ocean Edge Golf Course (✉ Villages Dr., off Rte. 6A, ☎ 508/896–5911), an 18-hole, par-72 course winding around five ponds, has Scottish-style pot bunkers and challenging terrain. Three-day residential and commuter golf schools are offered in spring and early summer.

HORSEBACK RIDING

Instruction and trail rides to riders of all levels are available at **Moby Dick Farm** (✉ 179 Great Fields Rd., ☎ 508/896–3544).

Woodsong Farm (✉ 121 Lund Farm Way, ☎ 508/896–5800) has instruction and day programs but no trail rides; it also has a horsemanship program for children 5–18.

TENNIS

The **Ocean Edge** resort (✉ 2907 Main St. [Rte. 6A], ☎ 508/896–9000) has five clay and six Plexipave courts. It offers lessons and round-robins and hosts a tennis school, with weekend packages and video analysis.

Run by the town and open to the public at no charge are four **public tennis courts,** all just behind the fire and police stations on Route 6A. Two basketball courts are also for public use.

WATER SPORTS

Cape Cod Sea Camps (✉ Box 1880, Brewster 02631, ☎ 508/896–3451) teaches team sports, archery, art, drama, sailing, and water sports to children ages 7–17.

Jack's Boat Rentals (✉ Flax Pond, Nickerson State Park, Rte. 6A, ☎ 508/896–8556) rents canoes, kayaks, Seacycles, Sunfish, pedal boats, and sailboards; guide-led kayak tours are also offered.

Shopping

B. D. Hutchinson (✉ 1274 Long Pond Rd., ☎ 508/896–6395), a watch- and clock maker, sells antique and collectible watches, clocks, and music boxes.

Brewster Book Store (✉ 2648 Main St. [Rte. 6A], ☎ 508/896–6543) prides itself on being a special Cape bookstore. It's filled to the rafters with all manner of books by local and international authors and has an extensive children's section. A full schedule of author signings and children's story times continues year-round.

Kemp Pottery (⊠ 258 Main St. [Rte. 6A], ☎ 508/385–5782) has functional and decorative stoneware and porcelain, fountains, garden sculpture, pottery sinks, and stained glass.

Kingsland Manor (⊠ 440 Main St. [Rte. 6A], ☎ 508/385–9741) has ivy covering the facade, fountains in the courtyard, and everything "from tin to Tiffany"—including English hunting horns, full-size antique street lamps, garden and house furniture, weather vanes, jewelry, and chandeliers.

Kings Way Books and Antiques (⊠ 774 Main St. [Rte. 6A], ☎ 508/896–3639) sells out-of-print and rare books, including a large medieval section, plus small antiques, china, glass, silver, coins, and linens.

Lemon Tree Village (⊠ Main St. [Rte. 6A, about 1 mi west of town center]) is a cheery shopping complex filled with many unusual stores. You'll find garden statuary, top-of-the-line cooking implements, locally made arts and crafts, pottery, birding supplies, clothing, gifts, jewelry and toys. There's even a nice café next door if all that shopping makes you hungry.

Open from April through October, the **Satucket Farm Stand** (⊠ 76 Harwich Rd. [Rte. 124], just off Rte. 6A, ☎ 508/896–5540) is reminiscent of the well-stocked and freshly fragrant side-of-the-road farm stands that make us all nostalgic. Most produce is grown on the premises, and you can fill your basket with the finest of the harvest, from home-baked scones and breads to fruit pies, produce, herbs, and flowers.

The **Spectrum** (⊠ 369 Main St. [Rte. 6A], ☎ 508/385–3322) carries a great selection of imaginative American arts and crafts, including pottery, stained glass, art glass, and more.

Sydenstricker Galleries (⊠ 490 Main St. [Rte. 6A], ☎ 508/385–3272) stocks glassware handcrafted by a unique process, which you can watch in progress.

Harwich

❺ *3 mi east of Dennisport, 6 mi south of Brewster.*

Originally known as Setucket, Harwich separated from Brewster in 1694 and was renamed for the famous seaport in England. Like other townships on the Cape, Harwich is actually a cluster of seven small villages, including Harwich Port. Historically, the villages of Harwich were marked by their generous number of churches and the styles of worship they practiced—small villages often sprang up around these centers of faith.

Harwich and Harwich Port are the commercial centers, and although the two have very different natures, both have graceful old architecture and a rich history. Harwich Port is the more bustling of the two: Brimming with shops, calm-water beaches, restaurants, and hotel complexes, it packs all manner of entertainment and frivolity along its roadways. Harwich is more relaxed, its commerce more centered, and its outlying areas graced with expanses of greenery, large shade trees, and historic homesteads. The Harwich Historical Society has a strong presence here, maintaining exhibits and artifacts significant to the town's past.

The Cape's famous cranberry industry took off in Harwich in 1844, and Alvin Cahoon was its principal grower at the time. Each September Harwich holds a great **Cranberry Festival** to celebrate the importance of this indigenous berry; the festival is usually scheduled during the week after Labor Day. There are cranberry bogs throughout Harwich.

Three naturally sheltered harbors on Nantucket Sound make the town, like its English namesake, popular with boaters. You'll find dozens of elegant sailboats and elaborate yachts in Harwich's harbors, plus plenty of charter fishing boats. Each year in August the town pays celebratory homage to its large boating population with a grand regatta, Sails Around the Cape.

Beaches are plentiful in Harwich, and nearly all rest on the warm and mild waters of Nantucket Sound. Freshwater ponds also speckle the area, ideal for swimming as well as small-scale canoeing and kayaking. Several conservation areas contain miles of secluded walking trails, many alongside the vivid cranberry bogs that have made the town famous.

Once the home of a private school offering the first courses in navigation, the pillared 1844 Greek Revival building of the **Brooks Academy Museum** now houses the museum of the **Harwich Historical Society**. In addition to a large photo-history collection and exhibits on artist Charles Cahoon (grandson of cranberry grower Alvin), the sociotechnological history of the cranberry culture, and shoemaking, the museum displays antique clothing and textiles, china and glass, fans, toys, and much more. There is also an extensive genealogical collection for researchers. On the grounds is a powder house used to store gunpowder during the Revolutionary War, as well as a restored 1872 outhouse that could spur your appreciation for indoor plumbing. ⊠ *80 Parallel St.,* ☎ *508/432–8089.* 🖃 *Donations accepted.* ☉ *June–mid-Oct., Wed.–Sat. 1–4.*

ᘓ **Brooks Park** on Main Street (Rte. 28) is a good place to stretch your legs, with a playground, picnic tables, a ball field, tennis courts, and a bandstand that's the site of summer concerts.

ᘓ **Grand Slam Entertainment** has softball and baseball batting cages and pitching machines, including one with fastballs up to 80 mph, a Wiffle-ball machine for younger children, a bumper-boat pool, and a video-arcade room. ⊠ *322 Main St. (Rte. 28), Harwich Port,* ☎ *508/430–1155.* 🖃 *$1.50 for 10 pitches, $5 for 40 pitches, or $10 for 100 pitches; $5 per bumper-boat pool ride.* ☉ *Apr.–May and Sept.–mid-Oct., Mon.–Sat. 11–7, Sun. 11–9; June–Aug., daily 9 AM–10 PM.*

For children who have spent too much time in the car watching you drive, a spin behind the wheel of one of 20 top-of-the-line go-carts at ᘓ **Bud's Go-Karts** may be just the thing. ⊠ *9 Sisson Rd., off Rte. 28, Harwich Port,* ☎ *508/432–4964.* 🖃 *$5 for 5 mins.* ☉ *June–Labor Day, Mon.–Sat. 9 AM–11 PM, Sun. 1–11.*

ᘓ The **Trampoline Center** has 12 trampolines set up at ground level over pits for safety. ⊠ *296 Main St. (Rte. 28), West Harwich,* ☎ *508/432–8717.* 🖃 *$4 for 10 mins.* ☉ *Apr.–mid-June, weekends (hrs vary widely, call ahead); mid-June–Labor Day, daily 9 AM–11 PM.*

Dining and Lodging

$$–$$$$ ✕ **L'alouette.** Owners Danielle and Jean-Louis, who hail from France, serve authentic French cuisine in their casual restaurant. Look for traditional and rich selections such as duckling and rack of lamb; veal chops with Portabello mushrooms; and the favorite, chateaubriand. ⊠ *787 Rte. 28, Harwich Port,* ☎ *508/430–0405. AE, DC, MC, V. Closed late-Feb.–mid-Mar.*

$$–$$$ ✕ **Cape Sea Grille.** Because it's settled primly on a side street off hec-
★   tic Route 28, this culinary gem stays free of thundering hordes. Fresh flowers, beautiful wood tables, colorful linens, and vibrant wall murals delight the eye while dinner teases the palate—specialties always include local fish, dressed in such fineries as applewood-smoked bacon

When you pack your MCI Calling Card, it's like packing your loved ones along too.

Your MCI Calling Card is the easy way to stay in touch when you travel. Use it to call to and from over 125 countries. Plus, every time you call, you can earn frequent flier miles. So wherever your travels take you, call home with your MCI Calling Card. It's even easy to get one. Just visit **www.mci.com/worldphone**.

EASY TO CALL WORLDWIDE

1. Just enter the WorldPhone® access number of the country you're calling from.
2. Enter or give the operator your MCI Calling Card number.
3. Enter or give the number you're calling.

Aruba ✤	800-888-8
Bahamas ✤	1-800-888-8000

Barbados ✤	1-800-888-8000
Bermuda ✤	1-800-888-8000
British Virgin Islands ✤	1-800-888-8000
Canada	1-800-888-8000
Mexico	01-800-021-8000
Puerto Rico	1-800-888-8000
United States	1-800-888-8000
U.S. Virgin Islands	1-800-888-8000

✤ Limited availability.

EARN FREQUENT FLIER MILES

MCI®

SEE THE WORLD
IN FULL COLOR

Fodor's Exploring Guides bring all the great sights vividly to life with hundreds of photographs, fascinating historical background, and colorful anecdotes. Detailed maps and practical information keep you headed in the right direction.

Pair a **Fodor's** Exploring Guide with your trusted Gold Guide for a complete planning package.

or an orange-and-ginger marinade. The menu changes frequently in order to feature the freshest ingredients. Save room for dessert—the bananas Foster Napoléon is heavenly. Dinner is served nightly from 5 in the height of summer; call for hours in the slower season. ⊠ *31 Sea St., Harwich Port,* ☎ *508/432–4745. AE, DC, MC, V. Closed Nov.– mid-Apr.*

$$–$$$ ✕ **Country Inn Restaurant and Tavern.** The main dining room has wide-plank floors and looks out onto the inn's 6 acres of greenery. Fresh flowers, candlelight, and—in the off-season—firelight set a romantic mood. The tavern room is darker and smaller, but still comfortable. Menu specials include the Country Inn Platter for Two—filet mignon, lobster, scallops, and shrimp scampi—and the local favorite, Lazy-Man's Lobster; it arrives dismantled, so you get all the meat without the mess. Friday and Saturday evenings meals are accompanied by live piano serenades; lots of folks push back their napkins and hit the dance floor on Saturday night, when music is liveliest. ⊠ *86 Sisson Ave. (Rte. 39), Harwich Port,* ☎ *508/432–2769. AE, MC, V.*

$$–$$$ ✕ **400 East.** This big, dark restaurant buzzing with conversation is in a nondescript shopping plaza. The menu includes teriyaki tuna and chicken, prime rib, and baked scrod, but also has excellent pizza, with toppings such as wild mushrooms, blue cheese, and Cajun chicken and corn. Eating at the busy, U-shape bar can be a great alternative to waiting for a table, provided you don't mind a television set in the picture. The 400 has a cousin restaurant (also called the 400) on Main Street that is not as much fun. ⊠ *1421 Rte. 39,* ☎ *508/432–1800. AE, D, MC, V.*

$–$$ ✕ **Ay! Caramba Cafe.** You can fill up on authentic Mexican fare without cleaning out your wallet at this tiny but vibrant café. Choose from tasty quesadillas, burritos, tostadas, and tacos, or go for one of the large combination plates, complete with rice and either refried beans or vegetables. The fish tacos and seafood quesadillas are especially good. Once you have your food, sidle up to the salsa bar, where three varieties are made throughout the day—but be sure to have your water handy for the hottest stuff. ⊠ *703 Main St., Harwich,* ☎ *508/432– 9800. AE, DC, MC, V.*

$–$$ ✕ **Brax Landing.** In this local stalwart perched alongside busy Saquatucket Harbor, you'll get a menu tip-off as you pass by tanks full of steamers and lobsters in the corridor leading to the dining room. The restaurant sprawls around a big bar that serves drinks such as the Moxie (pink lemonade and vodka, "calm seas guaranteed"). The swordfish and the Chatham scrod are favorites, both served simply and well. There's a notable children's menu, and Sunday brunch, served from 10 to 2, is an institution. ⊠ *Rte. 28 at Saquatucket Harbor, Harwich Port,* ☎ *508/432–5515. Reservations not accepted. AE, DC, MC, V.*

$$$–$$$$ 🏠 **Augustus Snow House.** This grand old Victorian is the epitome of ★ elegance. Common areas include the oak-paneled front room, with tall windows and a fireplace, and a wicker-filled screened porch. The stately dining room is the setting for the three-course breakfast, with dishes such as baked pears in raspberry and cream sauce. Guest rooms have Victorian-print wallpapers, luxurious carpets, and fine antique and reproduction furnishings. All have quilts, TVs, fireplaces, and antique brass bathroom and lighting fixtures; three rooms have whirlpool tubs. The Carriage House Suite has a fireplace, dining area, kitchenette, and living room. Downstairs, a gardenlike tearoom is open to the public on Thursday, Friday, and Saturday for afternoon tea. ⊠ *528 Main St. (Rte. 28), Harwich Port 02646,* ☎ *508/430–0528 or 800/320–0528,* 🖷 *508/432–6638 Ext. 15,* 🕸 *www.augustussnow. com. 5 rooms. Air-conditioning. AE, D, MC, V. BP.*

$$$–$$$$ 🏠 **Dunscroft by the Sea.** Romantic amenities include antique sleigh, laced canopy, and four-poster beds; two-person whirlpool tubs; terry robes; and some working fireplaces. The calming waters of Nantucket Sound are just a few paces away. ⊠ *24 Pilgrim Rd., Harwich Port 02646,* ☎ *508/432–0810 or 800/432–4345,* WEB *www.dunscroftbythesea.com. 8 rooms, 1 cottage. Beach. AE, D, MC, V. BP.*

$$$–$$$$ 🏠 **Winstead Inn and Beach Resort.** Reminiscent of an earlier era, the beach resort has a turret and a wraparound porch and elegant guest rooms include antiques. Some baths have whirlpool tubs. From umbrella tables on the deck you can watch the sweep of coast and surrounding grasslands while enjoying a generous Continental breakfast. Off-season, there's a fire burning in the common room. ⊠ *328 Bank St., 02645;* ⊠ *4 Braddock La., Harwich Port 02646,* ☎ *508/432–4444 or 800/870–4405,* WEB *www.winsteadinn.com. 14 rooms. Restaurant, pool. MC, V. CP.*

$$–$$$$ 🏠 **Sea Heather Inn.** Resting majestically amid sculptured lawns with views of Nantucket Sound, this is one of the grand dames of the area. The main house, a stately and rambling Cape-style building built in the 1840s, is in the perpetual process of renewing itself; currently the owners are adding painted wainscoting and wide-plank flooring. The eight rooms in the main house are filled with antiques and reproductions and several have water views. A larger, hotel-style complex on the property provides rooms with more modern furnishings in a decidedly hotel-style area, complete with game room for those in need of entertainment. The inn is a short walk from several beaches. ⊠ *28 Sea St., Harwich Port 02646,* ☎ *508/432–1275 or 800/789–7809,* WEB *www.seaheather.com. 20 rooms. Air-conditioning. AE, D, MC, V. CP.*

$–$$$ 🏠 **Seadar Inn.** Although it won't win any awards for elegant decor,
★   the friendly Seadar has a great location. The only thing between you and the beach on Nantucket Sound is the small parking lot and possibly the ice cream truck. The homey, motel-style rooms are unfussy and practical in a colonial style, with knotty-pine walls and frilly curtains; some have water views. Suites are available for larger groups. There are outdoor grills for alfresco cooking. ⊠ *Braddock La. at Bank St. Beach, Harwich Port 02646,* ☎ *508/432–0264 or 800/888–5250,* WEB *www.seadarinn.com. 23 rooms. Air-conditioning. AE, D, MC, V. Closed mid-Oct.–May. CP.*

Nightlife and the Arts

THE ARTS

The **First Congregational Church** (⊠ Main St. at corner of Rtes. 39 and 124, Harwich, ☎ 508/432–1053) closes its day of worship with Sunday-evening Candlelight Concerts at 7:30 from July through September.

Harwich Junior Theatre (⊠ 105 Division St., West Harwich, ☎ 508/432–2002) gives theater classes for children year-round and presents four family-oriented summer productions.

Town-band concerts in Harwich take place in summer on Tuesday at 7:30 in Brooks Park (☎ 508/432–1600).

NIGHTLIFE

Country Inn (⊠ 86 Sisson Rd. [Rte. 39], West Harwich Port, ☎ 508/432–2769) complements its dinner menu with dancing every Friday and Saturday evening. You can dance between courses to music of the 1940s with a piano player on Friday night and a pianist and bass player on Saturday evening after 7.

Irish Pub (⊠ 126 Main St. [Rte. 28], West Harwich, ☎ 508/432–8808) has dancing to bands—playing Irish, American, and dance music—as well as sing-alongs, pool, darts, sports TV, and pub food in the bar.

Jake Rooney's Pub (⊠ 119 Brooks Rd., off Rte. 28, Harwich Port, ☎ 508/430–1100) has a comfortable pub atmosphere, keno, and live entertainment five nights a week.

Outdoor Activities and Sports

BASEBALL

The **Harwich Mariners** (⊠ Harwich High School, Oak St., ☎ 508/432–0662), of the collegiate Cape Cod Baseball League, play home games at Whitehouse Field from mid-June through mid-August.

BEACHES

Harwich has 22 beaches, more than any other Cape town. Most of the ocean beaches are on Nantucket Sound, where the water is a bit calmer and warmer. Freshwater pond beaches are also abundant.

BOATING

Whether you're in the mood to sail under the moonlight, hire a private charter or learn to navigate yourself, **Cape Sail** (⊠ 337 Saquatucket Harbor, off Rte. 28, Harwich Port, ☎ 508/896–2730) can accommodate any whim.

Cape Water Sports (⊠ 337 Main St. [Rte. 28], Harwich Port, ☎ 508/432–5996) rents Sunfish, Hobie Cats, Lasers, powerboats, surf bikes, day sailers, and canoes and gives instructions.

In late-August, the **Sails Around Cape Cod** regatta (☎ 508/430–1165) circumnavigates the Cape, a distance of 140 nautical mi, beginning at the east end of the Cape Cod Canal and ending at the west end.

FISHING

Fishing trips are operated on a walk-on basis from spring through fall on the **Golden Eagle** (⊠ Wychmere Harbor, Harwich Port, ☎ 508/432–5611).

The **Yankee** (⊠ Saquatucket Harbor, Harwich Port, ☎ 508/432–2520) invites passengers aboard its 65-ft party boat in search of fluke, scup, sea bass, and tautog. Two trips depart daily Monday through Saturday, and there's one on Sunday. Reservations are recommended.

GOLF

Cranberry Valley Golf Course (⊠ 183 Oak St., ☎ 508/430–7560) has a championship layout of 18 well-groomed holes surrounded by cranberry bogs.

Harwich Port Golf Club (⊠ South and Forest Sts., Harwich Port, ☎ 508/432–0250) has a nine-hole course that's great for beginners.

Shopping

Cape Cod Braided Rug Co. (⊠ 537 Main St. [Rte. 28], Harwich Port, ☎ 508/432–3133) specializes in braided rugs made on the premises in a variety of colors, styles, and sizes.

Carriage House Designs (⊠ 100 Main St. [Rte. 28], West Harwich, ☎ 508/432–7800) has a fine selection of dried and silk flower arrangements, folk art, and antiques.

820 Main Gallery (⊠ 820 Main St. [Rte. 28], Harwich Port, ☎ 508/430–7622) sells original works in oil, acrylics, watercolors and photography, as well as limited-edition prints by established local artists. The gallery specializes in regional land- and seascapes.

The **Potted Geranium** (⊠ 188 Main St. [Rte. 28], West Harwich, ☎ 508/432–1114) stocks a wide selection of country-inspired gifts and home-related items, including colorful wind flags, handcrafted items, and wind chimes.

Pottery Plus (⊠ 551 Main St. [Rte. 28], Harwich Port, ☎ 508/430–5240) sells the pottery of artist Scott Sullivan, as well as other works by local artists.

Wychmere Book & Coffee (⊠ 587 Main St. [Rte. 28], Harwich Port, ☎ 508/432–7868) is a place to savor the comforts of browsing, reading, and sipping good coffee. Special events with authors and a children's summer reading hour further enhance the scene.

Chatham

6–**11**   *5 mi east of Harwich, 8 mi south of Orleans.*

Originally populated by Native Americans, Chatham came into the hands of white settlers from Plymouth when, in 1656, William Nickerson traded a boat for the 17 square mi of land that make up the town. In 1712 the area separated from Eastham and was incorporated as a town; the surnames of the Pilgrims who first settled here still dominate the census list. Although Chatham was originally a farming community, the sea finally lured townspeople to turn to fishing for their livelihood, an industry that has held strong to this day.

At the bent elbow of the Cape, with water nearly surrounding it, Chatham has all the charm of a quietly posh seaside resort, with relatively little commercialism. And it is charming: gray-shingle houses with tidy awnings and cheerful flower gardens, an attractive Main Street with crafts and antiques stores alongside homey coffee shops, and a five-and-dime. It's a traditional town, where elegant summer cottages share the view with stately houses of purebred Yankee architecture, including some of the finest bow-roof houses in the country. There's none of Provincetown's flash, yet it's not overly quaint—just well-to-do without being ostentatious, casual and fun but refined, and never tacky (unless you feel that a few large new "trophy houses" qualify as tacky).

Because of its location at the elbow, Chatham is not a town you just pass through—it's a destination in itself. The atmosphere is casual and quaint in the New England way, yet there's also that quiet essence of privilege and class here. Summer is truly beautiful in Chatham, when the streets are lined with exquisite hydrangea bushes in varying shades, from cobalt blue to indigo and deep violet.

Its position on the confluence of Nantucket Sound and the Atlantic Ocean makes Chatham especially vulnerable to the destructive wrath of stormy seas. Many a home and beachfront have been lost to the tumultuous waters. But like any stalwart, New England character, Chatham will continue to hold on to its fortunes, its past, and its future.

6   Authentic all the way, the **Railroad Museum** is set in a restored 1887 depot. Exhibits include a walk-through 1910 New York Central caboose, old photographs, equipment, thousands of train models, and a diorama of the 1915 Chatham rail yards. ⊠ *153 Depot Rd.,* ☎ *no phone.* 🖼 *Donations accepted.* ☉ *Mid-June–mid-Sept., Tues.–Sat. 10–4.*

The **Play-a-round,** a multilevel wooden playground of turrets, twisting tubular slides, jungle gyms, and more, was designed with the input of local children and built by volunteers. There's a section for people with disabilities and a fenced-in area for small children. ⊠ *Depot Rd., across from Railroad Museum.*

On **Queen Anne Road** around Oyster Pond, half-Cape houses, open fields, and rolling pastures reveal the area's colonial and agricultural history.

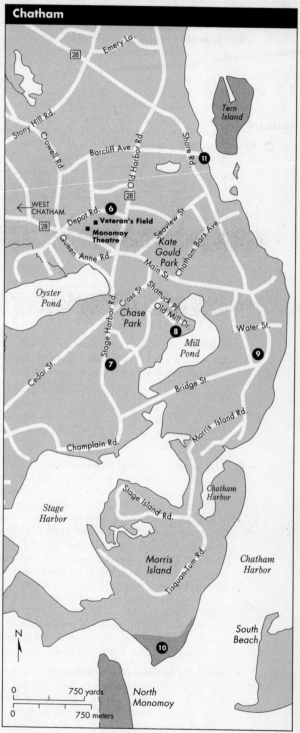

Built by sea captain Joseph C. Atwood in 1752 and occupied by his descendants until it was sold to the Chatham Historical Society in 1926,

❼ the **Atwood House Museum** has a gambrel roof, variable-width floor planks, fireplaces, an old kitchen with a wide hearth and a beehive oven, and some antique dolls and toys. The New Gallery displays portraits of local sea captains. The Joseph C. Lincoln Room has the manuscripts, first editions, and mementos of the Chatham writer, and in the basement is an antique tool room. The 1974 Durand Wing houses collections of seashells from around the world and threaded Sandwich glass, as well as Parian ware figures, unglazed porcelain vases, figurines, and busts. In a remodeled freight shed are murals (1932–45) by Alice Stallknecht Wight portraying religious scenes in Chatham settings. On the grounds are an herb garden, the old turret and lens from the Chatham Light, and a simple camp house rescued from eroding North Beach. ✉ *347 Stage Harbor Rd.,* ☎ *508/945–2493,* WEB *www.atwoodhouse.org.* 🎟 *$3.* ☉ *Mid-June–Sept., Tues.–Fri. 1–4.*

❽ The **Old Grist Mill,** one of a number of windmills still on the Cape, was built in 1797 by Colonel Benjamin Godfrey for the purpose of grinding corn. How practical the mill actually was is a matter of debate: for it to work properly, a wind speed of at least 20 mph was necessary, but winds more than 25 mph required the miller to reef the sails or to quit grinding altogether. The mill was moved to its present location from Miller Hill in 1956 and extensively renovated. ✉ *Old Mill Dr.* ☉ *July–Aug., weekdays 10–3.*

Mill Pond is a lovely place to stop for a picnic. There's fishing from the bridge, and often the bullrakers can be seen at work, plying the pond's muddy bottom with 20-ft rakes in search of shellfish.

Stage Harbor, sheltered by Morris Island, is where Samuel de Champlain anchored in 1606. The street on its north side is, not surprisingly, called Champlain Road. A skirmish here between Europeans and Native Americans marked the first bloodshed in New England between Native people and the new arrivals.

★ ❾ The famous view from **Chatham Light** (✉ Main St., near Bridge St., ☎ 508/945–0719)—of the harbor, the offshore sandbars, and the ocean beyond—justifies the crowds that gather to share it. The lighthouse is especially dramatic on a foggy night, as the beacon's light pierces the mist. Coin-operated telescopes allow a close look at the famous "Chatham Break," the result of a fierce 1987 nor'easter that blasted a channel through a barrier beach just off the coast; it is now known as North and South beaches. The Cape Cod Museum of Natural History in Brewster has a display of photos documenting the process of erosion leading up to and following the break. The U.S. Coast Guard auxiliary, which supervises the lighthouse, offers tours on the first and third Wednesdays, April–September. The lighthouse is also open by appointment, and on three special occasions during the year: Seafest, an annual tribute to the maritime industry held in mid-October; mid-May's Cape Cod Maritime Week; and June's Cape Heritage Week.

★ **Monomoy National Wildlife Refuge** is a 2,500-acre preserve including the Monomoy Islands, a fragile 9-mi-long barrier-beach area south of Chatham. Monomoy's North and South islands were created when a storm divided the former Monomoy Island in 1978. Monomoy was itself separated from the mainland in a 1958 storm. A paradise for birdwatchers, the island is an important stop along the North Atlantic Flyway for migratory waterfowl and shore birds—peak migration times are May and late July. It also provides nesting and resting grounds for 285 species, including gulls—great black-backed, herring, and laughing—and several tern species. White-tail deer also live on the islands, and harbor and gray seals frequent the shores in winter. The only structure on the islands is the **South Monomoy Lighthouse,** built in 1849. If you want to spend a night in the house and on the island, contact Brewster's Cape Cod Museum of Natural History (☎ 508/896–3867, WEB www.ccmnh.org), which organizes such trips.

Monomoy is a quiet, peaceful place of sand and beach grass, of tidal flats, dunes, marshes, freshwater ponds, thickets of bayberry and beach plum, and a few pines. Because the refuge harbors several endangered species, activities are limited. Certain areas are fenced off to protect nesting areas of terns and the threatened piping plover. The Massachusetts Audubon Society in South Wellfleet, the Cape Cod Museum of Natural History in Brewster, and other groups conduct tours of the islands, many with a focus on bird-watching. The *Rip Ryder* (☎ 508/945–5450) will take you over from Chatham in season for some lone bird-watching. Rates vary greatly: if you catch a ride out with the seal-watching cruise, it's $14 per person; if you charter a private ride, rates are $45 per person round-trip or $10 per person for three or more passengers round-trip.

⑩ The **Monomoy National Wildlife Refuge headquarters,** on the misleadingly named Morris Island (it is connected to the mainland), has a visitor center and bookstore (⊠ off Morris Island Rd., ☎ 508/945–0594), open daily 8–4, with gaps, where you can pick up pamphlets on Monomoy and the birds, wildlife, and flora and fauna found there. A ¾-mi interpretive walking trail, closed at high tide, around Morris Island gives a good view of the refuge and the surrounding waters. The area itself is open for exploring daily, from dawn to dusk.

⑪ The **Fish Pier** (⊠ Shore Rd. and Barcliff Ave.) bustles with activity when Chatham's fishing fleet returns, sometime between noon and 2 PM daily, depending on the tide. The unloading of the boats is a big local event, drawing crowds who watch it all from an observation deck. From their fishing grounds 3–100 mi offshore, fishermen bring in haddock, cod, flounder, lobster, halibut, and pollack, which are packed in ice and shipped to New York and Boston or sold at the fish market here. You might also see sand sharks being unloaded. Typically they are sent, either fresh or frozen, to French and German markets. Also here is *The Provider,* a monument to the town's fishing industry, showing a hand pulling a fish-filled net from the sea.

The **Eldredge Public Library** (⊠ 564 Main Street, ☎ 508/945–5170) has a special genealogy department.

Known for their artful contemporary treatment of blown glass, Jim Holmes and Deborah Doane of the **Chatham Glass Company** create everything from candleholders to unique vases in a vast spectrum of colors. You can watch the fascinating process of glassblowing here. ⊠ *758 Main St.,* ☎ *508/945–5547,* WEB *www.capecod.net/chathamglass.* ☉ *Memorial Day–Labor Day, Mon.–Sat. 10–5; Labor Day–Memorial Day, daily 10–5.*

NEED A BREAK?

If you're looking for a fat and fancy sandwich, a morning bagel, or an afternoon cappuccino pick-me-up, stop in at the **Chatham Village Café** (⊠ 400 Main St., ☎ 508/945–2525) and choose from an impressive selection of food. Eat inside at one of the few tables for some good street-side people-watching or head over to the Village Green for an impromptu picnic.

Dining and Lodging

$$–$$$ ✕ **Chatham Squire.** If you order anything local here, you can't go
★ wrong. The fish is as fresh and good as you get on Cape Cod, and the
kitchen continues to innovate while not forgetting its Cape roots. The
calamari is always tender, the oysters a lovely mouthful. Expect a long
wait in season, in which case you can visit the bar. ⊠ *487 Main St.,*
☎ *508/945–0945. Reservations not accepted. AE, D, MC, V.*

$$–$$$ ✕ **Christian's.** French and New England influences are found at this
landmark town restaurant. The menu includes boneless roast duck with
raspberry sauce and flaky sautéed sole with lobster and lemon-butter
sauce. The mahogany-paneled bar and deck upstairs serve a lighter menu
that remains strong on seafood but adds some Mexican influences, such
as tacos and quesadillas, that are well suited to the summer. As attractive
as the formal downstairs is, the upstairs is more of a happening scene.
⊠ *443 Main St.,* ☎ *508/945–3362. AE, D, DC, MC, V. Closed weekdays Jan.–Mar.*

$$–$$$ ✕ **High Tide Restaurant.** A long-established (and typically crowded)
favorite, this high-spirited place has an ample and varied menu. Local
seafood is generously represented, as are several creative meat dishes,
daily specials, and Italian entrées. A classic is the Neptune High Tide:
shrimp, scallops, and lobster bathed in a creamy garlic sauce and
heaped over pasta. There's also a children's menu. Live entertainment
is offered on the weekends. ⊠ *1629 Main St.,* ☎ *508/945–2582. AE,
MC, V.*

$$–$$$ ✕ **Marley's.** Shaking up traditional New England fare with interna-
tional flavors, this restaurant is not afraid to be a little creative. Try
the scallops Barbados, prepared with pineapple, rum, and brown sugar
and topped with a coconut-macaroon crust. More traditional entrées
include steaks, chicken potpie, lobster, and steamers; there are also several vegetarian options. This is also a comfortable and good bet for
weekend breakfast; try to get a seat out on the garden patio when the
weather cooperates. It seems the owners are as inventive with their hours
of operation as they are with the menu—after late October, you need
to call to see if the restaurant is open. ⊠ *1077 Main St.,* ☎ *508/945–
1700. AE, MC, V.*

$$–$$$ ✕ **Pate's.** This popular spot has been grilling up meats and local
seafood since 1957. You can expect such items as succulent lamb
chops, filet mignon, sirloin, and swordfish to arrive marked with the
telltale stripes of the open flame. Seafood is taken seriously here; that
baked lobster on your plate weighs in at more than 2 pounds. The setting is comfortable and casual, and dinner is consistently good. ⊠ *1260
Main St.,* ☎ *508/945–9777. AE, MC, V. Closed mid-Jan.–Apr.*

$$–$$$ ✕ **Vining's Bistro.** An exceptionally inventive menu and a determina-
★ tion not to rest on its laurels make this restaurant a standout. The wood
grill is the center of attention here, where the chef uses zesty rubs and
spices from all over the globe. The wonderful Bangkok fisherman's stew
has almost too much seafood crammed in; spit-roasted Jamaican
chicken competes with a Portobello mushroom sandwich as the restaurant's signature dish. Go for the Mahogany Fire Noodles, an awe-inspiring shrimp and chicken dish. The restaurant is upstairs at the
Gallery Building, and many windows look out on the art below. ⊠ *595
Main St.,* ☎ *508/945–5033. Reservations not accepted. AE, D, MC,
V. Closed mid-Jan.–Apr.*

$–$$ ✕ **The Sou'wester.** You're more likely to see someone in a yellow
slicker and rubber boots than a sports jacket and loafers in this small
spot, the most unpretentious bar-restaurant in Chatham, if not the Lower
Cape. The decor, if you can call it that, is eight booths, low light, and
what look like fake Oriental rugs for wall hangings. The handwritten
menu is heavy on steak tips, sirloin, and pork chops, with fish cakes

and beans for the fishermen patrons who haven't had their fill of fish for the day. On weekends there's good, loud, get-down live music in the bar, known as the Lincoln Lodge. ⊠ *1563 Main St.,* ☎ *508/945–4424. AE, MC, V.*

$$$$ ✗ ⌂ **Chatham Bars Inn.** This 1914 landmark inn is an oceanfront resort in the old, extravagant style. High above the beach on a windswept bluff, the inn claims a stunning view of the ocean through floor-to-ceiling windows. The formal dining-room menu includes seared foie gras and steamed swordfish with clams. The Tavern is open for a more casual lunch and dinner, and the Beach House Bar opens in season for breakfast and lunch down by the water. The inn consists of a main building flanked by wings—on the ground floor the grand lobby gives way to the formal restaurant on one side and a porch-fronted lounge on the other—with 26 one- to eight-bedroom cottages on 22 landscaped acres overlooking the ocean. Under seemingly perpetual renovation, the once-bland rooms are now filled with hand-painted furnishings by local artists and colorful fabrics depicting sunny seaside scenes. Although the ocean views from some rooms may be spectacular, when push comes to shove, the value for the money is not exceptional. ⊠ *Shore Rd., 02633,* ☎ *508/945–0096 or 800/527–4884,* FAX *508/945–5491,* WEB *www. chathambarsinn.com. 205 rooms. 3 restaurants, bar, lobby lounge, pool, putting green, 4 tennis courts, gym, volleyball, beach, baby-sitting, children's programs. AE, DC, MC, V.*

$$$$ ⌂ **Cranberry Inn.** Although close to the heart of town, the inn has a protected marsh area in its backyard—a fine spot from which to spy great blue herons and the occasional deer or fox. Billed as the oldest continuously operating lodging establishment in Chatham, it's no surprise to find antique and reproduction furniture and an array of handmade quilts. Rooms have telephones and televisions; some have fireplaces or balconies. ⊠ *359 Main St., 02633,* ☎ *508/945–9232 or 800/332–4667,* FAX *508/945–3769,* WEB *www.cranberryinn.com. 18 rooms. Restaurant. AE, D, MC, V. BP.*

$$$$ ⌂ **Wequassett Inn Resort & Golf Club.** This exquisite traditional resort
★ offers first-rate accommodations in 20 Cape-style cottages and an attractive hotel complex. Partly surrounded by the mild waters of Pleasant Bay and shaded by oaks and pines on its 22 acres, the Wequassett provides luxury in an informal setting. Along with attentive service and evening entertainment, you'll find plenty of sunning and sporting opportunities, including the very exclusive Cape Cod National Golf Club (guests have golf privileges). Spacious rooms have fresh pine furniture, floral bedcovers, or handmade quilts and such homey touches as overflowing window boxes and duck decoys. ⊠ *173 Orleans Rd. (Rte. 28), Pleasant Bay, 02633,* ☎ *508/432–5400 or 800/225–7125,* FAX *508/432–5032,* WEB *www.wequassett.com. 102 rooms, 2 suites. Restaurant, grill, piano bar, room service, pool, 4 tennis courts, gym, windsurfing, boating. AE, D, DC, MC, V. Closed Nov.–Apr. FAP.*

$$$–$$$$ ⌂ **Captain's House Inn.** A Victorian tile ceiling, wide-board floors, and
★ elaborate moldings and wainscoting are just part of what makes Jan and Dave McMaster's inn one of the Cape's finest. Each room in the four inn buildings has its own personality. Some are quite large, and most have fireplaces. The gorgeous Hiram Harding Room, in the bow-roof Captain's Cottage, has 200-year-old hand-hewn ceiling beams; a wall of raised walnut paneling; and a large, central working fireplace. The luxury suites in the former stables are particularly spacious and have every amenity imaginable, including whirlpool baths, fireplaces, TV/VCR, mini-refrigerators, and private patios or balconies. ⊠ *371 Old Harbor Rd., 02633,* ☎ *508/945–0127 or 800/315–0728,* FAX *508/ 945–0866,* WEB *www.captainshouseinn.com. 16 rooms, 3 suites. Croquet, bicycles. No smoking. AE, D, MC, V. BP.*

$$$–$$$$ ⊡ **Chatham Wayside Inn.** Once a stop on a turn-of-the-20th-century stagecoach route, the inn may still be an oasis for weary travelers. Everything is crisp and colorful here, from the floral comforters and wallpapers to freshly painted walls and bright wall-to-wall carpeting. Some rooms have balconies, fireplaces, and whirlpool tubs. The great location is smack in the center of town: you may not have to leave your room to hear the sounds of the weekly town-band concerts. ⊠ *512 Main St., 02633,* ☎ *508/945–5550 or 800/391–5734,* FAX *508/945–3407,* WEB *www.waysideinn.com. 56 rooms. Restaurant, pool. AE, D, MC, V.*

$$$–$$$$ ⊡ **Queen Anne Inn.** Built in 1840 as a wedding present for the daugh-
★   ter of a famous clipper-ship captain, the building first opened as an inn in 1874. Some of the large guest rooms have working fireplaces, balconies, and hot tubs. Lingering and lounging are encouraged—around the large heated outdoor pool, at the tables on the veranda, in front of the fireplace in the cozy sitting room, and in the plush parlor. The restaurant, which serves a delicious breakfast, is open to the public for dinner. ⊠ *70 Queen Anne Rd., 02633,* ☎ *508/945–0394 or 800/545–4667,* FAX *508/945–4884,* WEB *www.queenanneinn.com. 31 rooms. Restaurant, bar, air-conditioning, pool, 3 tennis courts. AE, D, MC, V.*

$$–$$$ ⊡ **Hawthorne Motel.** This popular motel overlooks Pleasant Bay, the Atlantic, and Chatham Harbor. Nearly all the rooms, whether they are the spotless no-nonsense, simply decorated motel rooms or the fully equipped efficiency units, have stunning water views. The center of town is just a short walk away. ⊠ *196 Shore Rd., 02633,* ☎ *508/945–0372,* WEB *www.thehawthorne.com. 16 rooms, 10 efficiencies, 1 cottage. AE, D, MC, V. Closed mid-Oct.–mid-May.*

$$–$$$ ⊡ **Moses Nickerson House.** Each room in this 1839 house has an in-
★   dividual look: one with dark woods, leathers, and English hunting antiques; another with a high canopy bed and a hand-hooked rug. Others have handmade quilts, floral wall-coverings, and canopy or four-poster beds. Some rooms have gas-log fireplaces. The constants are the queen-size beds, televisions, telephones, and complete modem and computer hookups. Breakfast is served in a pretty glassed-in sunroom with views of the garden and fishpond. ⊠ *364 Old Harbor Rd., 02633,* ☎ *508/945–5859 or 800/628–6972,* FAX *508/945–7087,* WEB *capecodtravel.com/mosesnickersonhouse. 7 rooms. Air-conditioning, in-room data ports. No smoking. AE, D, MC, V. BP.*

$$ ⊡ **Chatham Highlander.** A great bargain considering its location near the center of Chatham, this motel offers generously sized rooms on attractive grounds. Most rooms have double beds, though one has a king-size bed, and there are two efficiencies and a suite for larger families. All the standard amenities are offered, from cable TV to small refrigerators, and there are two outdoor pools on the grounds. ⊠ *946 Main St., 02633,* ☎ *508/945–9038,* WEB *capecodtravel.com/highlander. 28 rooms. Air-conditioning, 2 pools. No smoking. AE, D, MC, V. Closed Thanksgiving.–Apr.*

$$ ⊡ **Ridgevale Beach Inn Resort Motel.** This complex, just a few miles from Chatham's town center, is nestled on 6 acres of wooded green land. The warm waters of Nantucket Sound are not far, nor are all the in-town activities. Standard rooms have two double beds while the condolike suites are equipped with kitchens, dining areas, fireplaces, and private decks. For larger groups, there are two-bedroom suites, and cottages are available on the grounds for weekly rentals. ⊠ *2045 Main Street, West Chatham, 02633,* ☎ *508/432–1169,* FAX *508/432–1877,* WEB *capecodtravel.com/ridgevalebeachinn. 8 condos, 23 rooms. AE, D, MC, V. Closed late-Oct.–Apr.*

Nightlife and the Arts

THE ARTS

Chatham Drama Guild (✉ 134 Crowell Rd., ☎ 508/945–0510) stages productions year-round, including musicals, comedies, and dramas.

The **Creative Arts Center** (✉ 154 Crowell Rd., ☎ 508/945–3583) thrives year-round with classes, changing gallery exhibitions, demonstrations, lectures, and other activities.

In July and August the **Guild of Chatham Painters** presents an outdoor art gallery on Thursday and Friday from 9:30 to 5 on the lawn of the Main Street School (✉ Main St.).

The **Monomoy Theatre** (✉ 776 Main St., ☎ 508/945–1589) stages summer productions—thrillers, musicals, classics, modern drama—by the Ohio University Players.

Chatham's summer **town-band concerts** (✉ Kate Gould Park, Main St., ☎ 508/945–5199) begin at 8 on Friday and draw up to 6,000 people. As many as 500 fox-trot on the roped-off dance floor, and there are special dances for children and sing-alongs for all.

NIGHTLIFE

Chatham Squire (✉ 487 Main St., ☎ 508/945–0945), with four bars including a raw bar, is a rollicking year-round local hangout, drawing a young crowd to the bar side and a mixed crowd of locals to the restaurant.

Wequassett Inn Resort & Golf Club (✉ 173 Orleans Rd. [Rte. 28], Pleasant Bay, ☎ 508/432–5400) has a jazz duo or piano music nightly in its lounge in July and August (jacket requested).

Sou'wester (✉ 1563 Main St., ☎ 508/945–4424) maintains an active schedule of live music—rock and roll, the blues, oldies, and swing—in a raucous and locally flavored setting.

Outdoor Activities and Sports

BASEBALL

The **Cape Cod Baseball League,** begun in 1885, is an invitational league of college players that counts Carlton Fisk, Ron Darling, and the late Thurman Munson as alumni. Considered the country's best summer league, it is scouted by all the major-league teams. Players have included Mo Vaughn and Nomar Garciaparra. Ten teams play a 44-game season from mid-June to mid-August; games held at all 10 fields are free. The **Chatham A's** games (✉ Veterans' Field, Main and Depot Sts. by rotary, ☎ 508/996–5004 for schedule) are great entertainment.

Baseball clinics (✉ Veterans' Field, Main and Depot Sts. by rotary, ☎ 508/432–6909) for children 6 through 8, 9 through 12, and 13 through 17 are offered in one-week sessions by the Chatham A's in summer. The other nine town teams in the Cape league also conduct clinics (☎ 508/996–5004 for information).

BEACHES

If you're looking for a crowd-free sandy beach, boats at Chatham Harbor—such as the *Rip Ryder* (☎ 508/945–5450)—will ferry you across to North Beach ($10–$12 per person), which is a sand spit adjoining Orleans's Nauset Beach, to South Beach ($10), or to Monomoy ($45, or $10 per person for three or more passengers).

Outermost Harbor Marine (✉ Morris Island Rd., ☎ 508/945–2030) runs shuttles to South Beach; rides cost $10 round-trip for adults. The cost includes parking.

THE CAPE COD BASEBALL LEAGUE

AT THE BASEBALL HALL OF FAME in Cooperstown, New York, you'll find a poster announcing a showdown between arch rivals Sandwich and Barnstable. The date? July 4, 1885. In the 100-plus years since that day, the Cape's ball-playing tradition has continued unabated, and if you're a sports fan, a visit to a Cape Cod Baseball League summer game is a must. Seeing a game on the Cape is to come into contact with baseball's roots. You'll remember why you love the sport, and you'll have a newfound sense of why it became the national pastime.

As they have since the 1950s, top-ranked college baseball players from around the country descend on the Cape when school lets out, in time to begin the season in mid-June. This is no sandlot, catch-as-catch-can scene. Each player joins one of the league's 10 teams, which are based in Bourne, Wareham, Falmouth, Cotuit, Hyannis, Dennis-Yarmouth, Harwich, Brewster, Chatham, and Orleans. The teams are the Bourne Braves, Wareham Gatemen, Falmouth Commodores, Cotuit Kettleers, Hyannis Mets, Dennis-Yarmouth Red Sox, Harwich Mariners, Brewster Whitecaps, Chatham Athletics (A's), and the Orleans Cardinals.

Players lodge with local families and work day jobs cutting lawns, painting houses, or giving baseball clinics in town parks. In the evening, though, their lives are given over to baseball, as they don uniforms and head for the field.

To judge by the past, Cape League veterans are tomorrow's major-league stars. By latest count, one of every eight active major-league ballplayers spent a summer in the Cape League on the way up. Boston Red Soxers Mo Vaughn, John Valentin, Tim Naehring, and Nomar Garciaparra all played in the Cape League in different years, for different teams.

Add names such as Frank Thomas, Jeff Bagwell, Albert Belle (before he lost his manners), Will Clark, and Walt Weiss, and you could build an all-star roster.

To enshrine these heroes past, the Cape League inducted its first members into its Hall of Fame at the Heritage Plantation in Sandwich in January 2001. Among the 12 players honored were Thurman Munson, Mike Flanagan, Jeff Reardon, Mo Vaughn, and Frank Thomas.

Yet as good as the baseball is—and you'll often see bunches of major-league scouts at a game—another great reason to come out to the ballpark is. . . the ballpark. Chatham's Veterans Field is the Cape's 3Com Park at Candlestick Point because, much like the San Francisco version, fog tends to engulf the games. Orleans's Eldredge Park is a local favorite—immaculate, cozy, and comfortable. Some parks have bleachers, while in others it's up to you to bring your own chair or blanket and stretch out behind a dugout or baseline. Children are free to roam and can even try for foul balls—which they are, however, asked to return because, after all, balls don't grow on trees. When hunger hits, the ice cream truck and hot-dog stand are never far away.

Games start at either 5 or 7, depending on whether the field has lights; there are occasionally afternoon games. Each team plays 44 games in a season, so finding one is rarely a problem (www. capecodbaseball.org. has information). And, best of all, they're always free. The Cape's baseball scene is so American, the ambience so relaxed and refreshing, it's tempting to invoke the old *Field of Dreams* analogy. But the league needs no Hollywood comparison. This is the real thing. It was built a long time ago, and they are still coming.

— Seth Rolbein

Harding's Beach (✉ Harding's Beach Rd., off Barn Hill Rd.), west of Chatham center, is open to the public and charges daily parking fees to nonresidents in season. Lifeguards are stationed in summer. This beach can get crowded, so plan to arrive early or late.

Bert & Carol's Lawnmower & Bicycle Shop (✉ 347 Orleans Rd. [Rte. 28], North Chatham, ☎ 508/945–0137) has a variety of bikes for rent.

Bikes & Blades (✉ 195 Crowell Rd., ☎ 508/945–7600) rents all manner of bikes as well as in-line skates.

Monomoy Sail & Cycle (✉ 275 Orleans Rd., North Chatham, ☎ 508/945–0811) rents sailboards and Sunfish.

Chatham Seaside Links (✉ Seaview St., ☎ 508/945–4774), a nine-hole course, is good for beginners.

The Lower and Outer Cape beaches, including North Beach in Chatham, are the best for surfing, which is tops when there's a storm offshore. Chatham does not have any surf shops, but you'll find them in nearby Orleans.

Chatham Bars Inn (✉ Shore Rd., ☎ 508/945–0096 Ext. 1155) offers three waterfront all-weather tennis courts, open to the public by reservation for $30 an hour. You can also take lessons and visit the pro shop.

The town maintains two public tennis parks, one on Depot Road next to the Railroad Museum at No. 153 and the other at the middle school on Crowell Road.

Shopping

Main Street is a busy shopping area, with upscale and conservative merchandise. Here you'll find galleries, crafts, clothing stores, bookstores, and a few good antiques shops.

Aquitaine Antiques (✉ 35 Cross St., ☎ 508/945–5787 or 945–9746) has a good selection of marine and Americana antiques.

Cabbages and Kings Bookstore (✉ 628 Main St., ☎ 508/945–1603) is a good independent bookstore. In addition to a full stock of literary and regional books, look for a host of unusual games, cards, and toys and a regular schedule of author appearances.

Cape Cod Cooperage (✉ 1150 Queen Anne Rd., at Rte. 137, ☎ 508/432–0788), in an old barn, sells woodenware made in a (more than) century-old tradition by an on-site cooper (barrel maker), as well as hand-decorated furniture, crafts supplies, and more. Daily classes are available in everything from stenciling to basket making, from decorative painting to birdhouse building. Another location in Chatham (on Rte. 28) sells antiques and finely crafted Shaker furniture.

Chatham Glass Company (✉ 758 Main St., ☎ 508/945–5547) is a glassworks where you can watch glass being blown and buy it, too. Objects include marbles, Christmas ornaments, jewelry, and art glass.

Chatham Jam and Jelly Shop (✉ 10 Vineyard Ave., at Rte. 28, West Chatham, ☎ 508/945–3052) sells preserves such as cranberry with strawberries and Maine wild blueberry, nutty conserves, and ice cream toppings, all made on-site in small batches.

Clambake Celebrations (✉ 1223C Main St., ☎ 508/945–7771 or 877/ 792–7771) prepares full clambakes, including lobsters, clams, mussels, corn, potatoes, onions, and sausage, for you to take out; it'll even loan a charcoal grill. The company also delivers, via air if necessary, year-round. The food is layered in seaweed in a pot and ready to steam.

The **East Wind Silver Co.** (✉ 878 Main St., ☎ 508/945–8935) specializes in artful silver jewelry but also sells watercolor paintings, pottery, fountains, and Tiffany-style lighting.

Journey on a Small Planet (✉ 746 Main St., ☎ 508/945–1771) has a good selection of antique prints, books, and unique gifts.

Marion's Pie Shop (✉ 2022 Main St. [Rte. 28], West Chatham, ☎ 508/ 432–9439) sells homemade and home-style fruit breads; pastries; prepared foods such as lasagna; Boston baked beans; chowder base; and, of course, pies, both savory and sweet.

S. Wilder & Co. (✉ 304 Rte. 28, North Chatham, ☎ 877/794–5337) displays old-style colonial crafts. Handcrafted brass and copper lanterns are made here.

The **Spyglass** (✉ 618 Main St., ☎ 508/945–9686) carries telescopes, barometers, writing boxes, maps, and other nautical antiques.

Yankee Ingenuity (✉ 525 Main St., ☎ 508/945–1288) stocks a varied selection of unique jewelry and lamps and a wide assortment of unusual, beautiful trinkets at reasonable (especially for Chatham) prices.

Yellow Umbrella Books (✉ 501 Main St., ☎ 508/945–0144) has an excellent selection of new books, many about Cape Cod, as well as used books.

En Route   North of Chatham, Route 28 winds through wooded upland toward **Pleasant Bay,** from which a number of country roads will take you to a nice view of Nauset spit and the islands in the bay.

Orleans

⑫   *8 mi north of Chatham, 4 mi southwest of Eastham, 35 mi east of Sagamore Bridge.*

Named for Louis-Philippe de Bourbon, *duc d'Orléans* (duke of Orléans), who reputedly visited the area during his exile from France in the 1790s, Orleans was incorporated as a town in 1797. Historically, it has the distinction of being the only place in the continental United States to have received enemy fire during either world war. In July 1918 a German submarine fired on commercial barges off the coast. Four were sunk, and one shell is reported to have fallen on American soil.

Today Orleans is part quiet seaside village and part bustling center with strip malls. The commercial hub of the Lower Cape, Orleans is one of the more steadily populated areas, year-round, of the Lower Cape. Yet the town retains a fervent commitment to preserving its past, and residents, in support of local mom-and-pop shops, maintain an active refusal policy of many big-time corporations.

Orleans has a long heritage in fishing and seafaring, and many beautifully preserved homes remain from the colonial era. Much of this beauty is found in the small village of East Orleans, home of the town's Historical Society and Museum. In other areas of town, such as down by Rock Harbor, more modestly grand homes stand near the water's edge. The dramatic cathedral of the Community of Jesus stands watch over the bustle of fishing fleets at Rock Harbor; this religious community owns a large portion of the prime real estate in the area.

As you head north, this is the first Cape town to touch both Cape Cod Bay and the Atlantic Ocean. Nauset Beach, on the Atlantic, is enormously popular. Backed by towering dunes dotted with sea grass and colorful *rosa Rugosa*, this beach begins what could be a long but beautiful trek clear to the very tip of the Cape. Skaket Beach, just south of Rock Harbor, is the main bayside beach and affords both scenic views and calm, warm waters for swimming.

A walk along Rock Harbor Road, a winding street lined with gray-shingle Cape houses, white picket fences, and neat gardens, leads to the bay-side **Rock Harbor,** a former packet landing and site of a War of 1812 skirmish in which the Orleans militia kept a British warship from docking. In the 19th century Orleans had an active saltworks and a flourishing packet service between Rock Harbor and Boston developed. Today the former packet landing is the base of charter-fishing and party boats in season, as well as of a small commercial fishing fleet whose catch hits the counters at the fish market and small restaurant here. Sunsets over the harbor are spectacular.

The 1890 **French Cable Station Museum** was the stateside landing point for the 3,000-mi-long transatlantic cable that originated in Brittany. Another cable laid between Orleans and New York City completed the France–New York link, and many important messages were communicated through the station. In World War I it was an essential connection between army headquarters in Washington and the American Expeditionary Force in France, and the station was under guard by the marines. By 1959 telephone service had rendered the station obsolete, and it closed. The equipment is still in place. ⊠ *41 S. Orleans Rd.,* ☎ *508/240–1735.* 🖾 *Donations accepted.* ☉ *June, Fri.–Sun., 1–4; July–Labor Day, Mon.–Sat. 1–4.*

The **Jonathan Young Windmill,** a pretty if somewhat incongruous sight on the busy highway, is a landmark from the days of salt making in Orleans, when it would pump saltwater into shallow vaults for evaporation. A program explaining the history and operation of the mill demonstrates the old millstone and grinding process. ⊠ *Rte. 6A and Town Cove.* ☉ *July–Aug., daily 11–4; June and Sept., weekends 11–4.*

Ⓒ The **Academy of Performing Arts** (⊠ 5 Giddiah Hill Rd., ☎ 508/255–5510, Ⓦᴱᴮ www.apa1.org) offers two-week sessions of theater, music, and dance classes to children ages 8–12, with a show at the end of each session. It also schedules year-round classes for ages four to adult in dance, music, and drama. The academy's theater is at 120 Main Street.

NEED A
BREAK? **Sunset Grill** (⊠ 84 Rte. 6A, ☎ 508/240–3282) is great for takeout or a quick sit-down bite. This smoky (from the barbecue grill, that is) little place has a large menu that includes big burgers, tacos, and barbecued chicken and beef. Cold salads and sandwiches are also available, as are beer and wine.

Snow Library (⊠ Main Street and Rte. 28, ☎ 508/240–3760) has been in operation since around 1876; today there are children's story hours and numerous lecture programs.

Dining and Lodging

$$$–$$$$ ✕ **Nauset Beach Club.** Though a longtime fixture here, this intimate
★ little restaurant has new owners, and locals say it has never been better. The kitchen produces seasonally inspired, regional Italian cuisine with an emphasis on locally harvested seafood and produce. Choose from a fixed-price option (offered daily at two early seatings) or the regular menu for such favorites as pistachio-crusted roast rack of lamb

or tagliatelle with lobster. The off-season warms up with the wood oven–fired dishes; in fall and winter, truffles appear artfully in various presentations. Pastas and desserts are all homemade, and the large Italian and American wine selection is excellent. ⊠ *222 Main St., East Orleans,* ☎ *508/255–8547. Reservations essential. AE, D, DC, MC, V. No lunch.*

$$–$$$ ✕ **Abba Cafe.** This place has brought a much-needed dash of flavor to the Orleans restaurant scene. Specializing in Mediterranean cuisine, the café serves robust sandwiches and pizzas unlike anything else you can get around here. Try the Gran Huevon—a sandwich of eggs, saffron-basil mayonnaise, onions, and capers—or La Bruja pizza, topped with walnut-and-spinach ricotta, marinated wild mushrooms, and Gorgonzola. An impressive range of salads is also available, including such treats as tabbouleh and baba ghanouj. Other good choices are falafel, *shawarma,* and anything from the extensive bakery selection. All items are made on the premises. ⊠ *West Rd. and Old Colony Way,* ☎ *508/255–8405. No credit cards.*

$$–$$$ ✕ **The Beacon Room.** Adorned with crisp linens, frilly curtains, and handsome wood furnishings, this little bistro serves a nice mix of seafood and meats enhanced with sophisticated and inventive flavors. The Gorgonzola, pear, and walnut salad is especially nice and makes for a rich beginning to such delights as potato-crusted salmon or the house favorite, chicken saltimbocca. There's a bit of everything here, from quesadillas to calamari, and each dish is treated with the same care and attention to quality. In the warmer months dinner out on the lantern-lighted garden patio is particularly gracious. An ambitious wine list complements the fine selection. ⊠ *23 West Rd.,* ☎ *508/255–2211. Reservations not accepted. D, MC, V.*

$$–$$$ ✕ **Kadee's Lobster & Clam Bar.** Kadee's serves good clams and fish-and-chips that you can grab on the way to the beach from the take-out window. Or sit down in the dining room for steamers and mussels, pasta and seafood stews, or the famous Portuguese kale soup. There's also a gift shop as well as a miniature golf course out back. The only serious drawback here is the prices. ⊠ *212 Main St.,* ☎ *508/255–6184. Reservations not accepted. MC, V. Closed day after Labor Day–week before Memorial Day and weekdays in early June.*

$$–$$$ ✕ **Mahoney's Atlantic Bar and Grill.** The chef, a Mahoney who cooked for years at one of Provincetown's busiest restaurants, really knows his stuff. The lunch and dinner menu are taking appetizers to new heights, emphasizing grilled vegetables and polenta; drunken littlenecks steamed in ale; and a New Orleans classic, oyster po'boys. The bar is long and comfortable, and you can sip your California wine to the tunes of live jazz and piano on weekends. ⊠ *28 Main St.,* ☎ *508/255–5505. AE, D, DC, MC, V.*

$$–$$$ ✕ **The Old Jailhouse Tavern.** The symbol next to the entrance of this rambling restaurant, added on to what was an old stone lockup, is a big set of golden jailer's keys. The theme continues, with a light touch, throughout the decor and menu. On the long, varied menu are headings such as "A Light Sentence," for salads and appetizers, and "The Lineup," for the sandwich list. Foods for sharing include a whole wheel of baked Brie with Boursin cheese, crackers, and fruit; and deep-fried fresh vegetables with ranch dip. Entrées lean toward basic seafood, steak, veal, and chicken dishes. There's a flower-hung atrium, a long oak bar, and the Courthouse addition for group events. ⊠ *28 West Rd.,* ☎ *508/255–5245. Reservations not accepted. D, MC, V.*

$$–$$$ ✕ **Rosina's Cafe.** Originally a classic mom-and-pop Italian restaurant off Main Street, Rosina's has expanded into a full-blown full-service place. Some feel that the food, which was some of the best home-style Italian cooking on Cape Cod, has not survived the move all that well.

The pasta primavera makes the grade, as does Angela's stuffed halibut (often on special), a good chunk of fish stuffed with scallops, cheeses, pine nuts, bread crumbs, and garlic. The spaghetti puttanesca remains a rewarding signature dish. The wine list veers toward the conventional. ⊠ *15 Cove Rd.,* ☎ *508/240–5513. AE, D, MC, V.*

$$ ✕ **The Yardarm.** Orleans's version of a roadhouse, the Yardarm feels smoky even though smoking is not allowed anymore. The tube over the bar is likely to be tuned to a sports game, and the only pool table in town is always busy (though not in use when dinner is being served). The hearty, well-cooked food is a great value, especially the baked sole, barbecued ribs or chicken, and the pot roast; thanks to the big portions, you can expect to take some of your dinner home. It's also a great place to stop in for a burger-and-beer lunch. ⊠ *48 Rte. 28,* ☎ *508/ 255–4840. Reservations not accepted. AE, DC, MC, V.*

$–$$ ✕ **Land Ho!** The scene at Orleans's flagship local restaurant is definitely fun and boisterous even if the typical tavern fare on the blackboard menu doesn't always live up to the atmosphere. Dozens of homemade wooden signs hang from the rafters. The burgers and the sea-clam pie are both excellent—much better than the fish-and-chips. This is a good place for a rainy-day lunch. On weekend nights, it livens up even more with the music of local bands. ⊠ *Rte. 6A and Cove Rd.,* ☎ *508/ 255–5165. Reservations not accepted. AE, MC, V.*

$–$$ ✕ **Lobster Claw.** If you're over 6 ft tall, keep an eye out for the fishnets hanging from the ceiling in this goofy little seafood spot. Tables are lacquered turquoise, portions are huge, and the lobster roll is one of the best. You can get all the Cape basics here: fish and seafood poached, broiled, baked, or fried, along with an assortment of steaks. The children's menu includes seafood and chicken tenders. The place gets packed to the gills, especially during its popular Early Bird dining hours. ⊠ *Rte. 6A,* ☎ *508/255–1800. Reservations not accepted. AE, D, DC, MC, V.*

$–$$ ✕ **Sir Cricket's Fish and Chips.** For a beautifully turned-out fish sandwich, you can pull off the highway into this tiny local favorite, a hole-in-the-wall attached to the Nauset Lobster Pool. Built mainly for takeout, this no-frills fried-food joint does have three or four tiny tables and a soda machine. Try the fresh oyster roll or go for a full fisherman's platter. Be sure to check out the chair seats as you gobble those fries. Each is an exquisitely rendered minimural of Orleans history or a personality painted by legendary local artist Dan Joy. ⊠ *Rte. 6A, near Stop & Shop,* ☎ *508/255–4453. Reservations not accepted. No credit cards.*

$$–$$$ ✕⊞ **Barley Neck Inn.** Spacious rooms are available in the hotel-like lodge, adjacent to the restaurant building. Modern conveniences such as televisions and small refrigerators are standard. It took a little time, but the inn's restaurant, in a restored 1850s sea captain's house, has shucked off its staidness and become a popular destination. The fairly formal main dining area and a buzzing, relaxed bar called Joe's have equally satisfying menus (the bar is cheaper); the chef updates classic Cape fish dishes with a French influence. The kitchen is innovation and particularly known for its salsas and sauces. Off-season, there is often live jazz on Sunday afternoon and a good fire burning in the huge stone fireplace. ⊠ *5 Beach Rd., East Orleans 02643,* ☎ *508/255–8484; 508/ 255–0212 for restaurant,* FAX *508/255–3626,* WEB *www.barleyneck.com. 18 rooms. 2 restaurants, refrigerators, pool. AE, MC, V. CP*

$$ ⊞ **Kadee's Gray Elephant.** A mile from Nauset Beach, next to shops, ★ a grocery store, a farm stand, a post office, and Kadee's Lobster & Clam Bar, this centuries-old house offers small vacation studio and one-bedroom apartments. They're a cheerful riot of color, from wicker painted lavender or green to bright pink bows and flowers painted on furniture to beds layered in quilts and comforters mixing plaids and florals.

Kitchens are fully equipped with microwaves, attractive glassware, irons and boards—even lobster crackers. ⊠ *216 Main St., Box 86, East Orleans 02643,* ☎ *508/255–7608,* ℻ *508/240–2976. 6–8 apartments. Restaurant, miniature golf, shop. MC, V.*

$$ 🏨 **Orleans Holiday Motel.** Smack in the middle of a commercial area, this complex is not a totally peaceful place, but its position does put you in the midst of restaurants and other services; it's also an easy walk from the center of town. Motel rooms are set around the giant outdoor pool and are furnished with either two double, one queen-size, or two queen-size beds. There's a complimentary boat shuttle to Nauset Beach. ⊠ *Rtes. 6A and 28, 02643,* ☎ *508/255–1514 or 800/451–1833,* ℻ *508/255–7284,* 🕸 *www.orleansholiday.com. 45 rooms. Picnic area, air-conditioning, refrigerators, pool. AE, MC, V. CP.*

$–$$ 🏨 **Nauset House Inn.** You could easily spend a day trying out all the places to relax here. There's a parlor with comfortable chairs and a large fireplace, an orchard set with picnic tables, and a lush conservatory with a weeping cherry tree in its center. Rooms in both the main building and the adjacent Carriage House have stenciled walls, quilts, and unusual antique pieces, as well as hand-painted furniture, stained glass, and prints done by one of the owners. The beach is only ½-mi distant (they'll set you up with beach chairs and towels), and the attractions of town are close but not too close. ⊠ *143 Beach Rd., Box 774, East Orleans 02643,* ☎ *508/255–2195,* 🕸 *www.nausethouseinn. com. 14 rooms. Breakfast room. D, MC, V. Closed Nov.–Mar. BP.*

$ 🏨 **Sea Breeze Motel.** In the historic area of East Orleans and about a
★ mile from famed Nauset Beach, you can walk to town restaurants, shops, and a post office from here. Guest rooms are nothing fancy, but each has either a queen-size or two twin-size beds, wall-to-wall carpeting, cable TV, radio, and a decent-size tile bathroom. A Continental breakfast is offered for weekend visitors. ⊠ *Nauset Beach Road, 02643,* ☎ *508/240–5500 or 877/648–6732,* 🕸 *capecodtravel.com/seabreeze. 16 rooms. Picnic area, air-conditioning, refrigerators. MC, V. Closed late Sept.–Memorial Day.*

$–$$ 🏨 **Skaket Beach Motel.** Rooms in this convenient-to-everything motel
★ on a busy roadside are well sized and available in standard, deluxe, or poolside variety. Outdoors is a number of distractions—from horseshoes to a heated pool to grills. ⊠ *203 Rte. 6A, 02643,* ☎ *508/255–1020 or 800/835–0298,* ℻ *508/255–6487,* 🕸 *www.skaketbeachmotel.com. 46 rooms. Pool, croquet, horseshoes. MC, V. Closed late Nov.–Mar. CP.*

Nightlife and the Arts

The **Academy Playhouse** (⊠ 120 Main St., ☎ 508/255–1963), one of the oldest community theaters on the Cape, stages 12 or 13 productions year-round, including original works.

The **Cape & Islands Chamber Music Festival** (⊠ Box 2721, 02653, ☎ 508/255–1386) presents three weeks of top-caliber performances, including a jazz night, at various locations in August.

The 90-member **Cape Symphony Orchestra** (☎ 508/362–1111) sails into Orleans in late August for one of two Sounds of Summer Pops concerts (the other is in Mashpee in July). The performance takes place at the Eldredge Park, adjacent to the Nauset Middle School. (⊠ Rte. 28 and Eldredge Pkwy.). Call for a year-round schedule of events.

Joe's Beach Road Bar & Grille (⊠ Main St. at Beach Rd., ☎ 508/255–0212) features live piano on Thursday through Sunday nights in summer; check for off-season entertainment schedules.

Land Ho! (⊠ Rte. 6A and Cove Rd., ☎ 508/255–5165) has live local bands frequently and throughout the year.

Mahoney's Atlantic Bar and Grill (⊠ 28 Main St., ☎ 508/255–5505) schedules live jazz and blues in the bar area on a regular basis; call for times.

Free ocean-side concerts are held in the gazebo at **Nauset Beach** each Monday evening from 7 to 9 in July and August. The resident fried-clam shack stays open until 10.

Outdoor Activities and Sports

BASEBALL

The **Orleans Cardinals** (☎ 508/240–2867) of the collegiate Cape Cod Baseball League play home games at Eldredge Park (⊠ Rte. 28) from mid-June to mid-August.

BEACHES

The town-owned **Nauset Beach** (⊠ Beach Rd., ☎ 508/240–3775)—not to be confused with Nauset Light Beach, up a ways at the National Seashore—is a wide 10-mi-long sweep of sandy ocean beach with low dunes and large waves good for bodysurfing or board surfing. The beach has lifeguards, rest rooms, showers, and a food concession (something the National Seashore beaches lack). Despite its size, the massive parking lot often fills up when the sun is strong; it's best to arrive quite early or in the late afternoon if you want to claim a spot. The beach is open to off-road vehicles with a special permit. Daily parking fees of $8 are charged, or you can buy a one-week pass for $25, a two-week pass for $45, or a season pass for $65. Entrance is free with a resident sticker. For more information call the parks department.

Freshwater seekers can access **Pilgrim Lake** (⊠ Pilgrim Lake Rd. off Monument Rd. and Rte. 28) with the same parking and sticker fees as Nauset Beach.

Skaket Beach (⊠ Skaket Beach Rd., ☎ 508/240–3775) on Cape Cod Bay is a sandy stretch with calm warm water good for children. It's a good place to watch motorboats, fishing charters, and sailboats as they leave the channel at Rock Harbor, not to mention the spectacular evening sunsets. There are rest rooms, lifeguards, and a snack bar. Daily parking fees are the same as at Nauset Beach. For more information call the parks department.

BOATING

Arey's Pond Boat Yard (⊠ 43 Arey's La., off Rte. 28, South Orleans, ☎ 508/255–0994) has a sailing school with individual and group lessons.

FISHING

Many of Orleans's freshwater ponds offer good fishing for perch, pickerel, trout, and more. The required fishing license, along with rental gear, is available at the **Goose Hummock Shop** (⊠ 15 Rte. 6A, ☎ 508/255–0455).

The **Osprey** (☎ 508/255–4212) leaves Rock Harbor for both half- and full-day sportfishing trips. All tackle, bait, and cleaning services are provided.

Rock Harbor Charter Boat Fleet (⊠ Rock Harbor, ☎ 508/255–9757; 800/287–1771 in MA) goes for bass and blues in the bay from spring through fall. Walk-ons and charters are both available.

ICE-SKATING

Ice-skating, lessons, hockey, clinics, and camps are available at the **Charles Moore Arena** (⊠ O'Connor Way, ☎ 508/255–5902). Children ages 9 through 14 ice-skate to DJ-spun rock and flashing lights at Rock Night, which takes place Friday from 8 to 10.

SPORTING GOODS—RENTALS

Nauset Sports (⊠ Jeremiah Sq., Rte. 6A at rotary, ☎ 508/255–4742) rents surf, body, skim, and wake boards; kayaks; wet suits; in-line skates; and tennis racquets.

For bike rentals just across the way from the Cape Cod Rail Trail, head to **Orleans Cycle** (⊠ 26 Main St., ☎ 508/255–9115).

SURFING

The Lower and Outer Cape beaches, including Nauset Beach in Orleans, are the best spots for surfing, especially when there's a storm offshore. For a surf report—water temperature, weather, surf, tanning factor—call ☎ 508/240–2229.

Pump House Surf Co. (⊠ 9 Rte. 6A, ☎ 508/240–2226) rents wet suits and sells other surf gear.

Shopping

Baseball Shop (⊠ 26 Main St., ☎ 508/240–1063) sells licensed products relating to baseball and other sports—new and collectible cards (and nonsports cards) as well as hats, clothing, and videos.

Bird Watcher's General Store (⊠ 36 Rte. 6A, ☎ 508/255–6974 or 800/562–1512) stocks nearly everything avian but the birds themselves: feeders, paintings, houses, books, binoculars, calls, bird-theme apparel—ad infinitum.

Compass Rose Bookshop (⊠ 43 Main St., ☎ 508/255–1545) is just what an independent bookstore should be: friendly, comfortable, and full of books on all kinds of subjects, including works by local authors and those of regional interest. You'll also find a generous collection of unique greeting cards and specialty items. Internet access is available on a sign-up fee basis.

Countryside Antiques (⊠ 6 Lewis Rd., East Orleans, ☎ 508/240–0525) specializes in European and Asian antique furniture, home-accent pieces, china, and silver.

Fancy's Farm Stand (⊠ 199 Main St., East Orleans, ☎ 508/255–1949) sells local produce, fresh sandwiches and roll-ups, salads (salad bar or prepared varieties), homemade soup, ice cream, fresh-baked breads, and other supplies for a great picnic. A wide assortment of flowers, both dried and fresh, are sold, adding great color to the beautiful, beamed old-style barn.

Hannah (⊠ 47 Main St., ☎ 508/255–8234) carries women's casual dresses, scarves, and hats with flair by such labels as Hannah, No Saint, and Angel Heart.

Heaven Scent You (⊠ 13 Cove Rd., ☎ 508/240–2508) offers massage, spa services, and beauty treatments—everything you need for some relaxation and rejuvenation.

Karol Richardson (⊠ 47 Main St., ☎ 508/255–3944) sells fine contemporary clothing. There's also a selection of silk wraps and scarves, hats, shoes, handbags, and handcrafted jewelry. You'll pay well for the quality, but if you're fortunate enough to be around for one of the off-season warehouse sales, you'll hit the jackpot.

Kemp Pottery (⊠ 9 Rte. 6A, ☎ 508/255–5853) displays functional and decorative stoneware and porcelain, fountains, garden sculpture, sinks, and stained glass.

Oceana (⊠ 1 Main St. Sq., ☎ 508/240–1414) presents a beautiful selection of nautical-theme home accents, gifts, and jewelry, as well as colorful hooked rugs made by Cape artist Claire Murray.

The **Orleans Farmers' Market** (✉ Cape Cod Five Operations Center, 19 West Rd.), held Saturday morning throughout the summer, features local delicacies such as fresh shellfish, produce, flowers, and homemade goodies. It opens at 8, and early birds get the best selection—things tend to disappear quickly.

XO Clothing (✉ 50 Main St., ☎ 508/255–4407) carries a full stock of designer warehouse excess at unbeatable prices. The inventory changes frequently, but expect scores of casual linen dresses, pants sets, shirts, and colorful cotton pieces.

ART AND CRAFTS GALLERIES

The **Addison Holmes Fine Art Gallery** (✉ 43 Rte. 28, ☎ 508/255–6200), in four rooms of a brick-red Cape house, represents more than two dozen regional artists and sells a broad range of contemporary works, many of which are inspired by life on Cape Cod. The sculpture garden in the side yard is a perfect complement to the tasteful gallery. Receptions, where you can often meet the week's featured artist, are held from 5 to 7 Saturday night.

The **Hogan Art Gallery** (✉ 39 Main St., ☎ 508/240–3655) features the colorful white-line woodblock, paintings, and pastels by artist Ruth Hogan, as well as 20th-century American regional paintings by her husband, Frank. There's also a nice selection of painted furniture.

Left Bank Gallery (✉ 8 Cove Rd., ☎ 508/247–9172) carries an eclectic mix of handcrafted jewelry, fine art by both local and national artists, hand-painted furniture, pottery, and handmade clothing.

In July and August, **Nauset Painters** presents outdoor juried art shows every Tuesday (✉ Depot Sq. at Old Colony Way) from 10 to 5 and Sunday (✉ Sandwich Cooperative Bank, 51 Main St.) from 10 to 5.

The **Orleans Art Association** holds outdoor art shows from 10 to 5 each Thursday and Friday in July and August on the grounds of the American Legion Hall (✉ 137 Main St.).

At various times in June, July and August, the **Orleans Professional Arts and Crafts Association** sponsors a giant outdoor show featuring the works of more than 100 artists and craftsmen on the grounds of the Nauset Middle School (✉ Rte. 28). For specific dates and times check the free town chamber of commerce guide.

The **Star Gallery** (✉ 76 Rte. 6A, ☎ 508/240–7827) specializes in contemporary and less traditional art by artists both local and beyond; watch for Saturday-evening artist receptions in July and August.

Tree's Place (✉ Rte. 6A, at Rte. 28, ☎ 508/255–1330), one of the Cape's best and most original shops, has a collection of handcrafted kaleidoscopes, as well as art glass, hand-painted porcelain and pottery, hand-blown stemware, jewelry, imported ceramic tiles, and fine art. Tree's displays the work of New England artists including Robert Vickery, Don Stone, and Elizabeth Mumford (whose popular folk art is bordered in mottoes and poetic phrases). Champagne openings are held on Saturday night in summer.

Eastham

⑬ *3 mi north of Orleans, 6 mi south of Wellfleet.*

Often overlooked on the speedy drive up toward Provincetown on U.S. 6, Eastham is a town full of hidden treasures. Unlike the other towns, it has no official town center or Main Street; the highway bisects Eastham, and the town is spread out on both Cape Cod Bay and the Atlantic. Stocked with gas stations, convenience stores, restaurants, and large motel complexes, it takes a little exploring to find Eastham's wealth of natural beauty.

One such gem is the National Seashore, which officially begins here. Beyond the commercial buildup are thousands of acres of wooded areas, salt marshes and wild, open ocean beaches. The Salt Pond Visitor Center rests just off U.S. 6 and is one of Cape Cod National Seashore's main centers. This is a fine place to stop for information on the area; the center also hosts numerous nature and history programs and lectures and maintains a paved bike path. Nearby is the much-beloved Nauset Light, the red-and-white-stripe lighthouse moved from its perilous place on the cliffs of the Atlantic back in 1996. The Fort Hill area is another pretty spot, with lots of walking trails and the stately old mansion called the Penniman House.

It was here in 1620 that an exploring band of *Mayflower* passengers met the Nauset tribe on a bayside beach, which was then named First Encounter Beach. The meeting was peaceful, but the Pilgrims moved on to Plymouth anyway. Nearly a quarter century later, they returned to settle the area, which they originally called by its Native American name, Nawsett. Eastham was incorporated as a town on June 7, 1651.

Like many of the towns on the Cape, Eastham started as a farming community and later turned to the sea and to salt making for its livelihood; at one time there were more than 50 saltworks in town. A more atypical industry here was asparagus growing; from the late 1800s through the 1920s, Eastham was known as the asparagus capital of the United States. The runner-up crop, Eastham turnips, are still the pride of many a harvest table.

⑭ The road to the Cape Cod National Seashore's **Fort Hill Area** (✉ Fort Hill Rd., off U.S. 6) winds past the **Captain Edward Penniman House,** ending at a parking area with a lovely view of old farmland traced with stone fences that rolls gently down to **Nauset Marsh** and a red-maple swamp. Appreciated by bird-watchers and nature photographers, the 1-mi **Red Maple Swamp Trail** begins outside the Penniman House and winds through the area, branching into two separate paths, one of which eventually turns into a boardwalk that meanders through wetlands. The other path leads directly to Skiff Hill, an overlook with benches and informative plaques that quote Samuel de Champlain's account of the area from when he moored off Nauset Marsh in 1605. Also on Skiff Hill is Indian Rock, a large boulder moved to the hill from the marsh below. Once used by the local Native American tribe as a sharpening stone, the rock is cut with deep grooves and smoothed in circles where ax heads were whetted.

The French Second Empire–style **Captain Edward Penniman House** was built in 1868 for a whaling captain. The impressive exterior is notable for its mansard roof; its cupola, which once commanded a dramatic view of bay and sea; and the whale-jawbone entrance gate. Though still in the process of renovation, the interior is open for guided tours or for browsing through changing exhibits. Call ahead to find out when tours are available. ✉ *Fort Hill Rd., Fort Hill Area,* ☎ *508/255–3421.* ⌑ *Free.* ☉ *Weekdays 1–4.*

The park at Samoset Road has as its centerpiece the **Eastham Windmill,** the oldest windmill on Cape Cod. A smock mill built in Plymouth in the early 1680s, it was moved to this site in 1793 and is the only Cape windmill still on the site where it was used commercially. The mill was restored by local shipwreck historian William Quinn and friends. The park often comes alive with town festivals and concerts, and occasionally demonstrations are given on the inner workings of the mill. Each September, just after Labor Day, Eastham celebrates its history and the change of the season with the annual Windmill Weekend, an event with a full roster of activities for all ages. ⊠ *U.S. 6 at Samoset Rd.* ⌹ *Free.* ☾ *Late June–Labor Day, Mon.–Sat. 10–5, Sun. 1–5.*

Frozen in time, the 1741 **Swift-Daley House** was once the home of Gustavus Swift, founder of the Swift meatpacking company. Inside the full Cape with bow roof you'll find beautiful pumpkin-pine woodwork and wide-board floors; a ship's-cabin staircase that, like the bow roof, was built by ships' carpenters; and fireplaces in every downstairs room. The colonial-era furnishings include an old cannonball rope bed, tools, a melodeon, and a ceremonial quilt decorated with beads and coins. Among the antique clothing is a stunning 1850 wedding dress. Out back is a tool museum. ⊠ *U.S. 6, next to Eastham post office,* ☎ *no phone.* ⌹ *Free.* ☾ *July–Aug., weekdays 1–4; Sept., Sat. 1–4.*

A great spot for watching sunsets over the bay, **First Encounter Beach** (⊠ *end of Samoset Rd. off U.S. 6*) is rich in history. Near the parking lot, a bronze marker commemorates the first encounter between local Native Americans and passengers from the *Mayflower,* led by Captain Myles Standish, who explored the entire area for five weeks in November and December 1620 before moving on to Plymouth. The remains of a navy target ship retired after 25 years of battering now rest on a sandbar about 1 mi out.

★ ☙ The Cape's most expansive national treasure, the **Cape Cod National Seashore** was established in 1961 under the administration of President John F. Kennedy, for whom Cape Cod was home and haven. The 27,000-acre seashore, extending from Chatham to Provincetown, encompasses and protects 30 mi of superb ocean beaches, great rolling dunes, swamps, marshes, and wetlands, pitch pine and scrub oak forest, all kinds of wildlife, and a number of historic structures. Self-guided nature trails, as well as biking and horse trails, lace through these landscapes. Hiking trails lead to a red-maple swamp, **Nauset Marsh,** and to **Salt Pond,** in which breeding shellfish are suspended from floating "nurseries"—their offspring will later be used to seed the flats. Also in the seashore, the Buttonbush Trail is a nature path for people with vision impairments. A hike or bike ride to Coast Guard Beach leads to a turnout looking out over marsh and sea. A section of the cliff here was washed away in 1990, revealing remains of a prehistoric dwelling.

⑮ **Salt Pond Visitor Center** is the first visitor center of the Cape Cod National Seashore; the other, the **Province Lands Visitor Center,** is in Provincetown. The Salt Pond center, overlooking pretty Salt Pond, offers guided walks, tours, boat trips, demonstrations, and lectures from mid-April through Thanksgiving, as well as evening beach walks, campfire talks, and other programs in summer.

The center includes a museum with displays on whaling and the old saltworks, as well as early Cape Cod artifacts including scrimshaw, the journal that Mrs. Penniman kept while on a whaling voyage with her husband, and some of the Pennimans' possessions, such as their tea service and the captain's top hat. A good bookstore and an air-conditioned auditorium showing films on geology, sea rescues, whaling, Henry David Thoreau, and Marconi are also here. Something's up most summer evenings at the outdoor amphitheater, from slide-show talks to military-band concerts. ⊠ *Doane Rd. off U.S. 6,* ☎ *508/255–3421,* WEB *www.nps.gov/caco/places/saltpondvc.html.* ⌹ *Free.* ☾ *Mar.–June and Sept.–Dec., daily 9–4:30; July–Aug., daily 9–5; Jan.–Feb., weekends 9–4:30.*

Roads and bicycle trails lead to **Coast Guard and Nauset Light beaches** (⊠ off Ocean View Dr.), which begin an unbroken 30-mi stretch of barrier beach extending to Provincetown—the "Cape Cod Beach" of Thoreau's 1865 classic, *Cape Cod.* You can still walk its length, as Thoreau did, though the Atlantic continues to claim more of the Cape's eastern shore every year. The site of the famous beach cottage of Henry Beston's 1928 book, *The Outermost House,* is to the south, near the end of Nauset spit. Designated as a literary landmark in 1964, the cottage was, alas, completely destroyed in the Great Blizzard of February 1978.

Moved 350 ft back from its perch at cliff's edge in 1996, the much-photographed red-and-white **Nauset Light** (⊠ Ocean View Dr. and Cable Rd., WEB www.nausetlight.org) still tops the bluff where the Three Sisters Lighthouses once stood; the Sisters themselves can be seen in a little landlocked park surrounded by trees, reached by paved walkways off Nauset Light Beach's parking lot. How the lighthouses got there is a long story. In 1838 three brick lighthouses were built 150 ft apart on the bluffs in Eastham overlooking a particularly dangerous area of shoals (shifting underwater sandbars). In 1892, after the eroding cliff dropped the towers into the ocean, they were replaced with three wooden towers. In 1918 two were moved away, as was the third in 1923. Eventually the National Park Service acquired the Three Sisters and brought them together here, where they would be safe, rather than returning them to the eroding coast. The Fresnel lens from the last working lighthouse is on display at the **Salt Pond Visitor Center.** Lectures on, and guided walks to, the lighthouses are conducted throughout the season. In 2001, tours of Nauset Light were given on Sunday between 4:30 and 7:30 in July and August, on Sunday from 1 to 4 after Labor Day, and by appointment; call in advance (☎ 508/240–2612) to confirm.

Dining and Lodging

$–$$ ✕ **Capone's.** Come for a huge selection of pasta, including such favorites as fettuccine Alfredo, linguini and clam sauce, and eggplant and chicken Parmesan. Everything is made on the premises, from the rich red sauce to the flaky and spiced focaccia bread. Freshly baked bread comes with each dish, and the portions are generous while the prices remain very reasonable. You won't leave hungry. ⊠ *Four Points Sheraton, 3800 U.S. 6,* ☎ *508/240–7828. AE, D, DC, MC, V.*

$–$$ ✕ **Fairway Restaurant and Pizzeria.** The family-run Fairway serves up Italian comfort food in a casual, friendly setting. Attached to the Hole in One Donut Shop (very popular among locals), the Fairway puts a jar of crayons on every paper-covered table and sells its own brand of root beer. Entrées come with salad and homemade rolls. Try the orange tequila shrimp and scallops with a little Cajun heat, eggplant Parmesan, or a well-stuffed calzone. You can order from the extensive breakfast menu from 6:30 to 11:30. ⊠ *4295 U.S. 6,* ☎ *508/255–3893. Reservations not accepted. AE, D, DC, MC, V.*

$–$$ ✕ **The Friendly Fisherman.** Not just another roadside lobster shack with buoys and nets for decoration, this is a place serious about its fresh seafood. It's both a great place to pick up ingredients to cook at home—there's a fish and produce market on hand—and a good bet for dining out on such favorites as fish-and-chips, fried scallops, and lobster. The market also sells homemade pies, breads, soups, stews, and pasta. ⊠ *Rte. 6, North Eastham,* ☎ *508/255–6770 or 508/255–3009. AE, MC, V.*

$ ✕ **Beach Break Grill and Lounge.** All in all, this is an affordable and fun place to eat. The decor is all Hawaiian surfer, complete with old photos, long boards on the ceiling, and grassy adornments on the bar. The menu is basic and varied, with seafood (even a raw bar), lots of burgers, fajitas, pasta, and steak. Pub food and late-night bites can be had in the lively bar, which also has a pool table. As a bonus, children under age 10 eat free at dinner. In fair weather there's an outdoor deck for dining. ⊠ *Main St. Mercantile off Rte. 6,* ☎ *508/240–3100. AE, D, DC, MC, V.*

$$$$ 🏨 **Four Points Sheraton.** This hotel is at the entrance to the National Seashore. Rooms have views of the tropical indoor pool (with lush plants, pirate-theme bar, and resident live parrot), the parking lot, or the woods. Outside rooms are a little bigger and brighter and have mini-refrigerators. ⊠ *3800 U.S. 6, 02642,* ☎ *508/255–5000 or 800/533–3986,* FAX *508/240–1870,* WEB *www.fourpoints.com/eastham. 107 rooms, 2 suites. Restaurant, lobby lounge, no-smoking rooms, room service, 2 pools, saunas, 2 tennis courts, gym, video games. AE, D, DC, MC, V. BP.*

$$$–$$$$ 🏨 **Whalewalk Inn.** Named for the widow's walk atop the building, this 1830 whaling master's home is on 3 acres of rolling lawns, gardens, and meadows. Lots of windows give the place an open, airy feeling, while wide-board pine floors, fireplaces, and 19th-century country antiques provide historical appeal. Guest rooms in the main inn are spacious, with four-poster twin, double, or queen-size beds; floral fabrics; and antique or reproduction furniture. There are suites with fully equipped kitchens in the converted barn and guest house. A secluded saltbox cottage has a fireplace, kitchen, and private patio. Deluxe rooms in the carriage house have fireplaces, whirlpool tubs, and air-conditioning. Breakfast is served each morning in the cheerful sunroom or on the garden patio. ⊠ *220 Bridge Rd., 02642,* ☎ *508/255–0617,* WEB *www.whalewalkinn.com. 11 rooms, 5 suites. Bicycles. No smoking. MC, V. BP.*

$$–$$$$ 🏨 **Penny House Inn.** Tucked behind a wave of privet hedge, this rambling gray-shingle inn offers mostly spacious rooms, furnished with antiques, collectibles, and wicker. Captain's Quarters, the grandest room, has a sitting area with a wood-burning fireplace, a king-size brass bed, a miniature library, and a lovely view of the garden. Common areas include the Great Room, with a fireplace and lots of windows, a combination sunroom-library, and a garden patio set with umbrella tables. A full homemade breakfast starts the day, and afternoon tea is available. ⊠ *4885 County Rd., U.S. 6, 02642,* ☎ *508/255–6632 or 800/554–1751,* FAX *508/255–4893,* WEB *www.pennyhouseinn.com. 12 rooms. Air-conditioning, library. No smoking. AE, D, MC, V. BP.*

$$–$$$ 🏨 **Overlook Inn.** If it weren't for the vivid yellow paint job on this three-story inn, it would be lost among the trees, even though it's right along U.S. 6. Both the Cape Cod Rail Trail and the Salt Pond Visitor Center are just across the road from this 19th-century refuge. Victorian touches include graceful high ceilings and intricate interior wood molding. Each room has antiques, brass beds, and soft down comforters; some have genuine claw-foot tubs, which are great to slide into after a day at the beach. ⊠ *3085 U.S. 6, 02642,* ☎ *508/255–1886,* FAX *508/240–0345,* WEB *www.overlookinn.com. 14 rooms. AE, D, MC, V. BP.*

$$ 🏨 **Ocean Park Inn.** Rooms are clean, simple, and straightforward. There are larger family units available—one with a fireplace—but most rooms are for double occupancy, with full or queen-size beds. Take advantage of the adjacent Sheraton's indoor pool and tennis courts. ⊠ *Next to Four Points Sheraton, U.S. 6, 02642,* ☎ *508/255–1132 or 800/862–5550,* FAX *508/255–5250,* WEB *www.oceanparkinn-eastham.com. 55 rooms. Picnic area, no-smoking rooms, 2 pools, sauna, 2 tennis courts, gym, video games, laundry facilities. AE, D, DC, MC, V. Closed Nov.–Mar.*

$–$$ 🏨 **Cove Bluffs Motel.** Nestled among the trees and very near the waters of Town Cove and several nature trails is this old-fashioned haven for families. Choose from standard motel rooms and fully equipped one- to two-bedroom housekeeping units. Grounds include basketball courts, shuffleboard, swing sets, a playhouse, a sandbox, grills, and swinging hammocks in the shade. ⊠ *U.S. 6 and Shore Rd., 02642,* ☎ *508/240–1616,* WEB *www.capecod-orleans.com/covebluffs. 5 rooms, 8 housekeeping units. No-smoking rooms, pool, basketball, shuffleboard, laundry facilities. MC, V. Closed Nov.–Mar.*

$ 🏠 **Hostelling International–Mid Cape.** On 3 wooded acres near the Cape Cod Rail Trail and a 15-minute walk from the bay, this hostel has cabins that sleep six–eight each; two can be used as family cabins. It has a common area and a kitchen, and there are a number of guest programs. ⊠ *75 Goody Hallet Dr., 02642,* ☎ *508/255–2785,* WEB *www. usahostels.org. 8 cabins. Ping-Pong, volleyball. MC, V. Closed mid-Sept.–mid-May.*

$ ⛺ **Atlantic Oaks Campground.** This campground in a pine and oak forest is less than a mile north of the Salt Pond Visitor Center and minutes from Cape Cod National Seashore. Primarily an RV camp, it offers limited tenting as well. There are bikes for rent and direct access to the Cape Cod Rail Trail. Movies for children are shown at night. RV hookups, including cable TV, cost $42 for two people; tent sites are $28 for two people. Showers are free. ⊠ *3700 U.S. 6, 02642,* ☎ *508/255–1437 or 800/332–2267,* WEB *www.atlanticoaks.com. 100 RV sites, 30 tent sites. Bicycles, playground, laundry facilities. D, MC, V. Closed Nov.–Apr.*

Nightlife and the Arts

The **Cape Cod National Seashore** (☎ 508/255–3421 for information) sponsors summer-evening programs, such as slide shows, sunset beach walks, concerts by local groups or military bands, and campfire sing-alongs.

The **Eastham Painters Guild** holds outdoor art shows every Thursday, Friday, and holiday weekend from 9 to 5, July through October, at the Schoolhouse Museum (⊠ next to Salt Pond Visitor Center, off U.S. 6).

First Encounter Coffee House (⊠ Chapel in the Pines, Samoset Rd., ☎ 508/255–5438) presents a mixture of professional and local folk and blues in a no-smoking, no-alcohol environment, with refreshments available during intermission. National acts are booked for the second and fourth Saturdays. It's closed May and December.

Outdoor Activities and Sports

BEACHES

On the bay side of the Outer Cape, **First Encounter Beach** (⊠ end of Samoset Rd. off U.S. 6) is open to the public and charges daily parking fees of $5 (weekly and season passes are also available; call the town hall at ☎ 508/240–5972) to nonresidents in season. Parking fees or passes also apply to several other bay beaches and ponds, both saltwater and freshwater.

Coast Guard Beach (⊠ off Ocean View Dr.), part of the National Seashore, is a long beach backed by low grass and heathland. A handsome former Coast Guard station is also here, though it is not open to the public. The beach has no parking lot of its own, so park at the Salt Pond Visitor Center or at the lot up Doane Road from the center and take the free shuttle to the beach. At high tide the size of the beach shrinks considerably, so watch your blanket. There are showers, and lifeguards are posted between June and August. A daily charge of $7 for cars or a season pass (by far the best bargain) for $20 grants admission to all seven National Seashore beaches.

Nauset Light Beach (⊠ off Ocean View Dr.), adjacent to Coast Guard Beach, continues the National Seashore landscape of long, sandy beach backed by tall dunes, grass, and heathland, with the lighthouse for a little extra Cape atmosphere. It has showers and lifeguards in summer, but as with other National Seashore beaches, there is no food concession.

BIKING

The **Idle Times Bike Shop** (✉ U.S. 6 and Brackett Rd., ☎ 508/255–8281) provides bikes of all sizes and kinds and is right near the Cape Cod Rail Trail.

The **Little Capistrano Bike Shop** (✉ Salt Pond Rd. across from Salt Pond Visitor Center, ☎ 508/255–6515) rents a variety of bikes and trailers and is conveniently located between the Cape Cod Rail Trail and the National Seashore Bike Trail.

Nauset Trail, maintained by the Cape Cod National Seashore, stretches 1.6 mi from Salt Pond Visitor Center through groves of apple and locust trees to Coast Guard Beach.

HEALTH AND FITNESS CLUBS

The **Norseman Athletic Club** (✉ 4730 U.S. 6, North Eastham, ☎ 508/255–6370 or 508/255–6371) has four racquetball courts, two squash courts, and six indoor tennis courts; one NBA indoor basketball court; an Olympic-size, heated indoor pool; swimming lessons; aerobics and children's self-defense classes; plus Nautilus, free weights, and cardiovascular machines. You can relax in the whirlpool, steam room, or sauna; you'll also find a pro shop and a restaurant. There are daily and weekly guest membership passes.

THE LOWER CAPE A TO Z

To research prices, get advice from other travelers, and book travel arrangements, visit www.fodors.com.

BIKE TRAVEL

The few parking lots along the Cape Cod Rail Trail are useful for those who'd rather ride a segment of the trail than tackle all 25 mi. In Harwich there's a lot on Route 124, just off Exit 10 from U.S. 6 and directly across from the Pleasant Lake Store. In Orleans, park on West Road across from Old Colony Way. Another small parking area is on Rock Harbor Road, between Bridge Road and the U.S. 6 traffic rotary.

BOAT AND FERRY TRAVEL

The Freedom Cruise Line runs express 90-minute ferries from Harwich Port to Nantucket between May 15 and October 15, allowing you to explore the rose-covered isle without having to brave the crowds of Hyannis. Parking is free for the first 24 hours; then it's $10 per day. Sightseeing and seal cruises are also offered daily. Admission is $39 round-trip, $10 extra with bicycle; $25 one-way, $5 extra with bicycle.
➤ BOAT AND FERRY INFORMATION: **Freedom Cruise Line** (✉ Saquatucket Harbor, Harwich Port, ☎ 508/432–8999).

BUS TRAVEL

The Cape Cod Regional Transit Authority operates several buses between Cape towns. The lower Cape route, which operates year-round, begins in Hyannis and follows Route 28 all the way to Orleans, stopping in Harwich Port and Chatham; buses will stop according to passenger discretion. Rates vary.
➤ BUS INFORMATION: **Cape Cod Regional Transit Authority** (☎ 508/385–8326; 800/352–7155 in MA; WEB www.capecodtransit.org).

CAR TRAVEL

On the north shore, the Old King's Highway, Route 6A, parallels U.S. 6 but is a scenic country road passing through equally eye-pleasing towns.

When you're in no hurry, use back roads—they're less frustrating and much more rewarding. Route 28, which begins at the upper Cape in Woods Hole and continues all the way to Orleans on the south side of the Cape, is notorious for its heavy traffic and slow going. Once past Harwich Port, the route is not as frustrating, and it even becomes scenic from Chatham to Orleans, winding past the shores of Pleasant Bay. In Orleans, when heading east, the large rotary can create problems. Remember, when approaching a rotary, you must yield to drivers already in the circle, and once within the rotary, you should not stop your vehicle.

EMERGENCIES

For rescues at sea, call the United States Coast Guard in Chatham. The closest hospital is in Hyannis (☞ The Mid Cape A to Z *in* Chapter 4).
➤ DOCTORS AND DENTISTS: **Long Pond Medical Center** (⊠ 525 Long Pond Dr., Harwich, ☎ 508/432–4100). **Outer Cape Health Services** (⊠ 81 Old Colony Way, Orleans, ☎ 508/255–9700).
➤ EMERGENCY SERVICES: **Ambulance, fire, police** (☎ 911 or dial township station). **United States Coast Guard** (☎ 508/945–0164).

LODGING

APARTMENT AND HOUSE RENTALS

Commonwealth Associates can assist in finding vacation rentals in the Harwiches, including waterfront properties. Great Locations Inc. specializes in vacation rentals in Brewster, Dennis, and Orleans. Vacation Cape Cod is one of many realtors with a listing of available apartments and houses on the Lower Cape.
➤ LOCAL AGENTS: **Commonwealth Associates** (⊠ 551 Main St., Harwich Port 02646, ☎ 508/432–2618, FAX 508/432–1771, WEB www.commonwealthrealestate.com). **Great Locations Inc.** (⊠ 2660 Rte. 6A, Brewster 02631, ☎ 508/896–2090, WEB www.greatlocationsre.com). **Vacation Cape Cod** (⊠ Main St. Mercantile Unit 19, U.S. 6, Eastham 02642, ☎ 508/240–7600 or 800/724–1307, FAX 508/240–6943, WEB www.vacationcapecod.com).

CAMPING

Nickerson State Park (☞ Brewster) is huge—almost 2,000 acres— and hugely popular. It has plenty of facilities and guest programs. Because of its immense popularity, significant advance registration is necessary if you want a site.
➤ CONTACTS: **Nickerson State Park** (⊠ 3488 Rte. 6A, Brewster, ☎ 508/896–3491; 877/422–6762 for reservations, WEB www.state.ma.us/dem/parks/nick.htm).

TAXIS

John's Taxi & Limousine picks up only in Dennis and Harwich but will take you anywhere on the Cape.
➤ TAXI COMPANIES: **Always Available Transport** (⊠ Orleans, ☎ 508/255–7557 or 800/339–9732). **Eldredge Taxi** (⊠ Chatham, ☎ 508/945–0068). **John's Taxi & Limousine** (☎ 508/394–3209).

TOURS

The Cape Cod Museum of Natural History offers a two-hour cruise from Orleans through Nauset Marsh. Early morning cruises include breakfast in a nearby restaurant; evening tours feature cocktails and appetizers on board. Tours run daily, Tuesday through Friday until Labor Day, and then weekends until Columbus Day. Guided natural history tours of Chatham's Monomoy Islands are also available through the museum.

To sightsee from the air, contact Chatham Municipal Airport.

➤ FEES AND SCHEDULES: **Cape Cod Museum of Natural History** (☎ 508/896–3867, WEB www.ccmnh.org). **Chatham Municipal Airport** (✉ George Ryder Rd., West Chatham, ☎ 508/945–9000).

VISITOR INFORMATION

Some local chambers of commerce are open only in season. The Brewster Chamber of Commerce is in the Brewster town offices building. The office includes a visitor center and the offices of the Brewster Chamber of Commerce and Board of Trade United.

➤ TOURIST INFORMATION: **Brewster** (✉ 2198 Main St. [Rte. 6A], Box 1241, 02631, ☎ 508/896–3500, WEB www.brewstercapecod.org). **Chatham** (✉ Box 793, 02633, ☎ 508/945–5199 or 800/715–5567, WEB www.chathamcapecod.org; visitor center ✉ 2377 Main St., South Chatham; information booth ✉ 533 Main St., Chatham). **Eastham** (✉ U.S. 6 at Fort Hill Rd., Box 1329, 02642, ☎ 508/240–7211, WEB www.easthamchamber.com). **Harwich** (✉ Box 34, Harwich Port 02646, ☎ 508/432–1600 or 800/441–3199, WEB www.harwichcc.com). **Orleans** (✉ Box 153, 02653, ☎ 508/255–1386; information booth ✉ Eldredge Pkwy. off Rte. 6A, ☎ 508/240–2484, WEB www.capecod-orleans.com).

6 THE OUTER CAPE

As the large trees and greenery fade to twisted pitch pine and sandy terrain, so too does the essence of the Outer Cape seem to grow a little wilder, a little less traditional than that of its neighbors. Though still proud of their histories, the towns of Wellfleet, Truro, and Provincetown are flavored by a more spirited attitude, one that seems more focused on the raw beauty of this area and the creativity it so often inspires.

TECHNICALLY PART OF THE LOWER CAPE, the Outer Cape is nonetheless its own entity, forming the wrist and fist of Cape Cod. There's a sense of abandon here, in the hedonistic summertime frenzy of Provincetown and out on the windswept landscape of dunes and marshes. As you drive down here, the land flattens out, vegetation gets sparser and more coniferous, and the sea feels closer as the land narrows. Much of the region is undeveloped, protected by the Cape Cod National Seashore. Long, straight, dune-backed beaches appear to go on forever; inland, trails wind through wind-stunted forests of scrub pine, beech, and oak. Wellfleet is a quiet town, with art galleries, upscale shops, and a calmly active harbor. With an expanse of high dunes, estuaries, salt marshes, pine forests, rivers, and winding back roads, Truro is the least-populated, least-developed town on the entire Cape.

Revised by
Laura V. Scheel

The promise of solitude has long drawn artists and writers out here. Provincetown has two faces—a quiet little fishing village in winter and a magnet for throngs of pleasure seekers (including a substantial gay and lesbian community) in summer, who come for the rugged beaches, photogenic streets lined with historic homes, zany nightlife, shops selling everything from antiques to zoot suits, and the galleries, readings, and art classes that carry on Provincetown's rich history as an art colony.

Pleasures and Pastimes

Beaches

Ocean beaches on the Cape Cod National Seashore have cold water and serious surf and are backed by dunes. They're also contiguous: you can walk from Eastham to Provincetown if you've got the stamina.

On the Cape Cod Bay side, you'll find warmer and more gentle waters. The tides are pivotal here: at low tide the flats expose vast sandy expanses, and to get thoroughly wet, you'll have to trek out a ways. Bay-side beachgoers also get more time in the sun—the majestic dunes on the ocean side block the descending late-afternoon sun—and sunsets on the Bay are spectacular.

Biking

The Cape Cod National Seashore maintains three bicycle trails. Head of the Meadow Trail is 2 mi of easy cycling between dunes and salt marshes from High Head Road, off Route 6A in North Truro, to the Head of the Meadow Beach parking lot. Province Lands Trail is a 5¼-mi loop off the Beech Forest parking lot on Race Point Road in Provincetown, with spurs to Herring Cove and Race Point beaches and to Bennett Pond. The paths wind up and down hills amid dunes, marshes, woods, and ponds and offer spectacular views—on an exceptionally clear day, you can see the Boston skyline. There's a picnic grove at Pilgrim Spring.

South Wellfleet is the beginning (or the end, depending on how you look at it) of the Cape Cod Rail Trail, a 25-mi flat, paved route to Dennis that winds past cranberry bogs and ponds and through wooded areas. A good-size parking lot is open to cyclists just behind the South Wellfleet General Store, off LeCount Hollow Road.

Dining

Dining on the Outer Cape means everything from humble fried-clam shacks to candlelight elegance. Most restaurants have withstood the test of time and fashion and have developed a loyal following that keeps their doors open year after year. Menus frequently feature local seafood as a staple. In Wellfleet restaurants are known more for their creative cuisine than reasonable prices—going out with the whole family won't come cheap. Truro lacks a concentration of restaurants (the town itself has no real center); its offerings are spread out along the byways. Provincetown opens a world of great variation to the eager diner. There are a number of elegant restaurants in town, all aglow with candles, crystal, and fine linens, but you'll find an equal number of lively and boisterous café spots. Many have outdoor seating, providing for a good view of the town's constant the action.

In the height of the summer season, expect a long wait for a table, sometimes despite a reservation—the sheer volume of visitors is to blame. To make matters worse, in the last few years Cape Cod has been experiencing a labor shortage, so good help is at a premium, leading more than a few restaurants to close their doors. Others have been forced to shorten their season.

CATEGORY	COST*
$$$$	over $26
$$$	$19–$26
$$	$11–$18
$	under $11

*per person for a main course at dinner

Lodging

Lodging options on the Outer Cape are diverse. Wellfleet has several cozy inns and bed-and-breakfasts in the center of town, with a few larger motels on busy U.S. 6. Despite the strict building codes, there are a surprising number of large (though not so imposing) hotel complexes and cottage colonies spread out along Cape Cod Bay in North Truro. It's crowded, but it's also right on the sand, with commanding views of sunsets and the Provincetown skyline.

Provincetown lodging varies from bare-bones lodging in a tiny room in an old house to the utmost luxury in one of the many meticulously restored and grand homes. Although it seems that every other building is an inn or guest house, a place to spend the night is not so easy to come by. Provincetown fills up fast and has a longer season than its neighbors. Minimum stays of at least three nights are often the norm during the peak season and holiday times.

CATEGORY	COST*
$$$$	over $200
$$$	$150–$200
$$	$100–$150
$	under $100

*All prices are for a standard double room in high season, excluding 5.7% state tax and gratuities. Some inns add a 15% service charge.

Nightlife and the Arts

Many credit the unusual light and extraordinary beauty of the Outer Cape with creating such a strong and vibrant artistic tradition. In Wellfleet's town center are nearly two dozen art galleries, all representing local and national artists. The works aren't limited to sea and landscapes either; you'll also find abstract works and fine crafts.

Truro has fewer art galleries, but its history is rich. Painter Edward Hopper spent many years here in his modest home overlooking Cape Cod Bay; numerous recognizable scenes of Truro exist among his work. The Center for the Arts at Castle Hill is a longtime organization that for more than 30 years has been holding summer classes in art, writing and crafts.

Today Provincetown remains a center for the arts. Its history is great; many world-famous artists made their homes here—some started art schools still in operation. Provincetown may have more galleries per block than any other New England town. Friday night is gallery night; stroll the streets and pop in on one of many champagne artist receptions.

Provincetown also has an active nightlife, from pulsating dance clubs to pool halls, with lots of live entertainment. Drag shows, theater, comedy routines, and music happen on a continual basis throughout the summer season. Wellfleet has a few more peaceful options such as restaurant taverns that occasionally feature live music. Truro seems to prefer the silence, leaving the revelry to its bordering towns.

Outdoor Activities and Sports

The waters off Provincetown are one of the finest whale-watching areas in the world. The Cape Cod National Seashore has nine walking trails through varied terrain. In winter, ponds and shallow flooded cranberry bogs sometimes freeze hard enough for skating—but you should check conditions with the local fire department before venturing into unfamiliar territory.

Shopping

Shoppers on the Outer Cape never have to worry about the uniqueness of their purchases—all stores are individually owned and are one of a kind.

Wellfleet shoppers will find a wealth of fine art and crafts to choose from as well as a healthy dose of chic, small designer-clothing stores. On one street, you could walk away with a funky Indonesian sarong for the beach and a handcrafted, multi-thousand-dollar gold and gem-studded ring. Out on U.S. 6, far from the sophistication of town, are a few shops specializing in the $2 T-shirt, plastic lawn ornaments, and saltwater taffy. The Wellfleet Flea Market—great for bargain hunting—is held four days a week in summer.

From the most civilized and expensive art gallery to the sunglasses hut, there's a little bit of everything in Provincetown. Commercial Street, aptly named, is a tightly packed thoroughfare dominated by pedestrians ambling in and out of the shops and galleries. In the off-season you can benefit from some fine sales, when shops are eager to clean out their inventories before winter sets in.

Exploring the Outer Cape

Numbers in the text correspond to numbers in the margin and on the Lower and Outer Cape, Wellfleet, and Provincetown maps.

The Outer Cape refers to the wrist and fist of Cape Cod, the towns that rooted and grew amid dunes and marshland—Wellfleet, Truro, and Provincetown. **Wellfleet** ①, with pleasant shops and galleries along Main Street, is also rich in dune-backed ocean beaches and marshes great for canoeing and kayaking. Historic **Marconi Station** ② was the landing point for the transatlantic telegraph early in the 20th century, and its White Cedar Swamp Trail is quite beautiful. In Wellfleet visit art galleries, browse through great bookstores, take a dip in the bay or the ocean, rent a canoe or kayak and tour the marshes, and have dinner at one of the fine area restaurants. Don't leave without visiting the **Massachusetts Audubon Wellfleet Bay Wildlife Sanctuary** ③, especially if you're a bird-watcher. It's a fantastic place to catch a sunset over the bay. **Truro** ④ solidly represents the quietude of this end of the Cape, at least until you reach the seasonally bustling **Provincetown** ⑦–⑱, out at the tip. Catch a whale-watch boat from P-town (as Province-

The Outer Cape

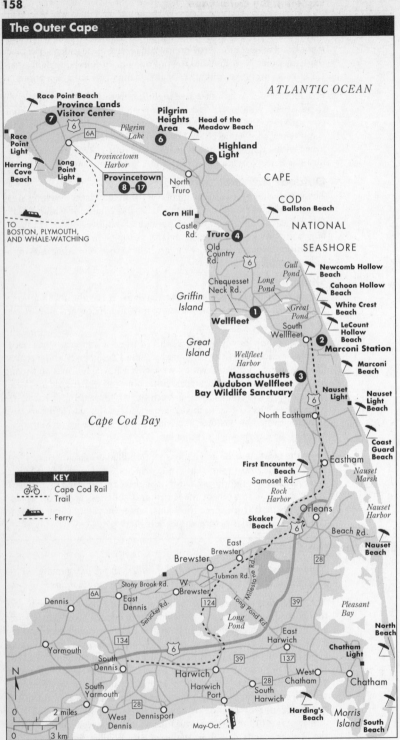

ATLANTIC OCEAN

Race Point Beach

Province Lands Visitor Center

7

Pilgrim Lake

Race Point Light

6A

Pilgrim Heights Area

6

Head of the Meadow Beach

Provincetown Harbor

Highland Light

5

Herring Cove Beach

Long Point Light

Provincetown

8 **17**

North Truro

CAPE

Corn Hill

Castle Rd.

Truro **4**

COD

Ballston Beach

NATIONAL

TO BOSTON, PLYMOUTH, AND WHALE-WATCHING

Old Country Rd.

6

SEASHORE

Gull Pond

Chequesset Neck Rd.

Long Pond

Newcomb Hollow Beach

Cahoon Hollow Beach

Griffin Island

Great Pond

White Crest Beach

Wellfleet **1**

LeCount Hollow Beach

South Wellfleet

2 **Marconi Station**

Great Island

Wellfleet Harbor

Marconi Beach

Massachusetts Audubon Wellfleet Bay Wildlife Sanctuary **3**

Nauset Light

6

Nauset Light Beach

North Eastham

Cape Cod Bay

Coast Guard Beach

First Encounter Beach

Samoset Rd.

Eastham

Nauset Marsh

Rock Harbor

Orleans

Nauset Harbor

Skaket Beach

6

Beach Rd.

Nauset Beach

KEY

🚲 Cape Cod Rail Trail

⛴ Ferry

East Brewster

Brewster

Tubman Rd.

28

Stony Brook Rd.

W. Brewster

Long Pond Rd.

Pleasant Bay

Dennis

6A

East Dennis

124

Long Pond

39

East Harwich

North Beach

Sesuckett Rd.

134

6

Milestone Rd.

39

137

West Chatham

Chatham Light

N

South Dennis

Harwich

South Harwich

Chatham

0   2 miles

South Yarmouth

28

Harwich Port

28

South Harwich

Morris Island

South Beach

0   3 km

West Dennis

Dennisport

May-Oct.

Harding's Beach

Yarmouth

town is almost universally known)—the Cape ranks fourth in the world for sighting whales. Take a trolley tour in town or bike through the National Seashore on its miles of trails. Climb the Pilgrim Monument for a spectacular view of the area—on an exceptionally clear day you can see the Boston skyline. Visit the museums and shops and art galleries, or spend the afternoon swimming and sunning on one of the beaches. To escape the crowds, walk across the breakwater to Long Point. Rent a sailboat or relax in the sand, taking in the splendid views of the bay. Then choose from an abundance of restaurants and the Cape's wildest nightlife.

When to Tour the Outer Cape

Prime time on the Outer Cape—when everything is open—is from Memorial Day to around Columbus Day. July and August are by far the most crowded times. The shoulder seasons of late May and June, and after Labor Day, have become more and more popular with visitors who aren't locked into a school schedule. Rates are lower during these times, and restaurants and shops are open. If the weather has been generous, swimming is still a pleasant possibility.

Wellfleet pretty much seals itself up after Columbus Day; most galleries and restaurants close, leaving just a handful of year-round businesses. But there's the entire outside world to explore, now free of thousands of others trying to do the same thing. Ocean climates keep winters milder than on the mainland. It's quiet—beautifully so—and distractions and pleasures take on a more basic flavor.

Provincetown clears out as well, but not as fully as Wellfleet. Various theme weekends throughout the year have boosted tourism in the off-season, and there are always readings, films, and places to eat. The off-season is truly a time to discover the essence of the place, see its changing natural beauty, and experience a more restful and relaxed pace.

Wellfleet and South Wellfleet

❶ *6 mi north of Eastham, 13 mi southeast of Provincetown.*

Still famous for its world-renowned and succulent namesake oysters and, with Truro, a colonial whaling and cod-fishing port, Wellfleet is also a center for artists and writers. Less than 2 mi wide, it's one of the more tastefully developed Cape resort towns, with a number of fine restaurants, historic houses, art galleries, and a good old Main Street in the village proper. South Wellfleet borders North Eastham and is home to a wonderful Audubon sanctuary and a drive-in theater that doubles on weekends as a flea market.

The downtown center of Wellfleet is quite compact, so it's actually best to leave your car in one of the public parking areas and take off on foot. Historic buildings that once housed oyster and fish drying shacks or stately residences are now home to upscale art galleries, clothing designers' stores, and restaurants. Wellfleet's small-town nature still somehow accommodates the demands of a major tourist industry; the year-round population of around 3,000 residents explodes to more than 18,000 people in July and August.

Tourism isn't the only industry, though. Fishing boats still head out from the harbor daily in search of scallops, cod, and other fish. Shell-fishing accounts for a major portion of the town's economy and many of its residents' livelihoods. Whaling played a role in the 18th and 19th centuries; out on the now-sunken Billingsgate Island, a raucous whaling tavern once thrived. The wealth of world-traveling sea captains found its way to Wellfleet as well, its impact evident in many of the grand old houses that line the narrow streets of town. The Wellfleet Historical Society is a fine stop for those who wish to see the town as it was in its early days.

Natural splendor, as well as history and sophisticated artistic culture, accounts for Wellfleet's popularity. The beaches of Wellfleet are spectacular, with their towering sand dunes, bracing surf, and miles of unfettered expanse. Seemingly endless wooded trails in the domain of the National Seashore provide terrific walking and hiking opportunities, and the sheltered waters of the tidal Herring River and Wellfleet Harbor are a favorite destination for canoeists, kayakers, windsurfers, and sailors.

② **Marconi Station,** on the Atlantic side of the Cape's forearm, is the site of the first transatlantic wireless station erected on the U.S. mainland. From here Italian radio and wireless-telegraphy pioneer Guglielmo Marconi sent the first American wireless message to Europe—"most cordial greetings and good wishes" from President Theodore Roosevelt to King Edward VII of England—on January 18, 1903. The station broadcast news for 15 years. An outdoor shelter contains a model of the original station, of which only fragments remain as a result of cliff erosion; parts of the tower bases are sometimes visible on the beach below, where they fell. The Cape Cod National Seashore's administrative headquarters is here, and though it is not an official visitor center, it can provide information at times when the centers are closed. Inside there is a mock-up of the spark-gap transmitter used by Marconi. Off the parking lot a 1¼-mi trail and boardwalk lead through the **Atlantic White Cedar Swamp**; it's one of the most beautiful trails on the seashore. Free maps and guides are available at the trailhead. **Marconi Beach,** south of the station on Marconi Beach Road, is another of the National Seashore's ocean beaches. ⊠ *Marconi Site Rd., South Wellfleet,* ☎ *508/349–3785.* ⊡ *Free.* ⊙ *Daily 8–4:30.*

For a **scenic loop** through a classic Cape landscape near Wellfleet's Atlantic beaches—with scrub and pines on the left, heathland meeting cliffs and ocean below on the right—take LeCount Hollow Road just north of the Marconi Station turnoff. All the beaches on this strip rest at the bottom of a tall grass-covered dune, which lends dramatic character to this outermost shore. The first of the four, **LeCount Hollow,** is restricted to residents or temporary residents in season, as is the last, **Newcomb Hollow,** with a scalloped shoreline of golden sand. In between, **White Crest** and **Cahoon Hollow** are town-managed public beaches. On breezy days hang gliders fly from the cliffs. Cahoon has a hot restaurant and dancing spot, the Beachcomber. Backtrack to Cahoon Hollow Road and turn west for the southernmost entrance to the town of Wellfleet proper, across U.S. 6.

Wellfleet's **First Congregational Church** (⊠ 200 Main St., ☎ 508/349–6877), a handsome 1850 Greek Revival building, is said to have the only town clock in the world to strike on ship's bells. The church's interior is lovely, with pale blue walls, a brass chandelier hanging from an enormous gilt ceiling rosette, subtly colored stained-glass windows, and pews curved to form an amphitheater facing the altar and the 1873 738-pipe Hook and Hastings tracker-action organ. To the right is a Tiffany-style window depicting a clipper ship, with a dedication to the memory of a sea captain. Concerts are given in July and August on Sunday at 8 PM.

For a glimpse into Wellfleet's past, the **Wellfleet Historical Society Museum** exhibits furniture, paintings, shipwreck salvage, needlework, navigation equipment, early photographs, Native American artifacts, clothing, and more. The society's Samuel Rider House is no longer open to the public. In July and August short guided walks around the center of town are given Tuesday and Friday mornings at 10:15 for $3. ⊠ *266 Main St.,* ☎ *508/349–9157.* ☞ *$1.* ☉ *Late June–mid-Sept., Tues.–Sat. 1–4.*

The **Wellfleet Public Library** (⊠ 55 W. Main St., ☎ 508/349–0310, WEB www.wellfleetlibrary.org), a great place to spend a rainy afternoon, reflects the literary life of Wellfleet, and the collection of books for adults and children is impressive. Also available are videos, books on tape, and Internet access. A full schedule of readings, yoga classes, and lectures is offered year-round. Among the writers who have spent time here are Mary McCarthy, Edmund Wilson, Annie Dillard, and Marge Piercy.

Main Street is a good place to start if you're in the mood for shopping. **Commercial Street** has all the flavor of the fishing town that Wellfleet remains. Galleries and shops occupy small weathered-shingle houses, some of which look like fishing shacks. A good stroll around town would take in Commercial and Main streets, ending perhaps at **Uncle Tim's Bridge** (⊠ off E. Commercial St.). The short walk across this arching landmark—with its beautiful, much-photographed view over marshland and a tidal creek—leads to a small wooded island.

Commercial Street leads to the **Wellfleet Pier,** busy with fishing boats, sailboats, yachts, charters, and party boats. At the twice-daily low tides you can fish on the tidal flats for oysters, clams, and quahogs (☎ 508/349–9818 for a permit).

Chequessett Neck Road makes for a pretty 2½-mi drive from the harbor to the bay past Sunset Hill—a great place to catch one. At the end, on the left, is a parking lot and wooded picnic area from which nature trails lead off to **Great Island** (⊠ off Chequessett Neck Rd.), perfect for the beachcomber and solitude seeker. The "island" is actually a peninsula connected by a sand spit built by tidal action. More than 7 mi of trails wind along the inner marshes and the water; these are the most difficult on the seashore because they're mostly in soft sand. In the 17th century lookout towers for shore whaling as well as a tavern stood here. The residents pastured animals and engaged in oystering and cranberry harvesting. By 1800 the hardwood forest that had covered the island had been cut down for use in ship- and home building. The pitch pines and other growth you see here (and all over the Cape) today were introduced in the 1830s to keep the soil from washing into the sea. Cape Cod National Seashore offers occasional guided hikes on Great Island and, from February through April, seal walks. To the right of the Great Island lot, a road leads to **Griffin Island,** with its own walking trail.

★ ❸ A trip to the Outer Cape isn't complete without a visit to the **Massachusetts Audubon Wellfleet Bay Wildlife Sanctuary,** a 1,000-acre haven for more than 250 species of birds attracted by the varied habitats found here. The jewel of the Massachusetts Audubon Society, the sanctuary is a superb place for walking, birding, and looking west over the salt marsh and bay at wondrous sunsets.

The Audubon Society hosts various naturalist-led wildlife tours around different parts of the Cape, including the Monomoy Islands, year-round. There are bay cruises; bird, wildlife, and insect walks; hikes; snorkeling; winter seal cruises; and birding, canoe, and kayak trips. The sanctuary also has camps for children in July and August and week-long field schools for adults. Phone reservations are required ahead of time, as some programs are very popular. ⊠ *Off U.S. 6, Box 236, South*

Wellfleet 02663, ☎ 508/349–2615, WEB *www.wellfleetbay.org.* 🖼 *$3.* ☉ *Daily 8 AM–dusk.*

Chances are, you've seen this place before. The popular franchise **Box Lunch** (⊠ 50 Briar La., ☎ 508/349–2178) serves up hot and cold roll-up sandwiches, a style it claims to have invented and perfected. For breakfast, lunch, or dinner, the fillings vary, but they're always tasty. This tiny place gets ferociously busy in the summer season—call your order in ahead of time if you can.

Dining and Lodging

$$–$$$$ ✕ **Aesop's Tables.** Inside this 1805 captain's house are five dining
★ rooms; aim for a table on the porch overlooking the center of town. The signature dish is bouillabaisse with mounds of fresh-off-the-boat seafood in a hot saffron broth; the homemade sourdough bread is the perfect accompaniment. The marinated duck breast is another favorite. When it's time for dessert, you might want to tempt fate with Death by Chocolate, a heavy mousse cake. Some nights in summer there's live jazz in the tavern, where the mood and the menu are more casual; the chairs are so comfortable, you may have trouble getting up. ⊠ *316 Main St.,* ☎ *508/349–6450. AE, DC, MC, V. Closed Columbus Day–Mother's Day. No lunch.*

$$–$$$ ✕ **Finely JP's.** This unassuming little roadside spot right on U.S. 6 gives
★ no hint that chef John Pontius consistently turns out wonderful food full of the best Italian influences and ingredients. The dining room is small and noisy, but the fish and pasta dishes (which emphasize good olive oil and plenty of lemon) silence all. Appetizers are especially good, among them a warm spinach-and-scallop salad or blackened beef with charred pepper relish. The Wellfleet paella draws raves and a steady handful of locals, but the chef is not afraid to cook a Delmonico steak, either. Be sure not to confuse this place with PJ's. ⊠ *U.S. 6, South Wellfleet,* ☎ *508/349–7500. Reservations not accepted. D, MC, V. Closed Mon.–Wed. Thanksgiving–Memorial Day; Mon.–Tues. Memorial Day–mid-June and Oct.–Thanksgiving; Tues. Labor Day–Oct.*

$$ ✕ **Captain Higgins.** Fish is the obvious specialty at this popular spot at the turn of the road across from Wellfleet's town pier. Besides being close to the fishing fleet and town beach, Captain Higgins has a broad outdoor deck overlooking a beautiful green and gold marsh. You can watch the slender reeds sway in the breeze as you sip an icy Seabreeze and finish a plate of fresh Wellfleet oysters or a marinated calamari appetizer. This is a good place to get a big boiled lobster dinner or fresh bluefish with a sweet mustard glaze. A more surprising option is a delicious 100% ostrich burger, similar to beef but lower in fat and calories. Reservations are accepted if you call before 6. ⊠ *Across from Wellfleet Town Pier,* ☎ *508/349–6027. MC, V. Closed Nov.–Apr.*

$$ ✕ **Mac's Seafood.** Right at Wellfleet Harbor, this ambitious little spot has some of the freshest seafood around. There's not a whole lot of seating here—some inside and some out on picnic tables—but when you've got a succulent mouthful of raw oyster in your mouth, who cares? The lunch and dinner menu includes all types of seafood, plus a sushi bar and a raw bar for your perusal. For takeout there are deli items, a selection of smoked fish, pâtés, fish, and lobster. You can even order a full traditional lobster clambake to go. ⊠ *Wellfleet Town Pier,* ☎ *508/349–0404. MC, V. Closed Columbus Day–Memorial Day.*

$–$$ ✕ **High Toss Pizza and Cafe.** Despite its name, this casual, family-friendly spot is a full-service bakery and restaurant with a full bar. There are no servers, so you grab a menu and a table, order and pay for your food, and then wait for the meal. The kitchen turns out plenty of seafood, including fresh Wellfleet oysters and littleneck clams. Steak, salads, soup, pasta such as mushroom ravioli, homemade desserts, and, yes, pizza, round out the menu. Off-season, order a pizza and curl up with free popcorn for Saturday's movie nights. ⊠ *50 Main St.,* ☏ *508/ 349–0005. Reservations not accepted. No credit cards. No lunch. No dinner Tues.*

$–$$ ✕ **PJ's Family Restaurant.** There's always a good-size but fast-moving line in front of this entrenched Wellfleet tradition, waiting for a heap of steamers or a creamy soft-serve cone. The inside is airy and unpretentious, with an open kitchen, slanting knotty-pine paneling, swirling overhead fans, and the ubiquitous starfish-studded fishnet. At PJ's you place your order and take a number. Food is served in utilitarian style: Styrofoam soup bowls, paper plates, plastic forks. The lobster-and-corn chowder doesn't have much lobster in it, so stick to the traditional clam chowder. Fried calamari and clam or oyster plates are generous and fresh. Try the dense, spicy stuffed clams and a pile of crispy homemade onion rings, but stay far, far away from the veggie burger. ⊠ *U.S. 6 at 1st turn into town,* ☏ *508/349–2126. Reservations not accepted. No credit cards. Closed mid-Oct.–mid-Apr.*

$–$$ ✕ **Lighthouse Restaurant.** There are no culinary fireworks, but a line still snakes out the door on summer mornings for a classic bacon-and-egg breakfast. Try a plate of steamers and a beer for lunch, and perhaps chowder, a burger, and another beer for dinner. ⊠ *Main St.,* ☏ *508/349–3681. Reservations not accepted. D, MC, V.*

$–$$ ✕ **Moby Dick's.** A meal at this good-natured, rough-hewn fish shack named for you-know-who is an absolute Cape Cod tradition for some people. There's a giant blackboard menu (order up front, and food is brought to you); a big, breezy screened-in porch in which to eat; and red-check tablecloths. The frying oil is filtered twice daily—essential for light and crisp clams, fish, and scallops. Go for the Nantucket Bucket: one pound of Monomoy steamers, one pound of native mussels, and corn on the cob served in a bucket. Don't miss the unique Outer Cape Onion, a whole onion cut in such a way that it opens like a flower when dipped in batter and deep-fried. ⊠ *U.S. 6 on Truro side of town center,* ☏ *508/349–9795. Reservations not accepted. Closed Oct.–Apr.*

$ ✕ **Serena's.** A family place that caters to children, Serena's (Italian for "mermaid") offers an assortment of blackboard specials every night. The Italian menu is short on the contemporary northern cuisine you'll find at many other places; red sauces still prevail here. Try the seafood *fra diavolo,* a bouillabaisselike stew that can be ordered hot or extremely hot. Reservations are essential for parties of 7 or more. ⊠ *U.S. 6, South Wellfleet,* ☏ *508/349–9370. AE, D, DC, MC, V. No lunch.*

$$–$$$$ ▥ **Wellfleet Motel & Lodge.** A mile from Marconi Beach, opposite the Audubon sanctuary, is this well-maintained and tasteful highway-side complex, which sits on 12 wooded acres. Rooms in the single-story motel are renovated each winter; rooms in the two-story lodge are bright and spacious, with king- or queen-size beds, TV with HBO, and balconies or patios. The property offers direct access to the Cape Cod Rail Trail. ⊠ *146 U.S. 6, Box 606, South Wellfleet 02663,* ☏ *508/349–3535 or 800/852–2900,* ℻ *508/349–1192,* ⓦⒺⒷ *www.wellfleetmotel. com. 57 rooms, 8 suites. Bar, coffee shop, air-conditioning, 2 pools, hot tub, basketball, meeting room. AE, DC, MC, V. Closed Dec.–Mar.*

$$–$$$ ▥ **Surf Side Colony Cottages.** There's very little in the way of accom-
★ modations on the Atlantic shore of the Outer Cape, so these one- to three-bedroom cottages are an especially good find. Scattered on either side of Ocean View Drive, they range from units in a piney grove to well-equipped ocean-side cottages; the two closest to the water have the best views. The cottages are a one-minute walk from Maguire's Landing town beach (Le Count Hollow), a beautiful, wide strand of sand, dunes, and surf. Though the exteriors are retro Florida, with pastel shin-

gles and flat roofs, cottage interiors are Cape style, including knotty-pine paneling. All units have phones, wood-burning fireplaces, screened porches, kitchens, (mostly) tile baths, rattan furniture, carpeting, and grills. Some have roof decks with an ocean view and outdoor showers. Ocean-side cottages have dishwashers. ✉ *Ocean View Dr., Box 937, South Wellfleet 02663,* ☎ *508/349–3959,* FAX *508/349–3959,* WEB *www.capecod.net/surfside. 18 cottages. Picnic area, laundry facilities. 1- to 2-wk minimum in summer. MC, V. Closed Nov.–Mar.*

$–$$$ **Even'tide.** Long a summer favorite, this motel is set back off the main road, surrounded by trees and sitting close to the Cape Cod Rail Trail. A central attraction is the 60-ft indoor pool (although Wellfleet's beaches are not far). Rooms are simple and have queen-size or double beds, two-room family suites, and efficiencies with kitchens. Speckled about the property are cottages, available for stays of a week or longer. ✉ *650 U.S. 6, South Wellfleet 02663,* ☎ *508/349–3410,* FAX *508/349–7804,* WEB *www.capecod.net/eventide. 31 units, 10 cottages. Air-conditioning, refrigerators, indoor pool, playground. 1- or 2-wk minimum for cottages in summer. MC, V.*

$$ **Holbrook House.** This inn, set in an immaculate and crisply elegant 1818 home, is surrounded by gardens and brick patios. A mixture of antiques, sea-grass floor coverings, and artwork adorns the interior (keep an eye out for the beautifully painted furnishings created by one of the owners). Because there are only two rooms and a studio apartment, privacy is guaranteed and cherished. The room on the first floor has a private entrance and twin beds that can be converted to a king. Upstairs, the second room has a sitting area and a large bedroom with a queen-size bed. Leave your car in the lot while in Wellfleet—the inn is close to town and to the harbor. ✉ *223 Main St., Wellfleet 02667,* ☎ *508/349–6706,* WEB *www.holbrookwellfleet.com. 2 rooms, studio apartment. MC, V. BP.*

$–$$ **Holden Inn.** If you're watching your budget and can deal with modest basics, try this old-timey place just outside the town center. Rooms have hardwood floors and are simply decorated with grandma's house–type wallpapers, ruffled sheer or country-style curtains, and antiques such as brass-and-white-iron or spindle beds or a marble-top table. Private baths with old porcelain sinks are available in adjacent 1840 and 1890 buildings. A suite has a queen-size bed and two twins, suitable for a small family. The lodge has shared baths, an outdoor shower, and a large screened-in porch with a lovely view of the bay and Great Island, far below. The main house has a common room and a screened front porch with rockers and a bay view through trees. There are picnic tables and gardens in the backyard. ✉ *140 Commercial St., Box 816, Wellfleet 02667,* ☎ *508/349–3450. 25 rooms, 10 with bath. No credit cards. Closed mid-Oct.–mid-Apr.*

$ **Inn at Duck Creek.** Set on 5 wooded acres by a duck pond, creek, and salt marsh, this old inn consists of the circa-1815 main building and two other old houses. Rooms in the main inn (except rustic third-floor rooms) and in the Saltworks house have a simple charm. Typical furnishings include claw-foot tubs, country antiques, lace curtains, chenille spreads, and rag rugs on hardwood floors. The two-room Carriage House is cabinlike, with rough barn-board and plaster walls. There's formal dining at Sweet Seasons or pub dining with entertainment at the Tavern Room. ✉ *70 Main St., Box 364, Wellfleet 02667,* ☎ *508/349–9333,* FAX *508/349–0234,* WEB *www.capecod.net/duckinn. 25 rooms, 17 with bath. 2 restaurants. 2-night minimum weekends July–Aug. AE, MC, V. Closed mid-Oct.–mid-Apr. CP.*

Nightlife and the Arts

THE ARTS

Jim Wolf, Master Storyteller (✉ Main St., ☎ 508/349–0103 for information) beguiles folks of all ages with his dramatic tales of both past and present Cape Cod lore and legend. July and August show times are Wednesday through Friday at 7:30 PM at the Wellfleet United Methodist Church.

During July and August the First Congregational Church (✉ 200 Main St., ☎ 508/349–6877) trades the serenity of worship for **Sunday evening concerts.** The music begins at 8 PM and has included opera, blues, jazz, and chamber music.

The drive-in movie is alive and well on Cape Cod at the **Wellfleet Drive-In Theater** (✉ 51 U.S. 6, South Wellfleet, ☎ 508/349–7176 or 508/255–9619). Films start at dusk nightly in season, and there's a miniature golf course.

On Saturday evening in July and August during the **Wellfleet Gallery Crawl,** art galleries are open for cocktail receptions to celebrate show openings. You can walk from gallery to gallery meeting the featured artists and checking out their works.

The well-regarded **Wellfleet Harbor Actors Theater** (✉ Kendrick St. past E. Commercial St., ☎ 508/349–6835) presents world premieres of American plays, satires, farces, and black comedies in its mid-May–mid-October season. This is the place for provocative experimental theater.

NIGHTLIFE

Beachcomber (✉ Ocean View Dr., Cahoon Hollow Beach, off U.S. 6, ☎ 508/349–6055) is big with the college crowd. It's right on the beach, with national touring acts most nights, weekend happy hours with live reggae, and dancing nightly in summer. Indoors or at tables by the beachfront bar, you can order from a menu of fun appetizers, salads, burgers, seafood, barbecue, and frozen drinks. There's also a raw bar.

A number of organizations sponsor outdoor activities at night, including the **Massachusetts Audubon Wellfleet Bay Wildlife Sanctuary**'s night hikes and lecture series.

The **Tavern Room** (✉ 70 Main St., ☎ 508/349–7369), set in an 1800s building with a beam ceiling, a fireplace, and a bar covered in nautical charts, has live entertainment from jazz to pop to country to Latin ensembles. Munchies are served alongside the menu of traditional and Latin/Caribbean-inspired dishes.

Kick up your heels and grab a twirling partner for a long-standing Wellfleet tradition, the **Wednesday Night Square Dance.** Down at the town pier in July and August, the music and live calling by master caller Toots begins at 7 and lasts as long as *you* can.

Outdoor Activities and Sports

State-of-the-art Skateboard Park down at **Baker's Field** (✉ Kendrick Ave. just past Wellfleet Town Pier) was professionally designed for tricks and safety, and is manned by local teens. For the little ones, the town has built a good-size play area with all kinds of slides, tunnels, and places to climb.

BEACHES

Public Beaches. The spectacular dune-backed Atlantic beaches White Crest and Cahoon Hollow charge daily parking fees of $10 to nonresidents in season only. Extensive storm-induced erosion has made the cliffs to most of Wellfleet's ocean beaches quite steep—so be prepared for an exerting trek up and down the dune slope. White Crest is a prime surfer hangout where the dudes often spend more time waiting for waves than actually riding them. Cahoon Hollow has lifeguards, rest rooms, and a restaurant and music club on the sand. Both beaches tend to attract younger and slightly rowdier crowds; Cahoon Hollow in particular is known as a big Sunday afternoon party place. Marconi Beach, part of Cape Cod National Seashore, charges $7 for daily parking or $20 for a season pass that provides access to all seven National Seashore beaches. Mayo Beach just west of Wellfleet Harbor is free. But swimming here is only pleasant around high tide—once the water recedes, it's all mud and sharp shells. You can park free at the small lot by Great Island on the bay.

Restricted Beaches. Resident or temporary resident parking stickers are required for access to Wellfleet beaches in season only, from the last week of June through Labor Day (some hotels and rental agencies give parking stickers to their guests or to people renting houses). To get a weekly ($25) or season ($75) pass, visit the Beach Sticker Booth on the town pier with your car registration in hand and a proof-of-stay form, available from rental agencies and hotels. For the rest of the year anyone can visit the beaches for free. Note that people arriving on foot or by bicycle can visit the beaches at any time; the sticker is for parking only. LeCount Hollow and Newcomb Hollow are the restricted ocean beaches; the Indian Neck harbor beach and the Duck Harbor bay beach past Great Island are also restricted. For information about restricted beaches, call the **Wellfleet Chamber of Commerce** (☎ 508/349–2510).

The **Wellfleet Ponds,** nestled in the woods between U.S. 6 and the ocean, were formed by glaciers and are fed by underground springs. Mild temperatures and clear, clean water make swimming pleasant for the whole family, a refreshing change from the bracing salty surf of the Atlantic. They are also perfect for canoeing, sailing, or kayaking (boats are available from Jack's Boat Rentals). These fragile ecosystems have called for restricted use, and a Wellfleet beach sticker is required in season. The sticker is only for cars, however; anyone can walk over or ride a bike to the ponds. Motorized boats are not allowed.

BIKING

The Cape Cod Rail Trail ends at the South Wellfleet post office. Other scenic routes for bicyclists include the winding, tree-lined Old County Road, just outside Wellfleet center at the end of West Main Street. Ambitious riders can bike all the way to Truro on this often bumpy road, but do watch for vehicular traffic around the tight curves. Ocean View Drive, on the ocean side, provides for many miles of cycling in wooded areas. If you get too hot, there are several ponds along the route perfect for a quick dip.

The Wellfleet Chamber of Commerce publishes a pamphlet, "Bicycling in Wellfleet," with an annotated map.

Black Duck Sports Shop (⊠ U.S. 6 at LeCount Hollow Rd., South Wellfleet, ☎ 508/349–9801; 508/349–2335 off season) rents a variety of bikes.

Idle Times Bike Shop, Inc. (⊠ U.S. 6, just west of Cahoon Hollow Rd., ☎ 508/349–9161) opens Memorial Day and rents bikes, trail-a-bikes (a tandem bike with a backseat for children who are big enough to pedal), and trailer attachments for the littler passengers. The shop also handles repairs and sells parts and assorted accessories. Depending on the crowds and weather, it usually remains open until Columbus Day.

BOATING

Fun Seekers (☎ 508/349–1429) offers windsurfing instruction and guided mountain-bike and kayak tours by appointment. Children's programs are available; the company closes in the off-season.

Jack's Boat Rentals (✉ Gull Pond, ☎ 508/349–7553; ✉ U.S. 6, ☎ 508/349–9808 for long-term rentals) provides canoes, kayaks, sailboards, Sunfish, pedal boats, surfboards, boogie boards, and sailboards. Guided tours are also available.

Wellfleet Marine Corp. (✉ Wellfleet Town Pier, ☎ 508/349–2233) rents motorboats in various sizes and sailboats by the hour or the day.

FISHING

You can climb aboard the charter boat *Jac's Mate* (✉ Wellfleet Town Pier, ☎ 508/255–2978) for fishing expeditions in search of bass and blues.

Fishing trips are operated on a walk-on basis from spring through fall on the *Navigator* (✉ Wellfleet Town Pier, ☎ 508/349–6003). Rods, reels, and bait are included.

Licenses are not required for saltwater fishing, and many anglers hit the outer beaches to surf-cast for bluefish and striped bass. Rods, bait, and some advice are available at the **Black Duck Sports Shop** (✉ U.S. 6 at LeCount Hollow Rd., South Wellfleet, ☎ 508/349–9801; 508/349–2335 off season).

GOLF AND TENNIS

Wellfleet maintains several tennis courts down at **Baker's Field** near the Town Pier. Court time, from late June until the end of August, is $10 per hour for singles and $12 per hour for doubles; call the Recreation Department to reserve (☎ 508/349–0330).

Chequessett Yacht Country Club (✉ Chequessett Neck Rd., ☎ 508/349–3704) is a semiprivate club (public use on space-available basis) with a nine-hole golf course and five hard-surface tennis courts by the bay. Lessons are available.

Oliver's (✉ U.S. 6, ☎ 508/349–3330) has one Truflex and seven clay courts, offers tennis lessons, and arranges matches.

SURFING

The Atlantic-coast **Marconi** and **White Crest** beaches are the best for surfing. Surfboard rentals can be arranged at Jack's Boat Rentals.

Shopping

ART GALLERIES

Blue Heron Gallery (✉ 20 Bank St., ☎ 508/349–6724) is one of the Cape's best galleries, with contemporary works—including Cape scenes, jewelry, sculpture, and pottery—by regional and nationally recognized artists, among them Steve Allrich and Del Filardi.

Cape Impressions Gallery (✉ 313 Main St., ☎ 508/349–6479), one of the few shops open year-round in Wellfleet, carries a nice selection of fine art, gifts, and the beautiful stained-glass works of Thomas Brophy.

Cove Gallery (✉ 15 Commercial St., ☎ 508/349–2530) features the works of John Grillo, Tomi dePaola, and Leonard Baskin, among others, with Saturday night artist receptions in July and August.

Davis Gallery (✉ 2766 U.S. 6, ☎ 508/349–0549) makes its home in what was once a hideously ugly building on the highway. The owners have turned the place into a very respectable and attractive gallery showing contemporary art and fine crafts.

Jacob Fanning Gallery (✉ 25 Bank St., ☎ 508/349–9546) represents the work of several established local artists, including Joyce Zavorskas, Jane Lincoln, and Lynn Shaler.

Kendall Art Gallery (✉ 40 E. Main St., ☎ 508/349–2482) carries contemporary art, including Harry Marinsky's bronzes in the sculpture garden, John French's brightly colored ceramic renderings of real and whimsical building facades, and watercolors by Walter Dorrell.

Left Bank Gallery (✉ 25 Commercial St., ☎ 508/349–9451; ✉ 3 West Main St., ☎ 508/349–7939) has two branches. The larger one, on Commercial Street, has a display of the larger works of local and national artists and sells fine crafts in the back room facing Duck Creek. The other gallery has fine handcrafted jewelry, silk and chenille scarves, hats, and small works of original art and photography.

Nicholas Harrison Gallery (✉ 275 Main St., ☎ 508/349–7799) is relatively new but is making a name for itself in the area of lovely and unusual American crafts. Owners Mark and Laura Evangelista are also accomplished potters, so you'll see their vibrant ceramic works.

SPECIALTY STORES

Eccentricity (✉ 361 Main St., ☎ 508/349–7554) keeps the corner of Main and Briar offbeat. One of the most interesting stores on the Cape, it sells gorgeous kimonos, ethnic-inspired cotton clothing, African carved-wood sculptures, barbershop paintings, odd Mexican items, and trinkets.

Herridge Books (✉ 11 E. Main St., between U.S. 6 and town center, ☎ 508/349–1323) is a perfect store for a town that has hosted so many writers. Its dignified literary fiction, art and architecture, literary biography and letters, mystery, Americana, sports, and other sections are full of used books in very nice condition. Herridge also carries new books on the Cape and its history.

I Used to Be a Tree (✉ 326 Main St., ☎ 508/349–1234) may seem like an odd name considering conservation and preservation are the themes here. At any rate, the little barn is full of all manner of curious games, toys, frames, puzzles, jewelry, gadgets, clocks, and carved figures all made from—you guessed it—wood.

Jules Besch Stationers (✉ 15 Bank St., ☎ 508/349–1231) has an extraordinary collection of cards, fine stationery, journals, papers, and pens. Proprietor Michael Tuck's warm and welcoming nature is as beautiful as his products. He also offers full calligraphy services.

Karol Richardson (✉ 11 W. Main St., ☎ 508/349–6378) fashions women's wear in luxurious fabrics and sells interesting shoes, hats, and jewelry.

Off Center (✉ off Main St., diagonally across from Eccentricity, ☎ 508/349–3634), another of the Eccentricity owners' enterprises, sells mainstream yet stylish women's clothing.

Pickle and Puppy (✉ 355 Main St., ☎ 508/349–0606) found a niche for itself by offering a bit of everything: housewares, T-shirts, gourmet foodstuffs, ceramics, luxury bath and beauty-parlor items, and a selection of unusual children's toys, games, and puzzles.

Puritan of Cape Cod (✉ Main St.) represents a family-owned chain of sportswear stores that sells brands such as Tommy Bahama, Sperry Top-Sider, C.C. Collection, and Woolrich from Memorial Day to Labor Day. Watch for some good sales.

Secret Garden (⊠ Main St., ☎ 508/349–1444) doesn't waste any precious space—from floor to ceiling are whimsical folk art pieces, handbags, clothing, decorative accessories, and good buys on sterling silver jewelry. In the back room are the gallery pieces, prints, and paintings from the old Wellfleet Collection, now closed.

FLEA MARKET

The giant **Wellfleet Flea Market** (⊠ 51 U.S. 6, South Wellfleet, ☎ 508/349–2520) sets up shop in the parking lot of the Wellfleet Drive-In Theater mid-April–June and September–October, weekends and Monday holidays 8–4; July and August, Monday holidays, Wednesday–Thursday, and weekends 8–4. You'll find antiques, sweat socks, old advertising posters, books, Beanie Babies, Guatemalan sweaters, plants, trinkets, and plenty more. On Monday and Tuesday in July and August the vendors make way for large arts and crafts shows. A snack bar and playground keep fatigue at bay.

En Route   If you're in the mood for a quiet, lovely ride winding through what the Cape might have looked like before Europeans arrived, follow **Old County Road** from Wellfleet to Truro on the bay side. It's bumpy and beautiful—let's hope it stays that way—with a stream or two to pass. So cycle on it, or drive slowly, or just stop and walk to take in the nature around you.

Truro

❹   *2 mi north of Wellfleet, 7 mi southeast of Provincetown.*

Settled in 1697, Truro has had several names. It was originally called Pamet after the local Indians, but in 1705 the name was changed to Dangerfield in response to all the sailing mishaps off its shores. "Truroe" was the final choice, and Truro became the namesake of a Cornish town that homesick settlers thought it resembled. The town relied on the sea for its income—whaling, shipbuilding, and cod fishing were the main industries.

Today a town of high dunes, estuaries, and rivers fringed by grasses, rolling moors, and houses sheltered in tiny valleys, Truro is a popular retreat of artists, writers, politicos, and numerous vacationing psychoanalysts. Edward Hopper summered here from 1930 to 1967, finding the Cape light ideal for his austere brand of realism.

One of the largest towns in terms of area—almost 43 square mi—it is the smallest in population, with about 1,400 year-round residents. If you thought neighboring Wellfleet's downtown was small, wait until you see—or don't see—Truro's. It's a post office, a town hall, a shop or two. You'll know it by the sign that says DOWNTOWN TRURO at a little plaza entrance. Truro also has a library, a firehouse, and a police station, but that's about all. It's the Cape's narrowest town, and from a high perch you can see the Atlantic Ocean on one side and Cape Cod Bay on the other.

NEED A BREAK?   **Jams** (⊠ 14 Truro Center Rd., off U.S. 6 in Truro Center, ☎ 508/349–1616) has the answer for whoever is looking for a great picnic lunch, sandwiches, fresh produce, a bottle of wine or Evian, or a sweet treat. You won't be able to stay for lunch unless you're content getting your knees knocked on the bench outside, but with the best part of the Cape just outside the door, who would want to?

Ⓢ   For a few hours of exploring, take the children to **Pamet Harbor** (⊠ Depot Rd.). At low tide you can walk out on the flats and discover the creatures of the salt marsh. A nearby plaque identifies the plants and animals and tells of the ecological importance of the area.

On **Corn Hill** (⊠ off Corn Hill Rd.), near the beach area of the same name, a tablet commemorates the finding of a buried cache of corn by Miles Standish and the *Mayflower* crew. They took it to Plymouth and used it as seed, returning later to pay the Native Americans for the corn they'd taken.

The **Truro Center for the Arts at Castle Hill,** housed in a converted 19th-century barn, offers summer arts-and-crafts workshops for children, as well as courses and single classes in art, crafts, photography, and writing for adults. Teachers have included notable New York– and Provincetown-based artists. ⊠ *10 Meeting House Rd.; or write to Box 756, Truro 02666,* ☎ *508/349–7511.*

Built at the turn-of-the-20th-century as a summer hotel, the **Truro Historical Museum** is a repository of 17th-century firearms, mementos of shipwrecks, early fishing and whaling gear, ship models, a pirate's chest, scrimshaw, and more. One room exhibits wood carvings, paintings, blown glass, and ship models by Courtney Allen, artist and founder of Truro's historical society. The museum also hosts some ambitious local art and artifact shows each year. ⊠ *6 Lighthouse Rd., off S. Highland Rd., North Truro,* ☎ *508/487–3397,* WEB *www.capecod.net/ ths.* ☞ *$3.* ☼ *Memorial Day–Sept., daily 10–4:30.*

❺ Truly a breathtaking sight, **Highland Light,** also called Cape Cod Light, is the Cape's oldest lighthouse. It was the last to have become automated, in 1986. The first light on this site, powered by 24 whale-oil lamps, began warning ships of Truro's treacherous sandbars in 1798— the dreaded Peaked Hills Bars alone, to the north, have claimed hundreds of ships. The current light, a white-painted 66-ft tower built in 1857, is powered by two 1,000-watt bulbs reflected by a huge Fresnel lens. Its beacon is visible for 20 mi.

One of four active lighthouses on the Outer Cape, Highland Light has the distinction of being listed in the National Register of Historic Places. Thoreau used it as a stopover in his travels across the Cape's backside, as the Atlantic side of the Outer Cape is called. Erosion threatened to cut this lighthouse from the 117-ft cliff on which it stood and drop it into the sea. Thanks to a concerted effort by local citizens and lighthouse lovers, the necessary funds were raised, and the lighthouse was moved back 450 ft to safety in 1996; it is still surrounded by the Highland Links golf course, however. Twenty-five-minute tours of the lighthouse are given daily in the summer. Children must be 51" tall to climb the tower. ⊠ *Off S. Highland Rd.,* ☎ *508/487–1121.* ☞ *$3.* ☼ *Mid-June–Sept., daily 10–sunset.*

The gardens of **A Touch of Heaven** are a beautiful place and, unlike most other gardens, are meant to be picked. The lawns are set with benches and birdbaths. The flowers are so abundant you don't feel guilty gathering a bunch to take home. ⊠ *Pond Village Heights, North Truro,* ☎ *no phone.* ☞ *Free.* ☼ *Daily, dawn–dusk.*

❻ At the **Pilgrim Heights Area** of the Cape Cod National Seashore (⊠ off U.S. 6), a short trail leads to the spring where members of a Pilgrim exploring party stopped to refill their casks, tasting their first New England water in the process. Walking through this still-wild area of oak, pitch pine, bayberry, blueberry, beach plum, and azalea gives you a taste of what it was like for these voyagers in search of a new home. "Being thus passed the vast ocean . . ." William Bradford wrote in *Of*

Plimoth Plantation, "they had no friends to welcome them, no inns to entertain them or refresh their weather-beaten bodies; no houses, or much less towns to repair to, to seek for succour."

From an overlook you can see the bluffs of High Head, where glaciers pushed a mass of earth before melting and receding. Another path leads to a swamp, and a bike trail leads to Head of the Meadow Beach, often a less crowded alternative to others in the area.

Dining and Lodging

$$–$$$ ✕ **Adrian's.** Adrian Cyr's restaurant crowns a high bluff overlooking Pilgrim Lake and all of Provincetown; his cooking also hits the heights. Cayenne-crusted grilled salmon with maple-mustard sauce is one of the well-prepared dishes. Tuscan salad is a constant hit, with tomatoes, olives, fresh basil, plenty of garlic, and balsamic vinegar. Pizzas, too, are standouts, especially one made with cornmeal dough and topped with shrimp and artichokes. The outdoor deck, always enjoyable, bursts at the very popular breakfasts and brunches, served every day in season. ✉ *Outer Reach Hotel, 535 U.S. 6, North Truro,* ☎ *508/ 487–4360. Reservations not accepted. AE, MC, V. Closed mid-Oct.– Memorial Day.*

$$–$$$ ✕ **Blacksmith Shop.** Here's where Truro locals like to linger at the bar, gossiping about what's going on in town while choosing from an eclectic menu with everything from seafood to Mexican items. The restaurant looks like it might have once been a place to bring your horse for a shoeing, but these days it's a nice out-of-the-way spot for company. There are excellent steaks as well as greens and gently cooked vegetables. A short bar menu has moved south of the border, listing wraps and bean dishes that could use a little more salsa heat. Local shellfishermen deliver excellent quahogs and oysters, then hang around for the latest gossip. ✉ *Off Rte. 6A, Truro center,* ☎ *508/349–6554. AE, D, MC, V. Closed weekdays Nov.–May.*

$$–$$$ ✕ **Montano's.** This friendly, cavernous Italian-style restaurant with vaulted ceilings and hanging plants looms on the side of U.S. 6. Old harpoons, fish barrels, and lobster-pot "chandeliers" add the requisite nautical touch, and the ever-smooth Tony Bennett croons in the background. Built to handle a tour bus crowd, Montano's serves comfortable, predictable Italian-American fare with a leaning toward seafood and a solid selection of steaks. You can't go wrong with classics such as linguine and mussels in a red or white sauce or a simple thick, center-cut filet mignon with roasted garlic butter. The 14-inch pizzas are made on fresh dough, and you can taste the difference. Montano's is one of those endangered species that still offer an unlimited salad bar. ✉ *481 U.S. 6,* ☎ *508/487–2026. AE, MC, V. No lunch.*

$$–$$$ ✕ **Terra Luna.** An insider's favorite for a special breakfast, Terra Luna has become a wonderful choice for dinner as well. The dining room may lean toward cramped instead of intimate, but the food is stylish and well presented, with surprising sauces for both fish and meat dishes. The striped bass is grilled but not over-grilled, and spicy stuffed lamb chops are an excellent alternative to the usual fish. ✉ *104 Shore Rd. (Rte. 6A), North Truro,* ☎ *508/487–1019. AE, MC, V. Closed late Oct.–May.*

$$–$$$ 🏠 **Shoreline Motel.** Although the motel itself won't win any awards for beauty, the location is majestic. Because it's perched right on the sands of Cape Cod Bay with views of daily sunsets and the glimmering lights of Provincetown beyond, you won't even notice the decor. There are standard motel rooms, suites, and a few efficiencies from which to choose; all come with stunning water views. Efficiencies have full kitchens and suites have kitchenettes. Upstairs rooms have private balconies from which to contemplate the tides. ⊠ *Rte. 6A, Box 761, North Truro 02652,* ☎ *508/487–9109,* WEB *www.capecodtravel.com/ shoreline. 24 rooms. Air-conditioning, refrigerators, beach. AE, MC, V. Closed Columbus Day–late Apr.*

$–$$ 🏨 **East Harbour.** This meticulously maintained complex outside Provincetown has simple accommodations ranged around a manicured lawn and separated from the bay beach by low grasses. The two-bedroom cottages have paneled walls, colonial-style furnishings, and full kitchens. Motel rooms have large picture windows, mini-refrigerators and coffeemakers, light paneling, and 1960s furnishings. A newer apartment is all white and bright, with skylights, Shaker-reproduction furnishings, a modern kitchen, and second-floor views of the harbor from a private deck. All units have microwaves and cable TV. ⊠ *618 Shore Rd. (Rte. 6A), Box 183, North Truro 02652,* ☎ *508/487–0505,* FAX *508/487–6693,* WEB *www.eastharbour.com. 7 cottages, 9 rooms, 1 apartment. Picnic area, beach, laundry facilities. In season, 1-wk minimum for cottages, 2-night minimum for rooms. AE, D, MC, V. Closed Nov.–Mar.*

$–$$ 🏨 **Moorlands Inn.** The creative works of innkeepers Bill and Skipper Evaul—artists and musicians—fill the walls and rooms of this Victorian beauty. Antiques adorn the bright, uncluttered rooms in the main house; the spacious penthouse has a full kitchen, two bedrooms, plenty of living space, and a deck. The Carriage House guests have their own outdoor whirlpool, and other guests can gather in the communal hot tub out back. ⊠ *11 Hughes Rd., North Truro 02652,* ☎ *508/487–0663. 5 rooms, 1 apartment, 3 cottages. Croquet, outdoor hot tub. MC, V. BP.*

$–$$ 🏨 **Sea Gull Motel.** Right on the beach, this motel's location is the real draw. Lodging is in standard motel rooms, motel studios, and beach apartments—the latter two are rented weekly, but you can rent rooms by the night. Because it's been family run for decades, you may feel like you're spending time in someone's living room. Most rooms have splendid water views. ⊠ *Rte 6A, Box 126, North Truro 02652,* ☎ *508/ 487–9070,* WEB *www.capecodtravel.com/seagullmotel. 26 rooms. Refrigerators. AE, D, MC, V. Closed Oct. 15–May 1.*

$–$$ 🏨 **Truro Vineyards of Cape Cod Inn.** On 5 acres of working vineyard, this 1836 former farmstead has been transformed into an elegant inn. Antique casks and presses stand in the corners of the rooms, and deep greens and burgundies predominate. Guest rooms have four-poster king- and queen-size beds and modern tile baths. The luxury room includes a king-size bed and a two-person whirlpool bath. Homegrown berries often garnish dishes at breakfast, which is served in the sunroom or, in nice weather, outside on the patio. A large common sundeck has sweeping views of the vineyard. ⊠ *11 Shore Rd. (Rte. 6A), North Truro 02652,* ☎ *508/487–6200,* FAX *508/487–4248. 5 rooms, 4 with bath. No smoking. MC, V. BP.*

$ 🏨 **Hostelling International–Truro.** In a former Coast Guard station right on the dunes, this handsome, well-placed hostel has kitchen facilities, a common area, and naturalist-led programs. It's also right by the ½-mi-long Cranberry Bog Trail, which takes you by a refurbished cranberry bog and an old bog house. ⊠ *N. Pamet Rd., Box 402, Truro 02666,* ☎ *508/349–3889,* WEB *www.usahostels.com. 42 beds. MC, V. Closed Labor Day–mid-June.*

Outdoor Activities and Sports

BEACHES

A number of Truro's **town beaches,** including Coast Guard Beach and Ballston Beach on the Atlantic, are reserved for residents and renters in season, although anyone can walk or bicycle in. Ask at the town hall (☎ 508/349–3635) about a seasonal sticker.

Corn Hill Beach (⊠ Corn Hill Rd.), on the bay, has beautiful views of Provincetown. The waters are generally calm and warm, typical of bay beaches. There are rest rooms on site as well. Parking requires a Truro beach sticker or a $5 daily fee.

Truro has several other accessible beaches stretched along Cape Cod Bay. All are beautiful and ideal for long, lazy days of watching the boats go by, with views of Provincetown in the distance. These beaches all require the Truro beach sticker to park. **Cold Storage Beach,** (⊠ Pond Rd. off Rte. 6A [Shore Rd.]) is just as popular with anglers looking for passing blues and stripers as it is with sunseekers and swimmers. Just off one of Truro's back-country roads, **Fisher Beach** (⊠ Fisher Rd.) is usually quiet, due to its smaller parking capacity. To get to **Great Hollow Beach** (⊠ Great Hollow Rd.) you must be ready to scale some moderate stairs from the parking lot to the sands below. **Ryder Beach** (⊠ Ryder Beach Rd. off Old County Rd.) rests just below a rise in the small dunes.

On the ocean side, three spectacular beaches are marked by massive dunes and bracing surf. Truro beach stickers are required for all parking. **Ballston Beach** (⊠ Pamet Rd.) lies at the end of the winding and antique home–spotted Pamet Road, and is backed by the golden hills artist Edward Hopper made famous in his Truro paintings. **Coast Guard Beach** (⊠ Coast Guard Rd.) sits just down the road from Highland Light. The parking area is small and tends to fill quickly. A not-so-secret favorite of nude sunbathers, **Long Nook Beach** (⊠ Long Nook Rd.) shares the senses of wildness and isolation synonymous with Truro's outer reaches.

Head of the Meadow Beach (⊠ Head of the Meadow Rd. off U.S. 6) in North Truro, part of Cape Cod National Seashore, is often less crowded than other beaches in the area. Since the bathhouse burned down, it has only temporary rest-room facilities available in summer and no showers. The daily parking fee is $7 in season, or the beach can be accessed with the purchase of a season pass ($20) good for all National Seashore locations.

BIKING

The **Head of the Meadow Trail** provides 2 mi of easy cycling between dunes and salt marshes from High Head Road, off Route 6A in North Truro, to the Head of the Meadow Beach parking lot. Bird-watchers also love the area.

Bayside Bikes (⊠ 102 Rte. 6A, North Truro, ☎ 508/487–5735) rents bicycles by the hour, day, or week, with easy access to the Head of the Meadow Trail.

Cape Outback Adventures (☎ 508/349–1617 or 800/864–0070) offers friendly instruction and guided tours for kayakers, mountain bikers, and beginning surfers. Times and location are arranged by phone, and owner Richard Miller and staff provide equipment. Kayak trips explore areas in both Wellfleet and Truro, while off-road mountain-biking excursions take place in the vast wooded areas within the National Seashore. Surfing instruction is available by the hour. These trips are designed for those of all ages and skill levels.

GOLF

The **Highland Golf Links** (⊠ Lighthouse Rd., North Truro, ☎ 508/487–9201), a nine-hole, par-36 course on a cliff overlooking the Atlantic and Highland Light, is unique for its resemblance to Scottish links instead of to the well-manicured and less-challenging courses that are more typically found in the United States.

Long Nook Beach (⊠ end of Long Nook Rd., off U.S. 6) is good for surfing.

Shopping

Atlantic Spice Co. (⊠ U.S. 6 at Rte. 6A, North Truro, ☎ 508/487–6100) stocks a fragrant array of spices, teas, and potpourris, as well as herbs, dried flowers, locally made soaps, sauces, and kitchenware items.

Whitman House Gift Shop (⊠ County Rd. just off U.S. 6, North Truro, ☎ 508/487–3204) sells Amish quilts and other country items.

Provincetown

❼–❶⓻ *7 mi northwest of Truro, 27 mi north of Orleans, 62 mi from Sagamore Bridge.*

The Cape's smallest town in area and the second-smallest in year-round population, Provincetown is a place of liberating creativity, startling originality, and significant diversity. In the busy downtown, Portuguese-American fishermen mix with painters, poets, writers, whale-watching families, cruise-ship passengers on brief stopovers, and gay and lesbian residents and visitors. In summer Commercial Street is packed with sightseers and shoppers hunting for treasures in the overwhelming number of galleries and crafts shops. At night raucous music and people spill out of bars, drag shows, and sing-along lounges galore. It's a fun, crazy place, with the extra dimension of the fishing fleet unloading their catch at MacMillan Wharf, in the center of the action.

The town's 8 square mi are also rich in history. The curled fist at the very tip of the Cape, Provincetown has shores that curve protectively around a natural harbor, perfect for visitors from any epoch to anchor. Historical records show that Thorvald, brother of Viking Leif Erikson, came ashore here in AD 1004 to repair the keel of his boat and consequently named the area Kjalarness, or Cape of the Keel. Bartholomew Gosnold came to Provincetown in 1602 and named the area Cape Cod after the abundant codfish he found in the local waters.

The Pilgrims remain Provincetown's most famous visitors. On Monday, November 21, 1620, the *Mayflower* dropped anchor in Provincetown Harbor after a difficult 63-day voyage from England; while in the harbor they signed the Mayflower Compact, the first document to declare a democratic form of government in America. One of the first things the ever-practical Pilgrims did was to come ashore to wash their clothes, thus starting the ages-old New England tradition of Monday wash day. They stayed in the area for five weeks before moving on to Plymouth. Plaques and parks commemorate the landing throughout town.

During the American Revolution, Provincetown Harbor was controlled by the British, who used it as a port from which to sail to Boston and launch attacks on colonial and French vessels. In November 1778 the 64-gun British frigate *Somerset* ran aground and was wrecked off Provincetown's Race Point. Every 60 years or so, the shifting sands uncover its remains.

Incorporated as a town in 1727, Provincetown was for many decades a bustling seaport, with fishing and whaling as its major industries. In the late 19th century, groups of Portuguese fishermen and whalers began

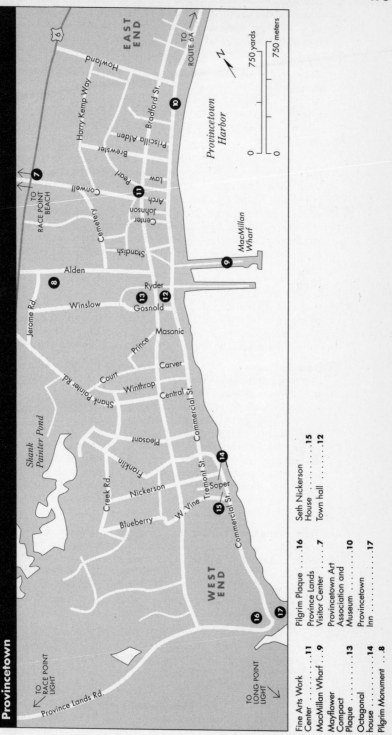

175

Provincetown

EAST END

Provincetown Harbor

MacMillan Wharf

WEST END

Shank Painter Pond

TO RACE POINT LIGHT

TO LONG POINT LIGHT

Province Lands Rd.

Fine Arts Work Center 11
MacMillan Wharf ...9
Mayflower Compact Plaque 13
Octagonal house 14
Pilgrim Monument ...8

Pilgrim Plaque 16
Province Lands Visitor Center 7
Provincetown Art Association and Museum 10
Provincetown Inn 17

Seth Nickerson House 15
Town hall 12

to settle here, lending their expertise and culture to an already cosmopolitan town. Fishing is still an important source of income for many Provincetown locals, but now the town ranks fourth in the world as a whale-watching, rather than -hunting, mecca.

Artists began coming here in 1899 for the unique Cape Cod light—in fact, Provincetown is the nation's oldest continuous art colony. Poets, writers, and actors have also been part of the art scene. Eugene O'Neill's first plays were written and produced here, and the Fine Arts Work Center continues to have in its ranks some of the most important writers of our time.

During the early 1900s, Provincetown became known as Greenwich Village North. Artists from New York and Europe discovered the town's unspoiled beauty, special light, lively community, and colorful Portuguese flavor. By 1916, with five art schools flourishing here, painters' easels were nearly as common as shells on the beach. This bohemian community, along with the availability of inexpensive summer lodgings, attracted young rebels and writers as well, including John Reed (*Ten Days That Shook the World*) and Mary Heaton Vorse (*Footnote to Folly*), who in 1915 began the Cape's first significant theater group, the Provincetown Players. The young, then unknown Eugene O'Neill joined them in 1916, when his *Bound East for Cardiff* premiered in a tiny wharfside East End fish house. After 1916 the Players moved on to New York. Their theater, at present-day 571 Commercial Street, is long since gone, but a model of it and of the old Lewis Wharf on which it stood is on display at the Pilgrim Monument museum.

Near the Provincetown border, **massive dunes** actually meet the road in places, turning U.S. 6 into a sand-swept highway. Scattered among the dunes are primitive cottages called dune shacks, built from flotsam and other found materials, that have provided atmospheric as well as cheap lodgings to a number of famous artists and writers over the years—among them poet Harry Kemp, Eugene O'Neill, e. e. cummings, Jack Kerouac, and Norman Mailer. The few surviving shacks are privately leased from the Cape Cod National Seashore, whose proposal to demolish the shacks was halted by their inclusion on the National Register of Historic Places in 1988. The dunes are fragile and should not be walked on, but paths lead through them to the ocean. You can see some of the shacks by van on Art's Dune Tours.

The **Province Lands** begin at High Head in Truro and stretch to the tip of Provincetown. The area is scattered with ponds, cranberry bogs, and scrub; unfortunately, this terrain provides optimal conditions for the deer tick, which can cause Lyme disease, so use extra caution. Bike and walking trails lace through forests of stunted pines, beech, and oak and across desertlike expanses of rolling dunes. Protected against development, the Province Lands are the "wilds" of the Cape.

A beautiful spot to stop for lunch before biking to the beach, the **Beech Forest picnic area** (⊠ Race Point Rd.) in the National Seashore borders a small pond covered with water lilies. The adjacent bike trails lead to Herring Cove and Race Point beaches, both part of the National Seashore.

❼ Inside the **Province Lands Visitor Center** in the Cape Cod National Seashore you'll find literature and nature-related gifts, frequent short films—on local geology, the U.S. Life Saving Service, and more—and exhibits on the life of the dunes and the shore. You can also pick up information on guided walks, birding trips, lectures, bonfires, and other current programs throughout the seashore, as well as on the Province Lands' own beaches, Race Point and Herring Cove, and the walking, biking, and horse trails. Don't miss the wonderful 360° view of the dunes and the surrounding ocean from the observation deck. ⊠ *Race Point Rd.,* ☎ *508/487–1256.* ⊙ *Apr.–Nov., daily 9–5.*

Not far from the present Coast Guard station is the **Old Harbor Station,** a U.S. Life Saving Service building towed here by barge from Chatham in 1977 to rescue it from an eroding beach. It is reached by a boardwalk across the sand, and plaques along the way tell about the lifesaving service and the whales seen offshore. Inside are displays of such equipment as Lyle guns, which shot rescue lines out to ships in distress when seas were too violent to launch a surfboat, and breeches buoys, in which passengers were hauled across those lines to safety. At 6:30 on Thursday night in summer there are reenactments of this old-fashioned lifesaving procedure. ⊠ *Race Point Beach, end of Race Point Rd.,* ☎ *no phone.* ⊠ *Donations accepted; Thurs. night $3.* ⊙ *July–Aug., daily 10–4.*

Provincetown's main downtown thoroughfare, **Commercial Street,** is 3 mi from end to end. In season, driving from one end of the main street to the other could take forever, so wear comfortable shoes and get ready to walk; even walking can be slow because of the crowds. You'll see signs for parking lots as you head into town. A casual stroll will allow you to see the many architectural styles (Greek Revival, Victorian, Second Empire, and Gothic, to name a few) used in the design of the impressive houses for wealthy sea captains and merchants. Be on the lookout for blue plaques fastened to housefronts explaining their historical significance—practically the entire town has been designated part of the Provincetown Historic District. The Historical Society puts out a series of walking-tour pamphlets, available for about $1 each at many shops in town, with maps and information on the history of many buildings and the more or less famous folk who have occupied them. You may also want to pick up a free Provincetown gallery guide.

The center of town is where the crowds and most of the touristy shops are. The quiet East End is mostly residential, with some top galleries, and the similarly quiet West End has a number of small inns with neat lawns and elaborate gardens. Narrated trolley sightseeing tours make the downtown circuit throughout the day, or the romantically inclined can hire a **horse-drawn carriage** from the stand in front of the town hall (⊠ 260 Commercial St.).

❽ The first thing you'll see in Provincetown is the **Pilgrim Monument** stretching into the sky. This grandiose edifice, which seems somewhat out of proportion to the rest of the low-rise town, commemorates the Pilgrims' first landing in the New World and their signing of the Mayflower Compact (the first colonial-American rules of self-governance) before they set off from Provincetown Harbor to explore the mainland. Climb the 116 steps and 60 ramps of the 252-ft-high tower for a panoramic view— dunes on one side, harbor on the other, and the entire bay side of Cape Cod beyond. On an exceptionally clear day you can see the Boston skyline. At the tower's base is a museum of Lower Cape and Provincetown history, with exhibits on whaling, shipwrecks, and scrimshaw, a diorama of the *Mayflower,* and another of a glass factory.

The tower was erected of granite shipped from Maine, according to a design modeled on a tower in Siena, Italy. President Theodore Roosevelt laid the cornerstone in 1907, and President Taft attended the 1910 dedication. On Thanksgiving Eve, in a ceremony that includes a museum tour and open house, 5,000 white and gold lights that drape the tower are illuminated—a display that can be seen as far away as the Cape Cod Canal. They are lighted nightly into the New Year. ⊠ *High Pole Hill Rd.,* ☎ *508/487–1310,* WEB *www.pilgrim-monument.org.* 🖂 *$6.* ⊘ *Apr.–June and Sept.– Nov., daily 9–5; July–Aug., daily 9–7; last admission 45 mins before closing.*

❾ MacMillan Wharf, with its large municipal parking facility, is a sensible place to start a tour of town. It is one of the remaining 5 of the 54 wharves that once jutted into the bay. The wharf serves as the base for P-town whale-watch boats, fishing charters, and party boats. The **Chamber of Commerce** is also here, with all kinds of information and events schedules. Kiosks at the wharf have rest-room and parking-lot locations, bus schedules, and other information for visitors.

The former Provincetown Marina building, on MacMillan Wharf, holds the **Expedition Whydah Sea Lab and Learning Center,** a home for artifacts recovered from the pirate ship *Whydah,* which sank off the coast of Wellfleet more than 265 years ago. The *Whydah* is the only pirate shipwreck ever authenticated anywhere in the world, and the museum is entertaining and educational, with one display on the restoration and conservation processes and another on the untold story of the 18th-century pirating life. The curators hope to collect all the recovered pieces eventually; some are on loan to other museums across the country. ⊠ *16 MacMillan Wharf,* ☎ *508/487–8899 or 800/ 949–3241.* 🖂 *$5.* ⊘ *Memorial Day–Labor Day, daily 10–7; Apr.– Memorial Day and Labor Day–Oct. 15, daily 10–5; Oct. 16–Dec., weekends 10–5.*

NEED A BREAK?

The **Provincetown Portuguese Bakery** (⊠ 299 Commercial St., ☎ 508/ 487–1803) makes fresh Portuguese breads and pastries and serves breakfast and lunch all day from March to October. Novices should ask the counterperson which pastries to try. It's open until 11 PM in summer.

❿ Founded in 1914 to collect and show the works of artists with Provincetown connections, the **Provincetown Art Association and Museum** (PAAM) houses a 1,650-piece permanent collection, displayed in changing exhibits that mix up-and-comers with established 20th-century figures. Some of the work hung in the four bright galleries is for sale. The museum store carries books of local interest, including works by or about area artists and authors, as well as posters, crafts, cards, and gift items. PAAM-sponsored year-round courses (one day and longer) offer the opportunity to study under such talents as Sal Del Deo, Carol Whorf Westcott, and Tony Vevers. ⊠ *460 Commercial St.,* ☎ *508/487– 1750.* 🖂 *$3.* ⊘ *Nov.–Apr., weekends noon–4 and by appointment; Memorial Day–Labor Day, daily noon–5 and 8–10; May and Sept.– Oct., Fri.–Sun. noon–5.*

⓫ To see or hear the work of up-and-coming artists, visit the gallery or attend a reading at the **Fine Arts Work Center** (FAWC). A nonprofit organization founded in 1968, the FAWC sponsors 10 writers and 10 artists from October through May each year with a place to live and work, a stipend on which to live, and access to artists and teachers. A summer program has open-enrollment workshops in both writing and the visual arts. The buildings in the complex around the center, which it owns, were formerly part of Day's Lumber Yard Studios, built above a lumberyard by a patron of the arts to provide poor artists with cheap accommodations. Robert Motherwell, Hans Hoffmann, and

CAPE COD'S MADAME BUTTERFLY

AMONG THE GENTLY SWAYING dune grasses, and beneath the waves of the Atlantic, waft the whispers of a legend. It's a classic tale with all the ingredients—true love, pirate treasure and a storm-wrought tragedy—and for nearly three centuries it has inspired fanciful embellishments and lustful searchings. Though she was wrecked in a treacherous storm back in April of 1717, the pirate ship *Whydah*, with cargo, captain, and legacy, still captivates.

As with any great legend, that of the *Whydah* has several versions, some conflicting. Many say the story began with an innocent love, when a dark, ambitious sailor named Sam Bellamy met the beautiful Maria Hallett in Wellfleet. From their brief acquaintance blossomed love, grand promises, and a child (the latter unknown to the wayward Bellamy), and the sailor gave his word that he would return, armed with riches.

He set off for England in hopes of finding fortune in shipping, but he soon realized that piracy was far more lucrative. Black Sam Bellamy, as he became known, and his men were wildly successful, taking over many dozens of ships. On a pirating jaunt in the Caribbean, Bellamy and his men captured a beauty—a slave ship loaded with gold and silver. Wealthy beyond their dreams, the men headed north with Bellamy at the helm of this exciting vessel, called the *Whydah*.

While the sailors grew rich and famous, young Maria Hallett was banished by her family because of her pregnancy. She fled to a small cabin in Eastham, awaiting the birth of her child and the return of her lover. She had a son, but he died in infancy, and the discovery of the dead child landed Maria in jail. Reputations were made swiftly in those days: It wasn't long before the townspeople decided Maria was a witch who had made an unholy pact with the devil. She suffered in isolation as Bellamy made his way back to Wellfleet.

Mariners have long feared the dangerous shoals, sand bars, and temperamental weather of the waters off Cape Cod. On the night of April 26, 1717, a sudden fierce storm interrupted Bellamy's homecoming, and the once sleek and swift *Whydah* was no match for the fury of the sea. Blasted by wave and wind, she met her demise in the form of a sturdy sandbar—nearly all hands were lost, and the ship lay broken, exposed to the tides.

At this point the legend sways wildly. The *Whydah* lay a mere 200 yards off the beach, within easy reach of eager treasure hunters. Historical records show that an officer, sent by the king to gather the spoils of the pirate ship, left the scene empty-handed, so the location of the gold, silver, and gems remains a mystery. Perhaps they were hidden by 18th-century scavengers; perhaps they still await discovery in the depths.

In 1984 modern-day pirate Barry Clifford and his crew uncovered some of the *Whydah*'s remains, but the promise of grand treasure has yet to unfold. In Provincetown, at the Expedition Whydah museum, you can see some artifacts from this ship and other historic wrecks.

And what of poor Maria? Some say her ghost still wanders among the dunes, wailing and cursing all sailors. Listen closely, on a foggy and ominous evening, to decide for yourself.

— Laura V. Scheel

Helen Frankenthaler have been among the studios' roster of residents over the years. ✉ *24 Pearl St.,* ☎ *508/487–9960,* WEB *www.fawc.org.* ⊘ *Weekdays 9–5.*

The former studios of two noted artists, Edwin W. Dickinson, at 46 Pearl Street, and Charles W. Hawthorne, at 48 Pearl Street, give an idea of the proliferation of now-famous artists who worked in the area. Hawthorne's **Cape Cod School of Art,** established here in 1899 (now managed by Lois Griffel, a former student of Henry Hensche, one of Hawthorne's disciples), put the town on its path to becoming a major art colony. The school runs weeklong workshops in summer; call ahead to get the catalog. The year 1999 marked the school's centennial, and the town celebrated being home to the nation's oldest continuous art colony. ✉ *22 Brewster St.,* ☎ *508/487–0101,* WEB *www.capecodschoolofart.com.* ⊘ *Late May–late Sept., call for hrs.*

⑫ The **town hall** was used by the Provincetown Art Association as its first exhibit space and still displays paintings donated to the town over the years, including Provincetown scenes by Charles Hawthorne and WPA-era murals by Ross Moffett. The Provincetown Repertory Theatre sometimes takes up residence here. ✉ *260 Commercial St.,* ☎ *508/487–7000.* ⊘ *Weekdays 8–5.*

⑬ In a little park behind the town hall is the **Mayflower Compact Plaque** (✉ *Bradford St.*), carved in bas-relief by sculptor Cyrus Dalin and depicting the historic signing.

NEED A BREAK?   The **Provincetown Fudge Factory** (✉ 210 Commercial St., ☎ 508/487–2850), across from the post office, makes silky peanut-butter cups, chocolates, saltwater taffy, yard-long licorice whips, custom-flavor frozen yogurt, and the creamiest fudge on the Cape—a must stop for those with a discriminating sweet tooth—and will ship goodies to you, too.

---

⑭ An **octagonal house** (✉ *74 Commercial St., between Soper and Nickerson Sts.*) built in 1850 is an interesting piece of Provincetown architecture in the West End. The house is not open to the public.

⑮ The oldest building in town, dating from 1746, is the small Cape-style **Seth Nickerson House** (✉ *72 Commercial St., at Soper St.*), still a private home. It was built by a ship's carpenter, with massive pegged, hand-hewn oak beams and wide-board floors. Renovated in 1998, the house does not offer the glimpse into centuries past that it once did, but it's still impressive.

⑯ The bronze **Pilgrim Plaque** (✉ *west end of Commercial St.*), set into a boulder at the center of a little park, commemorates the first footfall of the Pilgrims onto Cape soil—Provincetown's humble equivalent of the Plymouth Rock.

⑰ In the **Provincetown Inn** (✉ *1 Commercial St.,* ☎ *508/487–9500*) you can see a series of 19 murals, painted in the 1930s from old postcards, depicting life in the 19th-century town. The inn still operates as a hotel; the murals are in the lobby and hallways.

Dining and Lodging

$$$–$$$$ ✕ **Chester.** Understated and golden-hued, Chester, named for a pet terrier, is a seasoned veteran. The single-room restaurant in a Greek Revival sea captain's house serves beautifully presented meals from a small, contemporary menu that changes regularly. The menu lists locally procured meats and seafood, and the chef collects tomatoes, herbs, and

lettuces from a garden behind the restaurant. Try seasonal choices such as asparagus-and-fiddlehead risotto and lamb with cranberry *jus*, potatoes, and vegetables. The carefully crafted wine list has 160 selections. An outdoor, upper terrace patio has great views of Provincetown Harbor. ⊠ *404 Commercial St.,* ☎ *508/487–8200. Reservations essential. AE, MC, V. Closed part of Dec.–Mar, call for Dec. dates.*

$$–$$$$ ✕ **Dancing Lobster Café Trattoria.** Although the food is tending upscale, it remains among the best prepared in Provincetown. Presentations are innovative and sophisticated, outstanding in every way. Appetizers are pure classics—carpaccio is a favorite—and the *zuppa di pesce* (Italian seafood stew) with couscous is complex and filling. The chef can sometimes be a bit too generous with the olive oil, but think of it as more of a good thing. The lobster may not dance, but the customers will—sometimes joined by Robert the bartender, a great local favorite. ⊠ *371 Commercial St.,* ☎ *508/487–0900. AE, D, MC, V. Closed mid-Nov.–mid-May.*

$$–$$$$ ✕ **Martin House.** It's a relief to find this sanctuary of calm and cre-
★ ative contemporary fare right on bustling Commercial Street. Original 18th century woodwork lends a touch of history, and Provincetown paintings grace the walls. The menu leans toward colonial fare with a sophisticated touch, including unusually flavorful chutneys, risotto, and wild game. Some of the more interesting dishes include Oysters Claudia, which matches native Wellfleets-on-the-half-shell with an Asian dipping sauce, wasabi, and pickled ginger, and pan-roasted lamb rib eye with an exotic mint chutney and quinoa–wild rice tabbouleh. ⊠ *157 Commercial St.,* ☎ *508/487–1327. AE, D, DC, MC, V. Closed Wed.–Thurs. in Jan.–Mar.*

$$–$$$$ ✕ **Napi's.** No visit to Provincetown is complete without dinner at Napi's, an excellent Mediterranean-style restaurant. The food and the interior share a penchant for unusual, striking juxtapositions—a classical sculpture in front of an abstract canvas, for instance. On the gustatory front, look for sharp combinations such as shrimp flambé in ouzo and Metaxa, served with a tomato, garlic, and onion sauce. One specialty a vegetarian item with an international flair—rice heaped with spicy vegetables is one example. ⊠ *7 Freeman St.,* ☎ *508/487–1145. Reservations essential. AE, D, DC, MC, V. No lunch June–mid-Sept.*

$$–$$$ ✕ **Bubala's by the Bay.** Personality bubbles up at this funky joint in a bright yellow building adorned on top with campy carved birds. The kitchen rarely stops, serving breakfast, lunch, and dinner; it's strong on seafood bought directly off local boats and cut in back just hours before it's served. The Cuban cod has little to do with that cuisine (except the beans), but it's wonderfully fresh and tasty. The same thing can be said of the Jamaican fish stew. The wine list is priced practically at retail, and the U-shape bar picks up into the evening. Outdoor seating along Commercial Street is a social focal point, while quieter indoor seating reaches right down to the bay. ⊠ *183 Commercial St.,* ☎ *508/ 487–0773. AE, D, MC, V. Closed Halloween–April Fool's Day.*

$$–$$$ ✕ **Café Edwige.** Delicious contemporary American food, relaxed and
★ friendly service, and an eclectic, homey upstairs setting—Café Edwige delivers all this night after night. Begin with a Maine crab cake, warm goat cheese on crostini, or a refreshing field-green-and-wild-lettuce salad, and then consider lobster and Wellfleet scallops over pasta with a wild mushroom, Asiago, and tomato broth, or planked local codfish with roasted corn and shiitakes. Don't pass on the wonderful desserts, such as the Cape Cod cranberry crumble served with vanilla ice cream. Breakfast here is a local institution. ⊠ *333 Commercial St.,* ☎ *508/487–2008. AE, MC, V. Closed Nov.–May.*

$$–$$$ ✕ **Front Street.** Front Street is so good, so consistent, and so roman-
★   tic that many locals consistently rate it a contender for the title of best
         restaurant in P-town. Chef-owners Donna Aliperti and Kathleen Cot-
         ter link classic Italian cooking to offerings from other Mediterranean
         regions such as Greece and southern France and even North Africa.
         Duck smoked in Chinese black tea is dense and luscious, served with
         a different lusty sauce every day; a current favorite is fresh tropical fruit
         with mixed peppercorns. Littleneck clams and calamari with butter-
         nut squash in a roast garlic broth is essentially a simple dish, but its
         unique flavors show off these traditional ingredients in a new light. The
         wine list is also a winner. Call well ahead for a reservation, even dur-
         ing the shoulder seasons, when the menu turns purely Italian. ✉ 230
         Commercial St., ☎ 508/487–9715. Reservations essential. AE, D,
         MC, V. Closed Jan.–mid-May.

$$–$$$ ✕ **Lorraine's.** In its much bigger location in the East End, Lorraine's
         has a more robust than intimate feel, but the Mexican-inspired menu
         is as finely prepared as ever. Specials are always worth a listen. An ap-
         petizer of three large shrimp stuffed with cheese and fresh jalapeños
         packs a punch, and the *mujeres* clams (steamed littlenecks in a cilantro-
         citrus broth) are addictive. Also wonderful is a dish called simply *car-
         nitas,* slow-cooked pork tenderloin with fresh guacamole, salsa, sour
         cream, and lots of frilly greens. The vessel-shape bar draws a loyal,
         lively crowd. ✉ 463 Commercial St., ☎ 508/487–6074. Reservations
         essential. MC, V. Closed Jan.–Mar. No lunch.

$$–$$$ ✕ **The Mews.** This town favorite's menu focuses on seafood with a cross-
         cultural flair. Some popular entrées are rich and spicy scallops, shrimp-
         and-crab mousse in a wonton on grilled filet mignon, and a decadent
         French lentil ragout with chipotle aioli sauce. Downstairs, the main
         dining room opens onto magnificent harbor views. A piano bar up-
         stairs serves lunch (weekdays in summer) and dinner from a light café
         menu. The view of the bay from the bar is near perfect, and the gen-
         tle lighting makes this a romantic spot for a drink. Brunch is also served
         every day in season. The restaurant claims its vodka bar is New En-
         gland's largest. ✉ 429 Commercial St., ☎ 508/487–1500. Reserva-
         tions not accepted. AE, D, DC, MC, V. Closed Jan. No lunch weekdays
         off-season or Sat. between Columbus Day and Memorial Day.

$$–$$$ ✕ **Sal's Place.** Tucked away in the peaceful West End, this little wa-
         terfront place dishes up massive portions of southern Italian special-
         ties. Calamari and linguine, *vongole* (tiny clams) over pasta, and
         delicious vegetarian spinach lasagna are all longtime favorites. Deter-
         mined carnivores will want to tackle the steak *pizzaiola*: a massive 25-
         ounce rib-eye steak served with marinara sauce. The back dining room
         overlooks the harbor. ✉ 99 Commercial St., ☎ 508/487–1279. MC,
         V. Closed Nov.–Apr. and Mon.–Thurs. Oct. 2–mid-June. No lunch.

$–$$$ ✕ **Lobster Pot.** Provincetown's Lobster Pot is fit to do battle with all
         the Lobster Pots anywhere (and everywhere) on the Cape. As you
         enter, you'll pass through one of the hardest-working kitchens on the
         Cape, which turns out classic New England cooking: lobsters galore,
         generous and filling seafood platters, and some of the best chowder
         around. The upstairs deck overlooks the perpetual comings and go-
         ings of the harbor and is a great spot for lunch. There's also a take-
         out lobster market and bakery on the premises. The bad news is that
         you'll have to wait in line; the good news is that the line is in the cen-
         ter of town, great for people watching. ✉ 321 Commercial St., ☎ 508/
         487–0842. Reservations not accepted. AE, D, DC, MC, V. Closed Jan.

$–$$ ✕ **Mojo's.** This is Provincetown's fast-food institution, where any-
         body who knows anything about food and happens to be in a hurry

goes to grab a bite. The tiniest of kitchens turns out one of the most varied and eclectic menus in town, everything from fresh-cut french fries to fried clams with the bellies, steak subs, tacos, tofu burgers (and the regular kind), tacos, hummus, roll-up sandwiches, salads, and the best fried fish. There's some seating in the back at colorfully painted picnic tables. ⊠ *5 Ryder St. Extension,* ☎ *508/487–3140. Reservations not accepted. No credit cards. Closed mid-Oct.–early May, depending on weather and crowds.*

$–$$ ✕ **Spiritus.** The local bars close at 1 AM, at which point this pizza joint–coffee stand becomes the town's epicenter. It's the ultimate place to see and be seen, pizza slice in hand and witty banter at the ready. In the morning, the same counter serves up restorative coffee and croissants. ⊠ *190 Commercial St.,* ☎ *508/487–2808. No credit cards. Closed Nov.–Apr.*

$$–$$$ ✕🖾 **The Commons.** Built as an inn in the 1860s, this combination guest house and bistro run by Carl Draper and Chuck Rigg has tasteful rooms with wide-board floors, antique furnishings, Oriental carpets, and marble-tile baths. Most rooms can claim a view of the bay; some have balconies. All have TVs and fans or air-conditioning. The bistro's innovative, ever-changing Continental menu lists dishes such as seared halibut with lobster risotto. You can relax in the garden or at the deck bar that overlooks the bay. ⊠ *386 Commercial St., 02657,* ☎ *508/487–7800 or 800/487–0784,* FAX *508/487–0358,* WEB *www.capecod.net/commons. 14 rooms. Restaurant, bar. AE, MC, V. Restaurant closed Jan.–mid-Feb., guest house closed Jan.–Easter. CP.*

$$$$ 🖾 **Brass Key.** Close to restaurants, shops, galleries, and nightlife, this
★ complex is becoming Provincetown's most luxurious resort. The main house, originally an 1828 sea captain's home, is beautifully restored, and there are several other carefully groomed buildings and cottages. Rooms have antique furniture, floral wall-coverings, and modern amenities including Bose stereos, mini-refrigerators, and TV/VCRs (there's a videocassette library). Deluxe rooms also come with gas fireplaces and whirlpool baths or French doors opening out to wrought-iron balconies. A widow's-walk sundeck has a panoramic view of Cape Cod Bay. Complimentary cocktails are served in the courtyard; in winter, wine is served before a roaring fire in the common room. The Brass Key draws a largely gay clientele, but the owners and staff make everyone feel welcome and pampered. ⊠ *67 Bradford St., 02657,* ☎ *508/487–9005 or 800/842–9858,* FAX *508/487–9020,* WEB *www.brasskey.com. 36 rooms. Air-conditioning, in-room safes, in-room VCRs, pool. No smoking. AE, D, MC, V. CP.*

$$–$$$$ 🖾 **Beaconlight Guesthouse.** The English country interior includes designer wallpaper, freshly painted walls, antiques, extra pillows on your bed, and in-room televisions and VCRs. Outside, three decks provide varied, stunning views of the entire town and the harbor, and an outdoor hot tub invites soaks under the night skies. The guest house is between busy Commercial and Bradford streets, so it's close to everything but still a bit quieter than places on the main thoroughfares. ⊠ *12 Winthrop St., 02657,* ☎ *508/487–9603 or 800/696–9603,* WEB *www.beaconlightguesthouse.com. 7 rooms, 3 suites. In-room data ports, outdoor hot tub. AE, D, DC, MC, V. CP.*

$–$$$$ 🖾 **The Masthead.** Hidden away in the quiet west end of Commercial Street, the Masthead is a charming cluster of shingle houses that overlook a lush lawn, a 450-ft-long boardwalk, and a private beach. Accommodations include spacious rooms, efficiencies, apartments, and fully outfitted cottages. The cottages, which sleep four to seven, are an ideal choice for families or larger groups and for longer stays (kids under 12 stay free). The deepwater and in-shore moorings right on the property make this a great choice if you're boating into town. This is classic Provincetown—friendly, unpretentious, and homey. ☒ *31–41 Commercial St., Box 577, 02657,* ☎ *508/487–0523 or 800/395–5095,* FAX *508/487–9251,* WEB *www.capecodtravel.com/masthead. 7 apartments, 3 cottages, 2 efficiencies, 9 rooms. Beach, dock. AE, D, DC, MC, V.*

$$$ 🛏 **Best Western Chateau Motor Inn.** This may be part of a chain, but the personal attention of owners Charlotte and Bill Gordon, whose family has run the place for decades, shows in the landscaped grounds and in the well-maintained modern rooms with wall-to-wall carpeting and tile baths. Atop a hill with expansive views from picture windows of marsh, dunes, and sea, the motel is a longish walk to the center of town. ☒ *105 Bradford St. Extension, Box 558, 02657,* ☎ *508/487–1286 or 800/528–1234,* FAX *508/487–3557,* WEB *www.bestwestern.com/chateaumotorinn. 54 rooms. Pool. AE, D, DC, MC, V. CP. Closed Nov.–Apr.*

$$–$$$ 🛏 **Bayshore and Chandler House.** Formerly known as the Hargood
★ House, this apartment complex on the water, ½ mi from the town center, is a great option for longer stays. Many of the units have decks and large water-view windows; all have full kitchens, modern baths, and phones. Number 8 is like a light, bright beach house on the water, with three glass walls, cathedral ceilings, private deck, dining table, and chairs. Number 20 has a fireplace and a home-style kitchen. Rental is mostly by the week in season; there's a two-night minimum off-season. Pets are welcome. ☒ *493 Commercial St., 02657–2413,* ☎ *508/ 487–9133,* FAX *508/487–0520,* WEB *www.provincetown.com/bayshore. 25 apartments. Beach. AE, MC, V.*

$$–$$$ 🛏 **Fairbanks Inn.** This colonial-style inn on the next street over from Commercial Street includes the 1776 main house and auxiliary buildings. Guest rooms have four-poster or canopy beds, Oriental rugs on wide-board floors, and antique furnishings; some have fireplaces or kitchens. Many original touches remain here, from the 18th-century wallpaper to artifacts from the inn's first residents. The baths are on the small side, but they help preserve the colonial integrity of the home. The wicker-filled sunporch and the garden are good places for afternoon cocktails. ☒ *90 Bradford St., 02657,* ☎ *508/487–0386 or 800/324–7265,* FAX *508/487–3540,* WEB *www.fairbanksinn.com. 13 rooms, 1 efficiency. Free parking. AE, MC, V. CP.*

$–$$$ 🛏 **The Captain and His Ship.** Built in 1887 for a sea captain, this stately mansard-roof Victorian is only a short walk from the center of town and is across the street from Provincetown bay. Jim Baer, who has owned the house since 1980, fills his immaculate, spacious rooms with period antiques and Oriental carpets. Room 3, done in subtle earth tones, has a king-size bed, a gas fireplace, and private access to the garden. Most rooms have water views; all have color TVs, VCRs, mini-refrigerators, and hair dryers. Some have private decks. A Continental breakfast is included in July and August. There's a fee for the limited parking. ☒ *164 Commercial St., 02657,* ☎ *508/487–1850 or 800/400–2278,* WEB *www.captainandhisship.com. 9 rooms, 7 with bath. Air-conditioning. No smoking. MC, V. Closed Nov.–Apr.*

$–$$$ 🛏 **Christopher's by the Bay.** The rooms in this art-inspired inn are named after the greats—Rembrandt, Picasso, Monet, Van Gogh—and elegantly appointed with brass beds and rich fabrics. Many have great views of the bay. The building is a graceful old Victorian and is surrounded by carefully maintained gardens and brick patios. Rooms on the upper floors share bathrooms. Set back from the bustle, it's still a quick walk from the center of town. Like most other inns in town, Christopher's has a minimum stay requirement during holidays in peak season. ⊠ *8 Johnson St.,* ☎ FAX *508/487–9263,* WEB *www.christophersbythebay.com. 10 rooms, 5 with bath. Air-conditioning, in-room data ports. AE, MC, V. BP.*

$–$$ ⊡ **Dexter's Inn.** Just a block from the action of Commercial Street, the inn has simple and pretty rooms at some of Provincetown's more reasonable prices. Adorned with colorful quilts or lace bedspreads, beds are backed by wicker or brass headboards. Ceiling fans whir above the decent-size rooms, most of which have views of the Pilgrim Monument. The lowest-price accommodations share a bath, but most have their own. Relax in the keeping room by the warmth of a gas fireplace in winter. ⊠ *6 Conwell St.,* ☎ *508/487–1911 or 888/521–1999,* WEB *www. ptowndextersinn.com. 15 rooms, 12 with bath. Air-conditioning. MC, V. CP.*

Nightlife and the Arts

THE ARTS

The **Beach Plum Music Festival,** held in August at the Provincetown Town Hall (⊠ 260 Commercial St., ☎ 508/349–6874), is a series of popular folk and jazz concerts by performers such as Wynton Marsalis, Arlo Guthrie, Queen Ida, and Holly Near.

Provincetown Inn (⊠ 1 Commercial St., ☎ 508/487–9500) hosts several unusual theater productions in summer. Look for shows performed by C.A.P.E. Inc. Theatre and those offered during the Provincetown Fringe Festival. There are also nights of live music.

Begun in 1999, the annual **Provincetown International Film Festival** (WEB www.ptownfilmfest.com) has become so popular that most of the screenings sell out. Aside from a full schedule of independent films, it has guest appearances by such notables as director John Waters, Lily Tomlin, and Christine Vachon. The festival hits town in mid-June.

The **Provincetown Playhouse Mews Series** (⊠ Town Hall, 260 Commercial St., ☎ 508/487–0955) includes classical chamber, folk, ethnic, and jazz concerts in summer.

The **Provincetown Repertory Theatre** (☎ 508/487–0600) stages a summer lineup of classic and modern drama, presenting Equity actors and local talent. The theater has held performances in the town hall; call for current performance locations.

The **Provincetown Theatre Company** (☎ 508/487–8673) presents classics, modern drama, and new works by local authors year-round, as well as staged readings and playwriting workshops at the Provincetown Inn.

The **Provincetown Reservations System** (⊠ 293 Commercial St., ☎ 800/648–0364 or 508/487–2400, WEB www.ptownres.com) offers a quick and painless way to secure theater and show tickets. The system also handles lodging and travel reservations.

NIGHTLIFE

Atlantic House (⊠ 6 Masonic Pl., ☎ 508/487–3821), the grandfather of the gay night scene and the only gay bar open year-round, is frequented mostly by men. It has several lounge areas and an outdoor patio.

Boatslip Beach Club (⊠ 161 Commercial St., ☎ 508/487–1669) holds a gay and lesbian tea dance daily from 4 to 7 on the outdoor pool deck. The club has indoor and outdoor dance floors. There is ballroom dancing here as well, in addition to two-stepping Thursday through Sunday nights.

The **Cape Cod National Seashore** schedules summer evening programs, such as slide shows, sunset beach walks, concerts (local groups, military bands), and sing-alongs, at its Province Lands Visitor Center (✉ Race Point Rd., ☎ 508/487–1256), and sunset campfire talks on the beaches in Provincetown.

Club Euro (✉ 258 Commercial St., ☎ 508/487–2505) has weekend concerts by big names in world music, including African music, Jamaican reggae, Chicago blues, and Cajun zydeco. The venue itself is fantastic: the 1843 Congregational church, later a movie theater, is an eerie ocean dreamscape with oceanic sea-green walls with a half-submerged three-dimensional mermaid spouting fish, and a black ceiling high above. Pool tables and a late-night menu are available.

The **Crown & Anchor Complex** (✉ 247 Commercial St., ☎ 508/487–1430, WEB www.onlyatthecrown.com) has plenty of action with several bars and restaurants, a cabaret with drag shows, and a game room. There are also 18 rooms and suites.

Governor Bradford Restaurant (✉ 312 Commercial St., ☎ 508/487–9618) is perhaps better known as a sometimes-rowdy pool and dance hall. In the afternoon you can play chess or backgammon at the tables by the window. After 8 PM the place revs up with live music or a DJ spinning everything from hip-hop to disco. On weekend nights get set for a raucous evening of drag-hosted karaoke.

Napi's (✉ 7 Freeman St., ☎ 508/487–1145) offers easy-listening piano in its upstairs lounge on weekends, nightly in season.

Pied Piper (✉ 193A Commercial St., ☎ 508/487–1527) draws hordes of gay men to its post–tea dance gathering at 6:30 every evening in July and August and weekends in the shoulder seasons. Later in the evening, the crowd is mostly, though not exclusively, women. The club has a deck overlooking the harbor, a small dance floor with a good sound system, and two bars.

Vixen (✉ 336 Commercial St., ☎ 508/487–6424), a lively women's club, gets packed with dancers. On most nights, before the dance crowd sets in, there are both national and local women entertainers. Look for live music and comedy. There are also a couple of pool tables in the front room.

Whalers' Wharf (✉ 237–241 Commercial St.) resembles an old European marketplace, with a brick pathway that leads straight to the beach and a rotunda theater alive with street performers and entertainment. The first floor of the building holds shops; upstairs are artists' studios and a museum dedicated to the town's history.

Outdoor Activities and Sports

BEACHES

The entire stretch of Commercial Street is backed by the waters of Provincetown Harbor, and most hotels have private beaches. Farther in town there are plenty of places to settle on the sand and take a refreshing dip. Just be mindful of the busy boat traffic.

Race Point Beach (✉ Race Point Rd.), one of the Cape Cod National Seashore beaches in Provincetown, has a wide swath of sand stretching far off into the distance around the point and Coast Guard station. Behind the beach is pure duneland, and bike trails lead off the parking lot. Because of its position, on a point facing north, the beach gets sun all day long, whereas the east-coast beaches get fullest sun early in the day. Parking is available, there are showers and rest rooms, and lifeguards are stationed in season. From mid-June through Labor Day, parking costs $7 per day, or $20 for a yearly pass good at all National Seashore beaches.

Herring Cove Beach, a National Seashore beach, is calmer (and a little warmer) than Race Point Beach, though it's not as pretty since the parking lot isn't hidden behind dunes. But the parking lot to the right of the bathhouse is a great place to watch the sunset. There's a hot dog stand, showers, and rest rooms. Lifeguards are on duty in season. From mid-June through Labor Day, parking costs $7 per day, or $20 for a yearly pass good at all National Seashore beaches.

For a day of fairly private beachcombing and great views, you can walk across the stone jetty at low tide to **Long Point,** a sand spit south of town with two lighthouses and two Civil War bunkers, named Fort Useless and Fort Ridiculous because they were hardly needed. It's a 2-mi walk across soft sand—beware of poison ivy and deer ticks if you detour from the path—or hire a boat at Flyer's (☎ 508/487–0898) to drop you off and pick you up.

BIKING

The **Province Lands Trail** is a 5¼-mi loop off the Beech Forest parking lot on Race Point Road, with spurs to Herring Cove and Race Point beaches and to Bennett Pond. The paths wind up and down hills amid dunes, marshes, woods, and ponds, affording spectacular views. More than 8 mi of bike trails lace through the dunes, cranberry bogs, and scrub pine of the National Seashore, with many access points, including Herring Cove and Race Point.

The **Beech Forest** bike trail (✉ off Race Point Rd.) in the National Seashore offers an especially nice ride through a shady forest to Bennett Pond.

Arnold's (✉ 329 Commercial St., ☎ 508/487–0844) rents all types of bikes, children's included.

Nelson's Bike Shop and Rentals (✉ 43 Race Point Rd., ☎ 508/487–8849), across from the Beech Forest bike trail, rents a variety of bikes, including trailers, and has a deli with picnic-ready food; parking is free.

Ptown Bikes (✉ 42 Bradford St., ☎ 508/487–8735) has Trek and Mongoose mountain bikes at good rates; the shop also provide free locks and maps.

BOATING

Bay Lady II Excursion Schooner (✉ MacMillan Wharf, ☎ 508/487–9308), a beautiful 73-ft sailing vessel, heads out for two-hour cruises three times daily. You're welcome to bring your own spirits and snacks for this scenic and peaceful sail.

Flyer's Boat Rental (✉ 131A Commercial St., ☎ 508/487–0898) has kayaks, surfbikes, Sunfish, Hobies, Force 5s, Lightnings, powerboats, and rowboats. Flyer's will also shuttle you to Long Point.

Schooner Hindu (✉ MacMillan Wharf, ☎ 508/487–3000) takes you on a graceful sail in the waters around Provincetown; trips leave four times daily.

FISHING

You can go for fluke, bluefish, and striped bass on a walk-on basis from spring through fall with **Cap'n Bill & Cee Jay** (✉ MacMillan Wharf, ☎ 508/487–4330 or 800/675–6723).

HORSEBACK RIDING

The **Province Lands Horse Trails** lead to the beaches through or past dunes, cranberry bogs, forests, and ponds.

Bayberry Hollow Farm (⊠ 27 W. Vine St. Extension, ☎ 508/487–6584) has pony rides year-round.

KAYAKING

Kayaking has become increasingly popular on the Cape, and **Off the Coast Kayak Company** (⊠ 3 Freeman St., ☎ 508/487–2692 or 877/785–2925) offers guided kayak tours as well as equipment rentals for those who wish to venture out on their own. Choose a tandem kayak or go solo; all skill levels are welcome. Several tours are offered, including sunset paddles, town harbor tours, clinics, and the special Kayak Clambake tour.

TENNIS

Bissell's Tennis Courts (⊠ 21 Bradford St. Extension, ☎ 508/487–9512) has five clay courts and offers lessons. It's open from Memorial Day to September.

Provincetown Tennis Club (⊠ 286 Bradford St. Extension, ☎ 508/487–9574) has several outdoor clay courts open to nonmembers; you can also take lessons with the resident tennis pro.

TOURS

Art's Dune Tours (⊠ Commercial and Standish Sts., ☎ 508/487–1950 or 800/894–1951, WEB www.artsdunetours.com) has been taking eager passengers into the dunes of Province Lands for more than 50 years. Bumpy but controlled rides are peppered with lively tales of legend and history. These popular 1- to 1½-hour tours are offered several times daily; especially intriguing are the sunset and moonlight tours.

King of the Hill Adventures (⊠ Standish St., ☎ 508/487–1296 or 877/738–6377) has off-road vehicles that take you into the dunes for narrated rides several times daily.

Y & C Harbor Tours (⊠ MacMillan Wharf, ☎ 508/487–4330) offers 40-minute narrated cruises around Provincetown Harbor daily on the hour.

WHALE-WATCHING

One of the joys of Cape Cod is spotting whales while they're swimming in and around the feeding grounds at Stellwagen Bank, about 6 mi off the tip of Provincetown. On a sunny day the boat ride out into open ocean is part of the pleasure, but the thrill, of course, is in seeing these great creatures. You might spot minke whales; humpbacks (who put on the best show when they breach); finbacks; or perhaps the most endangered great whale species, the right whale. Dolphins are a welcome sight as well; they play in the boat's bow waves. Many people also come aboard for birding, especially during spring and fall migration. You can see a great variety of birds at sea—gannets, shearwaters, and storm petrels, among many others.

Several boats take you out to sea—and bring you back—with morning, afternoon, or sunset trips lasting from three to four hours. All boats have food service, but remember to take sunscreen and a sweater or jacket—the breeze makes it chilly. Some boats stock seasickness pills, but if you're susceptible, come prepared.

The municipal parking area by the harbor in Provincetown fills up by noon in summer. Consider taking a morning boat to avoid crowds and the hottest sun. And although April may be cold, it is one of the better months for spotting whales, who at that time have just migrated north after mating and are very hungry. Good food is, after all, what brings the whales to this part of the Atlantic.

Cape Cod Whale Watch's naturalist-narrated trips leave three times daily from MacMillan Wharf. *SeaVentures* sets sail on select Sundays, offering a full day of wildlife watching. ✉ *Ticket office at MacMillan Wharf or 293 Commercial St.,* ☎ *508/487–4079 or 877/487–4079,* WEB *www.capecodwhalewatch.com.* 🎫 *$20 (seasonal variations).* ☉ *Tours Apr.–Oct.*

Dolphin Fleet tours are accompanied by scientists from the Center for Coastal Studies in Provincetown who provide commentary while collecting data on the whale population they've been monitoring for years. They know many of the whales by name and will tell you about their habits and histories. Reservations are required. ✉ *Ticket office in Chamber of Commerce building at MacMillan Wharf,* ☎ *508/349–1900 or 800/826–9300,* WEB *www.whalewatch.com.* 🎫 *$20 (seasonal variations).* ☉ *Tours Apr.–Oct.*

The **Portuguese Princess** sails with a naturalist on board to narrate. The snack bar sells Portuguese specialties. ✉ *Tickets available at 70 Shank Painter Rd. ticket office or at Whale Watchers General Store, 309 Commercial St.,* ☎ *508/487–2651 or 800/442–3188,* WEB *www. princesswhalewatch.com.* 🎫 *$15–$19.* ☉ *Tours May–Oct.*

Shopping

ART GALLERIES

Albert Merola Gallery (✉ 424 Commercial St., ☎ 508/487–4424) focuses on 20th-century and contemporary master prints and Picasso ceramics and features artists from in and around Provincetown, Boston, and New York, including James Balla and Richard Baker.

Bangs Street Gallery (✉ 432 Commercial St., ☎ 508/487–0743) represents contemporary artists as well those from the 1970s.

Berta Walker Gallery (✉ 208 Bradford St., ☎ 508/487–6411) specializes in Provincetown-affiliated artists, including Selina Trieff, Nancy Whorf, and many of the artists who migrated here from the now-defunct Long Point Gallery.

The **DNA Gallery** (✉ 288 Bradford St., ☎ 508/487–7700) represents artists working in various media, including many former fellows from the Fine Arts Work Center. The gallery also hosts readings, films, and concerts.

Julie Heller Gallery (✉ 2 Gosnold St., ☎ 508/487–2169) has a good combination of contemporary artists as well as some Provincetown icons. The gallery has works from the Sol Wilson estate, as well as those from such greats as Robert Motherwell and Blanche Lazzell.

Hilda Neily Art Gallery (✉ 432 Commercial St., ☎ 508/487–6300) is named for its featured artist, who was once a student of Impressionist painter Henry Hensche. Her oil paintings follow the same tradition of magical light and color.

The **Schoolhouse Center** (✉ 494 Commercial St., ☎ 508/487–4800) houses both the Driskel Gallery and the Silas Kenyon Gallery. It displays changing exhibitions of antiques as well as the works of local and national artists and photographers. A full range of performing- and visual-arts classes is available year-round, and the center has a Summer Reading Series on Thursday evening at 8. A true community organization, the center is open Thursday through Monday.

The **William Scott Gallery** (⌂ 439 Commercial St., ☎ 508/487–4040) primarily shows contemporary works such as John Dowd's reflective, realistic Cape 'scapes.

SPECIALTY STORES

Far Side of the Wind (⌂ 389 Commercial St., ☎ 508/487–3963) stocks New Age paraphernalia, including some unique Native American jewelry and artifacts, gifts, books, and music. Psychic readings are also available.

Giardelli Antonelli (⌂ 417 Commercial St., ☎ 508/487–3016) sells quality handmade clothing by local designers. Hand-knit sweaters are especially popular.

Impulse (⌂ 188 Commercial St., ☎ 508/487–1154) has contemporary American crafts, including jewelry and an extraordinary kaleidoscope collection. The Autograph Gallery exhibits framed photographs, letters, and documents signed by celebrities.

Kidstuff (⌂ 381 Commercial St., ☎ 508/487–0714) carries unusual, colorful children's wear.

Marine Specialties, Inc. (⌂ 235 Commercial St., ☎ 508/487–1730) is full of treasures, knickknacks, and clothing. Here you can purchase some very reasonably priced casual and military-style clothing, as well as sea shells, marine supplies, stained-glass lamps, candles, rubber sharks (you get the idea), and prints of old advertisements.

Moda Fina (⌂ 349 Commercial St., ☎ 508/487–6632) displays an eclectic selection of women's fashions, shoes, and jewelry—everything from flowing linen or silk night wear to funky and casual pieces. Unique Mexican crafts are also for sale.

Remembrances of Things Past (⌂ 376 Commercial St., ☎ 508/487–9443) deals with articles from the 1920s to the 1960s, including Bakelite and other jewelry, telephones, neon items, ephemera, and autographed celebrity photographs.

Silk & Feathers (⌂ 377 Commercial St., ☎ 508/487–2057) carries an assortment of fine lingerie, women's clothing, and jewelry.

Tim's Used Books (⌂ 242 Commercial St., ☎ 508/487–0005) has volumes of volumes—rooms of used-but-in-good-shape books, including some rare and out-of-print texts. It's a great place to browse for that perfect book to read on vacation.

Wa (⌂ 184 Commercial St., ☎ 508/487–6355) is an oasis of peace and Zenlike tranquillity. Unusual and Japanese-inspired items include fountains, home accent pieces, and even a collection of framed and sometimes frightening tropical insects.

West End Antiques (⌂ 146 Commercial St., ☎ 508/487–6723) sells everything from $4 postcards to a $3,000 model ship. Handmade dolls, better-quality glassware—Steuben, Orrefors, and Hawkes—are also available.

THE OUTER CAPE A TO Z

To research prices, get advice from other travelers, and book travel arrangements, visit www.fodors.com.

AIR TRAVEL

CARRIERS

Cape Air/Nantucket Airlines flies direct from Boston to Hyannis and Provincetown year-round and from New Bedford to Martha's Vineyard and Nantucket. Cape Air has joint baggage agreements with eight major U.S. airlines and with KLM.

➤ AIRLINES AND CONTACTS: **Cape Air/Nantucket Airlines** (☎ 508/771–6944 or 800/352–0714, WEB www.flycapeair.com).

AIRPORTS

Cape Air serves Boston year-round from Provincetown Municipal Airport.

➤ AIRPORT INFORMATION: **Provincetown Municipal Airport** (✉ Race Point Rd., ☎ 508/487–0241).

BOAT AND FERRY TRAVEL

Bay State Cruise Company makes the three-hour trip between Commonwealth Pier in Boston and MacMillan Wharf in Provincetown daily from mid-June to Labor Day, and then weekends only through Columbus Day. The company also runs a 90-minute express boat from Boston to Provincetown's Fishermen's Wharf daily from June to Columbus Day. The three-hour trip costs $18 one-way, $5 additional for bicycles; a same-day round-trip ticket costs $30, $10 additional for bicycles. The express boat costs $39 one-way, $5 additional for bicycles; a same-day round-trip costs $75, $10 additional for bicycles.

Capt. John Boats' passenger ferry makes the 1½- to 2-hour trip between Plymouth's State Pier and Provincetown from Memorial Day to mid-June, weekends; mid-June to Labor Day, daily. Schedules allow for day excursions. Fares are $27 for round-trip travel, $16 for one-way, and bicycles are an additional $2. One-way fares are only available in May, June, and September.

➤ BOAT AND FERRY INFORMATION: **Bay State Cruise Company** (☎ 617/748–1428 in Boston; 508/487–9284 in Provincetown, WEB www.baystatecruisecompany.com). **Capt. John Boats'** (☎ 508/747–2400; 800/242–2469 in MA, WEB www.provincetownferry.com).

BUS TRAVEL

Plymouth & Brockton Street Railway provides bus service to Provincetown from downtown Boston and Logan Airport, with stops en route. The Logan Direct airport express service bypasses downtown Boston and makes stops in Plymouth, Sagamore, Barnstable, and Hyannis. The company also has service between Boston and Provincetown, with stops at many towns in between, including Wellfleet center, Truro, and Provincetown.

The Shuttle, run by the Cape Cod Regional Transit Authority, provides a much-needed transportation boost. The shuttle begins its route at Dutra's Market in Truro and continues to Provincetown along Route 6A; it stops wherever a passenger or roadside flagger dictates. Once in Provincetown, the shuttle continues up Bradford Street, with alternating trips to Herring Cove Beach and Pilgrim Park. It runs every 20 minutes and is outfitted to carry bicycles. The service is popular and reasonably priced ($1), and the only trouble seems to be finding parking on the Truro end. Plans are in the works to find alternative areas for parking. The shuttle runs from the end of June until mid-September; from then until October 15, service is within Provincetown only.

➤ Bus Information: **Plymouth & Brockton Street Railway** (☎ 508/
746–0378, ẄEB www.p-b.com). **Shuttle** (☎ 800/352–7155, ẄEB www.
capecodtransit.org).

CAR RENTAL

Budget rents cars at Provincetown Municipal Airport in season.
➤ Major Agencies: **Budget** (☎ 508/487–4557).

CAR TRAVEL

From the Bourne Bridge to Provincetown, expect to be in your car for
a good hour and a half—and that's when traffic is light. During peak
driving times (Friday afternoon and Saturday), expect lengthy delays
on U.S. 6 at Exit 9 and then again just before the Wellfleet town line—
here U.S. 6 narrows to one lane. For a more pleasant drive that will
avoid aggravating delays (but won't get you there faster), detour on
historic Route 6A. From the bridge to Orleans the road ambles alongside some beautiful old sea captains' homes and dozens of antiques and
specialty shops.

Driving to Provincetown from other points on the Cape is mostly a
scenic adventure. The wooded surrounds of Truro break into a breathtaking expanse of open water and sand dunes, with the skyline of
Provincetown beyond. All of this is spectacular, unless you are caught
in horrendous traffic. The busiest time is early morning—especially on
days when the sun is reluctant to shine—when it seems that everyone
on Cape Cod is determined to make it to Provincetown. Traffic is heav-
iest around Wellfleet, and since the road is just one lane until North
Truro, it can be slow going. Except during the traffic-heavy season,
you'll find the drive from Wellfleet to Provincetown beautiful and
only 25 minutes in duration.

EMERGENCIES

The closest hospital is in Hyannis (☞ The Mid Cape A to Z *in* Chapter 4). For rescues at sea call the Coast Guard in Provincetown. Boaters
should use Channel 16 on their radios.

Adams Pharmacy, Inc. is open until 10 PM. A & P Pharmacy offers prescription service until 8 PM.
➤ Doctors and Dentists: **Outer Cape Health Services** (✉ 3130 U.S.
6, Wellfleet, ☎ 508/349–3131; ✉ 49 Harry Kemp Way, Provincetown,
☎ 508/487–9395). **Provincetown Dental Associates** (✉ 86 Harry
Kemp Way, ☎ 508/487–9936).
➤ Emergency Services: **Ambulance, fire, police** (☎ 911 or dial township station). **Coast Guard** (☎ 508/487–0070).
➤ Late-night Pharmacies: **Adams Pharmacy, Inc.** (✉ 254 Commercial St., Provincetown, ☎ 508/487–0069). **A & P Pharmacy** (✉ 28 Shank
Painter Rd., Provincetown, ☎ 508/487–3738).

LODGING

APARTMENT AND HOUSE RENTALS
Cape Cod Realty lists rentals for Wellfleet, and Atlantic Bay Real Es-
tate specializes in Provincetown rentals. Ruth Gilbert Real Estate also
lists Provincetown vacation rentals. Vacation Cape Cod is one of many
realtors with a listing of available apartments and houses on the Outer
Cape.
➤ Local Agents: **Atlantic Bay Real Estate** (✉ 168 Commercial Street,
Provincetown 02657, ☎ 508/487–2430, ẄEB www.atlanticbayre.com).
Cape Cod Realty (✉ Corner of Rte. 6 and Old County Road, Wellfleet
02667, ☎ 508/349–2245, ẄEB www.capecodrealty.net). **Ruth Gilbert**

Real Estate (✉ 167 Commercial Street, Provincetown 02657, ☎ 508/ 487–2004, WEB www.ruthgilbertrealestate.com). **Vacation Cape Cod** (✉ Main St. Mercantile Unit 19, U.S. 6, Eastham 02642, ☎ 508/240–7600 or 800/724–1307, FAX 508/240–6943, WEB www.vacationcapecod.com).

B&BS

In summer, lodgings should be booked as far in advance as possible— several months for the most popular cottages and B&Bs. Assistance with last-minute reservations is available at the Cape Cod Chamber of Commerce information booths. Off-season rates are much reduced, and service may be more personalized. Keep in mind that most lodging establishments require a minimum stay of three days during peak season and holiday times. Provincetown Reservations System makes reservations year-round for accommodations, shows, transportation, and more.

➤ RESERVATION SERVICES: **Provincetown Reservations System** (✉ 293 Commercial St., Provincetown 02657, ☎ 508/487–2400 or 800/648– 0364, FAX 508/487–6517, WEB www.ptownres.com).

CAMPING

Coastal Acres Camping Court, Inc., in Provincetown, is within walking distance of the town center. There are numerous tent and RV sites, with showers, rest rooms, and a small general store for supplies. It's open until November. The only camping permitted on the Cape Cod National Seashore itself is in nonrented, self-contained RVs at Provincetown'sRace Point Beach.

➤ CONTACTS: **Coastal Acres Camping Court, Inc.** (✉ W. Vine St. Extension, ☎ 508/487–1700, WEB www.coastalacres.com). **Race Point Beach** (✉ Provincetown, ☎ 508/487–2100).

TAXIS

Mercedes Cab Co. offers local and long-distance service in vintage Mercedes sedans.

➤ TAXI COMPANIES: **Cape Cab** (✉ Provincetown, ☎ 508/487–2222). **Mercedes Cab Co.** (✉ 35 Alden St., ☎ 508/487–3333). **Provincetown Taxi** (✉ North Truro, ☎ 508/487–8294).

TOURS

The gaff-rigged schooner *Bay Lady II* makes two-hour sails, including a sunset cruise, across Provincetown Harbor into Cape Cod Bay; fares range between $10 and $15. Private charters are also available.

The Provincetown Trolley leaves from the town hall on the hour from 10 to 7 and on the half hour from 10:30 to 4:30; you can also hop on and off at the Provincetown Inn, Province Lands Visitor Center, and Provincetown Art Association. Points of interest on the 40-minute narrated tours include the downtown area and the Cape Cod National Seashore. Tours are available between May and October for $9.

For other tours, including whale-watching trips, *see* Outdoor Activities and Sports *in* Provincetown, *above.*

For aerial tours, contact Cape Air.

➤ FEES AND SCHEDULES: *Bay Lady II* (✉ MacMillan Wharf, Provincetown, ☎ 508/487–9308). **Cape Air** (Provincetown Municipal Airport, ✉ Race Point Rd., ☎ 800/352–0714). **Provincetown Trolley** (☎ 508/ 487–9483).

VISITOR INFORMATION

The Provincetown Chamber of Commerce is open from March until New Year's Day. The Provincetown Business Guild specializes in gay tourism, and the office is open year-round. The Truro Chamber of Commerce is open weekends only in June and September; daily in July and August. The Wellfleet Chamber is open from mid-May through Columbus Day.

➤ Tourist Information: **Provincetown** (✉ MacMillan Wharf, Box 1017, 02657, ☎ 508/487–3424, WEB www.ptownchamber.com). **Provincetown Business Guild** (✉ 115 Bradford St., Box 421, 02657, ☎ 508/487–2313, WEB www.provincetown.com). **Truro** (✉ U.S. 6 at Head of the Meadow Rd., Box 26, North Truro 02652, ☎ 508/487–1288, WEB www.trurochamber.com). **Wellfleet** (✉ Box 571, 02667, ☎ 508/349–2510; ✉ information center off U.S. 6 in South Wellfleet; WEB www.wellfleetchamber.com).

7 PORTRAITS OF CAPE COD

The Cape's Six Seasons

A Brief History of the Cape

Home, Sweet Rental Home

What to Read Before You Go

THE CAPE'S SIX SEASONS

So much has been made of the difference between "the season" and "the off-season" that you might think a magic switch flicks Cape Cod on and off. The truth is something more complicated. Far from having only two seasons, much less the traditional four, the Cape really has six identifiable seasons, each distinct and dramatic.

From early April until Memorial Day, it's spring—a season that can be beautiful, bursting with wildflowers and green grass. Locals shake out the kinks and get ready. In the old days you could smell tar and pitch as fishermen prepared their nets for another season at sea. Now, you're likelier to smell paint as bed-and-breakfast owners put on a fresh coat. Provincetown's exotic little gardens, nurturing unusual plants brought home from seaports around the world, are in their glory. And it's a great time to enjoy bird walks, nature hikes, and country drives, along with lower prices and a lack of crowds.

"The season" is generally thought to start on Memorial Day, but, in fact, the holiday is a quick and busy harbinger, nothing more. After the long weekend a lull sets in that lasts until the end of June, when schools finally let out. The weather is still iffy—balmy one minute, freezing the next—but everything is open, and not too many summer people have arrived yet. It's the calm before the rush—more anticipation than real hustle.

Then, all at once, comes the high tide of visitors—from late June through early September, with surges on July 4 and Labor Day. Inns, restaurants, beaches, and roads can be packed; everything is open and bustling, and the weather can be warm and beautiful. It's not a time for people who don't enjoy being in a crowd at least occasionally, although it's always possible to walk a bit farther on the beach and escape everyone.

Some people find the spell between Labor Day and Columbus Day the most intriguing time on the Cape. School's back in session, so families are gone. Yet summer often sticks around. And the ocean, not nearly as fickle as the air, holds on to its warmth. Many people not tied to summer vacations have discovered this so-called shoulder season.

Columbus Day to New Year's becomes a time of slow retraction. Under crisp blue skies in the clear autumn light, the lower Cape's cover of heather, gorse, cranberry, bayberry, box berry, and beach plum resembles, in Thoreau's words, "the richest rug imaginable spread over an uneven surface." Oaks and swamp maples burnish into beautiful, subtle tones, and fields of marsh grass that were green just a few weeks ago become tawny, like a miniature African savanna. Thanksgiving is a particularly evocative moment, when the Cape's Pilgrim history comes to the fore.

And then—winter. The mainland generally gets more snow than the Cape, but nonetheless, it's a stark, tough time. The landscape has a desolate, moorish quality, which makes the inns and restaurants that do remain open all the more inviting. Many museums and shops close, although a year-round economy has emerged, especially around Hyannis, Falmouth, and Orleans. The Cape's community-theater network continues throughout the year, and many golf courses remain open, except when it snows (some open their courses to cross-country skiers). Intimate B&Bs and inns make romantic retreats after a day of ice fishing or pond skating.

Still, the farther toward the fringes you get, the quieter life becomes. If you believe that less can be more, this is the time to discover what others never could have found during the hectic high-season months.

Many towns on the Cape celebrate Christmas in an old-fashioned way, with wandering carolers and bands, theatrical performances, crafts sales, and holiday house tours. The Cape's holiday season extends from Thanksgiving to New Year's, with celebratory activities including First Night celebrations in many towns.

— Seth Rolbein

A BRIEF HISTORY OF THE CAPE

The fortunes of Cape Cod have always been linked to the sea. For centuries fishermen in search of a livelihood, explorers in search of new worlds, and pilgrims of one sort or another in search of a new life—down to the beach-bound tourists of today—all have turned to the waters around this narrow peninsula arcing into the Atlantic to fulfill their needs and ambitions.

Although some maintain that Iceland Viking Thorvald broke his keel on the shoals here in 1004, European exploration of Cape Cod most likely dates from 1602, when Bartholomew Gosnold sailed from Falmouth, England, to investigate the American coast for trade opportunities. He first anchored off what is now Provincetown and named the cape for the great quantities of cod his crew managed to catch. He then moved on to Cuttyhunk, in the Elizabeth Islands (which he named for the queen); on leaving after a few weeks, he noted the crew was "much fatter and in better health than when we went out of England." Samuel de Champlain, explorer and geographer for the king of France, visited in 1605 and 1606; his encounter with the resident Wampanoag tribe in the Chatham area resulted in deaths on both sides.

None of these visits, however, led to settlement; that began only with the chance landing of the Pilgrims, some of whom were Separatists rebelling from enforced membership in the Church of England, others merchants looking for economic opportunity. On September 16, 1620, the *Mayflower*, with 101 passengers, set out from Plymouth, England, for an area of land granted them by the Virginia Company (Jamestown had been settled in 1607). After more than two months at sea in the crowded boat, they saw land; it was far north of their intended destination, but after the stormy passage and in light of the approach of winter, they put in at Provincetown Harbor on November 21. Before going ashore they drew up the Mayflower Compact, America's first document establishing self-governance, because they were in an area under no official jurisdiction, and dissension had already begun to surface.

Setting off in a small boat, a party led by Captain Myles Standish made a number of expeditions over several weeks, seeking a suitable site for a settlement in the wilderness of woods and scrub. Finally they chose Plymouth and there established the colony, governed by William Bradford, that is today re-created at Plimoth Plantation.

Over the next 20 years settlers spread north and south from Plymouth. The first parts of Cape Cod to be settled were the bay-side sections of Sandwich, Barnstable, and Yarmouth (all incorporated in 1639), along an old Indian trail that is now Route 6A. Most of the newcomers hunted, farmed, and fished; salt hay from the marshes was used to feed cattle and roof houses.

The first homes built by the English settlers on Cape Cod were wigwams built of twigs, bark, hides, cornstalks, and grasses, which they copied from those of the local Wampanoag people who had lived here for thousands of years before the Europeans arrived. Eventually, the settlers stripped the land of its forests to make farmland, graze sheep, and build more European-style homes, though with a New World look all their own. The steep-roof saltbox and the Cape Cod cottage—still the most popular style of house on the Cape and copied all over the country—were designed to accommodate growing families.

A newly married couple might begin by building a one- or two-room half-Cape, a rather lopsided 1½-story building with a door on one side of the facade and two windows on the other; a single chimney rose up on the wall behind the door. As the family grew, an addition might be built on the other side of the door large enough for a single window, turning the half-Cape into a three-quarter-Cape; a two-window addition would make it a symmetrical full Cape. Additions built onto the sides and back were called warts. An interesting feature of some Cape houses is the graceful bow roof, slightly curved like the bottom of a boat (not surprising, since ships' carpenters did much of the house building as well). More noticeable, often in the older houses, is a profusion of small, irregularly shaped and located windows in the gable ends; Thoreau wrote of one such house that it looked as if each of the various occupants "had punched a hole where his necessities required it." Many ancient houses have been turned into historical museums. In some, docents take you on a tour of the times as you pass from the keeping room—the heart of the house, where meals were cooked at a great hearth before which the family gathered for warmth—to the nearby borning room, in whose warmth babies were born and the sick were tended, to the relatively showy front parlors, where company was entertained. Summer and winter kitchens, backyard pumps, beehive ovens, elaborate raised-wall paneling, wide-board pine flooring, wainscoting, a doll made of corn husks, a spinning wheel, a stereopticon, a hand-stitched sampler or glove—each of these historic remnants gives a glimpse into the daily life of another age.

The Wampanoags taught the settlers what they knew of the land and how to live off it. Early on they showed them how to strip and process blubber from whales that became stranded on the beaches. To coax more whales onto the beach, men would sometimes surround them in small boats and make a commotion in the water with their oars until the whales swam to their doom in the only direction left open to them. By the mid-18th century, as the supply of near-shore whales thinned out, the hunt for the far-flung sperm whale began, growing into a major New England industry and making many a sea captain's fortune. Wellfleet, Truro, and Provincetown were the only ports on the Cape that could support deepwater distance whaling (and these were overtaken by Nantucket and New Bedford), but ports along the bay conducted active trade with packet ships carrying goods and passengers to and from Boston. Cape seamen were in great demand for ships sailing from Boston, New York, and other deep-water ports. In the mid-19th century the Cape saw its most prosperous days, thanks largely to the whaling industry.

The decline in whaling hit the economy hard, and the Cape began cultivating tourism in the 19th century. Whereas previously people traveled from Boston to and along the Cape only by stagecoach or

packet boat, in 1848 the first train service from Boston began, reaching to Sandwich; by 1873 it had been extended little by little to Provincetown. In the 1890s President Grover Cleveland made his Bourne residence (now gone) the Cape's first "summer White House" (to be followed in the 1960s by John F. Kennedy). Grand seaside resorts grew up for summering families, and Cape Cod began to court visitors actively.

Artists were drawn to Provincetown starting in the early part of the 20th century. In 1899 Charles W. Hawthorne opened the Cape Cod School of Art and taught the Impressionist *en plein air* style (outdoors) on the beach. It was the first of several art schools established over the next few years that promoted Provincetown as an art colony. Writers (including John Reed and the young Eugene O'Neill) started the Provincetown Players, which would be the germ of Cape community theater and professional summer-stock companies. The Barnstable Comedy Club, founded in 1922 and still going strong, is the most notable of the area's many amateur groups; novelist Kurt Vonnegut acted in its productions in the 1950s and 1960s and had some of his early plays produced by the group. Professional summer stock began with the still-healthy Cape Playhouse in Dennis in 1927, and its early years featured Bette Davis (who was first an usher), Henry Fonda, Ruth Gordon, Humphrey Bogart, and Gertrude Lawrence. In 1928 the University Players Guild (which later became the Falmouth Playhouse, and subsequently closed) opened in Falmouth, attracting the likes of James Cagney, Orson Welles, Josh Logan, Tallulah Bankhead, and Jimmy Stewart (who, while on summer vacation from Princeton, had his first bit part during Falmouth's first season).

The idea of a Cape Cod canal, linking the bay to the sound, was studied as early as the 17th century, but not until 1914 did the privately built canal merge the waters of the two bays. It was not, however, a thunderous success; too narrow and winding, the canal allowed only one-way traffic and created dangerous currents. The federal government bought it in 1928 and had the U.S. Army Corps of Engineers rebuild it. In the 1930s three bridges—two traffic and one railroad—went up, and the rest is the latter-day history of tourism on Cape Cod.

The building of the Mid Cape Highway (U.S. 6) in the 1950s marked the great boom in the Cape's growth, and the presidency of John F. Kennedy, who summered in Hyannis Port, certainly added to the area's allure. In 1961 President Kennedy signed the legislation that established Cape Cod National Seashore. Today the Cape's summer population is more than 500,000, 2½ times the year-round population.

Though tourism, construction, and light industry are the mainstays of the Cape's economy these days, the earliest inhabitants' occupations have not disappeared. There are still more than 100 farms on the Cape, and the fishing industry—including lobstering, scalloping, and oyster aquaculture, as well as the fruits of fishing fleets such as those in Provincetown and Chatham—brings in $2 million a month.

Visitors are still drawn here by the sea: scientists come to delve into the mysteries of the deep, artists come for the light, and everyone comes for the charm of the beach towns, the beauty of the white sand, the softness of the breezes, and the roaring of the surf.

HOME, SWEET RENTAL HOME

One of the joys of a Cape Cod vacation can be renting a furnished house—one with plenty of space to accommodate extended families or groups of friends, a backyard or deck where you can kick back with a cool drink, and a kitchen where you can boil up some lobsters. If a house rental is in your plans, you must act early. Cape realtors report it's not unusual to get bookings a year in advance, and by January in some years, the summer pickings in many prime beachfront areas may already be getting slim.

Most Cape Cod house rentals run weekly, from Saturday to Saturday—you can move in on Saturday afternoon, and you must be out the following Saturday morning. There may be some flexibility outside the peak summer season of July 4 through Labor Day, but otherwise you'll have to cross the bridges with the rest of the week-to-week renters. Two-week minimums for some choicer properties are not uncommon. Note that summer rental prices can vary, even from week to week, depending on the most popular times; early to mid-June and mid- to late September prices may be a bit lower.

If you're planning a summer rental, here are some tips on making arrangements:

Decide where you'd like to be. Most Cape realtors deal with a particular town or area, so narrow your search before you start asking about houses. Do you want to be on Cape Cod Bay or Nantucket Sound, or close to the beaches of the Cape Cod National Seashore? Will you stay put, or do you want a central location that lets you explore the Cape easily? The towns on the Cape have different personalities, and that will be part of your decision making.

Know what you'll need. How many bedrooms (with how many beds) and how many bathrooms? Is there a washer and dryer? What about a yard or a deck? How close to the beach? Is a water view important? Or a quiet street where the children can play? Do you want to be close to a supermarket and other stores, or are you willing to drive a bit?

Ask what's included. Most Cape rentals do not include linens, so you'll need to bring your own sheets and towels. Many do provide a cleaning service before you arrive and after you leave, but ask whether you're responsible for taking trash to the dump or for handling other cleanup tasks. Check ahead of time about any recycling regulations. Inquire about using the phone; some owners restrict their tenants to local calls, while others ask for a deposit to cover your phone bill. If you want anything special—a crib, bicycles, a barbecue grill, air-conditioning—be sure to ask.

Use the Internet. Many realtors post property listings—with photos—on their Web sites, and a growing number of property owners handle their own rentals via the Internet. If you can't visit properties in person, be sure to ask the realtor or owner for pictures of the house, either by post or by e-mail. What is described as cozy may turn out to be cramped, and old-fashioned may sometimes be run-down; photos will help avoid misunderstandings.

Don't forget the beach permits. Before you head for the Cape, ask your realtor or the local chamber of commerce about beach stickers. Many towns with resident-only beaches or ponds will sell you a weekly beach permit if you present a copy of your lease at the town hall or the town recreation department.

Then pack up the family, pick up some lobsters, and relax in that lawn chair. At least for the week, you're home.

— Carolyn Heller

WHAT TO READ BEFORE YOU GO

Cape Cod has inspired a vast number of books, from hard-to-find, locally published autobiographical reminiscences to handsomely illustrated coffee-table books from national publishers. You can explore some of these before your trip at your local library, bookstore, or on-line bookseller, but try to make time to visit some of the many excellent bookstores on the Cape. You may well make a special discovery that will illuminate your stay. For information about local newspapers and magazines, *see* Media *in* Smart Travel Tips A to Z.

General

The classic works on Cape Cod are Henry David Thoreau's readable and often entertaining *Cape Cod*, an account of his walking tours in the mid-1800s, and Henry Beston's 1928 *The Outermost House*, which chronicles the seasons during a solitary year in a cabin at ocean's edge. Both reveal the character of Cape Codders and are rich in tales and local lore, as well as observations of nature and its processes. *Cape Cod: Henry David Thoreau's Complete Text with the Journey Recreated in Pictures*, by William F. Robinson, is a handsome New York Graphics Society edition (currently out of print), illustrated with prints from the period and current photographs. *Cape Cod Pilot*, by Josef Berger (alias Jeremiah Digges), is a Works Progress Administration guidebook from 1937 that is filled with "whacking good yarns" about everything from religion to fishing, as well as a lot of still-useful information. *A Place Apart: A Cape Cod Reader* (1993), edited by Robert Finch, includes stories about the Cape from dozens of writers, from Melville to Adam Gopnik.

History

Cape Cod, Its People & Their History, by Henry C. Kittredge (first published in 1930), is the standard history of the area, told with anecdotes and style as well as scholarship. Now out of print, *Sand in Their Shoes*, compiled by Edith and Frank Shay, is a compendium of writings on Cape Cod life throughout history. *Of Plimoth Plantation* is Governor William Bradford's 17th-century description of the Pilgrims' voyage to and early years in the New World. *Art in Narrow Streets*, by Ross Moffett; *Figures in a Landscape*, by Josephine Del Deo; *Provincetown as a Stage*, by Leona Rust Egan; and *Time and the Town: A Provincetown Chronicle*, by Provincetown Playhouse founder Mary Heaton Vorse, paint the social landscape of Provincetown in the first half of the 20th century, concentrating on the lives and contributions of the many writers, artists, and actors that flocked to the town. More recently, Paul Schneider has written *The Enduring Shore: A History of Cape Cod, Martha's Vineyard, and Nantucket*, another look at the region's past. An illustrated history for children, *The Story of Cape Cod*, by Kevin Shortsleeve (available through *Cape Cod Life*, ☏ 800/645–4482), is written in rhyming verse and sure to entertain. *In the Footsteps of Thoreau: 25 Historic and Nature Walks on Cape Cod*, by Adam Gamble, is a useful guide for naturalists and Thoreau admirers. For baseball fans, Christopher Price's *Baseball by the Beach: A History of America's National Pastime on Cape Cod* provides a portrait of the Cape Cod Baseball League and the Cape's version of summer on the sandlots.

Fiction

Herman Melville's *Moby-Dick*, set on a 19th-century Nantucket whaling ship, captures the spirit of the whaling era. *Cape Cod*, by William Martin, is a historical novel and mystery following two families from the *Mayflower* voyage to the present, with lots of Cape history and flavor along the way. Norman Mailer's *Tough Guys Don't Dance* is a murder mystery set in Provincetown and Truro, and several other novels use Provincetown as a setting, including *Resuscitation of a Hanged Man*, by Denis Johnson, and Anne LeClaire's *Grace Point*. Other writers who have set books on the Cape are Margot Arnold, Rick Boyer, Philip A. Craig, Virginia Rich, Marie Lee, Alice Hoffman, Jane Langton, David Osborn, and Phoebe Atwood Taylor. *Cape Cod Stories*, edited by John Miller, is a collection of Cape-related short fiction by such luminaries as Edgar Allen

Poe, John Cheever, and Sylvia Plath. *Cape Discovery,* edited by Bruce Smith and Catherine Gammon, an anthology of poetry and fiction by former fellows of the Fine Arts Work Center in Provincetown, includes the work of noted contemporary American writers such as Louise Glück, Michael Cunningham, Dean Albarelli, and Maria Flook. Many of the poems in *Passing Through,* Pulitzer Prize–winning poet Stanley Kunitz's 1997 collection, evoke the natural beauty of the Cape, and several refer to his garden on Commercial Street in Provincetown.

Memoirs

In *Heaven's Coast,* Mark Doty, a Provincetown writer, recounts the death of his lover, Wally Roberts, from complications caused by AIDS. In a similar vein, David Gessner's *A Wild, Rank Place: One Year on Cape Cod* combines insights about the Cape with reminiscence about battling cancer and confronting his father's death. In *The Salt House: A Summer on the Dunes of Cape Cod,* Cynthia Huntington describes a summer during the first year of her marriage spent in a tiny Outer Cape beach shack called Euphoria, while Gladys Taber chronicles her life on the Cape at Still Cove in *My Own Cape Cod.* Journalist Alec Wilkinson portrays a different side of Cape life in *Midnights: A Year with the Wellfleet Police.*

Natural History

Robert Finch, editor of *A Place Apart,* has also written three lyrical books about natural history: *Outlands: Journeys to the Outer Edges of Cape Cod, Common Ground: A Naturalist's Cape Cod,* and *The Primal Place,* a meditation about life on the Cape, especially its natural rhythms and history. Finch is also the author of *Death of a Hornet and Other Cape Cod Essays* and the attractively illustrated *Cape Cod: Its Natural and Cultural History,* a National Park Service handbook about the National Seashore and the Cape. *In the Company of Light* traces John Hay's journey from Maine to Cape Cod, recounting his observations of light and luminescence—in nature and as revelation. Hay is a wonderful nature writer; his other titles include *The Run,* about the life cycle of alewives, and *Great Beach. A Guide to Nature on Cape Cod and the Islands,* edited by Greg O'Brien, has sections by a variety of experts on the area's flora and fauna.

Photography

A Summer's Day (winner of the 1985 Ansel Adams Award for Best Photography Book) and *Cape Light* present color landscapes, still lifes, and portraits by Provincetown-associated photographer Joel Meyerowitz.

INDEX

NOTES

NOTES

NOTES

NOTES

NOTES

NOTES

NOTES

NOTES

NOTES